RISK, RUIN & RICHES

ALSO BY JIM POWELL

An Investor's Guide to Art & Antiques

RISK, RUIN

&

RICHES

Inside the World of Big Time Real Estate

JIM POWELL

MACMILLAN PUBLISHING COMPANY

New York

Macmillan Publishing Company
866 Third Avenue, New York, N.Y. 10022
Collier Macmillan Canada, Inc.

Library of Congress Cataloging-in-Publication Data
Powell, Jim.
Risk, ruin, and riches.
1. Real estate developers—United States.
2. Real estate development—United States.
3. Real estate investment—United States.   4. Risk—United States.
5. Wealth—United States.   6. Success in business—United States.   I. Title.
HD1390.P68 1986   333.3'8'0973   86-7223
ISBN 0-02-598530-2

Macmillan books are available at special discounts for bulk purchases
for sales promotions, premiums, fund-raising, or educational use.
For details, contact:
Special Sales Director
Macmillan Publishing Company
866 Third Avenue
New York, N.Y. 10022

10 9 8 7 6 5 4 3 2 1

Printed in the United States of America

CONTENTS

CONTENTS

V. POWER PLAYS / 167

VI. SQUARE-FOOT PEDDLING / 213

VII. END GAME / 279

INDEX / 371

I

RISK-TAKERS

This is a story about daring entrepreneurs along the frontiers of real estate. I've traveled thousands of miles around the country to size up firsthand these people who are changing the environment where we work, live and play.

Many have gained fantastic wealth. The first great American fortune was amassed by John Jacob Astor who, among other things, was a real estate entrepreneur. Recently, I was fortunate to meet Albert and Paul Reichmann, the richest real estate men on the continent, whose profits are reportedly $700,000 per day. I've talked with plenty of entrepreneurs who, with just a single building, create more net worth than a chief executive at IBM, General Motors or any other Fortune 500 company will earn during an entire lifetime.

The rewards can be sweet. New York apartment king Sam LeFrak relaxes aboard his 85-foot yacht *Jonathan III*. Like a modern-day Medici, Houston entrepreneur Gerald Hines commissions the most fashionable architects to design his many stylish homes. Manhattan entrepreneur Donald Trump seems to love his New Jersey Generals football team as much as Indianapolis entrepreneur Melvin Simon loves his Indianapolis Pacers basketball team. The Detroit-based shopping center entrepreneur Alfred Taubman not only collects art, he controls Sotheby's, the world's largest art auction house begun more than two centuries ago. Boston's Mortimer Zuckerman collects major magazines, such as *Atlantic Monthly* and *U.S. News & World Report*. Columbus, Ohio office builder Dan Galbreath breeds horses at his Darby Dan Farm. One of them is a mare belonging to Queen Elizabeth II.

But potential ruin and humiliation await real estate entrepreneurs at practically every turn. The more I understood the risks of real estate development, the more I came to appreciate these bold, courageous, arrogant, persistent, resourceful, cunning and curious personalities.

Developing real estate is like trying to wrap your arms around an angry bull. Imagine assembling, then holding together all the independent people you need throughout a project—appraisers, architects, engineers, financiers, lawyers, title insurers, leasing agents and often more than a hundred subcontractors and consultants. All of these probably have their own ideas about doing things. Often they don't get along or don't communicate well with each other. So there are wrenching conflicts which threaten to wreck a project, as I show in this book.

The whole process begins with an idea like how to interpret the needs of a market. "Getting great ideas is probably the hardest challenge in real estate," a Los Angeles entrepreneur told me. In the following pages, you'll encounter some extraordinarily fertile minds.

How appealing a project will be to prospective tenants and neighbors depends very much on the architect. So I visited architects' offices to see how design ideas evolve. I'll tell you about a New Haven, Connecticut architect who's finishing the biggest office complex in the United States, a magnificent $1.5 billion project. He almost walked away from it.

To gain control of a desirable location may require spending millions and negotiating with difficult sellers for years. Yet often key parcels prove elusive, so the location has to be abandoned. You'll see what's involved as I recount the dramatic, secret assemblage of a downtown Dallas block.

It's easy for a real estate entrepreneur to founder amidst a blaze of bad guesswork. Since project financing may cost $50,000 to $100,000 per day, interest is a critical cost. During the time that a project is under construction, interest rates may jump, and what looked like a good deal initially may become a horrendous loser. In this book, I talk about an alarmed Manhattan entrepreneur who was losing $500,000 a month.

Securing needed government approval may involve considerable risk of delay. I describe a Boston property that was contested for almost a decade before anything was built there. Even the most respected, well-financed entrepreneurs may be helpless, as you'll see when I chronicle a Chicago battle.

Logistical foul-ups, materials shortages and strikes may throw construction behind schedule—and costs out of control. Such a situation jolted an Atlanta entrepreneur, and his chief money partner decided to pull out of their deal. There's a chapter that tells you what happened.

Because delay costs so much, real estate entrepreneurs are especially vulnerable to extortion. I know a Manhattan entrepreneur, for instance, who pays a no-show bulldozer operator an outrageous $205,428 annually rather than risk union violence and slowdowns. I tell you in the book how an unforgettable construction boss fought extortion on a mammoth Florida job.

If there are serious design or construction errors, a real estate project may be set back for years. Sometimes many people are killed because of deadly oversights—as you'll see in the Kansas City building disaster I recount here.

What will the market be like when a project is finished a couple years down the road? An entrepreneur may have predicted a million-square-foot building on an average lease rate of $35 per foot. But rates may tumble because of a recession or space glut. If space leases for perhaps $2 a square foot less, there'd be a heart-stopping $2 million annual shortfall.

More times than you may imagine, the market is so tough that not a single tenant can be signed up for a building, and it actually stands empty. There's a Manhattan building I talk about that lost more than $100 million, triggered three defaults and the liquidation of a famous real estate company.

Many real estate entrepreneurs succumb to the perils I talk about. Look what happened to Houston entrepreneur Mel Powers. He was long one of the highest high rollers in that dizzy boom town. One thing after the other, from aerospace to energy, propelled Houston upward through the 1960s and 1970s. While other places languished in recession, Houston continued to grow.

Sporting long hair and a wavy moustache, Powers bought his first Houston building in 1966. He paid $2,200 down, refurbished it, leased it up and sold it several months later for $110,000.

Before long, he was taking the risk of building new projects. He filled them with tenants and sold the properties at a profit. By 1979, he had built or started more than $200 million worth.

Powers was the talk of Houston. He had a chalet in Aspen, Colorado and a lakefront spread in Clear Lake, Texas. He launched Powers Center, a health club, and Powersair, an executive helicopter and jet service. He loved to hop in one of his helicopters for a Mexico weekend break or, better yet, climb aboard his 165-foot, $3 million yacht fitted with gold-plated sinks.

Entrepreneurs like Powers continued to build as fast as they could even while slumping oil prices were hitting oil companies hard, and suddenly they weren't in the market for fancy offices anymore. By 1983, almost a third of Houston's office space was vacant—some 40 million square feet altogether. Whole buildings were achingly empty. That year, at 46, Powers declared bankruptcy. I tried to track him down, but he had vanished.

Such are the risks of real estate development. If they were easy, then everybody would rush out to do a building and pocket all those million dollar bills.

Because real estate risks are frightening, I found the most successful entrepreneurs as formidable as any macho bullfighter or test pilot. They may not be your favorite people. Certainly they do their share of bad things. But they have what it takes to help our cities and country grow.

In this book, I explain the six major types of real estate risks. You'll see why some entrepreneurs lose, how others make fortunes and what difference it makes for the rest of us. Through their adventures, I hope to show you how ideas happen.

II

TURF
BATTLES

1.
BOLD VISION

RECENTLY I VISITED ATLANTA TO SEE ONE OF THE FIRST PLACES where the public fell in love with contemporary architecture. The place is the Atlanta Hyatt Regency Hotel designed by John Portman.

It's a structure 764 feet in circumference, with 800 balconied rooms surrounding a 22-story-high atrium, largest ever for a hotel when it opened in 1967. You approach it through a tunneled entrance, then suddenly see incredible soaring heights. This is the Jesus Christ Entrance, nicknamed after the exclamations of astonishment it inspires.

It's a fun place. Glass bubble elevators speed up and down one end of the atrium. Water cascades down from a 70-foot fountain. The atrium has a three-story-high aviary with macaws, parrots and cock of the rock birds. There's a cocktail lounge beneath what appears to be a gigantic faceted Tiffany lamp that hangs from the roof 200 feet above. Atop the hotel is a revolving restaurant. Now, two decades after opening, people still crowd into the bubble elevators that take you up for a panoramic view of the city of Atlanta.

As I was to learn from interviews in Atlanta, Chicago, Dallas and New York, the entrepreneurs who built this hotel are every bit as remarkable as the hotel itself. John Portman gained control of the location and figured out what to do with it. There was an intuitive genius named Trammell Crow who became a partner. Almost everybody in the hotel industry laughed at Portman's design idea, but not the Pritzkers, who agreed to invest in it and operate it, thus securing another of their fortunes.

Portman, now 61, was among the earliest architects to take on the risks of real estate development. If he didn't invent the atrium, he certainly raised it to a fine art here, and spectacular atriums—which he prefers to call "exploded spaces"—have become his trademark. They're now commonplace across the country, in shopping malls and office buildings as well as hotels, and they retain their popular appeal.

Portman, a tall man with long wavy brown hair and a soft southern twang, works on the second floor of Peachtree Center, one of many downtown Atlanta landmarks he built. In his offices, extending into what used to be the Midnight Sun Dinner Theater, he likes to surround himself with his own creations: his trim-line chrome-and-leather chairs, chrome-and-glass conference tables and a chandelier of delicate hand-blown glass tubes and globes. There are yellow chrysanthemums everywhere.

Portman designed his living environment, too. He built an airy 12,500-square-foot home atop a knoll on a 20-acre wooded tract about 15 miles northwest of Atlanta. It affords a splendid view of the city. Rather than using walls, Portman separated interior spaces with 24 8-foot-wide exploded hollow columns where he put stairs, closets and sculpture, including life-size statues of Plato, Aristotle and Sophocles which he salvaged from a British library. Lighted from above, they add a theatrical touch. A stream flows through Portman's living room, and the dining room table is on a little island.

It's said that Portman built this house for his blonde wife Jan, a high-school sweetheart, then built the Atlanta skyline for her to admire. Here they nurtured a family to match Portman's outsize ambitions: Michael Wayne, John Calvin III, Jae Phillip, Jeffrey Lin, Jana Lee and Jarel Penn. When somebody misbehaved, friends say, it was perhaps because there weren't any corners to send anyone to. Since Portman was away from home so much, preoccupied with his business, Jan gets most of the credit for the way their children turned out.

Portman is building a far more ambitious home on Sea Island, Georgia, where the family has summered for years. It is a secluded beachfront resort, with trees draped in sleepy Spanish moss. Nearby residents include chief executives Clifton Garvin of Exxon and Joseph Flavin of Singer.

"Perhaps the first thing you notice when you arrive at the beach," Portman says, "is umbrellas with people lying underneath partially shaded. The beach house took its form from this expression. The roof is like a giant umbrella. Beneath, the house is sprawled in an exploded fashion. The living room and dining room are on an island—there's more water, trees and flowers here than at the Atlanta house."

The house is a tremendous undertaking. More than 200 pilings were sunk to support the concrete structure—there's so much concrete that it took 14 months to pour. It will cost several million dollars.

"I designed it, first of all, to accommodate my six children and four grandchildren who like to visit," he smiles. "I also wanted a place to display my expanding art collection—modern paintings, wood masks from Uganda and Nigeria, Italian glass sculptures of designs by twentieth century artists like Picasso, Braque, Le Corbusier, Cocteau and Ernst. There will be my own sculptures, architectural forms, fashioned from concrete and aluminum."

Several of his children have followed him into his principal business, the architectural and engineering firm John Portman & Associates and his development firm Portman Properties. "When my son Jack, as a teenager, expressed an interest, I sent him to work in a different part of the world every summer—I always had a hankering to work overseas. I started a project in Brussels and opened an office in Paris. During the early 1970s, Jack noted that the Far East was sure to see the most dramatic growth, and we should be there.

"Well, we are doing projects in Hong Kong, Singapore, Kuala Lumpur and Jakarta. In Shanghai, we're building 400 housing units, a 200,000-square-foot office facility and 700-room hotel. The Chinese asked me how I felt about my hotel going up across from the giant Soviet-built Exhibition Hall. Thinking about the designs, I said, 'I feel sorry for the Russians!'"

Michael Portman is director of development for Portman Properties. Jae Portman is director of the Atlanta Decorative Arts Center, another family venture. Jarel Portman is preparing for the hotel business by working at the Hyatt on Union Square in San Francisco.

John Portman has the intense drive born of need. Originally from Walhalla, South Carolina, he's the son of a General Services Administration worker and a beautician. He studied architecture at Georgia Tech, paying expenses with many jobs, including work on store interiors for New York architect Morris Ketchum. It was during this period that he learned techniques to create drama and attract customers.

Having graduated in 1950, he landed a job with Stevens & Wilkinson, Atlanta's largest architectural firm. He's remembered as being brash back then. "John could give and take, but not much," says William Barnett, the firm's president. "He didn't want anybody between him and his designs." Joe Amisano, an Atlanta architect, says good-naturedly: "He has an incredible ego. He'd try to make you believe he came before the planet."

After three years at Stevens & Wilkinson, Portman got his architect's license, and, impatient, struck out on his own. He didn't have any connections to speak of, so he struggled along on meager architectural commissions from homes, drugstores and school annexes.

Portman decided that to generate the business he wanted, he had to become a developer himself. Through Atlanta executive Robert

Wilby, whom he had known as a client of Stevens & Wilkinson, Portman met John O. Chiles, a leader of the Atlanta real estate community who headed the city's largest firm, Adams-Cates Company. Portman proposed that he provide architectural advice to Chiles in exchange for letting him sit in on development meetings, so he could learn the real estate business. Chiles, intrigued by this brash, bold upstart, agreed. He jokingly referred to Portman as The Marijuana Kid because of his seemingly crazy ideas.

In 1954, Portman tried developing the Peachtree Medical building, a co-op deal. While it won a design award from *Progressive Architecture* magazine, Portman lost $7,500 because the realtor-partner he relied on didn't sell enough co-op units. He resolved to take full responsibility for his next venture.

After developing a number of small projects, Portman made a breakthrough with Al Hendley, the Managing Trustee of the Belle Isle Estate, who owned the downtown Belle Isle Garage. In January 1957, Hendley leased the place to Portman, who imagined it as some kind of an exhibition hall. When Portman discovered that the furniture industry was the biggest user of showroom space in the United States, a furniture mart seemed like a natural. The 250,000 square foot garage was filled within a year.

But after seeing Portman's success with the Belle Isle Garage, an established Atlanta developer named Robert Holder, known for building the city's biggest industrial project, started promoting a similar idea for his property 20 miles away in Gwinnett County. When he couldn't line up private financing, he began lobbying state officials to back it. Competition between Holder and Portman was intense, because everybody agreed there wasn't enough demand in Atlanta for two furniture marts.

Portman is tenacious. He recruited a team consisting of furniture salesman Randy Macon, product salesman John La Rue and trade show booker Herbert Martin. They went to High Point, North Carolina, mecca for furniture manufacturers. Meanwhile, Portman described his rapturous visions to Metropolitan loan officer Larry Benway. Convinced that the project was viable, Metropolitan provided an $8 million mortgage, largest ever granted in the state until then. This helped convince Atlanta's biggest developer, Ben Massell, to help finance the project. Construction began in 1959.

In 1958, while Portman was developing the 1-million-square-foot Merchandise Mart, Frank Carter, a local real estate broker, introduced him to a balding, bushy-browed Texan named Trammell Crow who was building marts for the furniture, gift and apparel industries in Dallas. Crow understood this business of delivering retail buyers to manufacturers and wholesalers at a permanent showroom facility. Crow and Portman got to know each other, and when the Atlanta Merchandise Mart opened in 1961, an immediate success, the two men bought out the other partners. Each ended up with a half interest. Together, they acquired land just south of the mart on Peachtree Street, and they developed an office building there. These projects attracted some 250,000 visitors a year, creating a demand for more hotel rooms.

Portman eyed a parcel diagonally opposite the Merchandise Mart on the north side of Peachtree Street. It was a great site where, with the right design, he could really make a reputation for himself. The owner, Ben Massell, didn't want to sell, but he agreed to lease it for 99 years. Portman took the deal with Phoenix Investment Company, a local group headed by Atlanta attorney Granger Hansel and advised by John O. Chiles.

"I didn't want the hotel to be just another set of rooms," Portman says. "The traditional central-city hotel had always been a cramped thing with a narrow entranceway, a dull and dreary lobby for registration, elevators over in a corner, a closed elevator cab, dimly lighted corridors, nondescript doorways and a hotel room with a bed, chair and hole in the outside wall."

Inspired by Europe's most fabled sights like Tivoli Gardens in Copenhagen, Portman says: "I wanted to explode the hotel, to create a grandeur of space, almost a resort, in the central city. The whole idea here is to create spaces which give people a feeling of uplift and exhilaration. Something to touch the spirit. The size and scale of interior space has an effect the ancients discovered long ago. You walk into St. Peters and wow!

"Everybody's first reaction to the design was that it would cost a fortune, but you must remember there are many ways to spend money. There is no fancy marble or terrazzo in this hotel. It's all concrete. The carpet, furniture and fittings are as luxurious as those of any other hotel, but everything else is simple, conventional construction, using a minimum of materials. Money saved by avoiding fancy finishes and the saving in labor are what help pay for the big atrium space."

Portman secured 60 percent of the financing from Phoenix Investment Company and 20 percent from Dallas investor Fritz Hahn. Portman was credited with 20 percent for putting the deal together. Then Hahn decided he didn't want to go forward, and in addition he had a falling out with Trammell Crow—Hahn, Crow and Portman were partners in an Atlanta shopping center called Greenbriar. They agreed that Hahn would swap his interest in the Portman hotel for Crow's interest in Greenbriar. Thus, Crow acquired a 20 percent stake in the hotel without any additional investment.

John O. Chiles and George Kennedy, President of Phoenix Investment Company, arranged for a well-known Atlanta hotel man named Joe Crocy to manage the hotel. He was with Dinkler, then Atlanta's largest hotel operator.

Portman and Crow clashed in many ways. Portman developed in central cities, while Crow was a suburban man—for years, even Crow's Dallas projects were decidedly outside the downtown core. Crow never did seem to feel comfortable taking risks in downtowns, which were deteriorating across the country.

Moreover, Portman received more recognition. He won architectural design awards. He got attention as an early architect-developer. His projects were more glamorous. Magazines and newspapers were always more interested in publishing articles about his ambitious downtown projects than Crow's suburban warehouses and office parks. Ten years older than Portman, Crow considered himself the senior partner, yet the spotlight glared on Portman, and this reportedly bothered Crow.

Crow then, as now, was unforgettable. He doesn't go for fancy offices, executive bathrooms and other prerequisites of top brass. His desk is on an open floor surrounded by dozens of other desks. "Since my staff can hear what I'm saying, I don't have to repeat myself," he told me. He encourages associates to go through his mail, so they'll keep abreast of things. Guided by his instincts, he often seems preoccupied, absentminded. On more than one occasion, when groping for ideas, he took off his shoes and stretched out on his office floor.

Crow exudes humility and has a knack for putting people at ease. His concern about a banker's problems has helped him win many backers. This is a straight-dealing Texan who can be counted on to honor his word.

Though he's a party to all major decisions, he has a kindly manner of delegating authority which inspires partners to earn his trust. Shrewd though he is, he used to sign many contracts which partners recommended without ever reading them. He agreed, on faith, to help back projects he knew little about.

His whims, if sometimes mysterious, are quite disarming. One afternoon, having negotiated a deal in Boise, Idaho, he insisted that he and an associate go fishing. Dressed in their business suits, they found a fishing store, bought licenses, rented poles and headed for a lake. On another occasion, wilting in Dallas's summer heat, he got a pair of scissors, cut the long sleeves off his shirt and accompanied friends to an elegant restaurant.

His favorite expressions reinforce the impression of a simple country boy. "Work is more fun than fun," he declares. "If it doesn't make money, it isn't pretty." And "the way to wealth is debt."

Crow, like Portman, is stirred by bold visions. He wants to be the biggest and best. He wants an empire. He wants to mingle with the powerbrokers—even the President of the United States.

Despite his ferocious drive, Crow accommodates the needs of his children Robert, Howard, Trammell S. Jr., Harlan, Lucy and Stuart. He handled late night feedings when they were infants. He gave up golf, since it took him away from them. He came home for dinner and, if there were unfinished business, he returned to the office with the children. Now, at 70, he dances with Lucy and talks about camping with her oldest son. Crow built a day care center at his company, so working mothers could be closer to their children.

Crow is spurred by recollections of his early years in poverty. During the Great Depression, he and his seven brothers and sisters grew up in a Dallas house with a kitchen, living room, bedroom, sleeping porch and toilet, and no bath or hot water. Just feeding all those mouths meant a continuing crisis. His father, a diligent, well-read, devout Christian Fundamentalist bookkeeper, "earned a little money doing accounts for a few small businesses," Crow recalls, "and the rest of us did what we could. We got two or three eggs a day, but one summer somebody stole our chickens.

"Though I didn't realize we were poor until I was about 16, there was a dull pain. Fortunately, I turned to work rather than resentment or self-degradation. Aside from 17 cents a week my father gave me for school lunch money, I earned all the money I have ever had. I've always managed, one way or another, to get by."

Crow certainly didn't show much early promise. He remembers his mother taking him to a child guidance counselor for being "fractious and sensitive." He was poor in art and writing, but arithmetic prepared the way for his salvation. He paid all his expenses at Southern Methodist University as a teller for Mercantile Bank and became a certified public accountant.

While he was in the Navy as an accountant during World War II, he married Margaret Doggett, daughter of a successful Dallas businessman. Her family was socially prominent, having lived in Dallas for five generations. Their home: fashionable Highland Park. It was an unlikely match.

Her parents were killed in a car crash several years before she met Crow, and she was left with an inheritance worth about $400,000. Among her holdings was a six-story warehouse and the building which housed the family firm, Doggett Grain Company. That's where Crow went to work after he left the military in 1946.

Soon he faced a crisis. More and more manufacturers were deciding that one-story warehouses were more efficient than multistory. The Doggett's biggest warehouse tenant vacated. Crow couldn't find a single tenant to take over the space, but he made a deal with a group of small rug manufacturers. Together, they were willing to occupy the space.

Unwittingly, he had made his first move into the merchandise mart and real estate business. His curiosity drove him to learn everything he could about how you finance, design and construct commercial property. He was instinctively attentive to the needs of his local market.

His next, much bigger, move began at a flower show where he met John and Storey Stemmons. They owned 11,000 acres several miles northwest of downtown Dallas. It would be an obvious site for real estate development, except that the nearby Trinity River had a long history of flooding. Nobody had confidence in the levees the Stemmonses had built. What to do with this idle land? Crow became interested because he was wondering how best to invest his wife's inheritance. They reached an understanding: the Stemmonses would contribute land, and they'd receive half interest in anything Crow constructed there.

Opportunity came when one of the rug manufacturers told Crow he wanted to move out of the Doggett warehouse and look for a new one-story building. Crow offered to develop whatever the manufacturer needed, and he agreed. Soon a 16,875-square-foot structure rose on Stemmons land, and more warehouses followed in quick succession.

Restless and competitive, Crow wasn't content to build like everybody else. He explored ways to produce a better product which could give him an advantage in the marketplace. The standard approach had loading docks in front and offices in the back, but Crow resolved to make the surroundings more pleasant. He located offices in front. He offered more windows and attractive landscaping. He built fast, and by the mid-1950s, he was the biggest warehouse operator in Dallas.

This wasn't enough though. He still wanted to be the biggest and best anywhere. He pondered the giant Merchandise Mart in Chicago, cornerstone of the Kennedy family fortune, which was a beehive of endless dim corridors. In 1955 he built the Decorative Center, the first design mart in the United States, which evolved into a 742,000-square-foot complex with more than 500 manufacturers.

He envisaged something for the entire homefurnishings industry. It would cost $6.5 million. To sign tenants, Crow and broker Bill Campbell traveled to the merchandising centers in Chicago and High Point, North Carolina. They didn't make advance appointments, since

Crow believed this just gave a prospect an opportunity to say no. "Trammell went in one direction," Campbell recalls, "I went in the other. We made a lot of calls, but nobody was interested in a Dallas mart. Back at the motel that night, Trammell asked me, 'What do you think we ought to do after this trip?' I said, 'Fold up our tent and forget the idea.' Trammell was lost in thought for several minutes, and then he spoke. 'I'm going to build the finest furniture mart in America, and you're going to lease it.' Then he went to sleep. Just like that."

The outside of Crow's 437,000-square-foot Homefurnishings Mart didn't look like much—it was a sprawling two-story brick warehouse building—but inside Crow provided amenities which mattered to people: open spaces for eating and relaxing, sculpture to refresh the eye, ample showrooms, neat bathrooms. Most of Crow's buildings were designed by a local architect named Harold Berry whose office was across the hall from Crow's. Berry worked out designs based on Crow's understanding of the marketplace.

Through persistent canvassing of the trade, Crow filled the Homefurnishings Mart, then his Trade Mart, Market Hall, Apparel Mart and World Trade Center, all on Stemmons land. His five-story, million-square-foot Trade Mart, which opened in 1959, reintroduced the atrium, an idea explored during the nineteenth century. Crow believed it would create an irresistible place for people to do their business. Besides providing a light and airy interior space as big as a football field, the Trade Mart had a pond, fountain, plantings and gazebo. Crow built an even bigger, 15-story-high Hall of Nations atrium at the 3.1 million-square-foot World Trade Center. By the 1960s, he was probably the biggest developer of merchandise marts in the world.

Crow is hard put to recall many details of his life, but he remembers when he got the idea for the atrium. "Margaret and I were touring Milan. We were at the palazzo, which is a square-doughnut building with a central outdoor plaza. It occurred to me that you could use high-strength steel to build a lightweight truss structure and move a wonderful place like this indoors. All you'd need was a roof on top."

Meanwhile, Portman's Atlanta hotel was hit by seven strikes which added a year to construction time and more than a million dollars of extra interest charges to construction cost. Richard Sorenson, the new president of Phoenix Investment Company, which owned a 60 percent interest in Portman's hotel, wanted out. Sorenson had come from Grant's, the variety store chain, and he preferred sticking with shopping centers, which he knew, rather than becoming involved with hotels. They took years to establish themselves in a market, and there was no way of telling how many more millions would have to be invested in this venture. The more optimistic market study estimated average room rates of $14.50, not nearly enough to break even.

Portman and Sorenson pitched more than a dozen major hotel operators who might be able to handle the financing, but decrepit, congested downtowns weren't the most attractive hotel sites. When urban violence erupted, which was often during the turbulent 1960s, occupancy rates plummeted, and many hotels gushed red ink. So hotel operators were more interested in suburban and airport locations. Moreover, hotel operators viewed Portman's atrium as a waste—costly space which should be used for income-generating rooms.

"We invited Conrad Hilton down," Portman told me, "and gave a big luncheon for him on top of the Merchandise Mart, out on the roof deck so that he could look over the hotel site. Hilton dismissed it by saying 'That concrete monster will never fly.' As you may imagine, such a gloomy assessment from the famous hotel man made my partners nervous."

Sorenson negotiated with the president of Chicago-based Pick Hotels, but it ran into trouble when the aging founder Albert Pick became involved. "He began nitpicking us with demands for free rent," Sorenson recalls. "If he was going to trade like that, we'd never get settled on the big issues. I think he really didn't like the deal, and his aim was to make us walk away."

Sorenson remembers meeting early one morning with a representative from a Teamsters pension fund which was investing considerable sums in hotels. A former bartender, the teamster wore an ill-fitting suit, white sweat socks and a cocked hat with a feather in it. He traveled all night from Chicago by train, got a couple hours sleep, arrived in Atlanta by 8 A.M. Sorenson tried to establish rapport by talking about his days at Chicago's Northwestern University. The teamster grumbled: "One of those rich people." The teamster was in a foul mood. Soon there was yelling. The teamster mashed his hat with his fist and stormed out.

Sorenson flew to New York for a meeting with balding, reserved Lawrence A. Tisch, a wizard of Wall Street who worked with his buoyant brother Preston Robert Tisch. They had started with $125,000 of family capital in 1946 and within two decades were worth more than $65 million. They built the glitzy Americana hotel in Miami Beach. They acquired Chicago's Ambassador Hotel, San Francisco's Mark Hopkins and the Warwick, Americana and Summit hotels in New York. They bought 118 Loews theaters from MGM.

Sorenson knew that the Tisches were tough, shrewd operators who ran their complex holdings rather straightforwardly like a candy store. At that time they were in spartan quarters on Broadway. Direct personal communications—rather than memos—were the norm. Lawrence and Robert Tisch had adjacent offices, and often they carried on conversations from their desks. They were surrounded by pictures of their families: Lawrence's wife Billie, their sons Andrew, Thomas, James and Daniel; Robert's wife Joan, their sons Jonathan and Steven, their daughter Laurie. Lawrence and Robert hoped some of their children would help build a dynasty.

While Lawrence Tisch spends most of his time watching television monitors displaying stock and commodity prices, Robert logs more than 120,000 miles a year, inspecting their various businesses, talking to hotel doormen, theater managers, warehousemen, foremen, even janitors who might help give him the pulse of what was going on. "In the end, it all comes down to instinct and feel," Robert says. "Like everything else, there's a knack to business."

Sorenson arrived for preliminary negotiations during the New York City blackout, July 1965. Since office lights and elevators weren't working, they met on the stairway leading from the lobby to the mezzanine of a Loews theater. Lawrence Tisch examined Sorenson's hotel blueprints and other papers. Soon they cut a deal. The Atlanta hotel would be named The Regency like the Tischs' New York Regency.

People from the operating side of Loews took over and began demanding design changes not contemplated in the contract—more than a million dollars' worth. Sorenson became alarmed as Tisch delayed signing the contract. Several months passed without any apparent action. The deal was terminated when Loews attorneys demanded an ice water line run to every room.

Then along came Ed Paulson, a slight, nervous, 70-year-old Chicago hotel broker with curly black hair. He was startled by an immense excavation along downtown Atlanta's West Peachtree Street. He visited the city, this summer day in 1965, to help sell what a businessman described as a "nice little hotel," but it turned out to be a flophouse. It wasn't Paulson's style, and the trip seemed wasted. But the excavation suggested tantalizing possibilities. His pulse quickened when the construction supervisor told him a high-rise hotel was going up, Atlanta's first in more than 40 years. The architect: a local guy named John Portman.

Paulson hurried to Portman's Danish modern office on the twenty-first floor of the Peachtree Center Building several blocks away. He remembers the architect hunched over a drafting table. Portman was cordial to this curious stranger and was glad to talk about his new project.

The frail Paulson didn't look like somebody who could handle a major deal. He was a chatty, self-effacing man who loved miniature poodles and took pills for his glaucoma. Yet it was soon apparent that he had tremendous knowledge of the hotel business. "I was too stupid to know anything else," he said to me. Paulson had a shrewd eye for good hotel locations. He knew how much flatware and linen to budget for any size hotel of whatever quality. He was on the phone almost around the clock with people interested in buying hotel properties—he didn't seem to sleep much. His clients included most of the major operators.

After discussing the options, Paulson ventured that he knew a Chicago family who might be interested in the Portman hotel. He called them and got an appointment for the next day. Paulson, Portman and Sorenson met at the second-floor offices of Pritzker & Pritzker, 134 North LaSalle Street, right across from Chicago's City Hall.

They reviewed the numbers of the deal with a tall, quietly self-assured man named Jack Pritzker and his brother Abram's son Donald. They said they'd think it over and get back to them soon. Sure enough, within a couple days, the Pritzkers agreed to assume the $8 million first mortgage at 6 percent which Sorenson had arranged with Massachusetts Mutual Insurance Company. Moreover, the Pritzkers would take a $4.5 million second mortgage in return for a payment of $3.75 million, giving the project a cash infusion.

Since neither Portman nor Sorenson had heard of the Pritzkers before, they wanted some assurances about the family's financial strength. They called First National Bank of Chicago, where the Pritzkers did much of their banking. Portman and Sorenson were amazed to learn that the Pritzkers had an unsecured line of credit for $70 million. Paulson smiled knowingly.

The Pritzkers are a remarkable family. Reigning patriarchs were Abram and Jack, sons of Nicholas and Anne who emigrated from Kiev, Russia. Nicholas became a pharmacist, trained himself as a lawyer and opened his Chicago practice in 1902. During the Great Depression, the cagy, resourceful Pritzkers often accepted stock in a client's company when there wasn't enough cash to pay their legal bill. They ended up taking over many distressed companies and rebuilding them. They discovered they could make more money from this than lawyering. So they left legal matters to their subordinates like Arthur Goldberg—later a Supreme Court Justice. In 1941, for instance, the Pritzkers bought Cory Corp., which manufactured coffee percolators as well as other appliances. That company cost $50,000, and they sold it in 1967 for $23 million to Hershey Foods. By then, the Pritzker family portfolio included an assortment of manufacturers, farmland, timberland, housing developments and shopping centers believed to be worth $500 million.

The Pritzkers adhere to the style that has served them so well: gain as big an interest as possible for the least amount of money. "The Pritzkers seldom risked much capital," an insurance company executive told me. "They'd take 90 percent of a deal for 10 percent of the money if they could."

The Pritzkers keep a low profile and run their affairs in what many would consider an informal manner—I find it quite appealing. A man with a light build, a shock of white hair, dark suspenders and a fresh cigar, A.N. carries almost everything he needs in a notebook protected by clear plastic. It has airline phone numbers, credit card numbers and a mortgage rate table. His secretary updates the names, addresses and phone numbers of business associates.

A.N. especially relishes striking deals in a corner of the Standard Club, an exclusive downtown gathering place for Chicago's Jewish business and professional elite. The Standard Club lobby is decorated with colorful prints by Picasso, Miro and Jasper Johns. You might compare the dining room with the Queen Mary—huge and stuffy. A.N. would scribble terms of a deal on a handy scrap of paper.

When his sons Jay, Robert and Donald were youngsters nearly a half-century ago, A.N. placed all his assets in trusts for them. "I got nothing!" A.N. told me proudly. "I remember Jay, at 13, telling me I was crazy to depend on them. I said if I couldn't raise you guys to do the right thing, I'd live in hell. I wanted money to be eliminated from our relationship. I didn't want anybody waiting for the old man to die."

Jay, a laundry service entrepreneur at Northwestern University, opted for the business world, and he began scouting for undervalued situations. He acquired a characteristic hoarseness from talking constantly on the telephone. A.N.'s middle son Robert, trained as an engineer, learned how to turn around ailing companies. He became a master. "We're a family unit," Robert stresses. "The things we do are so intertwined."

A.N. cultivated relationships with institutional lenders like Prudential Insurance Company, Ford Motor Land Company and the Rockefellers. He drafted every major contract. "Dad is the most brilliant lawyer you ever met," says Jay. "We assess risks and move fast without waiting for somebody else to advise us.

"Opportunities occur either when there's conflict which can only be resolved by a sale or when people are getting on in years and want to sell. You cannot buy on advantageous terms when a seller isn't anxious to sell.

"We buy where we can improve management and reduce the amount of assets needed to operate the business. Financial maneuvering is prologue. Management is all."

The Pritzkers never got involved with a hostile takeover. Their typical deal was surprisingly small. "We bought what we could afford," explains Robert Pritzker. "You go for little diamonds when you're married."

Jay got E. L. Bruce Company, a bankrupt plywood producer, by flipping a coin at First National Bank of Chicago. The bank held stock as collateral. Jay called heads and won against Henry Crown, a powerful Chicago industrialist who had just sold the Empire State Building. The Pritzkers reorganized Bruce, then sold it six years later at a profit. "That really wasn't worth the effort," Jay recalls, "but the experience did convince First National Bank that we knew how to run a business. A lot of people just thought of us as financial operators."

In 1957 Jay stayed in a four-year-old, 90-room Los Angeles airport motel called Hyatt House. It was the first comfortable airport motel he had ever known. He was startled to discover that its average occupancy was 98 percent—the industry considered 80 percent quite good—and the adjoining restaurant, Fat Eddie's, did a robust business. Pritzker envisioned great possibilities. He resolved to buy the place.

Owner Hyatt von Dehn had prospered by building motels near military installations, and that was how he happened to choose a site near Los Angeles International Airport. Jay offered him $2.1 million, and he agreed. The Pritzkers acquired more motel properties throughout the Midwest and Far West.

When Richard Sorenson and Portman called on the Pritzkers at their Chicago office, Hyatt was a $20 million company managing 6,000 hotel rooms. It was run by A.N.'s outgoing youngest son Donald who had graduated from Harvard before going on to the University of Chicago Law School. Donald was joined by his brother-in-law Skip Friend.

Sorenson and Portman hammered out a deal with Jack and Donald in less than three days. The Pritzkers could make any changes they wished, at their expense. They'd take title upon completion of the hotel. If it couldn't be completed, the Pritzkers owed nothing.

Donald Pritzker and his associates began reviewing the hotel plans. Then came the change orders. When they exceeded $700,000, Sorenson called Donald, reminding him that it was on the Pritzkers' tab. The word was passed to A.N.

Angered, he called Sorenson. "What's this about money," A.N. stormed, "you promised us a first class hotel."

"Jack agreed you were buying the hotel according to plan, and you'd pay for any changes," Sorenson retorted.

"I don't care what Jack did," said A.N. "I'm not paying for this stuff."

Sorenson, reflecting later: "Young Don was telling me what he wanted and left it for me to argue with his father. We used to call A.N. Daddy Rabbit—there were a lot of Pritzkers, and he was the daddy. I think one of the lawyers came up with that."

As a savvy attorney, A.N. had a good idea how far he could push Sorenson before the dispute would be worth a lawsuit. They sat down and agreed that Sorenson would be be liable for as much as $550,000 of changes. However, if accumulated profits for the first five years of operation exceeded $500,000, then $275,000 of that would be deducted from what he owed. In the event accumulated profits hit $1 million, the whole $550,000 would be forgiven.

Says A.N.: "The trick in making deals is first to establish credibility by treating people straight. Next, you must dream up ways to satisfy their requirements. I did that all the time."

Recalling that first hotel deal with the Pritzkers, Portman says, "I was so confident of success that I bet Donald Pritzker $1,000 to a cup of coffee the Atlanta Hyatt Regency would hit 90 percent occupancy within three months after opening. I won."

It opened May 1, 1967 with $40 million of advance bookings, an immediate success. Occupancy was 94.6 percent by September. A 200-room addition was soon underway. While hotels usually take years to establish themselves in a market, the Atlanta Hyatt Regency generated annual profits of more than $2 million during the first year.

In 1969 Portman's second hotel for the Pritzkers, near Chicago's O'Hare International Airport, exceeded the budget, and it became their last major collaboration. "He promised us no extra costs," A.N. claims, "but then I got a bill for an extra $800,000. The hotel had to be redesigned lower so it would conform with Federal Aviation Administration regulations which I believe he should have known about."

Portman remembers the experience a little differently, citing bureaucratic waffling over what the height limit should be. Since then, Hyatt executives have proposed working with Portman again, but A.N.'s long memory gets in the way.

Portman, Crow, David Rockefeller and Prudential Insurance Company were partners in a San Francisco project called Embarcadero Center. The Pritzkers got the operating contract for the Portman-designed hotel which the Pritzkers acknowledge as their most spectacular property. More than a decade after it opened, it still attracts some 2 million tourists a year who come to see the breathtaking 17-story atrium.

Crow's real estate empire, largest in the United States, grew to include 13 hotels. The biggest anywhere, and the one he's most proud of is the 1,620-room Anatole in Dallas. A city within a city, filling 45 acres, it has two huge atriums, extensive displays of oriental art and one of the best-appointed health facilities you'll see. Lockers are solid oak. The Anatole is operated by Loews, whose owners, Lawrence and Preston Robert Tisch, couldn't reach an agreement with John Portman in Atlanta. In August 1984, President Ronald Reagan came to the Anatole, where the Republican Convention nominated him as the party's candidate. He was the honored guest of Trammell Crow, chief Republican fund raiser. Crow fulfilled his dream of moving among the movers and shakers.

Equally satisfying, several of his children share his enthusiasm for the business. Trammell S. Crow Jr., 33, is chairman of the Dallas Market Center. Lucy Crow Billingsley, 31, is president. Their responsibility includes the Dallas Communications Complex for TV commercial and movie productions being built in Las Colinas, a new community near the Dallas–Fort Worth International Airport. Traveling throughout Europe, South America and the Far East, Howard Crow, 37, is chief buyer as well as manager for shops in family-owned hotels. Harlan Crow, 35, is the partner who handles the Trammell Crow Company's downtown Dallas office buildings. Recently, he took charge of development in New York and New Jersey.

Not everyone is in real estate, though. Stuart Crow, 29, races cars around the United States. Robert Crow, 42, moved to Los Angeles, where he heads Crow Productions, a movie production company. Thus far, Robert has finished two feature-length dramas, *Ordinary Heroes* and *Butterfly Revolution*.

Success and glamour hasn't changed Trammell Crow's lifestyle much. He gets up at 4:30 A.M. He exercises for at least an hour swimming or walking—until a knee injury several years ago, he jogged around his Highland Park neighborhood in Dallas. He eats a light breakfast with Margaret, arriving at the office by 8:30. He takes a 15-to-20 minute midday break in his company's lunch room. He's home by 6:30. After dinner, he reads or plays backgammon with Margaret. Asleep by 9:30.

Thanks largely to the success of the hotels Portman designed, the Pritzkers found themselves in the first-class hotel business. They were besieged with offers to do more hotels. Soon plans were underway

to build atrium hotels in downtown Houston, Knoxville and San Francisco. Within three years, Hyatt's sales tripled to $108 million. Profits quintupled to $5 million. That was just the beginning.

A. N. Pritzker announced a $12 million gift to the University of Chicago where A.N., his son Robert and nephew Nick had graduated. The gift funded what became known as the Pritzker School of Medicine. This along with Michael Reese Hospital, the Chicago Art Institute and the Jewish Federation of Chicago are his major philanthropic devotions.

A.N., gliding along at 88, grumbles about operational complexities of the far-flung family holdings. "You have to be nuts," he says. "I love the deals. I close one, delegate it to other people and move onto the next. Now even making deals is so involved. You got to consult an architect, interior design expert, builder, hotel person, finance person—I don't like it. My interest was always legal and finance."

To be sure, things weren't all up for the Pritzkers. They were devastated when Donald died of a heart attack on a Honolulu tennis court in May 1972. The driving force behind Hyatt's aggressive expansion, he was just 39. Seven months later, Jay and Marian Pritzker returned from a European trip to find their 24-year-old daughter Nancy in the garage, dead from carbon monoxide poisoning. A.N.'s brother Jack died in October 1979.

A.N. displayed remarkable resiliency. After his wife Fanny died, he remarried in 1972—Lorraine Colantonio, part owner and manager of the Hyatt Chalet, Elk Grove Village, near Chicago. A.N. wasn't a particularly religious man, and the ceremony was performed at his Lake Shore Drive residence by United States District Court Judge Hubert Will. The Pritzkers took off for the opening of the Plaza International Regency Hyatt House, Acapulco. That, A.N. quips, "must be the longest name in history for a hotel."

Despite his toughness in business, he sometimes seems a soft touch. When he got a fund-raising call from Gwen Henslee, principal of Chicago's Wicker Park Elementary School where he had graduated in 1910, he agreed to help. He donated thousands of dollars to after-school programs like cheerleaders, pompon girls, cooking, crafts, ceramics, basketball, volleyball and video games. Teachers selected students to accompany him on trips to New York, Washington and other places. Invariably for these kids reared in slums, it was their first adventure out of Chicago and their first night in a Hyatt hotel.

A.N. retains his lively sense of humor. "After all these years as a lawyer, I finally won a court case. My chauffeur was driving me through downtown Chicago south on Clark Street, and he made a left-hand turn onto Monroe. It was from the wrong lane. Got a ticket. Naturally, I agreed to represent him in court. The judge asked who the defense counsel was, and I stepped forward. He apologized for not recognizing me and said some nice things. I followed the number one rule of court procedure: When a judge appears sympathetic to your side, shut your mouth! Case was dismissed."

2.

CONTRARY THINKING

ONE OF THE MOST REMARKABLE FEATS IN REAL ESTATE IS TO AC-quire control of a potentially great site when it looks miserable. Perhaps it's out of the way or disfigured with decrepit buildings, or it may seem a poor bet because of land use restrictions. You need bold, contrary thinking to see beyond present realities and envision changes which will add value. Then you've got to back your convictions with cash.

North America's largest personal fortune involves three very great site deals. Albert and Paul Reichmann parlayed these into a $15 billion empire which extends across the United States, Canada and Europe. Their principal company, Olympia & York, is the biggest real estate developer on the continent. The Reichmanns' net worth is estimated at $5 billion. They're far richer than the Rockefellers, Hunts, Kennedys or anybody else you might name.

How do they spot potentially great sites other people miss? How do they assess the risks of real estate? How did they make the three site deals that are the cornerstones of their fortune? To answer these and other questions, I got on a plane for Toronto. I went downtown to the Reichmanns' white marble flagship building, One First Canadian Place, at 72 stories the tallest in Canada. Their offices are on the thirty-fourth floor, not the top floor, which would give them a smashing view. "Middle is better," Albert told me in his unassuming way.

Albert is somewhat heavy set, about 5 feet 9 inches tall, with thick brown hair.

Paul, more slender, is over 6 feet. He has prominent ears and a neatly trimmed beard. He was a chain smoker for years until he beat the habit in 1984.

The Reichmanns speak with a distinctive Eastern European accent.

They're models of sobriety. They favor plain black suits, narrow ties and black shoes. Though they have a formal manner, Albert enjoys a good laugh, and Paul seems illuminated by an inner mirth.

They're without pretense, I discovered. No corporate limousine or jet for the Reichmanns: They, who could afford to buy almost any commercial airline, wait with everybody else at airport ticket counters. They don't own any vacation homes or sports franchises. Unlike Donald Trump, Harry Helmsley, the Tishmans and other real estate entrepreneurs, they don't name buildings after themselves.

The Reichmanns display a quiet Old World charm. They'll go out to meet a visitor in the reception area rather than having a secretary do it. They're deferential to everyone.

Tenants, bankers and other real estate owners find them easy, responsive listeners. They're unusually straightforward to deal with— no egos needing to be stroked, no winning through intimidation. "The Reichmanns are the only Toronto developers who never got in a fight with city authorities," says Ron Soskolne, a former Toronto city planner and now an Olympia & York development executive.

The Reichmanns avoid the limelight, and this helps intensify curiosity about them. They don't belong to fashionable clubs or attend society affairs. They give very few press interviews. They decline requests to be photographed. Once when Albert went to Oakdale Golf and Country Club for a reception honoring the head of the Israeli air staff, he hid behind a column more than an hour to avoid a clutch of photographers.

They cultivate such a low profile that they aren't always recognized by their own people. Once after a dinner in Dallas, Albert wanted to show his wife Egosah their new building, but it was closed, and the guard refused to let them in.

Though they tithe a hefty portion of their vast income to charity, they seldom give to mainstream organizations like United Jewish Appeal, for instance, and they don't attend fund-raising dinners. Instead, they cut through organizational overhead and give directly to those causes they consider worthy. They've written some 3,000 checks for $1,000 to individual teachers, scholars and rabbis. They support a strict Orthodox Jewish boys school, Yesodai Hetorah, and a girls school, Junior Beth Jacob. They finance the construction of yeshivas—religious high schools—in Israel. They established a multimillion-dollar endowment to finance the largest wing of Toronto's Mount Sinai Hospital, and they're underwriting the cost of an affiliated medical laboratory where some 300 researchers will work. "I believe learning is more important than business," Paul says.

The Reichmanns insist on strict observance of the sabbath and Jewish holidays. They always wear yarmulkes. They live within walking distance of their temple, since they aren't permitted to do physical work like driving on the Sabbath. They vacation at a kosher resort in Switzerland.

They're equally observant in business, too. They are not known to eat at a fancy restaurant—lunch is prepared at their offices, in accordance with Jewish dietary laws. On the elevator doors of their offices are mezuzahs—little cylinders with a scripture inside. Their offices close early enough on Friday—3 P.M. in winter—for everyone to arrive home before sundown, the beginning of the sabbath. Construction contracts specify that no work is to be done on the sabbath, and on more than one occasion enforcing this provision has required a little yelling by John Norris, their cockney vice president for construction. The only strike against Olympia & York was by a Boston union that objected to losing pay during the Jewish holidays. In their usual conciliatory style, the Reichmanns settled the dispute when they agreed to an equivalent amount of overtime.

Their mother Rene, well into her 80s, remains board chairman of Olympia & York. She lives in the same modest yellow home she and her husband Samuel bought almost three decades ago.

The Reichmanns spend weekends with their families. Albert and Egosah have four children. Philip, the oldest, is the only one in the company—he took over development of Queen's Quay Terminal, a complex of festive shops, condominiums and offices on Lake Ontario. Paul and his wife Lea have five children, none old enough to enter the business.

They attribute much of their success to insights gained from the Talmud, the 63 volumes containing Jewish civil and canonical laws. Fathers and sons sit across from each other for hours, taking a passage and discussing its interpretation. "My teenage son," Paul says proudly, "can talk about real estate law with me as a result of our Talmudic studies." They taught conciliation rather than confrontation as a way of doing business.

Consummate masters of detail, the Reichmanns bring exceptional financial sophistication and discipline to a business well-known for freewheeling, highly leveraged, cash-strapped entrepreneurs. They display a remarkable ability to control their cost of money and their construction cost. Since these are the key factors influencing a developer's break-even point, the Reichmanns possess staying power in difficult times.

Although they make extensive investments in natural resource companies, plus own an interest in Cadillac Fairview, Trizec, Landmark Land, Ernest Hahn and The Rouse Company, which develop office buildings, shopping centers and residential property, the Reichmanns concentrate their own development energies on downtown office buildings. "We believe we can recognize value," explains Paul, "but we prefer applying ourselves to what we do best."

29

Each brother can handle the responsibilities of the other, though Paul is more interested in financial strategy and Albert likes construction. Paul concentrates his efforts on New York, while Albert attends to Olympia & York properties around the United States.

Their resourcefulness owes much to years of surviving by their wits. Their father, Samuel Reichmann, built a sizable business as an egg wholesaler in his native Beled, Hungary. His wife Rene was cousin of David Gestetner, the Hungarian-born British industrialist who invented the stencil printing process. Samuel did considerable export business with England, and he transferred savings there. Concerned, during the 1920s, that Russia might invade Hungary, he, Rene and their daughter Eva, sons Edward and Louis moved to Vienna where Albert, Paul and Ralph were born. Samuel was an adroit entrepreneur who bought and turned around a faltering Vienna glass factory. The Reichmanns were decisive, leaving within hours after Hitler invaded Austria in 1938. With Hungarian passports, they took a train to Hungary, then headed for Paris.

By June 1940, Hitler was invading France. The Reichmanns had an English visa, but it was impossible to go there. Nor was there an obvious means of fleeing South. They escaped on foot 36 hours before the Germans entered Paris. "Then for the equivalent of $3,000," Albert recalls, "we got a truck and drove 80 miles to Orleans where we caught a train south to Biarritz. We rented a station wagon, and though we had no Spanish visas, we were allowed to cross into Spain. The roads were jammed, but it was easier getting through Spain and across the Strait of Gibraltar to Morocco than it was getting out of France."

It was an extraordinary accomplishment, escaping with their families intact. Only a tiny percentage of European Jews managed that during the most dangerous years. The Reichmanns preserved most of their assets, too.

In turbulent Tangier, Samuel Reichmann started a lively curbside currency exchange business. "He could do all the calculations in his head incredibly fast," says Albert, who was the only one to work in the new family business. Samuel started a banking operation.

I was astonished to discover that Paul—now real estate's greatest financial genius—had no interest in business. He attended talmudic colleges in England for five years before deciding to work for an educational organization linked to the Hebrew International Aid Society. He helped with the education of Jewish immigrants who poured into Morocco. "We learned Hungarian, French, English, Spanish, Hebrew and Arabic," he reflects.

As Morocco moved toward independence from France, and the

prospect of currency controls threatened to end their business, the Reichmanns planned their next move. This time, to Canada. Oldest-son Edward scouted Montreal before recommending Toronto. The family arrived in 1956. While searching for opportunities, they saw an advertisement in *The Wall Street Journal* offering for sale a foun-dering Montreal company that manufactured plastic tiles. They bought it, and since Ralph relished ancient Greek history, they called it Olympia Floor & Wall Tile Co.

Within a year, the Reichmanns outgrew their rented warehouse. They decided to build a new 16,000-square-foot facility. The lowest bid they got from an outside contractor, $125,000, seemed high, and they did the job themselves for $70,000. They were in the con-struction business. They started a new company which they called York Developments, after the county where they operated.

While Ralph operated the building materials business, Paul and Albert began building warehouses for others. They sought advan-tages by offering a better product. "Industrial buildings used to have a big front with concrete blocks on three sides," Paul recalls. "The front was a brick wall with some windows for front offices. We felt it looked horrible. You could spend pennies more per square foot, not dollars, and have it look decent. We used a nice combination of materials and landscaping. Consequently, we could get 52 cents a foot per year, while competitors charged 50 cents, and before long we were building more warehouses than all the local vendors com-bined." The Reichmanns' fortune stems, in part, from their meticu-lous attention to 2-cent details like these.

They found their first great site amidst the ruins of William Zeck-endorf's crumbling empire. Zeckendorf was the most flamboyant de-veloper in modern times. He and his second wife Marion got choice theater tickets from their friend Lee Shubert to whom Zeckendorf sold a number of theaters. Zeckendorf backed Broadway shows like *Gentlemen Prefer Blondes* and movies such as *The Joe Louis Story*. Dur-ing the 1940s, he bought a building on Madison Avenue and 54th Street which housed the Monte Carlo Club, known for leggy dancers who did a roisterous revue called the *Monte Carlo Follies*. There Zeck-endorf held court at a corner table with private telephone, entertain-ing real estate people and reporters alike. "I make bananas out of peanuts," he boasted. "I make grapefruit out of lemons. What I like to do is recognize a great piece of land and conceive a suitable edifice for it."

A tall, husky, balding supersalesman for the brokerage firm Webb & Knapp, Zeckendorf made a name for himself by earning hefty real estate commissions during the Great Depression. In 1942, he persuaded the flamboyant Vincent Astor to let him manage a $50 million real estate portfolio which was losing money. Astor was heir to John Jacob Astor, the German immigrant who became an international fur trader and created America's first fabulous fortune. He plowed his profits into a marshy but promising place called Manhattan, where he owned more property than anybody else. "Could I begin again," John Jacob reflected to a friend in 1848, "knowing what I now know, and had the money to invest, I would buy every square foot of land on the island of Manhattan."

Within four years after taking over Vincent Astor's portfolio, Zeckendorf consummated some 150 deals which lifted Astor's portfolio value more than $15 million and turned losses into $2.5 million annual profits. Zeckendorf acquired 17 acres of East Side slaughterhouses and sold the property to John D. Rockefeller Jr., who donated it for the United Nations headquarters. Zeckendorf bought famous Manhattan properties like the Graybar Building and Chrysler Building. He built Park West Village, Lincoln Towers and Kips Bay Plaza, all of which house thousands of New Yorkers. He turned Long Island's 370-acre Roosevelt Field into a mammoth shopping center.

Encouraged by David Rockefeller, Zeckendorf engineered deals which helped preserve Lower Manhattan as a financial center. It was moribund during the 1950s—no new buildings had gone up there since the Wall Street crash—and many financial executives, restless in their cramped inefficient buildings, were considering a move uptown. Zeckendorf consolidated small properties, creating room for big new buildings. He helped bankers horse-trade their way out of long-standing lease obligations, so they'd be free to expand elsewhere. He assumed the risk of re-renting space they vacated. Then he moved Rockefeller's Chase Manhattan Bank. He also moved Chemical, Morgan, Hanover and Irving Trust. His was a virtuoso performance, and the value of these real estate transactions exceeded $250 million.

Zeckendorf expanded his operations throughout North America. He built giant projects such as Denver's Mile High Center and Montreal's Place Ville-Marie. When the federal government gave its blessing to urban renewal, Zeckendorf promoted it and became among the biggest U.S. builders of residential housing. During the 1950s, he built high-rise projects in Chicago, Philadelphia, Pittsburgh and Washington, D.C. He hired top design talent to guide these efforts—I. M. Pei, for instance, got his start in Zeckendorf's office.

Zeckendorf's ideas got wilder. In a seedy four-story walk-up, Zeckendorf bid $500 million to buy the reclusive Howard Hughes's empire of oil drilling bits, movie studios and airlines. Zeckendorf pushed to build the world's tallest building atop Grand Central Terminal. He committed himself to developing a $60 million office-retail-residential complex called L'Enfant Plaza in Washington, D.C., but political opponents squeezed him out, and others built it along the lines he had envisioned. Nothing ever came of his proposed $200 million Palace of Progress, promoted as the world's largest office building.

Chronic overtrading proved his undoing. Whatever cash he had was plowed into new deals, so he never had much margin for error. By the 1960s, he was scrambling. Losses from Denver's Mile High Center and the Roosevelt Field shopping center were draining his cash reserves. His Freedomland amusement park was a bust in the Bronx, and it was sold to make way for Co-op City, one of the largest U.S. housing developments.

In 1960, Zeckendorf promised New Yorkers "the greatest hotel ever built"—48 stories with 2,000 luxury guest rooms, 10 banquet halls and 15 private dining rooms. So on Sixth Avenue and 52nd Street he dug a hole 50 feet deep, 250 feet wide and 450 feet long. He ran out of cash, though, gave up on his dream and sold the hole to Percy and Harold Uris who were then reportedly Manhattan's largest builders. What was to have been the Zeckendorf Hotel became a modest office tower, the Sperry Rand Building.

In 1961, he bought 260 acres that had belonged to the bankrupt movie mogul William Fox, just west of Beverly Hills. But soon strapped for cash himself, Zeckendorf persuaded Alcoa President Frank McGee that a splendid office-retail-hotel development on that site could demonstrate the potential of aluminum as a building material. There Alcoa built the Century City complex of offices, stores, hotels and residences.

On May 7, 1965, Zeckendorf's chauffeur was driving him to Wall Street when his limousine phone rang. It was a *New York Times* reporter asking if Webb & Knapp were really bankrupt. Zeckendorf was stunned. A few minutes later, a *Wall Street Journal* reporter called, asking the same question. Then Zeckendorf's office called to say that Marine Midland Bank demanded immediate payment of the balance of an $8.5 million Webb & Knapp bond issue. Webb & Knapp was kaput.

As Canada's biggest real estate developer, Zeckendorf had property all around Toronto, and that's why Albert and Paul Reichmann happened to approach Webb & Knapp. "In 1965 we needed a half-acre parking lot," Albert recalls. "The most suitable land for a parking lot belonged to Zeckendorf.

"Webb & Knapp told us they couldn't sell us that little parcel, because it was encumbered with mortgages. We would have to buy all their Toronto property—over 500 acres. We offered $17.3 million, enough to clear up the mortgages, and we got the property. If we had offered a million less, they probably couldn't have made a deal.

"The property included apartments and raw land. The more we analyzed the situation, the less risk there seemed to be. We couldn't figure out why the land hadn't been picked up, because it was in the geographical center of Toronto. Its value was much greater than what they were asking.

"We negotiated the purchase in a couple weeks. We decided that the simplest thing was to get our money out right away. Have no more risk. Our main business was never residential building.

"Within about a month, we found an apartment investor who bought the hundred acres where most of the apartments were, and we recovered all our investment. We still had 400 acres, and we've been developing it ever since."

Thus Zeckendorf unknowingly helped the Reichmanns assemble their emerging empire. In August 1968, at age 63, Zeckendorf filed personal bankruptcy. He listed assets of $1,885,620 against $79,076,100 of liabilities. He died in 1976.

His personal legacy: son William Zeckendorf Jr., who started working in his father's business as a messenger boy during the 1940s. When he ventured out on his own three decades later, nobody was surprised that he tried his hand at real estate development. Stung by his father's embarrassing bankruptcy, he adopted a decidedly low profile. "I'm sure if I really wanted to do something else," he says, "nobody would have twisted my arm. But the 1940s and 1950s were the days of empire building, succession from father to son. I think I was lucky, because Webb & Knapp was large enough that as a young man, I had my own projects to run rather independently."

Since his father's death, William has developed primarily in Manhattan, to avoid becoming overextended like his father. He has a staff a tenth the size of his father's. He seldom talks to the press. But he, too, is attracted to run-down areas that seem ripe for redevelopment—the Upper West Side, the closed-down S. Klein Building on Union Square, the old Statler Hotel in the garment district.

William Zeckendorf Jr. married Guri Lie, daughter of Trygve Lie, first Secretary General of the United Nations, which his father helped bring to New York. They had two sons, William and Arthur, neither of whom was interested in real estate. This first marriage ended in divorce. Subsequently Zeckendorf married Nancy King, once a principal dancer at the Metropolitan Opera. They began to step out a little, and she became a trustee of the American Ballet Theater.

But it was the Reichmanns who really stepped into William Zeckendorf's seven-league boots. Until 1973, they had developed properties around the perimeter of cities. Then an unexpected opportunity enabled them to assemble a prime downtown site.

"We built new offices for the *Toronto Star* by Lake Ontario," Albert explains, and they were vacating their old building in the financial district. They had no further use for it. We bought it after a very straightforward negotiation, then tried to assemble the rest of the block between King Street on the south, Adelaide on the north, York on the west and Bay on the east."

The assemblage started easily enough. North American Life Insurance Company owned most of the block, and they were willing to sell. The Reichmanns acquired land from the Bank of Montreal by agreeing to give them space in their new building.

"Royal Trust vacated their building, so that looked simple, too," Albert continues. "But another developer was interested. Royal Trust decided to remain neutral and offer their building to the highest bidder. Each of us could submit a single bid in a sealed envelope.

"How much to bid was a crucial decision, because the Royal Trust property was in the middle of our assemblage. We could have built without it, but the project would be much smaller and less interesting. The envelopes were opened, and Royal Trust announced the other developer bid $1.5 million. We got the property with a bid of $1,537,000. As far as we could figure, both parties arrived at the same bid per square foot and multiplied this amount by the number of square feet involved. But they *rounded down* to arrive at an even amount, and we were content to bid an odd number. So the outcome depended on that $37,000, a 2 percent difference!

"Finally, there was a drugstore. It wasn't essential for our site, but the additional 2,500 square feet would give us room for a better project. The drugstore was owned by a developer who named his price, and we accepted. He had another small building elsewhere in town he wanted to dispose of, and he insisted we take it as part of the deal. We accepted that, too. We still have it, an empty building. As I remember, we paid about $180,000 for it, and it's worth more than $2 million. I expect it will be torn down to make way for larger development eventually."

Their site assembled, the Reichmanns built One First Canadian Place. At its base are three levels with 165 shops, boutiques and specialty restaurants. It sits astride perhaps the most valuable block in Toronto. Underground retail corridors similar to those at Rockefeller Center connect One First Canadian Place to adjacent buildings including a companion, Two First Canadian Place. "Half the money in Toronto is within a few blocks of here," Albert says.

They needed their financial reserves for One First Canadian Place because, opening amidst a recession, it took four years to fully lease— twice as long as they had anticipated. Though the first-year cash drain alone hit $20 million, they maintained their rent levels. The last tenants to move in paid $42 a square foot, almost four times more than the initial tenants.

This project, twice as big as anything the Reichmanns had attempted before, certified them as major developers. But they remained virtually unknown in the United States. They began to explore new investments, especially in New York.

They became intrigued with a group of office towers built by Percy and Harold Uris. The buildings were rather ugly glass-and-steel boxes, since the Urises weren't interested in fine architecture. But the structures were soundly built at good locations. Percy had died in 1971, and Harold, disconsolate, lost interest in managing the properties. None of the Uris children wanted to take over.

Warner Communications Chairman Stephen Ross, who controlled National Kinney, bid up prices for the properties against British Land Chairman John Ritblat, and the Reichmanns decided to bide their time. Ten Uris buildings went to National Kinney.

Then New York became a bad news city. Bankruptcy was averted only by a $2.3 billion bailout from Congress. Crime was in the headlines. Several major corporations moved their headquarters elsewhere. National Kinney needed cash, and the Uris buildings, with an average vacancy rate of 13 percent, were awash in read ink. National Kinney had lost $15 million on a 48-story tower at 1633 Broadway before defaulting on its construction loan from Irving Trust, Chemical Bank, Bankers Trust and Morgan Guaranty Trust. Those banks foreclosed—the first foreclosure against a big Manhattan office building since the 1930s. The empire the proud Uris brothers had created was in shambles.

"When I heard they let 1633 Broadway go," recalled Donald Davis of Prudential, which had mortgages on several Uris properties, "the first thing I thought of was our vulnerability. The crux of the matter is, how long can they hold on? We can't see these buildings as reasonable investments."

National Kinney had few choices. "There isn't any mortgage money around now," warned Michael Wechsler of Chemical Bank. "Savings banks don't have any money, and insurance companies don't want any more of New York, except in very special cases."

Several insurance companies declined a chance to buy the Uris buildings. Harold Grabino, responsible for selling the properties, recalled: "The truth was that most institutional buyers who could afford this kind of deal had already drawn a big red line around Manhattan. They were afraid of it."

Sam LeFrak, New York's biggest apartment builder, dickered for the Uris properties. He wanted to refinance the mortgages and stretch out payments. He resisted putting as much cash into the deal as the Uris people wanted. "I don't buy anticipation," he says, waving his arms with characteristic exuberance. "If you want to sell me anticipation, I'll give you anticipation money. When I get it, you get it." Nothing happened.

Pioneering real estate syndicator Harry Helmsley: "I certainly had a go at those buildings, but there just wasn't the interest. You couldn't convince anybody to invest in New York property then." Helmsley had his own worries with One Penn Plaza, a 2.2-million-square-foot office building that was a cash drain partially because a major company called Ebasco had signed a lease, then merged with Boise Cascade and broke the lease, never actually moving in.

The Reichmanns certainly didn't seem like hot prospects. "You look at a pair of Orthodox guys from Toronto," said Grabino, recalling his initial impression, "and you have to wonder if they are in a league to make this deal."

They were interested in making a major Manhattan real estate investment, because they retained their European faith in the future of central cities. "Despite the bad news, New York remained a diversified city, and we didn't believe it would lose its position as the world's leading financial center," Albert Reichmann explains.

In the summer of 1976, they were approached by Edward Minskoff, an investment banker who was a partner with their Canadian rival Cadillac Fairview, the largest publicly-held real estate developer controlled by the Bronfman family, which also controlled Seagram's. Cadillac Fairview, with its layers of corporate executives, wasn't in a position to make a fast decision on the Uris properties, but the Reichmanns could. Minskoff, with deep knowledge of Manhattan real estate, offered to help them evaluate the possibilities.

This involved analyzing leases in each building. While the buildings were almost all well-built structures in desirable locations, most leases were written in the 1960s, before inflation and high interest rates became a serious concern. The Uris brothers had negotiated long-term leases with rent ceilings, and rent included what turned out to be volatile expenses like taxes. Estimating the present worth of a building required considerable thought.

Soon one building—1301 Avenue of the Americas—was taken off

the market. It was the J.C. Penney headquarters, and the retailer exercised its option to buy.

Among the eight remaining properties was the Sperry Rand Building at 1290 Avenue of the Americas—what used to be William Zeckendorf's gaping hole. The 43-story building was owned 50 percent by National Kinney, 50 percent by Rockefeller Center Inc.; it had almost 1.9 million square feet, about 98 percent leased; and it was part of Rockefeller Center, which had a strong rental history.

Then there was 44-story 245 Park Avenue, an excellent location near Grand Central Station and many corporate headquarters. A Fortune 500 prime tenant, American Brands, had a third of the 1.6 million square feet. However, the company had a lease that ran for 13 more years and provided negligible rents—$6 a square foot, which was about a third of the then-current market.

The 34-story 320 Park Avenue was a similar situation: excellent location, but income severely limited by the lead tenant, ITT. They paid $9 a square foot for 90 percent of the space. Minskoff and the Reichmanns attributed negligible value to this building.

A block from the new Citicorp headquarters was 21-story 850 Third Avenue, where Western Publishing was the major tenant. This building had a mixed roster with the possibility of rolling over leases during the next several years and improving income.

The 37-story Harper & Row building, 10 East 53rd Street, was a small building in another superb midtown location. It, too, was virtually full, with tenants paying rents well below market levels.

A downtown property, 2 Broadway, was losing money because of the low rent levels. The building had 1.6 million square feet of space on 32 floors. The Reichmanns didn't want to pay much for this.

At 60 Broad Street, there was a 39-story tower with 900,000 square feet opposite Morgan Guaranty Trust's world headquarters. Almost all the space was leased by four tenants—Drexel Burnham, RCA, RCA Global Communications and Dresdner Bank. Here again, cheap leases had several years to run.

The most troubled of the Uris properties was downtown—the massive 51-story, 3.6-million-square-foot 55 Water Street. With almost 800,000 square feet of vacant space, this was losing about $2 million a year. Yet the Reichmanns viewed it as among the most valuable properties. That space was available for immediate leasing at market rates. The location was fine. The floors were large, ranging from 54,000 to 62,000 square feet—a definite plus, since the Reichmanns believed very large floors would be the choice of major corporations. Financial services companies couldn't operate efficiently on small floors.

The Uris properties had $288 million of conventional fixed-rate mortgages ranging from 5.125 percent to 9 percent. They were non-recourse, meaning that in the event of default, lenders would try to recover their loans by selling the buildings instead of going after the borrower's other assets. The Reichmanns could have the package if they'd assume these mortgages and pay $50 million cash.

They also recognized a recent history of laggard maintenance. Bringing the buildings up to the Reichmanns' standards would require an additional infusion of capital.

The land under several Uris buildings was owned by various institutions, and this was a drawback. In the event the Reichmanns wanted to build something different on the sites later, they might find themselves restricted. To acquire the land, if it ever became available, would require further investment.

Overall, the average rent for the Uris properties was under $10 a square foot. Likely acquisition cost would be about $31 a square foot, a third of estimated replacement cost. "If you believed that New York City was going to recover," Minskoff says, "then these properties were definitely undervalued."

Friday morning, September 19, 1977, at the Park Avenue law offices of Paul Weiss Rifkin Wharton & Garrison, the Reichmanns met for the closing. There was a zoo of attorneys, title insurance people, brokers, bankers and owners. Terms: $320 million, $50 million in cash. By midafternoon, the paperwork was finished, money was wired to the seller's bank account, and the deal was closed. A little over an hour later, Albert and Paul Reichmann were hustling to their rooms at the Waldorf-Astoria for Sabbath prayers.

The New York Times gave the story little space. Two weeks after the initial agreement to buy in March, they ran an article headlined "Foreign Bargain Hunters Seek Prime Office Space." There was no mention at all of the September closing. Nonetheless, the Reichmanns were now among New York's largest landlords.

Within six months, tenants in the Uris buildings noticed dramatic improvements in the way their buildings were maintained, for the Reichmanns poured millions into their new acquisitions. Systems worked. No more lobby litter. Vacant space began to fill.

Some tenants who couldn't get more space in their present building were glad to consider space in another Reichmann property. Merrill Lynch, Lehman Brothers, Bear Stearns and Dean Witter, for instance, all at 55 Water Street, leased additional space at 2 Broadway.

By 1979, New York's financial situation improved dramatically, and the Reichmanns looked like geniuses. Uris leases that had averaged $10 a square foot when the Reichmanns bought were renewed for more than $30. In 1981, new leases were being written at $60 a square foot. The value of those buildings climbed more than $2 billion, providing the wherewithal for even bigger deals. "New York turned around much faster than we expected," Albert smiles.

When a tall, tanned Californian named Victor Palmieri was liquidating properties of the bankrupt Penn Central Railroad, the Reichmanns seized opportunities to enlarge their holdings. Buying the 1-million-square-foot 237 Park Avenue Building, across the street from their American Brands Building, required some resourcefulness, because there was intense bidding—New York real estate millionaires like Harry Helmsley, Robert Tishman, Sam LeFrak and Paul Milstein were after it. To help clinch the deal, the Reichmanns agreed to buy from the railroad land under their buildings at 245 Park Avenue and 320 Park Avenue, which the Reichmanns wanted anyway. Other bidders weren't interested in matching this proposal.

The Reichmanns stripped 237 Park Avenue to the frame and had offices redesigned around a gleaming atrium that rose 23 stories above a 7,000-square-foot courtyard. It became a popular gathering spot, and major companies like the J. Walter Thompson advertising agency moved in.

As prime downtown sites became tougher to acquire everywhere, the Reichmanns entered the public bidding process. This involved urban renewal land belonging to municipal governments, cleared and ready for development. Typically, there was a lot of competition for the sites.

Among the choicest in the United States was Battery Park City, 93 acres of landfill resulting from the construction of New York's World Trade Center. Governor Nelson Rockefeller had promoted the idea, and in 1968 the Battery Park City Authority was created to develop the site. It floated $200 million of bonds. A lot of money was spent hatching grandiose plans by Harrison & Abramovitz, the architectural firm that had designed the monstrous Albany Mall. But the plans were bigger than any developer could handle, and political wrangling brought action to a standstill. Without action soon, there would be a calamitous bond default.

In 1980, Governor Hugh Carey appointed Richard Kahan chairman of the Battery Park City Authority. He had city planner Alex Cooper design a new master plan that extended the existing city street grid into the landfill so developers could bid on smaller, block-size properties.

One parcel, where 2 million square feet of office space could be built, had a tax abatement 50 percent greater than the other parcels. "This was because we believed the hardest parcel to lease was the first," says Kahan. "Once somebody stepped forward to take it, the other 4 million square feet would be more desirable, and leasing would follow." He invited proposals by October 15, 1980.

They required the most careful analysis, because there were huge risks. Until this time, the largest amount of lower Manhattan office space rented in a single year was a million and a half square feet. Even if the Reichmanns got every square foot up for grabs, leasing their project would take years. The last big downtown deal—World Trade Center—glutted the office market there throughout most of the 1970s.

A dozen developers responded. Some of New York's biggest were represented: Harry Helmsley, Sam LeFrak, Robert Tishman and Jerry Speyer. Smaller New York developers like Sheldon Solow, George Klein, Larry Silverstein and Cohen Brothers entered, too. Cadillac-Fairview was in, as was a Chicago deal-maker named Jerry Wexler.

Should the Reichmanns enter? They huddled with Michael Dennis, former Toronto housing commissioner who was Olympia & York's executive vice president for U.S. development, and Ron Soskolne, vice president of planning and development. He was formerly Toronto's chief city planner. Both understood how to deal effectively with public agencies that control land use.

They began by analyzing the market. The most powerful trend, they believed, was the consolidation of the financial services industry. Brokerage firms and banks, with offices scattered all around lower Manhattan, were merging. There was a growing demand for larger floors—more than 25,000 square feet—so firms could locate their operations close together. Comparatively few buildings satisfied this demand. Therefore, it was a good time for a new project offering large floors.

What to bid? The Reichmanns proposed ground rent that would start at a low $2 million and graduate as buildings were substantially completed. If the Reichmanns were successful at leasing the buildings, they would begin receiving income about the time they had to start writing hefty rent checks to the Battery Park City Authority. Developers had assembled some 10 million square feet of downtown land where big new buildings could go up, but building costs, the Reichmanns realized, were significantly higher than at Battery Park City. They would be in a position to offer space for an estimated $5 to $8 less per square foot than anybody else. This could translate to millions of dollars. Who knows, in a good market, the Reichmanns could keep much of this for themselves.

Bid on the initial parcel with the lush tax abatement or go for the whole site? "We believed that it could be difficult leasing a single building," says Paul Reichmann, "since people would be looking out at an unimproved site. Who could say what would happen with the rest of it? Tenants would be more comfortable knowing the whole site was being developed at once, and they would be part of a finished project."

Eleven developers gave elaborate presentations. Half a dozen bid for the whole site, but they proposed phasing in development over many years. Helmsley bid for 3 million square feet. Milstein and Wexler, for 2 million square feet. Cohen Brothers, 1.35 million square feet.

Paul Reichmann arrived without a briefcase. He pulled out a sheet of blue paper with a bond repayment schedule through the year 2014. "You have quite a lot of debt here to be paid off," he began, in his customary hushed tone.

"Yes, we do," Kahan nodded.

"If I were to guarantee the payments in that column," Reichman asked, "would I be on the right track to getting the job of developing Battery Park City?"

Kahan, apparently, was stunned. "What I really wanted to do then," he said, "was jump up from behind my desk and kiss the man on both cheeks. He was the only one in the procession of developers who understood my primary worry—paying off the bonds."

He bid a total of $189.1 million for the right to develop all 6 million square feet in five years—about half the time contemplated by others. This included a guarantee to cover the $50 million Battery Park City Authority owed bondholders, even if Olympia & York failed to complete the project. Paul brought letters of credit to back him up.

Suddenly, competitors were virtually wiped out. The mainstream development game was to do a deal with as little of your own money as possible, yet the Reichmanns had the brass to put $50 million on the line.

Moreover, although Kahan hadn't anticipated development of the whole site at once, he soon decided that not only could it be done, but it would be desirable. He wouldn't have to worry about making deals with anybody else. Olympia & York won.

There was grousing. Jerry Wexler protested that it wasn't clear developers could bid on the whole site. Sheldon Solow denounced as "outrageous" the selection of an "out of the country" developer. Kahan responded that Battery Park City Authority had a single asset, and it was his job to maximize it.

Just what the Reichmanns won was open to question. Expected to cost around $1.5 billion, this would be the most costly real estate project in the United States. Big projects were hard to control, and many broke the budget, something even the Reichmanns couldn't afford. The World Trade Center, for instance, was estimated to cost $650 million, but the final tab exceeded $900 million. It lost $10 million annually.

Battery Park City was among the most risky projects, a pure speculation. Perhaps most major developers irrevocably commit themselves to a venture only after they have a significant amount of space pre-leased—usually 25 percent to 50 percent—thereby reducing their financial risk. The worst nightmare was an empty building. This happened many times, most memorably at the 44-story 1166 Sixth Avenue, which cost $100 million to build, stood empty for five years, incurred $100 million of losses, was sold after foreclosure for $37 million and helped trigger liquidation of the venerable Tishman Realty & Construction Company in 1978.

Yet the Reichmanns made their commitment to build Battery Park City before they had a single tenant. This seemed daring if not reckless, since at the time the project was a sandbar that a planned expressway would separate from the financial district. Failure could drain all their profits from the Uris deal and mark an ignominious end to the Canadian invasion.

"I reached essentially the same conclusions as the Reichmanns," recalls feisty Kenneth D. Laub, a leading Manhattan office broker who represented Cadillac Fairview in the Battery Park City competition. "But I would never have put $50 million on the line like they did. Nor could I, in good conscience, have recommended that my client do it. We just didn't have the experience, composure and confidence of the Reichmanns."

Success would signal the arrival of new titans on the world stage, successors to John Jacob Astor and William Zeckendorf. Richard Kahan's assessment: "These are the biggest crapshooters Manhattan has ever seen."

3.
SECRET ASSEMBLAGE

ASSEMBLING PROPERTY DOWNTOWN IS AMONG THE TOUGHEST
challenges in real estate. A city block is typically divided into many
parcels held by banks, retailers, family trusts and individual investors
who may be scattered around the world. Often it's difficult just to
locate these people. Probably most aren't interested in selling. Different needs must be resolved before there can be a deal. If word of
an assemblage leaks out—which can happen at any time—asking prices
will skyrocket, dooming a project before it really gets underway.

Assembling major properties is the mission of a special breed of
brokers. The most successful have tremendous reserves of patience,
persistence and resourcefulness. They're as skilled at dealing with people
as they are at handling intricate real estate transactions. Their nerves
are carbon steel. Because they must be discreet, they tend to be little
known outside their profession.

I had heard that one of the most dramatic real estate assemblages
in recent years took place in Dallas, where two quiet brokers accumulated a downtown block for Cadillac Fairview, North America's
largest publicly-held real estate company. In addition to straightforward investors and retailers, the sellers included a con man, gun merchant and bag lady. I went to Dallas to find out for myself how a
secret assemblage works.

I began by learning about the people behind Cadillac Fairview.
Principal owners are Edgar, Charles, Minda and Phyllis Bronfman—
children of short, paunchy Samuel Bronfman, the volatile man who
built Seagram's into a multibillion-dollar liquor empire, the world's
largest distiller. In Yiddish, the family name means "liquorman."

The Bronfmans are much more a part of the mainstream than the
Reichmanns, partially because they arrived much earlier. Sam's father
Yechiel was a prosperous Russian tobacco farmer, an Orthodox Jew
who emigrated in 1889 to avoid anti-semitic pogroms of Czar Alexander III. With his wife Minnie, their children Abe, Harry and Laura,
a maid, a rabbi and the rabbi's family, they arrived at a settlement
near Moosomin, eastern Saskatchewan, Canada. Two more children,

Sam and Allan, were born there. Tobacco seed wouldn't grow in the bitter cold, and their first wheat crop froze. They turned to peddling logs, then sold waste wood from lumber mills as fuel. They sold frozen whitefish, traded horses and began buying hotels because of the enviable profit margins on serving drinks. Some people carped that the Bronfman hotels were really brothels, and Samuel retorted: "If they were, they were the best in the West!"

By 1916 all Canadian provinces but Quebec were establishing Prohibition. The Bronfmans noted that it was still legal to sell liquor by mail from Quebec, so they moved there and launched a thriving business. Outraged Drys pushed to close this loophole, and the Bronfmans thought their days might be numbered until they discovered they could obtain a license and sell alcohol to druggists. Whereupon the Bronfmans launched the Canada Pure Drug Company. Whoozy remedies like Dandy Bracer/Liver & Kidney Cure—36 percent alcohol—owed much to the enterprising Bronfmans. People with assorted afflictions reportedly lined up four deep at druggists, seeking relief.

During the 1920s, Canadians grasped the folly of Prohibition, and it was repealed. The Bronfmans became distillers. In 1927 they bought Joseph Seagram & Sons, a bigger distiller.

American Prohibition provided the Bronfmans with a windfall, for they exported huge volumes to U.S. bootleggers. They survived virtually unscathed, though Harry Bronfman was jailed briefly for trying to bribe a customs official. After Prohibition collapsed and open competition returned to the liquor trade, the Bronfmans realized they needed a superior product to achieve the dominance they craved. They promoted the first national brands of aged, carefully blended whiskey. Seagram's marketed more than 600 brands in 175 countries. Seagram's 7 Crown was the world's best seller.

Harry Bronfman was a key strategist, but it was his brother Sam who emerged the acknowledged ruler of the empire. Sam was quick to spot opportunities and ruthless in pursuing them. He bellowed at associates who wasted anything. He was a mercurial, sentimental, mostly absent father, who traveled on business almost three weeks of every month while his wife, Saidye, raised their children at a posh, guarded Montreal compound. When Sam was around, he'd assemble his children for a formal "lesson on life."

While he achieved wealth and power, it wasn't enough. Sam Bronfman wanted much more—social acceptance signified by membership in Montreal's Mount Royal Club, election to the Canadian Senate, appointment as governor of McGill University or director of the Bank of Montreal. These were denied, and the slights gnawed at him.

He poured considerable energies into Jewish philanthropy, and he was decidedly more public than the Reichmanns. Sam and his brother Allan led a fund-raising drive for the construction of Montreal's Jewish General Hospital. During World War II, he established the Refugee Committee of the Canadian Jewish Congress. The family gave a $1 million wing to the Israel Museum. For 16 years, Sam headed Montreal's Federation of Jewish Philanthropies.

The families of Sam and Allan came to despise one another after Sam insisted that his children succeed him at Seagram's. He didn't want anybody else around who could challenge him, even his brother or nephews. He amassed twice as much stock as Allan, and in 1952 he forced his way: Allan's sons Edward and Peter would be forever excluded from any role in the company. The two branches of the family have seldom spoken to each other since then. Allan's daughter Mona committed suicide.

Edward and Peter were banished with $10 million of stock apiece, sheltered in a trust called Edper. They traveled, skied, and contributed to Jewish philanthropies. Uncertain of purpose, Edward was shy and partially deaf in one ear. He was divorced, with three children. He had little interest in business. Peter, twice-married with three children, spent a quarter-century in psychoanalysis. He worked to master investment but conceded he really didn't know what he was doing.

Sam jolted his nephews' self-confidence again in 1960 when he demanded that they sell 600,000 of their Seagram's shares for $28 a share—$2 below market value. Edward and Peter didn't want to sell, finding the discount demeaning, so Sam threatened to push their father out of Seagram's. They sold the stock.

This gave them $15 million to play with, and somehow they had to become better at business. They dabbled in venture capital. While they didn't lose much, they weren't tough enough to negotiate deals that would give them a profit when a company they bet on succeeded. In 1969, two of Canada's largest banks agreed to finance their takeover of Great-West Life Assurance Company, but Sam declared he would take Seagram's business away from the banks if they went ahead. He didn't want his nephews upsetting the establishment whose respect he craved. "He felt the Bronfman family was *his* family," Peter reflected. "We were upstaging his boys." The debacle marked Edward and Peter as indecisive, weak bunglers.

While Sam was religious, he certainly wasn't strict. Orthodox practice called for a private funeral and opposed displaying the body, but when Sam died, July 10, 1971, his body was decked with a white shroud in the rotunda of the Canadian Jewish Congress in Montreal, where all could see. The funeral service was an event that attracted the movers and shakers in Canada. He was reportedly worth $400 million.

Recognizing that they didn't have business brains, Edward and Peter were sensible to pick an associate who did: Jack L. Cockwell, a South African-born accountant in his 30s. He had worked with Touche Ross, one of the Big Eight firms, and moved to Canada in 1967. He guided investments in banking, tin, timber, diamonds, oil and real estate. They gained a 33 percent controlling interest in Brascan Ltd., a diversified natural resources company with assets over $2 billion. Within a decade, their combined net worth was estimated to exceed $300 million—about $100 million more than it would have been if they had held onto their Seagram's stock.

Rivalry intensified with Sam's sons Edgar and Charles, who started the Montreal Expos baseball team.

Edward and Peter bought controlling interest in the Montreal Canadiens hockey team, and they gained control of Trizec, Canada's second largest publicly-held real estate developer that was started by William Zeckendorf.

Among Trizec's holdings were Zeckendorf's Place Ville Marie development in Montreal, a 20 percent stake in the Rouse Company and its 38 million square feet of shopping centers and festive market places, plus 100 percent ownership of Ernest Hahn Company, which had another 28.7 million square feet of shopping centers. Trizec was a well-run company.

Meanwhile, Edgar and Charles built Cadillac Fairview into a power with $1.5 billion of assets. Unlike the rival Reichmanns, who specialized in office buildings, the Bronfmans wanted to become a colossus—with office buildings, residential buildings, industrial parks, shopping centers and more.

To be sure, the Bronfmans had little to do on a day-to-day basis with Cadillac Fairview, relying on their financial wizard Leo Kolber, a dour dentist's son whose acumen made him one of Sam Bronfman's favorites. Kolber, in turn, assigned the empire-building mission to Ephriam Diamond, a resourceful financial executive. He was a lively public speaker who could convey a deep understanding of real estate and what makes cities grow—his personal fortune was estimated over $20 million.

In 1977 Cadillac Fairview made headlines when it bid $235 million for the Irvine Ranch, a tantalizing 73,000 acres of choice undeveloped land in Southern California. This was $35 million more than giant Mobil was willing to offer. Though Cadillac Fairview, in turn, lost to a consortium headed by Detroit-based shopping center tycoon A. Alfred Taubman and Henry Ford II—they bid $337 million—Diamond put people on notice that Cadillac Fairview had arrived as a power in North American real estate. Subsequently, the company was successful in gaining the go-ahead for several mammoth urban projects: Toronto's three-block-long Eaton Centre, Los Angeles's 11-acre California Plaza, the 33-block Houston Center and New York's 30-acre River Walk.

Diamond wanted to make his mark on Dallas, among the flashiest and lustiest American cities. To carry out this mission, he chose another intense competitor—the 6-foot-4-inch muscular Michael Prentiss from Tacoma, Washington, whom friends nicknamed The Bear and Godzilla. When at 27 he decided real estate was what he wanted, Prentiss enrolled at Harvard Business School and graduated in the top 3 percent. He joined Atlanta's Ackerman Development Company, rising from project manager to president within a year. In 1979 when he went to Cadillac Fairview, he was the first outsider immediately named an officer and a member of the company's senior management committee. Soon he was rated the number three executive. Prentiss never stopped striving to win. "If you play tennis, racquetball or basketball with him," said Michael Young, a Dallas commercial real estate broker and friend, "everything is for the gold medal."

Prentiss is equally devoted when it comes to his family. He'll interrupt intense work sessions to take a phone call from Paige, his teenage daughter who lives with his first wife Betty in Seattle. He and his second wife, Patricia, an interior designer he met in Atlanta, have a daughter, Kennedy, and a son, Brian, and he rarely lets business come between them on weekends. They live near Lovers Lane in North Dallas. During the summer, they rent a cottage in Siasconset on Nantucket, where they wiggle their toes in the sand.

During the late 1970s, Dallas was site-driven. Bankers especially elbowed one another to relocate their offices in prestigious new skyscrapers on the choicest sites. It was believed that since financial services were intangible, a building that created a powerful, forward-looking image would help a bank generate business and recruit top talent. Accordingly, if a developer could somehow acquire the right site, it was comparatively easy to sign a Dallas bank as lead tenant. This would attract other tenants and cut financial risks.

Cadillac Fairview got a jump on competitors by closing a deal with First City Bank, where it became the lead tenant in the gleaming 50-story pink granite First City Center. This is near the center of downtown, between Elm and Pacific, Ervay and St. Paul. Soon Republic Bank officials, long satisfied with their 1954 stamped aluminum tower, were talking about a new skyscraper across St. Paul Street—opposite First City Center. National Bank of Commerce agreed to move into

Thanksgiving Tower, a new 49-story skyscraper built by the wealthy Hunt brothers. It was a block west. The only Dallas bank insisting on the primacy of a west side location was InterFirst, which had built InterFirst One in 1965 and InterFirst Two a decade later. It was negotiating with Bramalea, another Canadian developer, for the construction of InterFirst Plaza, yet another block farther west.

Pressure mounted on a horse trader named Gene Bishop, chairman of Mercantile National Bank with assets approaching $5 billion. Bishop had to have a new building. "We wanted a full block which would enable us to project the right image for our bank," he says. "We aimed to be as close as possible to our present, central location."

Bishop's ideal choice was the block across the street, bounded by Elm, Main, Ervay and St. Paul. However, it consisted of 19 separate parcels. In a number of old, decrepit, small-scale retail buildings was a bridal shop, jeweler, Radio Shack, restaurant, several clothing shops and a boarded-up former Volks Department Store. "Rayburn Tucker, a broker we've used over the years," says Bishop, "wasn't able to assemble the site. We concluded it just couldn't be done.

"We considered many other possibilities. Thanksgiving Tower is central, but it occupies only about a quarter block. We decided to pass on a nearby site which involved complex rights-of-way, and Cadillac Fairfiew developed a new building there for First City. We were close to a deal with Ben Carpenter of Southland Life. He offered us an east side location, but we decided that was too far from the center of things."

When it was clear Bishop wouldn't take Carpenter's site, other developers approached him. Trammell Crow offered a site on the northeastern part of downtown, but that was too far away—a new building called 2200 Ross Avenue is going up there now. Mack Pogue of Lincoln Property Company, one of the largest U.S. developers, proposed a site several blocks north, but that wasn't acceptable either. An office tower called Lincoln Plaza was built there. Houston entrepreneur Gerald Hines didn't have a site, but he approached Bishop about being the bank's development partner wherever he wanted to build.

Industry observers noted that by holding out for an ideal site, Bishop risked ending up with lousy choices. "After all this back and forth, Mercantile Bank was left sucking the hind tit," a realtor says.

If somehow Cadillac Fairview could assemble the block Bishop coveted, he'd be sure to sign with them. Michael Prentiss together with Robert Short, the senior development officer in charge of this project, pursued the difficult assemblage with stealth. The effort got underway in late 1979.

Nobody from Cadillac Fairview could be directly involved, since this would signal the interest of a big player and property owners would begin demanding steep prices that would probably trigger cancelation of the project. Cadillac Fairview's Dallas attorney, John Johnson, had in mind a real estate broker named John Bradley who, with his brother Jerry, both bachelors, had worked in Dallas for years.

The Bradley brothers are unassuming, straightlaced men who share a brick house in North Dallas and keep pretty much to themselves. John reads mysteries and putters with a flower garden. Both enjoy a lively game of tennis. They entertain quietly at home. Though they had done some work for Ray Hunt's Woodbine Development Corporation, they weren't associated with any particular developer, so their doings wouldn't attract much attention. Ray Hunt confirmed they were discreet, an absolute essential for a big land assembly. But could Cadillac Fairview and the Bradleys work together?

"Johnson arranged for me to have dinner with a client who wouldn't give his name or the company he represented," John Bradley recalls. "So this fellow talked with me a while. Apparently, the chemistry was right, because in the middle of dinner, he excused himself from the table. When he came back, he introduced himself as David Fitch of Cadillac Fairview. Would we help them assemble a downtown Dallas block? Start tomorrow!"

The Bradleys, former naval officers, approached the task like a military campaign. From City Hall, they got a map showing the dimensions of each parcel on the block, and they evolved a battle plan.

How to approach property owners? Every week, a broker contacted a downtown Dallas property owner or tenant, asking whether they'd be interested in selling. Invariably, people say no. If the assemblage was to be completed fast, somehow they had to be convinced right away that the Bradleys were serious.

Moreover, it was important to minimize the outlay for Cadillac Fairview, because every expenditure magnified their risk. If they ended up with patchwork holdings scattered through the block, they might have a significant amount of square footage, but they couldn't build much on it. They'd be out millions of dollars.

A conventional approach was to pay property owners for an option on their property, then try to find tenants and arrange financing. If not enough tenants could be lined up, or financing wasn't available on acceptable terms, the option expired. But the Bradleys believed this approach would fail, because many of the parcels were held by old-line Dallas families who'd dismiss an option as frivolous. A serious person would come across with an actual offer to buy.

The Bradleys believed they had to approach property owners with a contract. Accordingly, they drew up a standard two-page contract approved by the Dallas Board of Realtors. They recommended that the contract require Cadillac Fairview to pay nonrefundable earnest money—a cash deposit which the owner would keep if the deal didn't close.

First, however, a title search. This identified problems early in the game so they could be dealt with most easily. The owner might turn out to be a minor, for instance, in which case the deal would be negotiated with a guardian. There were many family situations involving multiple owners. The owner may be an elderly person, and the buyer wouldn't want to make a deal only to be challenged later by children contending the owner was incompetent to pass title. City records may show that the boundaries of a parcel were disputed. Or there may be deed restrictions.

John Johnson retained Bill Kramer, the blond, bespectacled, gregarious president of Plano Title Company. Attorney Johnson had known Kramer for years, since they were attorneys together at another firm. Kramer was known as somebody who could keep confidential information strictly confidential. If an employee at a title company remarked casually to the wrong person that a lot of searches were being processed for a single downtown block, rumors of an assemblage might reach local real estate reporters, and owners would begin licking their lips at the prospect of a killing.

The Bradleys formed several corporations that would take over title to property in the event of a sale. Cadillac Fairview used names like Arundal Investments, Kon Company, Panyon Inc. and Evilo Corporation. The idea was to approach people who owned a cluster of parcels, big enough to build something on, in the name of one corporation. Then, representing another corporation, the Bradleys would approach the next cluster. When owners gossiped with each other, there would seem to be different buyers involved, allaying suspicions. Moreover, anybody who examined City Hall records would notice an unusual number of transactions on this block, but the different corporate names would make it difficult to determine just what was going on. Eventually, if and when the assemblage were consummated, titles would be transferred from the corporations to Cadillac Fairview.

Which parcels to go after first? Cadillac Fairview wanted four mid-block parcels which would be enough to build a modest structure and provide possible linkage to First City Center across Elm Street. The Bradleys marked parcels A, B, C and D on their map.

The Bradleys swung into action on a Friday afternoon. They had time to approach only one owner before the weekend. By chance, they decided on a man I'll call Slim Whipple (all the sellers' names are changed to protect their privacy). Whipple's family owned a corner parcel with a four-story building on it. "He couldn't believe we called," Jerry Bradley told me. "His family had the property since the early 1900s, and it was never for sale until this weekend. They were negotiating now with McDonald's. There was a verbal agreement. My heart sank, but still we had a shot.

"Though the family was well-to-do, Whipple, a man in his 50s, wanted to clear up the family estate. We got him a contract, and apparently it was a little better than the McDonald's offer. He sold the parcel to us for $525,000.

"We were lucky. If we had decided to work on parcels B, C or D, we wouldn't have reached Whipple until after the McDonald's deal was concluded. Since McDonald's had definite plans for the property, they would have been much tougher to deal with."

One parcel the Bradleys had no chance of acquiring was held by a so-called spendthrift trust, often used to prevent heirs from dissipating their assets. In this case, there were four beneficiaries. The leasehold on the parcel had 45 years to run—not long enough to secure financing for a new office building. So a new ground lease would have to be negotiated. Since the trustees needed to know the creditworthiness of the lessee, Cadillac's identity would be disclosed to them—a seller, by contrast, doesn't need to know the actual buyer in a cash transaction.

The incredible low-rent leasehold dated from the 1930s and provided for little rent escalation. It belonged to Woolf's department store, headquartered in Kansas City. Naturally, they weren't eager to give up their sweet deal—just persuading them to talk required persistence on the part of Cadillac's Robert Short who handled the negotiation. He identified other sites where Woolf's might move their business. Since it seemed Woolf's was primarily concerned about their rent level, Short proposed several ways Cadillac could absorb some of the huge rent increase that they would face.

After almost a month, Woolf's tall, strapping president told Short they would consider a cash deal—presumably because they had decided to close down this Dallas store. With the top two floors in the building unused, the place obviously wasn't a big money-maker. Short agreed to value the store around $2 million. Cadillac bought it, thereby removing the obstacle to renegotiating the leasehold—and giving a tremendous windfall for those Dallas heirs.

Meanwhile, the Bradleys negotiated for more parcels. One was owned by Gloria Stevens of a wealthy Dallas oil family. She certainly didn't need to sell. Nor did she welcome heavy taxes a sale would involve. Solution: Buy another desirable property of equivalent value, then swap it for hers. This the Bradleys did.

To clinch a deal for Billy Bob Jackson, a wealthy Dallas investor, the Bradleys offered to close late in the year, give him 25 percent down and a note for the balance. Half would be paid the following January, the balance a year after that. The idea was to spread the capital gain over three tax years.

Dr. Harold Thomas, a dentist specializing in reconstruction work for people who had suffered severe injuries, proved to be a tough negotiator. He insisted on $220 a square foot, an unprecedented price. Jerry Bradley visited him at his home and office many times, but he wasn't interested in anything less. Bradley persuaded Dr. Thomas to sign a ground lease with an option to purchase at $220. At least this locked up the property. More than a year later, when it became clear that they'd acquire all the parcels they sought, and the average price was within bounds, they exercised their option.

Daniel Morse, a local attorney, owned a parcel. He died without a will and the title appeared to be clear until a bank secretary stepped forward with a young man she claimed was her illegitimate son by Mr. Morse. To determine whether such a union might have taken place, detectives had to find maids who worked at the Adolphus Hotel and might remember the couple. This parcel was slow to close.

A Dallas investor named Roger Platt owned one of the parcels as well as a string of radio stations and a drive-in theater. Before discussions got far, the Dallas Historical Preservation League began to reconsider the merit of Platt's attractive six-story building. There was talk of giving it an historic designation, which would make demolition difficult. On the other hand, it wasn't a unique design, it was half empty, and if it weren't demolished a modern structure would be wrapped around it. Platt realized he wouldn't get his asking price if his building became a designated historic landmark, so he demolished it. Cadillac paid him $353 a square foot, more than double what comparable properties were worth.

There was a parcel with ownership divided among more than 20 family members scattered around the world. One person was on a naval ship, so communications with him were always slow. As in any case of divided ownership, everybody must agree to a sale. If anyone couldn't be reached, no deal. A single holdout would kill it.

Fortunately, a family patriarch named Otto Samuels had the stature to deal with all the relatives. He called a meeting, and the family property manager made his presentation. The Bradleys offered $170 per square foot. Samuels recommended the family go for it. A family member objected. He had only 1.5 percent interest, and he wanted to demand more. Samuels listened for a while, then ordered him to shut up, and they closed the deal.

The Bradleys weren't as lucky with a parcel that was held in the same family for almost a century. Its ownership was divided among a dozen people who faced very different financial situations. Some were affluent and didn't want to sell because the gains would be steeply taxed. Others were struggling, eager for the cash. One cousin, a doctor, refused to sell out of spite because he reportedly detested his cousins. His wife was willing to sell, but he remained adamant.

The deal seemed hopeless until some months later when he had a fatal heart attack in his swimming pool. Within a few weeks, his widow agreed to the deal, and the Bradleys bought the parcel.

A restaurant with boxing decor was owned by a man and wife originally from New York. Business was lousy. Though the wife's money had financed their restaurant, her husband did all the talking. He insisted the deal be concluded in a bank parking lot just off the North Central Expressway. Afterward, he cashed as much of the note as he could—$25,000—then disappeared. Later the Bradleys learned that the couple filed for divorce, and the husband tried to keep his wife from getting sale proceeds. Police were put on his trail.

One of the last people to close was a tough guy who operated a gun shop and owned the land underneath. If Cadillac Fairview could buy his property, they'd use it as part of the garage next to their planned office building. He didn't believe they could build the garage without his property, so he held out for $1 million, a price way above the market.

He wouldn't budge until the Bradleys acquired the parcel next door and began building the garage. "With dust in the air," Jerry Bradley remembers, "the man called. He asked us to meet him right away at the Statler Hilton. He was willing to negotiate."

One parcel, with a 25-foot-wide storefront, was owned in part by two sisters whose finances were managed by their Dallas brother, Edward Sage. One sister lived in Dallas, the other in San Francisco. Each owned a third interest. Their Dallas cousin, Thelma Wellington, owned the other third. These people were in their 60s and 70s. The two sisters didn't get along at all with Mrs. Wellington, because she refused to pay her share of building expenses. The sisters had eight children, and they wanted to sell so their children didn't have to deal with Mrs. Wellington.

No one here wanted to sign a contract first, because they were afraid a relative would get more money. One of the women told John Bradley she heard Hong Kong property was selling for $2,000 a square foot, and she expected that kind of money for her downtown Dallas parcel.

Just finding Mrs. Wellington presented obstacles. She didn't have a telephone. City tax records showed she owned a house in rundown East Dallas, but it was empty. Letters addressed there were unanswered.

A little asking around town brought some curious reports. There was a Mrs. Wellington who seemed to carry her possessions in a shopping bag. She had several million dollars which she moved from one bank to another almost every week, seeking the highest interest rates. Bank clerks reported that she'd wash her underwear in the bank bathroom, put it on and, soaking wet, sit down to grill a bank officer about business conditions. When she was through, she left a distinctive stain on the chair.

At last, Jerry Bradley discovered her at her house. She had wild frizzy hair, wore tennis shoes and a faded-silk polka-dot dress. "She scowled at a neighbor who might be eavesdropping and asked to talk privately in my car," he recalls. "She insisted her share of the downtown property wasn't for sale. But I had to keep talking with her.

"John had lunch with her several times. Not at your finer establishments, to be sure. A cafeteria, usually. She'd upend a shaker, fill a glass with sugar and dump it in her mouth. Since she didn't have many teeth, she'd gum her food. Once, she grabbed an unfinished piece of cake from somebody's tray and jammed it into her mouth. Before she left, she'd sweep unconsumed food into her shopping bag."

Once the Bradleys coaxed Mrs. Wellington and Mr. Sage into their office, but the relatives still didn't want to see each other. They were given different conference rooms. The Bradleys would go back and forth, letting each know what the other agreed to. When discussions were deadlocked, the relatives took separate doors out.

More than a year passed without an agreement on this parcel. Michael Prentiss decided to gamble: buy out Mr. Sage and his two sisters. If Mrs. Wellington held out, Cadillac Fairview could file a partition suit, claiming that there was divided ownership. Yet the property itself—a building—couldn't be divided like a piece of raw land. A judge might decide to order the property sold and the proceeds divided among the parties.

The deal with Mr. Sage and his sisters convinced Mrs. Wellington that she must reach an agreement. She wasn't the kind of person who'd want to endure court appearances or costs. Finally, the property changed hands for $600,000. This was about $200 per square foot, consistent with other market prices at the time.

After Mrs. Wellington signed the contract, she pointed to the pen holder on Bill Kramer's desk and asked if she could have a pen. As soon as he nodded yes, she grabbed all of them, swept them into her shopping bag and walked out the door.

So more than two years after it started, this assemblage was finished. Michael Prentiss had paid an average of $150 per square foot for the more than 80,000 square feet on the block. Cadillac Fairview's total outlay was $12 million before anyone put a spade in the ground.

As joint venture negotiations with Gene Bishop got underway, and it became clear he would gain control of the block, Prentiss approached New York architects Philip Johnson and John Burgee about a design. He wanted a tower with 1.4 million square feet of space. Johnson and Burgee proposed 60 stories of granite and glass. It would have a grand entrance: a 55-foot-high granite arch leading to a gallery—topped with a vaulted skylight—where visitors could view Mercantile's banking room floor. Vaulted setbacks would emphasize the verticality of the structure. It would climax with a copper-domed cross-vault, a distinctive signature on the skyline.

Gene Bishop and Michael Prentiss have reached a joint-venture agreement for this new headquarters building, which will be called Momentum Place. When moving day arrives in 1987, Bishop will walk across the street to the place he wanted all along—just as if it were easy.

III

GRAND
DESIGNS

4.

DISTINCTIVE STYLE

SINCE REAL ESTATE IS SO RISKY, FEW ENTREPRENEURS CAN AFFORD to develop a building unless they know beforehand they can sell or lease a significant amount of space. But potential occupants need confidence in something more than a plot of ground. Often success depends on how well an architect describes a dream.

These days, many major corporations want a distinctive presence on the skyline. Perhaps no architects better provide that than Philip Johnson and John Burgee. Each building they do has a unique skyline signature.

You never know what to expect from these architects. Their AT&T Building, recognized for its broken-pediment top, is among Manhattan's most famous landmarks. Johnson and Burgee have almost single-handedly reshaped Houston's skyline with a succession of contrasts—trapezoids, stately setbacks and spiked gables. Johnson and Burgee have made their mark in Boston, Minneapolis, Pittsburgh, Denver and San Francisco, too. Perhaps because each of their buildings is quite different from others, they lease well even in the most depressed real estate markets.

I wondered how Johnson and Burgee get their ideas and how they convince corporate titans to go along. So I visited them in their offices on the thirty-seventh floor of the Seagram Building, the sleek bronze Park Avenue icon of modernism. Mies van der Rohe designed it in 1958, and Johnson assisted him. Johnson designed the interiors, including the Four Seasons Restaurant, rated among the most beautiful in New York.

A part of Johnson and Burgee's daily routine is lunch at a corner table in the Bar Room, diagonally across from the entrance where they can see everyone who enters. They mix their own Americanos with equal parts of soda, sweet vermouth and Campari, which are already on their table. "It's delightful, yet it doesn't get you drunk," Burgee says. You'll never get much work done with Johnson and Burgee, though, because every few minutes somebody stops by their table to say hello. Much of the fun in this splendid setting is seeing and being seen.

One client, unaccustomed to their ways, called to arrange an appointment several days later and suggested a working lunch in the architects' offices. Johnson objected, but the client insisted. After getting off the phone, Johnson ordered sandwiches delivered immediately. They sat around, becoming stale and pasty. When at last they were served to the hungry client, the client conceded: "I get the point, Philip. Next time, we'll have it your way, in the Four Seasons." They did, and everybody was happy.

The Johnson/Burgee offices are a paradigm of modernism. The partners have simply furnished rooms facing each other across an open meeting area. There are light teak Knoll desks and behind each a Mies van der Rohe desk chair of steel and leather. Visitors sit in any of the four Wegener wood chairs. Since Johnson works on his designs in New Canaan at a white studio near his Glass House, there aren't any models or drawings about. Just a couple of Frank Stella paintings.

Johnson, at 79, cuts an elegant figure. He's tall, trim, with close-clipped white hair and a shining dome. His trademark glasses have big black circular frames, the same kind worn by his idol, the French architect Le Corbusier. Johnson dresses in dark conservative double-breasted suits tailored by Bernard Weatherill—the man who has done all his suits since he came to New York in 1930. Johnson is as dapper as the corporate brass he hopes will become his clients.

Johnson is witty, frank, infuriating. Though he began his career as an apostle of modernism, he concluded in the late 1960s that modernism had virtually run out of ideas, and he was appalled by what he considered mediocre, knock-off designs. He derides Skidmore, Owings & Merrill, which disciples of modernist pioneer Mies van der Rohe have built into a corporate behemoth—"three blind Mies" is how Johnson refers to the firm. He brushes off Edward Larrabee Barnes, an architect who has scored many corporate commissions, as "a sheep in sheep's clothing." Johnson calls Frank Lloyd Wright "the greatest architect of the nineteenth century." When Wright met him, Wright unleashed his fury: "Why, Philip, I thought you were dead."

Johnson met Burgee, a solid, genial, red-cheeked Irishman, in 1967 when the Chicago-based Burgee was 33—28 years younger than Johnson. The two met through a mutual friend and pitched a Philadelphia airport. Though they didn't get the job, they worked together well, and Johnson recognized that Burgee's wide practical experience would complement his own flair for dramatic design. Burgee had worked on the First National Bank of Chicago Building,

Chicago Civic Center, O'Hare International Airport and other huge projects. With those capabilities, Johnson/Burgee would be more than an arty boutique. They could go after the Fortune 500. They decided right away to become partners.

They're artists in the corporate world. "We've got to say yes to somebody if we want to stay in business," Johnson says. Yet they won't take a job they believe will result in a bad building. For instance, they were asked to design a skyscraper over Grand Central Station, but they refused the multimillion-dollar commission involved—Johnson, actually, had marched in pickets protesting the proposed demolition of that fabled landmark. Johnson and Burgee passed up more millions by declining to design an office tower that would replace another landmark, the Byzantine-style Community House connected to St. Bartholomew's Church at 50th Street and Park Avenue. Nor did they take on a condominium project that would entail demolition of a Christian Science Church at 63rd Street and Park Avenue. They declined to design an office tower that would replace Lever House, an early set piece of modern architecture at 53rd Street and Park Avenue.

Johnson is the unpredictable act corporate executives come to see. He can wow them with his dramatic design ideas. They feel creative just being in his charismatic presence.

Yet they won't necessarily authorize the spending of millions of dollars on his say-so alone. It's reassuring to huddle with Burgee afterward about engineering, budgets and other practical matters. Executives feel comfortable with Burgee, who tames Johnson's wild schemes so they'll work.

Johnson has enjoyed a bohemian bachelor life devoted to architecture, thanks to his father Homer H. Johnson, a successful Cleveland lawyer. Homer Johnson's biggest break came when a friend asked him to help get an invention patented and, instead of a conventional fee, offered stock in the company formed to market the invention. It was the Charles Martin Hall process for extracting aluminum from bauxite. The company: Aluminum Company of America—Alcoa. In 1926, Homer wanted to divide his estate while his children were young enough to enjoy themselves, so his daughters got downtown Cleveland real estate and Philip got the Alcoa stock. He became wealthier than his father, who did fine on a 3,000-acre farm near Cleveland.

Philip Johnson fell in love with architecture when he was 13. While traveling in France, his mother showed him Chartres Cathedral. "There was a funeral going on," he says. "I was so moved, I don't know why I wasn't dead."

He was a Harvard undergraduate longer than most students—seven years—because of a nervous breakdown. On the advice of a psychiatrist, he returned home. "I cried and read two detective stories a day," he laughs.

In 1929, while attending his sister Theodate's graduation ceremonies at Wellesley College, he met Alfred Barr, a professor there who taught what became known as modern art. Johnson and Barr talked for hours. Barr formed the Museum of Modern Art the following year.

During the summer of 1930, after Johnson graduated from Harvard—a Greek and philosophy major—he traveled around Europe with a Vassar College art professor named Henry Russell Hitchcock. They looked at significant examples of modern architecture and met modernist pioneers like Le Corbusier in France, Walter Gropius and Mies van der Rohe in Germany. They rejected architectural decoration and urged austere, functional designs.

When Johnson and Hitchcock returned, Barr asked Johnson to form the architecture department at the Museum of Modern Art. He did, cheerfully agreeing to pay his own salary, plus salaries of his assistant and the librarian. "We were all under 30, had marvelous people to work with and no bosses except for lovely Mrs. Rockefeller, whom we adored," Johnson says.

Even back then, he had a flair for getting attention. The conservative Architecture League rejected modern architects from their 1931 exhibition at Manhattan's Grand Central Palace. So Johnson, Barr and art dealer Julien Levy staged a counterexhibition, "Rejected Architecture," in a storefront at Seventh Avenue and 57th Street. They hired a man to walk back and forth in front of Grand Central Palace with a sandwich board saying "See Really Modern Architecture, Rejected by the League, at 907 Seventh Avenue." The League tried to have the man arrested, but this just excited controversy.

In 1932, Johnson mounted a far more important show called "Modern Architecture" which heralded a powerful new design trend. That year, he and Hitchcock went on to write the book *The International Style,* which spread the modernist gospel and is still in print after more than half a century.

He dabbled in politics for several years, embarrassing himself more than once before he resolved to become a professional. At 34, in 1940, he entered Harvard's School of Architecture. To fulfill requirements for his graduate thesis three years later, he built a $23,000 house on Ash Street in Cambridge. It was a wood rectangle with a glass wall, among the first houses designed according to the doctrine of Mies van der Rohe, who had fled the Nazis to the United States a half-dozen years earlier. Johnson hosted quite a few lively parties at his Ash Street house.

After graduation, Johnson kept flunking the New York State architectural licensing exam, so in 1948 he moved to New Canaan, Connecticut and designed the 32-by-56-foot Glass House, which remains one of the most famous modernist structures ever built. Some of my conversations with Johnson took place there. The walls are glass, the roof supported by eight black H-shaped steel columns. There are no interior walls—just a cylinder that houses a bathroom and fireplace. It's a shrine of the International Style for architects, artists and wealthy patrons who flock there.

Johnson loves collecting paintings and, with his father's inheritance, has become among the biggest benefactors to the Museum of Modern Art.

For a couple of decades, Johnson did one small architectural commission after another. Many were houses for prestigious clients like Mrs. John D. Rockefeller III, Nelson Rockefeller, Joseph Hirshhorn and Henry Ford II. He earned visibility by designing the Abby Aldrich Rockefeller Sculpture Garden at the Museum of Modern Art, the Amon Carter Museum of Western Art in Fort Worth, the New York State Pavilion at the 1964 World's Fair and the New York State Theater at Manhattan's Lincoln Center.

Johnson's first commission for a tall building came in 1967, soon after he and Burgee became partners. It was the $135 million, 51-story octagonal, reflective-glass IDS Center with its 20,000-square-foot Crystal Court of shops and markets. The hub of Minneapolis, IDS was critically acclaimed when it opened in 1973. But it was partially blamed for the financial troubles of Investors Diversified Services (IDS), and it helped give Johnson/Burgee a reputation as expensive architects. That scared away many potential clients.

Architectural commissions slowed to a trickle during the recessions of 1970 and 1974–75, and Johnson/Burgee let go a substantial number of their people. For Johnson, this was a particularly anxious time, because he spent the last of his Alcoa inheritance and had to make a living entirely on his architectural commissions. He closed down his Glass House when he couldn't afford to heat it.

Since Johnson and Burgee couldn't find many commissions in the United States, they opened an office in Teheran. They designed apartment buildings in Isfahan and did a master plan for the modernization of that city's downtown. But as the U.S. situation improved during the late 1970s, Johnson and Burgee found it harder to spend time in Iran. Consequently, they couldn't be sure of controlling quality. So they folded up shop and devoted all their energies to the United States, missing Ayatollah Khomeini's bloodbath in the process.

A tremendous opportunity came from an unexpected connection. During the mid-1950s, Johnson was dining in Houston with his friends Mr. and Mrs. John de Menil, art patrons whose house he had designed in 1950. Johnson met them through a sculptor named Mary Callery he had encountered at the Museum of Modern Art. At the Menils'—whose fortune came from Schlumberger, giant of the oil services business—Johnson became acquainted with Ruth Carter Johnson, daughter of the Fort Worth newspaper baron Amon Carter. Charmed by Johnson, she asked him to design her new museum—the Amon Carter Museum of Western Art in Fort Worth. Johnson agreed.

He wanted some teak for it. He discovered a Houston warehouseful belonging to a wily Palestinian immigrant named Isaac Brochstein, a manufacturer of fine furniture. Apparently Johnson impressed Brochstein. He owned some land on Post Oak Boulevard, about seven miles west of downtown Houston, where a developer named Gerald Hines wanted to put up several buildings. Brochstein agreed to sell Hines the land, provided Brochstein got part interest in the project and Johnson/Burgee were seriously considered as architects for the buildings.

Hines is a diffident, yet fiercely aggressive man with a lean build, conservative dress and wire spectacles. He grew up in Gary, Indiana, the son of a U.S. Steel factory hand. He graduated from Purdue University in 1948, a mechanical engineer. Seeking opportunities further afield, he moved to Houston and joined Texas Engineering, as a manufacturers' representative for air conditioning and other equipment used by office builders. He's a good salesman, but a Lincoln-Mercury dealership he invested in flopped.

He did better when he spent $16,000 to renovate an old house at 1309 Anita Street, Houston. Texas Engineering moved in. Hines began developing other small projects. "The first time I built a building," he told me, "I may have invested an extra $5,000. We used pure vinyl tile instead of asphalt tile and a special brick rather than sand brick. Several months later, in my second building, there were a lot of improvements which cost about $20,000 but distinguished us from other builders."

Hines struck out on his own as a real estate developer in 1957. He did warehouses, small office and factory buildings. He cultivated prospective tenants willing to pay premium rents for convenient location, easy parking, insulating glass, responsive climate control systems, quiet work environments and building security. Each year, he added new touches—solid-core full-height doors and granite counter tops in bathrooms, for instance. At his presentations, he showed prospects bronze lever door handles which had impressive heft.

During the mid-1960s, Hines began to appreciate the potential commercial value of fine architecture. While on a golf course in Point Clear, Alabama, he met brash, blunt Bruce Graham, senior design partner with the Chicago office of Skidmore, Owings & Merrill. Born in Bogota, Colombia, Graham is an olive-complexioned Spanish-Irishman with a fierce determination to become the most powerful architect around. He cultivates connections with Chicago moneymen and developers, and he's feared by many of his associates. If he's a doctrinaire disciple of functional modernism, he inspires confidence that he can design the very largest structures anybody might care to build.

Graham and Hines began talking about structural problems Hines had designing an apartment project. In 1966, Hines was ready to graduate from small jobs—his tallest was 16 stories. He had his eye on the skyscraper leagues.

Hines entered a competition to develop an office tower for Shell Oil in downtown Houston. They needed about 600,000 square feet, but to be economical on the available site, there would have to be more than one and a half times that amount of leasable space. This meant about a 50-story building.

Hines wanted that job, worth about $6 million, so badly that he was willing to guarantee personally 100 percent of the construction costs, which he estimated at about $40 million. If designs were faulty, if he encountered serious construction problems, if costs got out of control—if any of a number of things went wrong, he'd be bankrupt. Maybe nobody would trust him with another job. His career might be over just when it seemed so promising. He called on Bruce Graham, who was gaining recognition for mammoth projects like the 100-story John Hancock Center rising on Chicago's North Michigan Avenue.

While Hines was small fry by tall Texas standards, he could point to a record of dependable performance. His modest buildings—most around 50,000 square feet—earned him valuable goodwill with major companies like SCM Corporation, Fireman's Fund Insurance Company, Prudential Insurance Company of America, General Electric, Xerox and IBM.

He seemed a good bet for investors whom he brought into his deals. They contributed cash, and he delivered handsome buildings on time and within budget. Among his investors was John Duncan, a co-founder of Gulf & Western. Charles Duncan, who later realized millions selling his Duncan Coffee Company to Coca-Cola, was another. With wealthy limited partners like these, Shell executives were confident that even if construction problems exhausted Hines's own capital, he could tap resources needed to finish the job.

Hines offered Shell an irresistible lease for the 50 percent of the building they'd occupy, and they signed. He counted on their presence to help lease the rest at premium rates that would yield a profit. One Shell Plaza, a soaring slab of travertine marble, opened in 1971, and it was a big money-maker. Hines was ecstatic.

Then Shell asked him to provide more space in downtown Houston. Hines redoubled his efforts and built 29-story Two Shell Plaza nearby. He built One Shell Square, a 50-story, 1.5-million-square-foot building in New Orleans. Following this string of successes for Shell, Trans World Airlines asked him for a building—it was only 500,000 square feet, but it meant further expansion beyond Houston, to Kansas City. During the 1960s, Hines started a new project about every month and a half.

Hines nurtured perhaps his greatest single dream for the Post Oak neighborhood about seven miles west of downtown Houston. It was a convenient location that seemed ripe for ambitious development. His idea was the Galleria, a 1.4-million-square-foot complex of offices, stores, movie theaters, hotels and indoor skating rink. Around the roof of the hotel and shopping mall would be a running track, reflecting his passion for jogging. Such a multi-use complex would be lively from early in the morning until late at night, not just during business hours. If successful, it could be expanded over the years into a tremendous project. Having secured Neiman-Marcus as an anchor retail tenant and the architectural firm Neuhaus & Taylor as a lead office tenant, he was eager to plunge ahead.

Hines wanted to sign a high quality hotel operator, so he approached Western International Hotels, headquartered in Seattle. The chief executive promised him only 15 minutes. He didn't believe Hines could deliver, since nobody had attempted such an ambitious multi-use complex before. Hines's most preposterous idea was a skating rink in balmy Houston.

His presentation continued for two hours. By the time he finished, Western International executives agreed to visit Houston, inspect the proposed site and evaluate Hines's other projects. Eventually, they agreed to manage not one but two hotels at the Galleria.

Hines was equally determined several years later when he planned a Galleria expansion. He acquired most of the needed property easily enough, but a key parcel on the 5100 block of Westheimer belonged to Wildcat oilman Michel Halbouty. He had his offices there and refused to sell. Hines ordered excavation crews to dig a hole up to

Halbouty's driveway. That got Halbouty's attention. Hines kept offering more money, and when finally he offered a percentage of the Galleria, Halbouty agreed. Within a decade, the Galleria became one of the most valuable chunks of Texas real estate, securing Halbouty's fourth fortune.

Hines worked practically around the clock. When a leasing man named Joe Gilbert found himself alone one night, his wife and kids off visiting relatives, he returned to the office. He was grappling with some problems at 3 A.M. as Hines walked in. He just said "good morning" and headed for his own office, as if that were customary. Afraid to delegate much, Hines took on more and more.

As he expanded his developments throughout Post Oak, he eyed a conveniently located tract owned by furniture manufacturer Isaac Brochstein. It was big enough for several buildings. He wasn't yet able to sign any tenants in advance, thereby reducing his risk. He never had done a building before without some tenants, so he was quite nervous. But he wanted to proceed right away and take advantage of prime sites while they were available—before a major rival moved in. So the buildings he planned had to be economical. The less expensive, the more cushion against adversity.

He began thinking that a distinctive enough design might give him greater assurance of leasing a building, even though the materials weren't overly expensive. He already had used architects with a national reputation—Bruce Graham on several buildings, Helmuth, Obata & Kasabaum for the Galleria. For this project he was receptive to considering an even more imaginative designer like Philip Johnson.

Hines selected Johnson and Burgee to design the first building on Brochstein's site, a 25-story structure that would be called Post Oak Central. To minimize costs, Hines insisted on walls of glass, steel and aluminum.

Johnson and Burgee wanted to distinguish the building somehow. They gave it two setbacks for a more interesting shape. They designed it with alternating bands of silver reflective glass and charcoal anodized aluminum—inexpensive materials. "As an extra touch," Burgee explains, "we alternated these with narrow aluminum bands, to stagger the rhythm."

The narrow bands added cost, and several of Hines's zealous cost-cutters questioned whether it was worthwhile. Hines asked Johnson and Burgee to rate the importance of those bands on a scale of 1 to 10. They replied 8½ to 9. Hines turned to his staff: "O.K., they need the bands. Cut the $200,000 someplace else." As much as possible, he tried to give his architects a free hand.

Hines approved the design since he believed it had the appeal he was looking for. Projected to cost about $22 per square foot, it would be the least expensive tall building Johnson and Burgee would ever do, and it was reasonable by Hines's standards. He was delighted.

"We have found that sensitive planning, a concern for the human scale, and stimulating architecture are the elements that create the best working environment," Hines wrote in a foreword to his hardbound leasing brochure. "Designed by the highly respected firms of Philip Johnson and John Burgee, New York, and S. I. Morris Associates, Houston, Post Oak Central is an important architectural statement. It reflects the trendsetting pace of our time, our era."

S. I. Morris Associates? Si, as friends called him, was a local boy. His story illustrates the anguished rivalry among architects for choice commissions.

He graduated from Rice University in 1935 and by 1938 had formed a partnership with a school chum named Talbot Wilson. An amiable person, Morris made connections, cultivating business. Wilson was the designer. In Houston as in so many places, designers weren't expected to be creative mavericks; they got routine jobs done. They were paid little, because enthusiastic young designers could always be hired cheaply out of architecture school. Top salaries went to those who brought in the clients. Morris's big break came during the 1950s when, through a Rice classmate, he got a commission to redecorate the Houston Club. This didn't call for anything fancy, but it enabled him to meet important people much more easily. Many used architects. Morris came to serve on community boards, helped charities and knew everybody. He was probably the heaviest hitter in Houston.

That's the way local architectural firms got business until Philip Johnson came to town. Business people wouldn't risk a major investment like a building on a prima donna with a casual attitude toward cost.

To established Houston architects, Johnson didn't seem like anybody to take seriously. He had, after all, designed a model bungalow that the Museum of Modern Art displayed after World War II, and it lacked banisters on the stairs. Anybody with youngsters would anticipate trouble there, but Johnson thought they were an aesthetic nuisance. His famous Glass House had elegant lines partially because there was no back door. Consequently, during cocktail parties, the help had only one inelegant way to dispose of garbage—right past guests and out the front door.

When Johnson designed the de Menil home, he didn't even know how to do mechanical drawings. Blissfully unaware of Houston's suffocating summer heat and humidity, he didn't specify an air conditioning system. When asked for one, he struggled to develop a design that would keep fans and ducts unobtrusive. He approved extravagant expenditures for hardware that nobody would see. He seemed an impractical fellow.

Then during the 1960s, out-of-towner Skidmore, Owings & Merrill won big Houston jobs. Gordon Bunshaft, SOM partner in the New York office who had designed Lever House, the first notable skyscraper on Park Avenue, snatched the First City Bank headquarters commission away from S. I. Morris. Nat Owings, business-getter for the firm's San Francisco office, persuaded Gardner Simons, chairman of Tenneco, to have SOM design the new Tenneco building in downtown Houston. A local architect named Victor Neuhaus thought he had that one. Bruce Graham, of course, got the One Shell Plaza commission.

The invasion continued. The Galleria was an inexplicable loss, since that plum went to Gyo Obata, outsider from St. Louis. Johnson was back to snatch away the Post Oak business. This was an alarming trend, beyond anybody's control.

Increasingly, developers asked local architects to serve as associates—to do the grubby detail work. The limelight as well as the most lucrative commissions went elsewhere. For a while, local architects didn't want anything to do with this. They were accustomed to being the primary architects on a job. Most, however, came to accept the money and hoped for better luck the next time a major building was announced. So far, their luck hasn't turned.

Behind all this was the shadow of Philip Johnson, because he had beat the drums for modernism, which was sweeping through Houston. Modernism was an ideology that architects at SOM and elsewhere adopted as their credo. It made for persuasive presentations when competing against a local architect who didn't have strong convictions about design.

To the shock of Houston architects remembering Johnson's uncertain early days there, he proved to be far more potent when he returned in person during the 1970s. Though his first work was on Post Oak Central, that didn't deliver the most devastating blow, because it was put on hold. As the economy skidded into recession, the ever-cautious Hines decided he couldn't afford the risk of that speculative building without tenants already signed on.

But Hines had other projects underway. He acquired a full block downtown, and he found another prospect who was willing to sign as a lead tenant, if he had the right design. The man was J. Hugh Liedtke, the gruff, chunky entrepreneur who had founded Pennzoil in 1953—and who would threaten the destruction of mighty Texaco in 1985. He wanted a strong public presence for Pennzoil, because he believed it would help sell his products and make recruiting talented people easier. This didn't mean erecting the tallest building around, because in the future somebody would surely build taller. Liedtke wanted a striking presence on the skyline that could hold its own for years.

Hines turned to Bruce Graham. His design was straightforward modernism, the brand Skidmore, Owings & Merrill was known for. It resembled his previous Houston designs as well as those of partners from the other SOM offices. Liedtke rejected it. He didn't want what he derided as "an inverted cigar box." Unless Hines could produce an acceptable design, Liedtke would give the job to another developer.

Johnson and Burgee got a call. They considered a single building, but they weren't satisfied with the ideas they tried. They hit on a solution while flying from Houston back to New York. "We do a lot of work on airplanes," Burgee said to me. "That's time when you're away from telephones and other interruptions. We wondered if we should use materials similar to the courthouse down the block. How best to relate our project to adjacent buildings?

"Although the design we evolved for IDS Center didn't have a top, it did have a jagged look, because of the octagonal shape and sawtooth edges. We began to think about a jagged look for Pennzoil. We tried slicing off the top at an angle. That was interesting.

"At some point, we considered two shorter buildings with the same total amount of space, 1.8 million square feet. Two buildings would give Gerry the option of signing two lead tenants instead of just one. We explored more complex shapes until we arrived at trapezoids with their tops sliced off. We never could quite draw these. Airline martinis didn't help.

"It became clear that aligning two trapezoidal buildings in a certain way would make for dramatic effects. Your perspective would change as you moved around the buildings. There would be the marvelous experience of walking between two buildings close together— in our final scheme, they were 10 feet apart. We added a glass lean-to on either side, to shelter the entranceways from weather.

"When Philip and I got back to New York, I asked Joe Santaramo in our model shop to work on it. He started cutting up the Styrofoam. That afternoon we saw the results. Our ideas worked!"

Hines, however, worried that the roofs, sloping at a 45 degree angle, would be too complicated and costly to build. He asked that Johnson and Burgee make presentation models with sloping tops which could be removed, giving Liedtke the choice of a flat-topped building.

Hines took the tops off the buildings and recommended Liedtke go with the flat tops, because it would involve fewer problems, but that made Liedtke angry.

"Did I ask you how much it costs?" he roared. "I'll only take the building with the sloping tops."

Hines remembers the experience well. "There were complications, like avoiding leaks. How do you suspend window cleaning equipment, so it can be lowered down the building? Most cases, it's suspended from the flat top. But you can't do that here. Instead, we devised a $200,000 monorail scaffolding system."

While Pennzoil Place, as the project was called, did cost more than standard steel and glass boxes, it didn't cost much more. Hines, who doesn't reveal many numbers, told me that the structure cost $28 a square foot, a reasonable amount at that time. Overall cost was about $45 million.

Pennzoil agreed to take about half of one building, and Zapata, also an energy company, signed for part of the other. So Hines still had a considerable amount of space he'd be responsible for leasing. The buildings went up in 1973, an intensely competitive time when some 6 million square feet of office space was coming on the market.

The leasing effort he and Marketing Vice President Patricia Harris devised was different from anything the firm had attempted before. Until then, they emphasized practical issues like comfortable appointments, soundproofing, temperature control and security. Now, for the first time, they stressed fine architecture.

To be sure, many corporations and institutions prided themselves on sumptuous headquarters by name architects. But no real estate entrepreneur had made fine architecture a stock-in-trade. There didn't seem to be any experience which showed that enough tenants would pay premium rents to offset the higher costs of designer architecture. Tenants paid for tangible things.

Johnson and Burgee suggested making models of the exterior and setting up a typical office with a cyclorama showing what the views would be. Besides printing detailed, illustrated brochures, Hines and Harris leased a suite of rooms in One Shell Plaza, a block away. They commissioned elaborate large-scale models of the entire buildings, close-up models of the ground-floor exteriors and interior lobbies. Actual offices were set up. There was an elaborate slide and music presentation which used 30 computer-coordinated projectors. Hines spent $375,000 on this marketing center to make the unfinished building seem tangible, so prospects would more readily take space in it.

"Because demand was so great for Pennzoil," Hines says proudly, "we had to add two floors while construction was underway. Offices at the top, beneath the sloping roof, commanded such a premium that we had to ration them. For every office a tenant leased at the top, they had to lease a certain amount of space elsewhere in the building. On average, we got 25 cents to 50 cents more per square foot per year at Pennzoil compared to other buildings in the market. Space was 97 percent leased before the building was finished."

Pennzoil Place opened in 1975 amid astonishing critical raves. *New York Times* architectural critic Ada Louise Huxable declared it was "Houston's towering achievement." The building was considered important enough for a second article, this time by Paul Goldberger, who had become fascinated with Johnson during the architect's many lectures at Yale and later visited Johnson at the Glass House. Goldberger called Pennzoil "high design at a profit." Several years later, the *American Institute of Architects Journal* commented that Pennzoil Place "has played a crucial role in its city's growth and the skyscraper's evolution."

Hines was delighted he could tap the fertile talents of Johnson and Burgee at an economical cost, showing that an aesthetically pleasing result also would be a sound business proposition. If he could do it once, he could do it again—not just with Johnson/Burgee, but with other first-class design architects, too. Hines was intent on making Gerald D. Hines Interests a name to be reckoned with.

Johnson and Burgee, for their part, were exhilarated. Hines was the first developer they worked with, and they loved him. He enjoyed dealing with architecture more than almost any other aspect of building. He relished grappling with conceptual issues, finding a design to match the personality of his lead tenant. He took pains to master details and responded intelligently to their designs. He'd call Johnson and Burgee from almost anywhere when architecture was on his mind—as he did while trekking in Katmandu, Nepal.

Hines's battle cry became "the point of difference" prospective tenants could gain with his buildings. He gave Johnson and Burgee more assignments across the country. Each design is utterly different. Houston's 56-story RepublicBank Center is a fanciful red granite gothic confection with graceful obelisks, inspired by Flemish seventeenth century designs that Johnson told me he had seen in a book. The 64-story glass Transco Tower, looming over Hines's Galleria, is a sleek contemporary interpretation of Art Deco motifs that change colors throughout the day. As if to confound those who assume everything by Johnson and Burgee would involve some historic theme, they designed 101 California Street, San Francisco, as a tapering, faceted circular tower. For Hines's 53rd at Third, New York, Johnson and Burgee designed three stacked elliptical forms with alternating bands of polished imperial red granite, flame-finished imperial red granite, gray-tinted glass and brushed stainless steel. Thus far, Johnson and Burgee have done 11 buildings for Hines.

Hines is an exacting client. "Sometimes it requires six or seven designs to arrive at something which starts to make sense," Hines says. "We're interested in architects who aren't afraid to expose their egos in the evolution of an idea." Johnson and Burgee respond to Hines's challenges with remarkable speed. If they're with him in Houston when he voices an objection, they'll begin sketching on the spot. Or if they're at their New York office, they'll rush him new sketches by telefax.

This work for Hines demonstrates that while Johnson and Burgee are expensive architects, they can work within the constraints of a commercial budget. "With proper controls like we have," Hines says, "their designs may cost 2 percent to 4 percent more."

It's valuable testimony, because Johnson and Burgee's celebrated AT&T Building, credited with spurring new exploration of historical forms after the design was unveiled in 1979, became among the most expensive buildings ever—more than $180 per square foot. Johnson seemed to reinforce his reputation for monument-building when he quipped after receiving the American Institute of Architects' Gold Medal that year: "If you leave out the desire for immortality, you just get cheap design."

No doubt about it, Johnson and Burgee helped Hines secure his fortune, estimated at more than $300 million. RepublicBank Center and Transco Tower, for instance, opened as Houston tumbled into a devastating economic crisis, yet both buildings were soon 85 percent leased.

Hines is determined that his son, Jeff, will succeed him in the business, and this has caused friction among some experienced hands who resent what seems to be unearned promotion. Gradually, though, Jeff has grown more skillful and confident, and the issue has become less important than dealing with Houston's real estate crash.

Gerald D. Hines Interests continues to prosper. Hines funded the catalog for a 1983 exhibition by New York's Municipal Arts Society, "Philip Johnson: the First Forty Years," and Jacqueline Onassis and *New Yorker* theater critic Brendan Gill headed a celebrity crowd that paid $1,000 a plate for opening-night festivities at the Four Seasons. Among those present was Phyllis Bronfman Lambert whose father, liquor baron Samuel Bronfman, had commissioned Mies van der Rohe and Philip Johnson for the Seagram Building. Gerald Hines offered a toast.

For pleasure, Hines likes to spend some of his money on exquisitely designed homes. He asked Johnson about designing one in Aspen, Colorado, and the sage recommended a competition among younger design architects he favors—Michael Graves, Gwathmey Siegel, Charles Moore and William Turnbull. That commission went to Turnbull. Robert Stern designed Hines's home on Martha's Vineyard. Hines is considering architects for his new home in Houston's posh River Oaks neighborhood.

There are other name architects Hines retains to do his skyscrapers: I. M. Pei worked on Texas Commerce Tower in Houston; Kevin Roche, the new headquarters for E. F. Hutton in New York. In 1984, the American Institute of Architects elected Hines an honorary member. "He has changed the way architects work," noted the citation. "Architects now think like businessmen and find themselves therefore more profitably employed. He has changed the way the market responds to architecture."

In the process, though, his 30-year marriage to Dorothy crumbled. Soon, Hines fell in love with a sophisticated foreign-born woman—the former Barbara Fritzsche from West Germany, 24 years his junior. They were married, and associates report that Hines became more relaxed, less preoccupied by business.

He became quite the man about Houston. He gave a little dinner party at the Houston Petroleum Club for actress Samantha Eggar, actor David Hemmings and Princess Anne, who was president of the British Olympic Association. Hines gave $100,000 for a Celebration of Bayou Bend, a museum with one of the finest collections of American antique furniture, assembled by the late Ima Hogg. Among those who attended were oil services magnate Pierre Schlumberger, former Watergate prosecutor Leon Jaworski, oilman John Mecum, newspaper operator and banker Joe Allbritton, attorney and future Texas Governor Mark White. The Houston Symphony provided music.

Eventually competitors began retaining name architects, moving in on territory Hines had pioneered, and this annoyed him. Cadillac Fairview commissioned Philip Johnson and John Burgee for buildings in Dallas as well as Atlanta. New Yorker George Klein, who some call The Candy Man because of his Barton chocolate inheritance, commissioned Kevin Roche, Philip Johnson and John Burgee for his Manhattan projects. Klein adopted Hines's jazzy marketing techniques, from hardbound leasing brochures to million-dollar presentations. Hines reached agreement with his architects not to do a building near one of his.

Johnson has been showered with honors. The Pritzkers established an annual architecture prize, and they consulted Johnson about it.

"Jay wanted to give $75,000," Johnson laughs, "but I told him it had to be at least $100,000 if it were to make the front page of the *New York Times.*" Johnson won the first Pritzker Prize.

While Johnson savors all the praise, he acknowledges his debt to John Burgee for the tremendous success they share together. "It's no coincidence my best work was done with John," he says. He credits Burgee with ideas like the broken pediment atop the AT&T Building and the angular tops of Pennzoil. The firm is known now as John Burgee with Philip Johnson. "Creatively, they're interchangeable as far as I'm concerned," Hines says.

"Old age is wonderful," Johnson told me, "because it liberates you to do what you want. I don't get discouraged anymore when I'm stuck for an idea, either. I realize now that you just apply the seat of your pants to the chair. Then you play."

5.

PURSUIT OF ELEGANCE

DESPITE THE RECENT TREND TOWARD DISTINCTIVE ARCHITEC-tural forms like those designed by Philip Johnson and John Burgee, many executives still prefer the spare, elegant geometry of modernism. That's what Ieoh Ming Pei continues to design after more than three decades. He hasn't done stylistic flip turns. "Architecture isn't a matter of fashion," he told me. "You cannot have an architectural revolution every 20 years."

Pei, 68, is a short, trim, impeccably tailored man who wears the style of circular black glasses Le Corbusier made popular among architects including Philip Johnson.

He works in a surprisingly nondescript building at 600 Madison Avenue, New York, a few doors north of 57th Street, but his white-walled offices on the ninth floor are simple elegance. Visitors are greeted by a striking flower arrangement featuring a single variety like peony, azalea, orchid, amaryllis or tulip that changes every week. Along the corridor to Pei's quarters are color photographs of eight projects around the world, including the Portland (Oregon) Art Museum, an office building for IBM and the Fragrant Hills Hotel near Beijing. Pei has a large corner office with a five-by-five-foot black lacquer desk and four black-upholstered Brno chairs designed by Mies van der Rohe. Practically one whole wall is filled with an eight by fifteen foot Al Held black and white painting of geometric forms. Pei enjoys a pleasant view up Madison Avenue.

He displays considerable charm. He exudes enthusiasm, cheerful determination and quiet self-assurance. He's an attentive listener who waits until a client is through developing his thoughts before offering a reply. While voicing tactful disagreement, Pei deferentially expresses respect for a client's ideas. Pei pursues his goals with seemingly inexhaustible patience and persistence.

Characteristically, Pei discounts his talents as a presenter. "I'm certainly not a natural-born salesman like Bill Zeckendorf," he says. "I can hold my own when I talk about a design I believe in. But I've messed up presentations where I lacked conviction. I'd be terrible trying to sell socks or shirts!"

Although he's the biggest business-getter in his shop, he spends more time than ever on design. "I'm happy to report," he says, "that I no longer run around trying to get work. I run around to make sure that my designs are accepted by clients. This is quite time-consuming, but it is part of the design process, and design is my passion."

He's very much an international man. He has designed prestigious buildings across the United States, most notably in Boston, Dallas, New York and Washington, D.C. He has done projects in Canada, Mexico, Argentina, Uruguay, France, Spain, Teheran, Kuwait, China, Taiwan, Australia, Singapore and Hong Kong.

Pei was born in Canton in 1917, the son of a banker. His father later became governor of the Nationalist Chinese Central Bank. "My father and I talked a great deal about what I should devote my life to," Pei remembers. "The 23-story Park Hotel was under construction when I was in my last year of high school. I was greatly impressed by the sheer magnitude of this undertaking. It was then I decided to involve myself with the design and construction of buildings."

In 1935, Pei came to the United States with the idea of studying architecture at the University of Pennsylvania. But he decided he was not adequately prepared for architectural design, so he opted for architectural engineering instead. He enrolled at the Massachusetts Institute of Technology.

"I got restless when I was doing undergraduate work at MIT," he continues. "I had been knocking about the country in an old Chevy during summers, visiting landmarks of American architecture. Frank Lloyd Wright's designs had a deep appeal for me, especially his 1904 Larkin Building in Buffalo and his 1909 Robie House in Chicago. These are the kind of structures, worth as much for their humanistic principles as for their formal or technical innovations, that will be studied five centuries from now."

After graduating from MIT in 1940, Pei remained in the United States through World War II, working at the National Defense Research Committee, Princeton, New Jersey. Meanwhile, in 1938, a friend introduced him to a young woman named Eileen Loo, and they were married four years later, after she graduated from Wellesley College.

He planned on returning to China as soon as possible, but Bauhaus guru Walter Gropius persuaded him to accept a teaching job at Harvard University's Graduate School of Design. There he won a

Wheelright Fellowship. He thrived among zealous modernists like Gropius and Marcel Breuer. This was where Pei decided on the austere, geometric, functional approach to design which shaped his career. "We were together all the time, absorbing each other's ideas," Pei says. "I stayed at Gropius's house a whole summer, my wife Eileen and I. We spent many weekends with Breuer, talking, discussing, arguing, learning."

In 1948 Pei met real estate entrepreneur William Zeckendorf. Philip Johnson claimed to be the one who introduced Pei to Zeckendorf, but Zeckendorf wasn't sure. Zeckendorf would become a sponsor for Pei in the early years.

Thus, Pei wouldn't have to squeak by on a teacher's meager salary or grub for small jobs like most architects. He could tackle big challenges right away. Moreover, Zeckendorf offered to find a comfortable apartment for Pei and his wife in a residential tower on exclusive Beekman Place, plus an office near Zeckendorf's.

Pei said it would be for a limited time, because eventually he wanted to practice architecture in China, but Zeckendorf beckoned Pei anyway. He was 31. "The Urban Development Program of the U.S. was just getting started," Pei smiles, "and Bill wanted me as a kind of design conscience. This lasted until the end of the 1950s."

Pei began by redesigning an office for Zeckendorf at 383 Madison Avenue, New York. "Pei had already noted that the great majority of visitors came to see me and then went to see somebody else," Zeckendorf wrote in his autobiography. "His solution, therefore, was to start visitors off directly beside the place most of them wanted to go—my office. Within the great open lobby and display area of the top floor of our building, he built a 20-foot-diameter, wood-paneled, vertical cylinder, a headquarters within a headquarters: my office. On the roof above this self-encompassing cylinder we built a small penthouse dining room, which, in view of the transactions closed there, proved possibly the most remunerative investment I ever made. Down below, alongside my office, we laid out some open-air terraces with matched marble side walls and shrubbery and statuary. We ended up with a unique headquarters to which many prominent magazines devoted pages of pictures, all very useful publicity for our firm."

Pei discovered that working so closely with Zeckendorf had an unexpected drawback. "It was a principle then that an architect should not work for development companies," Pei explains. "So I couldn't get formally registered. My role from 1949 until 1960 was a one-to-one relationship with Zeckendorf."

Pei designed ambitious office complexes like Denver's Mile High Center and Place Ville Marie in Montreal. He did residential developments such as Society Hill in Philadelphia, and Kips Bay in New York. As was fashionable at the time, he favored tall box-buildings set amidst plazas accented with sculpture. Later, many people came to believe that box-buildings were boring, and the plazas were uncomfortable places to be.

While Zeckendorf pursued large proejcts, he didn't go for extravagant materials or design. Consequently, Pei gained a reputation for designing investment buildings. While this helped assure prospective clients that he was a practical man, it hampered his later efforts to do museums and other projects where clients often wanted an architect with a flair for striking, expressive design—an artist like Philip Johnson.

Nonetheless, this was an immensely successful collaboration for both Pei and Zeckendorf. "In 12 years, we built nearly a half-billion dollars' worth of work," Pei reflects. "I learned about his business. He learned as much as he needed about architecture. I became an organizer, spending 50 percent of my time flying over the country with him on his DC-3. It was 10 years out of my life as a designer, but looking back, I wouldn't swap that experience for anything. I learned things which serve me well today—the big picture, the flow of economic, political and civic decisions, the importance of seeing land as a precious raw material to be carefully used since urban land was worth millions and of being able to sense the influences which bear upon land as well as on what you want to do.

"Now when I'm shown a piece of land—I don't care whether it's Singapore, Australia, Dallas or Paris—I see a lot more than most architects because of the Zeckendorf education."

Pei began taking on projects for clients besides Zeckendorf in 1955, and he set out entirely on his own five years later. "It was not really until the early 1960s that I was able to spend more time on design myself," he told me. "Before that, I had always looked over the shoulders of the architects working with me, and I would participate in the concept and occasionally draw a line or two, to test an idea or help somebody consolidate his own direction in a design. But it really wasn't until I was asked in the early 1960s to do the National Center of Atmospheric Research, Boulder, Colorado, that I was totally involved with the design process.

"I began to realize how much I enjoyed this, and finding that out, I acquired an appetite for designing more. I slept in a sleeping bag on the site, getting the full force of the elements and the atmosphere. It's not a question of how you create a building which expresses the architect's personality, but how it can relate agreeably with people as well as the place."

In 1964, an international committee of 18 architects and designers selected Pei to design the John F. Kennedy Library. It was a prestigious commission which gave his firm a tremendous boost, even though the proposed Cambridge site triggered years of bitter opposition among neighbors anxious about traffic congestion and smog. Relocated at Columbia Point, just south of Boston, it opened in 1979.

Pei's firm got business from clients like John Hancock, Polaroid, National Airlines, Columbia University, Everson Museum of Art, Cornell University and the Christian Science Church. Pei's experience with all the urban renewal projects Zeckendorf did helped him land master-plan assignments from many community redevelopment agencies across the country.

Now that he was on his own, he had to divide this time between obtaining commissions and designing them. He and his partners would confer about the strategy to pursue for a prospective client, then he would lead the presentation. He's a master. He displays sensitivity toward the surroundings of a proposed building. He argues eloquently for elegant shapes, fine materials and open plazas.

With exceptions, one of Pei's partners assumes responsibility for a project. From time to time, Pei is asked for his advice, and he'll pass on a final design. He'll keep in touch with all projects.

This doesn't belittle the importance of his contributions, for most major design decisions are made in the early stages of a project. It's said that 2 percent of an architect's time involves overall design, and the rest is devoted to details and compromises—how to yield enough rentable floor space, how best to handle elevators, what kind of heating system, where to put plumbing.

The biggest project of Pei's career, the sleek glass rhomboid 60-story John Hancock Tower in Boston, became a disaster which nearly derailed his career. He started work on the project in 1967. As construction was being finished in November 1972, mirrored windows began popping out. For a couple years, it was a boarded-up eyesore, the butt of ridicule.

Though nobody was hurt, all 10,344 Thermopanes—two sheets of glass separated by a half inch of air—were replaced with 4½-by-11½-foot tempered half-inch-thick windows called "lites," which powder when broken so there won't be any dangerous shards. Some 1,500 tones of steel was added to elevator shafts and stairwells, providing more stability in high winds. The building cost millions more than anticipated, and didn't actually open until 1976.

More than a decade later, the case is still being litigated, with Pei, the glass manufacturer and contractors embroiled in lawsuits. If Pei wasn't actually at fault, being associated with such a botched job was bad enough, and many prospective clients wouldn't touch him. Business, already down because of the 1974–75 real estate recession, seemed to wither away. Pei was worried.

He took criticism about Hancock Tower stoically. While the building was designed by his partner Harry Cobb, Pei approved the blueprints, and he didn't duck the barbs. "Boston was a stormy place for me," Pei concedes with a little grimace.

Because he supported his partners in difficult times, let them design buildings and take credit for their triumphs, the partners worked with uncommon harmony. Pei, Cobb, Eason H. Leonard, James I. Freed, Leonard Jacobson and Werner Wandelmaier have been together more than a quarter-century.

After Hancock, Pei had to spend even more time than ever searching for new jobs. He traveled almost nonstop during the mid-1970s, wherever an entrepreneur, corporation, museum or government agency would give him a hearing.

The resourceful Pei applied his charms overseas. He used to turn down foreign inquiries, many inspired by his celebrated design for the Kennedy Library, but he purused those people now. He got a number of assignments in Singapore: the Overseas-Chinese Banking Corporation Center, the Collyer Quay/Raffles Square Development, Nathan Road Development Plan, Orchard Road Development Plan and Singapore River Master Plan. Pei worked in Europe, South America and the Middle East.

Pei's reputation revived, in part, because of a sketch he did with a red ball-point pen on the back of an envelope. He was flying from New York to Washington where he would meet with J. Carter Brown, director of the National Gallery of Art. The challenge: design a new East Wing on an unused nine acre trapezoidal site between Pennsylvania Avenue and the Washington Mall, Third and Fourth streets. How to approach such a difficult site?

Pei drew a line parallel to the Mall, a line parallel to Pennsylvania Avenue, a line parallel to Third Street and a line parallel to the west side of the National Gallery. "If the site has that geometry," Pei explains, "why shouldn't the whole building have it?" To make it function better, Pei cut his shape in two. The result was an isosceles triangle for museum exhibitions nested with a smaller right triangle for offices and a study center. Brown described these as "the most important lines of all."

Pei's initial meetings with the museum staff took place in 1969, several years before Hancock Tower became "Pei's Problem." The National Gallery was an immensely prestigious commission on a conspicuous site, guaranteed to receive critical attention around the world. The building would display the Gallery's growing art collection as well as traveling exhibitions.

Museum attendance had mushroomed since World War II, so the building would have to accommodate crowds easily, yet Brown didn't want an overwhelming, exhausting hulk. He asked for lively interest. He believed the optimum amount of time in a museum for most people was about 45 minutes.

Pei agreed, for he recalled how his children—daughter Liane and sons Chien Chung, Li Chung and Ting Chung—reacted to museums. "They'd refuse when I suggested going to the Metropolitan," he smiles. "They'd say 'Let's go to the Guggenheim.' " They wanted the excitement of Frank Lloyd Wright's coiled wonder rather than catacombs of corridors and galleries.

How should the design relate to all the monuments around? "We didn't want to be imperial, imposing," explains Pei. "Think about the Lincoln Memorial—it's imposing. We pay our respects, but we want to leave. Here we have other concerns. We must somehow make it an interesting and exciting place where people would want to return." He noted the experience of the Centre d'Art et de Culture Georges Pompidou. "I believe they had five million people in the first six months, but they'd go up the escalators, look at the skyline and leave. Only a fraction of the visitors made repeat visits."

Returning to his drawing board, Pei created four-story "houses" at each corner of the exhibition triangle. These afforded an intimate experience as at comfortable small-scale museums. He provided stairs or bridges for people to move among the houses. Pei linked the exhibition triangle to the office and study center triangle with a triangular skylit court.

The stark simplicity of Pei's design, like so many modern buildings, required meticulous workmanship if it was to look good. Museum trustees required that the East Wing be fashioned from two-by-five-foot blocks of the same pink Tennessee marble used in the National Gallery. But if the marble blocks weren't aligned precisely, or colors were off, finishes were uneven—the flaws would show for all to see. There was no decoration to distract the eye. The workmanship needed was difficult, time-consuming and costly. An early estimate for the original program was $20 million, but the space expanded substantially to 604,000 square feet. By the time the building was finished, after nine tedious years, costs had escalated to $83 million.

Pei didn't just have to satisfy Director Brown and patron Paul Mellon. He needed all his patience and charm to endure sessions with the National Capital Planning Commission, the Washington Fine

Arts Commission and the Pennsylvania Avenue Development Corporation, all of which had to approve the plans. This process alone took a year.

Pei's design received immense critical acclaim even before it opened in June 1978. Ada Louise Huxtable exulted in the *New York Times:* "Washington is finally going to have a great 20th-century building . . . the promise of these plans is enough to make one go dancing down Pennsylvania Avenue."

If the National Gallery triumph helped reestablish Pei as a design star, a 1977 meeting with Houston entrepreneur Gerald Hines proved to be perhaps even more important. Ben Love, chairman of Houston-based Texas Commerce Bancshares, wanted a new headquarters building. He was a former country boy from Paris, Texas whose phenomenal drive had made him the biggest wheel in Texas banking. He believed Texas Commerce needed a boost, because rivals like Bank of the Southwest, First International Bank and First City National had flamboyant new buildings. There were rumors that Allied Bank, another competitor, would unveil plans. Love had to move, so he acquired a full block downtown.

He considered three developers for the job: Hines, his flashy Houston rival Kenneth Schnitzer and sedate Galbreath-Ruffin in New York. Hines was a personal friend of Love's, and Texas Commerce had financed Hines's Houston Galleria, Three First National Plaza in Chicago, Pillsbury Center in Minneapolis and Seafirst Fifth Avenue Plaza in Seattle. Hines had done a lot of his banking at Texas Commerce ever since he began building modest warehouses in the early 1960s. While Hines was the leading contender, Texas Commerce was a public company, and Love couldn't justify recommending Hines unless he could produce the best deal for stockholders.

Hines and Love negotiated an agreement that would give Texas Commerce a share of profits. The bank would own the land and the building, and Hines would lease both for 65 years. As lead tenant, the bank would take 300,000 square feet of space.

Then Hines and Love arranged a design competition among seven architects. Each got a month and $15,000 to devise the most memorable skyscraper design in Houston. From all this, hopefully, Love would find a design he could approve.

Somehow it must be compatible with downtown landmarks of very different styles. It had to be at least 56 stories, one story higher than First International Plaza which, when it was finished, would be the tallest building downtown.

In December 1977, Love and Hines received the architects at Love's offices in the Gulf Building, an Art Deco celebration. Minoru Yamasaki, the Detroit-based architect who had done the twin tower boxes of New York's World Trade Center, showed models of three design ideas. After him came Romaldo Giurgola of the New York firm Mitchell/Giurgola, noted for low-key public buildings on the East Coast. A Houston architect named Ben Brewer gave a presentation. His firm, Lloyd Jones Brewer & Associates did major Houston projects like Allen Center, Greenway Plaza, Rice Stadium and the Houston Astrodome. J. V. Neuhaus III, president of 3D/International, had done extensive work in Saudi Arabia as well as a $1 billion project for the National Aeronautics and Space Administration, and he talked about his plans. "Tiny" Lawrence of the CRS Group, who designed buildings in 46 countries, proposed twin glass towers. He was known locally for his contribution to the well-received One Houston Center. Cesar Pelli, dean of Yale University's School of Art and Architecture, the designer of the Vivian Beaumont Theater at New York's Lincoln Center and other projects, made his case.

Pei revealed a simple small-scale model that showed the proposed design in its urban context. He recommended building it on the northeast corner of the block, so there would be an acre of open space for a plaza. By placing it at an angle, it would reflect light differently than other buildings and gain a point of distinction. The height of his proposed lobby would be 65 feet, same as nearby Jones Hall for the performing arts.

One of Pei's people had asked if it would be nice to have the building face Galveston, so tenants could look toward the Gulf of Mexico. Hines explained that nobody in Houston wanted to look at Galveston. The building should face southwest, enabling executives to see it as they drove downtown from the affluent suburbs, and that was how Pei presented his building to Love.

Pei captivated Love with his personable low-key manner. Yet Pei was a simmering caldron of enthusiasm. He walked around downtown Houston enough to absorb its possibilities. His proposal respected neighboring landmarks, offered open space to a downtown that had little and proposed a soaring height, which would fulfill Love's ego. Hines and Love gave Pei the nod. Reportedly a $100 million job, it was Pei's first major corporate commission since Hancock Tower.

Pei's associate partner Harold Fredenburgh was given charge of the project and did most of the day-to-day work. Hines was more interested than most developers in how the design was coming along, and he'd stop by Pei's 600 Madison Avenue office when he was in New York. He's drop in on Saturdays, observing the draftsmen. He always wore a suit. One Sunday morning, he called Fredenburgh from Geneva and discussed details about the elevators.

Hines was a meticulous detail man, far more concerned with the minutiae than anybody else Pei had encountered. Hines wasn't content to accept a plan as presented. He considered altering dimensions, for instance, calculating the cost of an additional inch of ceiling height. He determined how much more granite exterior wall would be needed, how many more office partitions, elevator cables, everything—before making his final decision.

Progress on this, as on most buildings, was marked by an endless succession of details. Love and Hines went to the Tyler elevator factory in Cleveland where Fredenburgh showed them a mock-up of the proposed $20,000 elevator cabs lined with stainless steel and woven horsehair. Curiously, the horsehair, which had a macho Tall Texas look, was from France. Hines, ever a practical man, wondered how well the horsehair would wear with people and parcels bumping against it. He pulled out his car keys. With all his might he pushed them into the horse hair and tried gouging it. There wasn't a scratch.

The stainless steel was a question mark because of its extra cost. Reluctantly, Love decided it looked so snazzy he had to go for it. But afterward he remarked that each meeting he had with Fredenburgh cost him another $600,000.

Pei and his people wanted the building to have solid granite corners, so there wouldn't be an unattractive caulking joint. Over the years, caulking cracked. Fresh caulking didn't prevent it from looking worse. Hines's Project Officer Clayton Stone, and Construction Officer John Harris resisted solid granite corners, because they meant substantially higher costs.

Fredenburgh proposed turning the opposing panels of granite four inches to achieve solid granite corners. "I explained," he told me, "that the building was more than the diagram of an idea. There was a certain element of craft which was important to the expression of the design, and this was a significant issue for us. Gerry thought about this overnight, then called to say that he decided he didn't want to be one of those developers who forfeited what might have become a more valuable long-term investment because he wasn't willing to put enough dollars into the project." Hines approved the solid granite corners.

Fredenburgh, Harris and the granite panel fabricators devised a solution. Instead of turning each granite panel four inches, they'd turn it two inches. To maintain the original effect, they'd glue two panels tight together and have them installed as a single piece.

Even though he had experienced the largesse of the Mellon family,

Pei was surprised at what Hines was willing to spend on tenant amenities. Pei had never designed nine-foot ceilings in an office building before, but that was what Hines wanted. Nor had Pei dared recommend granite in the elevator lobbies or marble counters in bathrooms. "Gerry, more than anyone else since Bill Zeckendorf," Pei notes, "recognized that fine architecture creates value and enhances the marketability of a building."

Love asked what Pei might propose for a 20-story companion building across Travis Street that would house a data processing center, health club and parking. Occupying a full block, it would extend to Main Street. The resulting design was a handsome departure from the usual eyesore garage. There were stores at ground level, which helped enliven seedy Main Street.

Then Love told Pei that he needed a drive-in facility. "What's that?" Pei asked.

Down Texas way, Love explained, banks provided one place for people who want to walk into a bank, another place for those who preferred to do their business from a car.

Pei wasn't interested in finding out how other architects designed drive-in banking facilities. He sketched a novel design with circular lanes, which channeled cars to a central teller booth, then dispersed them to the four surrounding streets.

Meanwhile, Hines scrambled to fill the 1.2 million square feet available in the main building. Howard Boyd, chairman of El Paso Company and a member of the Texas Commerce board, needed room to expand—he was in cramped quarters in the American General Building. So he, Love and Hines began talking. Hines hoped El Paso would occupy upper floors, which commanded premium rents. Boyd hoped to gain some recognition that would give his corporation a higher profile. He signed for 428,000 square feet.

Solution? Calling the site El Paso Place or El Paso Center would make people think it was in El Paso. Because Texas Commerce would continue using the popular Gulf Building for consumer banking, it didn't really need its name on the new building. El Paso's name would go on the new skyscraper. It would be El Paso Tower in Texas Commerce Plaza.

To hedge his bets further, the supercautious Hines searched for a major equity partner. Within a month, he made a deal with Netherlands Antilles Corporation. Hines got lower total interest costs than if he had raised the same amount of capital with a debt financing. Consequently, his break-even point was lower, and he could make money even if a recession resulted in low occupancy. He sacrificed potential profits to gain some peace of mind.

Yet he was a bold marketer. With two major tenants and an equity partner, Hines was ready to display his magic. In July 1978 he invited a thousand of Houston's politicians, bankers, potential tenants, architects, engineers and reporters to a reception at Jones Hall. It was hard to ignore his invitation: an eight-inch model of Pei's design on a block of granite like the kind that would be used on the building. These things cost $10 apiece, so his tab just for invitations exceeded $10,000. Those who attended the ceremony and eats were regaled with a spectacular two-story-high model, which cost $50,000. By 1980, a year before the building was to open, Hines had leased more than 80 percent of the space.

But Howard Boyd retired from El Paso Company, and new management was uneasy with a high profile represented by the new building. They didn't need the space anymore, for a large tenant had vacated the American General Building. If El Paso made a deal for it, they'd expand at less cost and without a disruptive move.

It would be embarrassing for the biggest tenant to walk out. On the other hand, the market had advanced since El Paso signed a long-term lease for the reported average rate of around $14 a square foot. Hines cultivated goodwill by letting El Paso out of its lease, and he re-leased the space for more money. His new anchor tenant was United Energy Resources, Inc., a company that needed more space than was available at Hines's Pennzoil Place across Milam Street. United Energy Resources Tower didn't have the right ring. The project became Texas Commerce Tower at United Energy Plaza.

The building was fully leased before the Houston real estate market crashed. Hines and Pei had a gratifying money-maker they could talk about.

Suddenly, in the 1980s, Pei once again seemed a logical choice for corporations whose executives wanted elegant architecture within a reasonable budget. He accepted commissions from IBM, Mobil, Johnson & Johnson. He did more traveling to Dallas than almost anywhere else, designing a gray trapezoidal office building for local developer Vincent Carrozza and an office tower for Arco, plus the Dallas City Hall and Dallas Concert Hall.

As construction was starting on Texas Commerce Tower, Pei got an irresistible offer to design a hotel in Beijing. It came because of a recent lecture he had given there. The commission would bring him back to the homeland he had seen little of for four decades. It represented an opportunity to make a dramatic contribution, because not much of China's architectural heritage has survived the ravages of twentieth century civil war, invasion and revolution. Until recently, anything beyond grim utilitarian structures was viewed as a frivolous violation of Communist decorum. Pei could lead in new, hopeful directions.

He wanted a contemporary design that drew inspiration from Chinese themes. "The Chinese must find an architectural language of their own," he said to me, "if they are to build towns and cities that are distinctively Chinese instead of the monotonous buildings the Russians put across their landscape."

The Chinese wanted a skyscraper, because, among other things, tall buildings symbolize progress. Furthermore, they were the basis of Pei's reputation. But Pei, summoning all his tact, explained why skyscrapers weren't for every place. They'd be wrong in the center of Beijing whose whole ambiance is formed by low buildings. Better, he suggested, not to have tall buildings that might seem to look down on the Forbidden City and Temple of Heaven. Officials accepted his advice, banning tall buildings around the historic district.

For his site, Pei chose Fragrant Hill Park, a seemingly remote region with lovely old trees and beautiful hills. Yet it was only 20 miles west of Beijing. Here he was free to explore a Chinese-style architecture.

"If you start by observing how people live," Pei says, "you will eventually find the right design solution for satisfying their needs. The Chinese desperately need new buildings and are correct in seeking something better than what was built during the past 50 years. They look admiringly at Western buildings but don't want them in their country, because they're too foreign. It's difficult for them to decide what they want."

The Chinese wondered how they could recruit foreign capital, but eventually they financed the project on their own. In that sense, it was a truly Chinese accomplishment.

Pei devised graceful three-story pavilions which form courtyards, mingled with centuries-old gingko trees, water-and-rock gardens and white pebble pathways. He designed a meandering stream for Liushui-yin (Music of Running Water), part of a traditional poetry-writing ceremony. There are decorative touches on the buildings and grounds that don't appear in anything else done by Pei. The hotel was called Xiangshan (Fragrant Hill).

He selected native Chinese materials like white stucco. He found an old craftsman who still knew how to make soft-colored tiles including a warm dark gray he wanted. Powerful-looking, ancient rocks for the gardens came from the Stone Forest in the province of Yunnan, more than a thousand miles away in southwest China. "I want to remind the Chinese of the intimate relationship between architecture and gardens, something they used to understand very well," Pei adds.

He acknowledges it was difficult finding trained, efficient workers, because most Chinese remained agricultural, ignoring the pressures of industrial civilization. They valued their leisurely tea breaks. "At one point," Pei says, "I abandoned the polite ceremonial approach of my ancestors in favor of blunt talk. The Chinese were shocked, but I got better work. I guess I'm not as Chinese as I imagined."

Fragrant Hill was widely hailed when it opened in 1983 but, state-owned, it was not properly operated and maintained. The grounds became shabby, litter filled the lobby, and shops were desolate. But now Fragrant Hill is reportedly restored to its original elegance.

Meanwhile, Pei is shuttling across the Atlantic to confer with French officials about his controversial new expansion of the Louvre. He designed an underground network of badly needed shops, cafeterias, conference rooms, storage rooms, restoration laboratories and parking facilities. This network is to connect the museum's main wings—cutting the distance visitors must walk from about 1,000 yards to 100. For the center of the grand courtyard, Pei has propsoed a 70.5-foot-high, 115-foot-wide glass pyramid that would form a distinctive entrance.

He needs all his charm to handle the ridicule from traditionalist-minded French critics—suggesting that it is impossible for a Chinese architect to understand things French. One newspaper branded Pei's entrance "The Astonishing Chinese Pyramid." Pei counters that because the proposed entrance would be simple, transparent and light-reflecting, it won't clash with the seventeenth century Baroque-style buildings. Pei's design survived, and the $200 million renovation is underway now.

Back home, at their Sutton Place, Manhattan townhouse, I. M. and Eileen Pei nurture plants, especially azaleas, and are surrounded by a personal collection of Chinese and modern art. They're serene.

6.

SHOPPERS' WORLD

IN MANY SURPRISING WAYS, THE PLACES WE LIVE, WORK AND SHOP are shaped more by real estate entrepreneurs than architects who do the actual design work. The initial concept of how spaces will be used, how they'll relate to one another, what key dimensions will be—these and myriad other decisions often spring from the practical observations of an entrepreneur rather than an architect's drawing board.

Certainly this is the case with James Rouse who, as founder of The Rouse Company, has conceived real estate projects worth a couple billion dollars. He prides himself on his practical knowledge of how people tend to behave in the spaces he builds. Shopping centers are his specialty. Among the earliest to tackle decrepit downtowns, he's credited with heartening urban revivals in Boston, Baltimore, Philadelphia and other cities. He even built a new town—Columbia, Maryland—where he lives in a modest five-bedroom glass-and-frame house overlooking Wilde Lake, one of three man-made lakes there.

In recent years, he has been phasing himself out of The Rouse Company, as he plunges into new ventures through the Enterprise Development Corporation which, by developing festive marketplaces around the country, helps finance his Enterprise Foundation, a private effort to help renovate housing for the very poor. I met him in his sixth floor offices at the white American City Building, just across the parking lot from The Rouse Company. He enjoys a cheerful view of Lake Kittamaqundi, which he also created. His desk is covered with papers, and his walls are full of design awards he has received over the years. Photographs record his proud moments with mayors and presidents.

With a yen for decidedly casual attire like loafers, madras and tweed sports jackets, the balding Rouse, 71, doesn't seem like a high-powered real estate entrepreneur who has netted $20 million. He's an affable 5-foot-11-inch man who drives a comfortable Buick Skylark rather than a flashy import. His idea of a fine lunch is walking to Baltimore's roisterous Lexington Market, where he can down a half-dozen raw oysters. Instead of a big yacht, he has a 26-foot fishing boat dubbed "Adequate" for outings in Chesapeake Bay.

As I discovered for myself, Rouse has a gift for conveying his ideas with eloquent missionary zeal. He's less interested in the artistic aspect of design, because he focuses on what buildings do for people. When he points to a pile of discouraging rubble, he conjures visions of eager shoppers, lively streets and a thriving community. Without a doubt, he has a greater impact on retail design than any critically acclaimed architect.

He certainly isn't a jet-setter. He relishes backpacking and fishing in Canada. He's an enthusiastic cook whose favorite dishes included terrapin, mock terrapin (made from muskrat), grilled quail and corn-meal pancakes. Taking a cue perhaps from the joyous James Beard, Rouse uses lots of fresh creamery butter.

He has an extraordinary energy level, as successful real estate people must, and it was tough for his wife Elizabeth Winstead to keep up. They were divorced after 31 years and three children: Lydia Robinson, married to a lawyer and living in Columbia; Winstead, a piano and oboe player who's a partner in a Baltimore development company; and James Wilson Jr., a Baltimore artist who owns Louie's Bookstore Cafe, which serves traditional Maryland dishes plus new ones his father concocted. Rouse has seven grandchildren.

In 1974, two years following his divorce, he married Patricia Traugott who, 12 years younger, was a former commissioner of the Norfolk, Virginia Redevelopment and Housing Authority. She became his partner in his improbable crusade to help poor people transform slums into clean, safe, affordable housing.

Rouse is motivated to do more than make money. He chides other millionaires for not helping the poor. He never forgets his rocky youth.

He is the fifth child of Lydia Robinson and Willard G. Rouse, a prosperous canned foods broker. He grew up in an eight-bedroom Victorian mansion in Easton, a placid town along Maryland's Eastern Shore.

He had the earmarks of enterprise from his earliest years. He tended radishes, beets and stringbeans in the family vegetable garden, then sold them to a local grocer. Later he worked as a caddie, cannery factory hand and Fuller Brush salesman. He was president of both his class and the student council at Easton High School.

Good times ended when his mother died in 1930, before his sixteenth birthday. Then his father died four months later, leaving so much debt that their house was foreclosed two months after that. Rouse drove across the country in a Model T Ford and shipped steerage class to Hawaii so he could live with his older sister, Mary Day, who had married a Naval officer. He attended the University of Hawaii for a year.

He longed for the East, however, and landed a scholarship at the University of Virginia. He couldn't afford to continue, so he quit in March 1933 and got a $13.50 a week job parking cars for the St. Paul Garage in Baltimore. He enrolled at the University of Maryland and studied law at night, paying his expenses by working as a legal clerk at the Baltimore office of the Federal Housing Administration.

After graduation, good jobs were hard to find, so he created one for himself by persuading Baltimore's Title Guarantee and Trust Company to open a mortgage department. He was hired to run it for three years, until 1939.

Then, restless, he, together with his partner Hunter Moss, borrowed $20,000 from family and friends to form a mortgage banking firm. Representing Connecticut General and Continental American Life Insurance Company, they wrote FHA mortgages on single-family homes. By 1942, when he joined the Naval Reserve as a lieutenant, Moss-Rouse Company had a $6 million loan portfolio.

After World War II, he returned to Baltimore and expanded their business to include mortgages on apartment buildings and shopping centers. He bought out Hunter Moss and formed James W. Rouse & Company in 1954. Alex Brown & Company, Baltimore, led an underwriting that sold $3 million of the firm's convertible debentures in 1957. Later, these were converted to common stock. By 1970, he represented about 70 life insurance companies and other lenders and managed a mortgage portfolio over $885 million.

But Rouse wasn't content just to finance real estate development. During the late 1940s, he wanted to become an entrepreneur himself. He was particularly fascinated with retailing. "I puzzled about how to create a successful retail environment," he recalls. "I told Bob Dowling, the president of City Investing who had helped revive downtown Pittsburgh, that I had a 46-acre site three miles from downtown Baltimore. I was sure it was a convenient retail site, but I didn't know how to develop it. Dowling said he didn't know much about Pittsburgh before he started work there, so he assembled a design panel and paid them by the day to generate ideas.

"That's what I did," Rouse continues. "I retained Pietro Belluschi, Dean of Architecture at the Massachusetts Institute of Technology; there was a New Hampshire landscape architect named Dan Kiley; a city planner, Steward Mott; a traffic expert, Al Vorhees.

"The genius of the group was a sleeper, Ken Welch, an architect on the staff of the Grand Rapids Store Equipment Company. He had studied retailing for nearly 50 years. He knew more about the movement of shoppers through a store than any man I ever met. He knew a mall shouldn't be more than 50 feet wide. I don't think anybody else knew that. He knew a parking bay should be 64 feet, an individual space should be nine feet, and parking should be only at right angles. In his pockets—which were always stuffed—he carried photographs of people trying to park, having a hard time angling into the space, backing out, going around. He showed action by flipping these photographs.

"We met every couple of weeks for a night and a day. I brought pages of questions about shopping. How wide should stores be? What kind of lighting works best? What kinds of stores should go together?

"Of course, we studied the local market. We asked people: Where did you buy your last coat? Your last men's suit? Shoes? Hat? Vacuum cleaner? Did you intend to buy it when you left home? What caused you to buy it? Where did you buy it?"

After six years of planning, in 1955, Rouse broke ground on his first project—Mondawmin Mall, a two-level retailing center. "We thought we should have an enclosed mall," he says, "but we lost our nerve because of the extra cost." He did build an enclosed mall, one of the earliest, three years later in Harundale, nine miles south of Baltimore. It provided comfortable shopping streets, heated in winter and cooled in summer.

Despite the press of business, Rouse was home almost every night while his children were growing up. When he brought home work from the office, he often did it on the living room floor, surrounded by his family. "All through our childhood," recalls daughter Robin, "he was the laughing, roughhousing one creating fun. He led everybody else on incredible adventures. If something didn't work, it was a new thing to be conquered, not something to get you down."

Once he interrupted a meeting with an Israeli architect about a possible project in Jerusalem to take a call from his son Jim who wanted to know how you find eggs inside a terrapin. Since cooking it was one of his specialties, he was eager to explain.

Rouse continued to encourage ideas from others. "In 1963," he says, "we set up a group for a critique of Cherry Hill Mall near Camden, New Jersey. In the group were nine merchants, nine professionals including city planners and architects, nine people from the community such as the high school principal, president of the high school senior class, editor of the Camden newspaper, head of Camden County mental health. We wanted to know what we could do to serve the community better. What could we add which wasn't there? How could the project have been planned better? We learned a lot about shopping."

Other developers usually landscaped only with money left over after a building was finished—seldom much—but Rouse was among the first to insist that landscaping be an integral part of a project. "I just thought it was depressing to see tired, forlorn plants," he says. "Rich, growing plants were so much better. But they must be nurtured. I had a sister who did the landscaping for a little center we built in Talbot County, because she lived nearby. The results were so good that we asked her to landscape all our centers. We experiemented with palm trees and other exotic indoor plants before we discovered what will survive and what won't. We established our own nursery in Florida to supply durable, appealing plants."

By the end of the 1960s, Rouse was a major retail developer with 17 malls finished and five under construction. He was among those who helped pull people from the cities to the suburbs.

Yet he was always concerned about the problems of cities. From 1949 to 1952, he chaired the Mayor's Advisory Committee on Housing in Baltimore, an early effort to help alleviate slums. President Dwight Eisenhower named Rouse to an Advisory Committee on Government Housing Policies and Programs. The resulting proposals were part of the 1954 Housing Act. In 1955, he coauthored a visionary tract called *No Slums in Ten Years*. The following year, with other Baltimore business leaders he started the Greater Baltimore Committee, which enlisted a hundred local businessmen to help revive the declining downtown. He served on the Maryland State Commission, which drafted legislation for a metropolitan Baltimore planning agency. With others he started the American Council to Improve our Neighborhood, which became ACTION Inc., to encourage thoughtful urban renewal across the country. During the 1960s, these efforts spurred the development of Charles Center, a complex of offices, stores and a theater. It was the city's first major redevelopment project.

He wondered about improvements that might be possible if a city were started from scratch. He imagined a city that mingled stimulating urban density with a lot of trees and lakes, a place where people could walk to work. It would be a racially mixed place with different kinds of people who thrived together. This was his dream for a new city called Columbia, which he hoped would grow to 110,000 people within 15 years.

"We had to get away from the separate cells with which we view urban life and problems," Rouse explains. "Each area—employment, health and education, for instance—must be understood as systems which reinforce each other. At Columbia, we attacked the whole urban problem. We never promised a perfect city, only a better one."

Through dummy corporations, the Rouse Company set about acquiring 147 farms for their 14,000 acres between Baltimore and Washington. He tapped his long association with Connecticut General Insurance Company for $23 million to finance land purchases. The Rouse Company put in $1 million.

As he had done before, he gathered a panel of urban planning experts, architects and engineers to develop ideas. The scheme that emerged was a cluster of seven villages around a downtown. Neighborhoods were oriented to their schools. Columbia, Rouse says, "was a very rational thing which emerged out of the irrationality of urban sprawl."

If the architecture was conventional, Columbia was hailed as a sensitive accomplishment. *New Yorker* critic Anthony Bailey: "For the first time on any such scale in this country, the design of single structures has been subordinated to the design of a larger work."

Despite acclaim like this, the 1973–75 recession hit Columbia hard. While many businesses located there—including major facilities for General Electric, Bendix, Pfizer and Toyota—land sales lagged. There were only 40,000 residents by the mid-1970s, and sales dropped more than 50 percent. Columbia had $80 million of short-term debt versus only $6 million of equity when interest rates skyrocketed.

"I think there is probably not a land development project in the United States that has not been in trouble during the past year and a half," Rouse told a congressional subcommittee. "Yes, Columbia has had severe financial troubles—that is, it has had to work out new financial arrangements."

Warren Fuller, a Connecticut General vice president, reported: "We sent a team of experts to analyze the whole situation. We came up with alternatives ranging from bankruptcy to refinancing, reorganizing and reordering management's priorities. We chose the latter, because we had confidence in Jim Rouse as an individual and businessman, and we believed in Columbia. We expected eventually we would realize a profit." With great boldness or recklessness, depending on your point of view, Connecticut General advanced Columbia $44.5 million, so he could survive until the market turned.

The Rouse Company experienced difficulties, too. It had ventured into the hotel business, launched a real estate investment trust, built industrialized housing and some office buildings, none of which were profitable at the time. The company's stock, issued at $5 a share in 1961, had hit $45 twice and split twice during dizzier days. By 1975, it plunged to 1⅜.

Rouse had hired Mathias J. DeVito, partner in the Baltimore law firm Piper & Marbury, to establish a general counsel's office at the company. Like Trammell Crow did when his empire collapsed during the 1973–75 crisis, Rouse asked his young attorney to unscramble the mess.

DeVito was born in Trenton, New Jersey, and his father, a house painter, wanted him to become an accountant. "In those days, you did what your parents told you, and I took that curriculum in high school," DeVito reflects.

"But my boyhood dream had always been to be a lawyer. This was born out of the movies. Every Saturday afternoon, we'd go to the movies, and somehow I got the idea this would be a great thing. But I was discouraged, because my parents couldn't really afford sending me to college. Well, I discovered that the University of Maryland would admit me, provided I took some courses for special enrichment. I graduated and went on through their law school. One thing led to another—I got a clerkship with Fourth Circuit Judge Morris Soper, which was considered one of the top clerkships after the Supreme Court. This experience made it possible for me to join Piper & Marbury. After six years there, I spent a year and a half at the Attorney General's office, then returned to the firm as a partner in 1965."

Piper & Marbury did legal work for the Rouse Company, and as its growth accelerated during the mid-1960s, so did the volume of legal work. Soon after DeVito was back, he was asked to take some on. "I really hadn't done much in real estate," he says, "but my very first assignment for Rouse was an enormous shopping center in northern New Jersey called Willowbrook. When I was handling the transaction, it was the biggest shopping center in America. We started with a swamp and had to relocate a stream if the project was to work. This required a complex array of approvals from federal, state and local government agencies. Then there were zoning issues, traffic issues. We negotiated with three powerful department stores—Sears, Macy's and Sterns—until they agreed to a single operating agreement. We got it done, then we did another and another.

"Rouse had some in-house lawyers who handled leasing for small tenants, but the company didn't have the capability for large transactions like these. For a lower salary than I was making at the firm, I agreed to spend full time for a while establishing a general counsel's operation and then return to Piper & Marbury.

"The Rouse Company was full of exciting, intriguing, surprising things. I was having more and more fun. Staying with Rouse was probably one of those decisions which was wrong if you added up the pros and cons as you knew them. People thought I was crazy—giving up a lucrative partnership in a growing firm, one of the most respected in the region, for this emerging company with a lot of risk. I was 39, and I figured that if I was going to try something risky, it had to be then. Later I realized you can make important decisions any time."

DeVito succeeded Rouse as president of The Rouse Company in 1973. He spent considerable time pondering what they should be doing and what they should pull out of. The profitable mortgage banking and shopping centers, he concluded, should be the core of the company. Virtually everything else except Columbia—a modular housing venture, a real estate investment trust and apartments—would be sold. The Rouse Company's two hotels would be run by a professional hotel management firm.

"We thought we could do anything because we had a lot of people," DeVito reflects. "We had very little long-term planning. We cut the staff in half and introduced vigorous discipline, and I believe it's largely responsible for our recovery. I'm more relaxed and can sleep easily at night."

"Even during the awful 1973–75 period," Rouse notes, "we survived. Our earnings were higher coming out of that recession than going into it. We had to sell a half interest in some projects, but we never defaulted on anything."

Though Rouse relied on DeVito to lead the turn-around, it was Rouse's own vision which gave the company a new direction. After making a fortune in suburban shopping centers, he insisted there was a future in the decaying downtowns he cared so passionately about.

He didn't recognize his big chance right away until, in 1975, a rumpled, wavy-haired Cambridge architect named Benjamin Thompson approached him with the idea of acquiring a 3.7-acre Boston property and renovating the three derelict nineteenth century Greek Revival buildings on it. They were known as Quincy Market, North Market and South Market. Each was two stories high and about 52 feet wide by 535 feet long. The wholesale food trade had abandoned these buildings nearly a decade before. For four years, Thompson had urged anyone who would listen that these might be adapted into a festive marketplace where people could sample many different foods and browse among boutiques. The proposed project was referred to as Faneuil Hall Marketplace after the adjacent Faneuil Hall, an historical structure belonging to the National Park Service.

It is easy to understand why people doubted the scheme would work. Very little in the way of new development had taken place in Boston for about 40 years. Boston had fewer hotel rooms than in

1960—it was hardly a tourist mecca. Moreover, without a department store as anchor, the idea was a risky departure from the standard shopping center formula. Nor was there much room for parking. Shopping centers were a suburban phenomenon which catered to cars, not pedestrians.

Thompson, though, was a restless visionary and a capable retail designer who appealed to Rouse. After graduating from the Yale School of Architecture in 1941, he joined with Bauhaus architect Walter Gropius, then chairman of Harvard's Department of Architecture, to form The Architect's Collaborative. When that became a hot shop with over 200 employees, Thompson moved on.

Inspired by bright Marimekko fabrics he discovered in Finland during the 1950s, he launched a store called Design/Research whose avowed aim was to integrate art with the home. He collected fabrics from 15 countries and fashioned them into a wide range of things from dresses to curtains and slipcovers. Despite the violence of the late 1960s, he built a vulnerable, virtually all-glass store in Cambridge. It did a burgeoning business. His wife Jane, a former editor of *Interiors* and founder of *Industrial Design,* took over when he returned to academia as chairman of Harvard's Department of Architecture.

Thompson was on a crusade. He upheld the modernist idea that architecture should have a social conscience and influence life for the better. He encouraged his students to tackle real urban problems rather than theoretical design ideas. But he became discouraged by petty academic politics, and he quit after four years. In 1970, after the Thompsons brought in a Wall Street whiz kid to help finance expansion of Design/Research, they lost control during a corporate maneuver, and it became part of the Crate & Barrel retail chain.

They recharged their spirits with a restored Victorian house in Cambridge—these modernists cheerfully acknowledged the heresy of eclectic Victorian decoration, but the place had charm. They became more concerned about how to revive a decaying city like Boston. They favored adapting great old structures rather than bulldozing whole blocks for numbing urban renewal projects.

Thompson appealed to Rouse's long-cherished dream of reviving downtowns. He began to imagine how Faneuil Hall Marketplace, if done right, could help stir Boston and bring profits to The Rouse Company. The crumbling market buildings were at the crossroads of traditional Boston—a few blocks from the waterfront, the financial district and the tight-knit North End Italian neighborhood. Nearby highways made this an easy place for people to reach from the suburbs.

"From the mid-1960s," Jane Thompson reflects, "when we first conceived the revitalization of Boston's market area, we knew there was no formula, no single existing prototype of the rich dynamic urban place we envisioned. Yet there were fragmentary sources: the native American tradition of county and state fairs; Boston's own tradition, now vanished, of neighborhood market houses; the markets of many cities abroad, from Marrakesh to Helsinki, which we visited often. Any successful realization would emerge, we believed, from countless small details in a new combination, to form a total environmental experience of indigenous character deeply satisfying to human needs."

The design that the Thompsons evolved with Rouse is open to the city. Instead of concentrating on the interior and presenting a boring blank wall to people outdoors, like many deadly downtown shopping centers, Faneuil Hall Marketplace faces outward. Accented with red, yellow, blue and green awnings, bright display windows and picturesque doors beckon people into the shops.

Moreover, Jane Thompson continues, "Pathways radiate out from, and into, the market area like spokes of a wheel, with people flowing along this multitude of pathways from all directions. Its edges melt into the city proper. There's not a single set of controlled or manipulated routes. The power of the Marketplace as the functional crossroads of downtown Boston lies in this multitude of inviting working connections."

From the beginning, food was seen as the central experience. Faneuil Hall Marketplace was designed so people would see fresh produce displayed, cookies being baked, coffee ground, ribs barbecued and dozens of other delectables prepared. The air would be full of a myriad of enticing fragrances. "The Marketplace," says Jane Thompson, "is a mothering place, welcoming and supportive, a source of sustenance. Its visual abundance gives assurance that growing, harvesting, preparing and consuming of food is being celebrated on a daily basis."

There would be plenty of comfortable places to sit, eat and chat around Faneuil Hall Marketplace. It would be a friendly environment where you're encouraged to linger—the very opposite of those forbidding corporate plazas whose high, narrow, sloping, spiked walls prod people on.

Attentive management would be crucial. To keep attracting people, Faneuil Hall Marketplace had to be safe and clean. Whatever might lurk in surrounding streets, this had to provide comfort, reassurance, pleasure.

Rouse wanted a lively mix of small merchants. A minority of businesses would belong to chains. He avoided standards like Mc-Donald's. To keep merchants from drifting in undesirable directions, he gave them a 54-page "manual" called *Retail Tenant Design Criteria,* which regulated the size, material, color, design and placement of everything involved with a store. Example: "The tenant may not use coy, rustic or unnaturally antiquated names or use imitations of old English or other scripts or affectations of spelling."

To achieve a critical mass that would help assure success, Rouse wanted to develop all the market buildings at once. He arranged $21 million of long-term financing from Teachers Insurance & Annuity Association. For short-term construction money, he called on just about all the banks in Boston, but they recoiled at the seemingly wild scheme. In New York, he persuaded Chase Manhattan to make a $10.5 million commitment, conditional on his going back to Boston and raising the balance there. Still they wouldn't touch the project.

Rouse decided to do the project in three phases. "The first was for $7.5 million," he says. "Teacher's stayed in for $7.5 million. Chase stayed in for $3.75 million. At last, from 12 Boston banks, we got a matching $3.75 million, and the Massachusetts Industrial Fund provided the last $350,000.

Renovation of the first market building started in October 1975, and opening day would be August 26, 1976—150 years to the day since Josiah Quincy had opened Quincy Market. It was not a date Bostonians took lightly, so missing it would be a highly visible sign that the project was in trouble. Yet two months before opening they had leased only 35,000 square feet of space. Rouse was urged to postpone opening, but he rejected that. On the other hand, opening with the place mostly empty would mean courting disaster.

"Better to figure out what we'd do before than after August 26th," Rouse remembers. He and his associates re-invented the pushcart. "We invited artists and craftspeople to come in. We'd provide attractive pushcarts with a one-page lease and a one-week term. They didn't need an architect, contractor, accountant or anybody. Just come and display their merchandise. Well, we leased 43 pushcarts in the last six weeks. They turned out to be crucial for the festive atmosphere.

"I recall sitting with Mayor Kevin White the night before opening. He tried to reassure me by saying that in Boston people tend to move slowly. 'Don't be disappointed if this project was slow,' he said.

" 'Kevin,' I replied, 'if this was slow, we're dead. It's got to be go right from the mark.' "

"That's how we opened. More than 100,000 people came, and the pushcarts obscured all the vacancies. That opening day may have had a bigger impact on reviving downtowns than any other single thing, because it made believers out of a tremendous number of people. It helped galvanize Boston, and it gave people across the country ideas for their cities."

To raise equity capital, so he could proceed with renovation of the other two market buildings, Rouse negotiated a deal with Chicago syndicator Neil Bluhm of JMB who agreed to take a 50 percent interest for an initial $2.5 million.

By 1978, Faneuil Hall Marketplace was complete, and annual sales exceeded $22 million, which translated to a hefty $350 per square foot. Perhaps surprisingly, almost half the merchandise there was sold to people who didn't come with the intention of buying. "People came to browse, stroll around, enjoy themselves," Rouse says. "Then they saw exciting things, and they began to buy."

To be sure, critics reacted against the tourist fare. Some retail developers asserted that Faneuil Hall Marketplace was really a food experience, not serious shopping. Robert Campbell, a Cambridge architect and architectural writer for the *Boston Globe* offered this reply in the *American Institute of Architects Journal:* "I think the snob view of Faneuil Hall Marketplace is the view of idiots. The markets have been an immense boon to Boston, a gift the city hardly deserved considering the fact that its own banks refused to finance a risk as dangerous as the markets were thought to be."

While other cities already had marketplaces with some of the elements seen at Faneuil Hall Marketplace—Salt Lake City's Trolley Square and San Francisco's Ghirardelli Square come to mind—none had the powerful national impact of the Boston experience. Why? "Diversity!" Rouse declares. "Faneuil Hall Marketplace has people who sell beef, fish, eggs, cheese, lettuce and tomatoes. Lots of different fast food, good restaurants. Pushcarts, kiosks, shops. The place is so full of life."

The Faneuil Hall Marketplace experience intrigued people in Baltimore. At a yuletide party, Baltimore housing commissioner Robert Embry asked his friend Rouse if he'd be interested in developing the former Pratt Street power plant, a four-story brick building at the edge of Baltimore's Inner Harbor, into a festive marketplace like Faneuil Hall Marketplace.

Rouse was skeptical. "First of all," he said then, "Baltimore was 2.5 million people compared to 3 million in Boston. Boston, too, was the sophisticated capital of New England, where you had about 11 million people. Baltimore was a blue collar city with very little hinterland. In fact, Washington, 35 miles away, was always drawing people out of Baltimore. Could Baltimore ever draw people from

Washington? Most people in Baltimore said no." Despite his doubts, Rouse agreed to join Embry and inspect the site the following day.

The inner Harbor was a vacuum. During the 1940s, the city had targeted it as an urban renewal area, and old wharves were demolished. By 1958, white ships of the United Fruit Line—known locally as banana boats—switched from Inner Harbor's Pier 1 to newer facilities further away at Locust Point. Conspicuous around Inner Harbor were a jumble of tomato wholesalers, poultry wholesalers and wino bars, the kind of businesses that spelled risk to developers. To help move things forward, the city leveled the area.

As Rouse surveyed the Inner Harbor, he noted that the power plant Embry talked about was east of the new World Trade Center and the site for a proposed aquarium. He became worried that it was too far from downtown. He told Embry that he'd be more comfortable with a site that could be reached easily by a lot of retail customers.

The next day, Embry suggested another site—an L-shaped 3.5 acres of shoreline that local people referred to as the "crotch" of the harbor, near the intersection of Pratt Street and Light Street, major downtown thoroughfares. Rouse agreed this was a promising location, but taking over the land would be a touchy issue. It was traditionally the place for ethnic festivals and the City Fair.

Mayor William Donald Schaefer, for one, had to approve the idea. A 59-year-old bachelor who lived with his 87-year-old mother, he spearheaded the city's efforts to emerge from its seedy slumber, and he looked favorably on downtown redevelopment. But he was a popular politician who didn't want to upset voters. Persuaded by how Faneuil Hall Marketplace had reinvigorated Boston, he became a Rouse enthusiast.

The proposal was announced at an August 1977 news conference, and it aroused vehement opposition. People who lived near the Inner Harbor objected that new buildings would block their water views. South Baltimore as well as Little Italy businesspeople feared sophisticated new competition would ruin them. In 1978 they maneuvered the issue onto a city referendum proposal for preserving all Inner Harbor land as a park. Feisty Mayor Schaefer countered with a referendum that would preserve all Inner Harbor as a park except the parcel Rouse wanted. Enough people voted "no" on the first proposal and "yes" on the second so that Harborplace could proceed.

How did Rouse adapt his ideas to Baltimore's situation? "We started by picking a group of people whom we believed had life, fire, imagination and taste, and we sent them to Boston," Rouse told me. "They spent a day and a half looking at Quincy Market, not as a committee to reach any decisions, just as a group of people. Then we spent a day and a half thinking how we could create the kind of delight they saw in Boston, only in Baltimore terms. Baltimore was 57 percent black, and we had to respond to that. Our site was right on the water, and it was much more a part of Baltimore than the waterfront was in Boston."

Rouse tapped Ben and Jane Thompson to design the project. Since they were starting with a bare site, they explored the tradition of waterfront building—ferry terminals, boathouses, warehouses, yacht clubs—which they hoped to combine with elements of traditional park architecture like exposition buildings, greenhouses, pleasure pavilions and bandstands.

Local regulations imposed constraints on design. There was a maximum height of 40 feet, so this meant the buildings couldn't be higher than two stories. Since the site was largely a public park, the buildings had to afford easy access to the water. Buildings had to be separated widely to assure a view of the U.S.S. *Constellation,* America's first commissioned warship, which is docked in the Inner Harbor.

The Thompsons developed a striking $18 million design that features two rectangular glass-enclosed market pavilions at right angles to one another. They have wide outdoor decks, balcony promenades and gabled green aluminum roofs. One pavilion is for merchandise and restaurants, the other is primarily for food. These pavilions are especially inviting, since people outside can look in at people and colorful displays of clothes, toys, crafts and other things, while people inside can see people outside and the Inner Harbor.

Famous after his success at Faneuil Hall Marketplace, Rouse was deluged with several thousand applicants for the 120 retail spaces available. But many prospects withdrew when they discovered they would have to keep their stores open from 9 in the morning until at least 9 at night, seven days a week—even a little mom and pop operation needed about 20 employees. Moreover, sophisticated accounting systems were required, and retailers had to satisfy The Rouse Company's strict quality standards. Finally, quite a few prospects were frightened by the big league rents. So leasing became another uphill battle for Rouse.

Nonetheless, Rouse got the lively mix he was looking for. Harborplace had purveyors of spicy Thai specialities, cotton candy, health salads, rich Italian ice creams, Texas-style barbecue, Indian cuisine, a plethora of baked goods and seafood. There were kites, books, posters, puzzles, stuffed animals, clothing and more.

Nobody could have predicted the tumultuous opening on July 2, 1980. Suddenly, Baltimore came alive. An astonishing 14 million people visited Harborplace during its first year—more than visited the Magic Kingdom at Disney World. "It would be hard to find anything else so small which has excited so many people," Rouse beams.

While Rouse is well known for these festive marketplaces, he also has been building conventional shopping centers, many in difficult downtown locations. His biggest successes include Philadelphia's Gallery at Market East and The Grand Avenue in Milwaukee.

Gradually, he has retired from the day-to-day affairs of The Rouse Company. He stepped down as chief executive officer in May 1979 and as board chairman in May 1984. The company had $25 million of stockholders' equity and $479 million of assets. It was administering a $1.4 billion mortgage portfolio and operated 53 shopping centers with 31 million square feet of space. By 1985 stock in the Rouse Company had soared 2,500 percent since DeVito began the turnaround. Dividends, $1.08 per share, are actually approaching the stock price at its low a decade ago.

The company has continued building festive marketplaces. After Harborplace came New York's South Street Seaport—Mayor Edward Koch decided he wanted it after seeing the crowds at Faneuil Hall Marketplace. The Thompsons did the the designs, and South Street Seaport won over critics who assumed the Big Apple already had everything.

Meanwhile, at 66 in 1981, Rouse started anew. He was inspired by a Washington, D.C. church which had formed a nonprofit group called Jubilee Housing Inc. to renovate old apartment buildings for very poor families. "When I first met with them," he acknowledges, "I didn't think they would succeed. I gagged from the stench in one of the buildings they proposed to renovate." But they restored eight buildings with 257 units, set up a health clinic and job center. They changed lives. "These weren't miracles, they were caring people," Rouse continues. "Maybe similar things could happen in other cities."

He launched The Enterprise Foundation whose mission was to help poor people refurbish run-down housing. His initial contribution was $1 million, and he draws no salary. He maintains a whirlwind schedule raising funds around the country. In its first three years, The Enterprise Foundation raised more than $16 million and gave support to 22 community groups including Jubilee Housing. "This is by all odds the most important thing I've ever done," he says.

To help provide financial staying power, he started The Enterprise Development Company as a subsidiary of the foundation to develop festive marketplaces in secondary cities and funnel earnings to the Enterprise Foundation. "I wanted to make a fortune," he says, "not for the rich, but for the poor."

The first projects to open were the $14-million, 80,000-square-foot Waterside in Norfolk, Virginia and the $14.5 million, 60,000-square-foot Portside in Toledo, Ohio. Enterprise Development has additional projects underway in Richmond, Virginia; Flint and Battle Creek, Michigan. Negotiations are well along for projects in 10 more cities. "When we first go to work in long-depressed cities like these, we encounter deep skepticism," Rouse says, with a youthful spring in his step. "But people yearn for their city to come alive, and as they see a project take shape, it helps build fires of enthusiasm and hope."

7.
GOOD NEIGHBORS

ARCHITECTS USED TO BE UTTERLY PREOCCUPIED WITH MAKING their artistic statements, but now more than ever their concern is to complement nearby buildings. If this involves less exuberant individualism, often the result is a more pleasing neighborhood.

Six-foot-two-inch Cesar Pelli has done his share of flamboyant set pieces, yet undeniably his greatest work—the World Financial Center—bows to the skyscraper tradition in lower Manhattan. He got the commission for the $1.5 billion project, in fact, because he had pondered more than anybody else how to achieve distinction within a stylish context.

I found him at 1056 Chapel Street, New Haven, on the second floor of an old building above Arnold's Boot Shop and Aloha Ice Cream. From the window of his modest office, Pelli looks out over Yale University's freshman quadrangle.

He's a sophisticated man, with lively brown eyes, a ready smile and resonant Spanish voice. His wife, Diana Balmori, a former history teacher he met while studying architecture in Argentina, works with him. She's an architect who's also involved with landscape design. Their son Rafael is an architecture student at Harvard. The Pellis' older son Denis is pursuing vision research.

Pelli, whose grandfather emigrated from Italy to Argentina more than a century ago, graduated cum laude in 1949 from the provincial Universidad Nacional de Tucuman. Then he got a job designing buildings for a government agency. "Instead of doing palaces and mausoleums and all sorts of building types of which there were no examples in the city, and no need for," he told me, "we became interested in hospitals, houses and schools—real buildings. We wanted to become architects who would contribute to the social body, not just make empty gestures in tired styles."

In 1952, Pelli moved to the United States, continuing his education with a scholarship at the University of Illinois. Within a year, he was working with Eero Saarinen, the acclaimed Finnish architect. Among Saarinen's best-known designs are the CBS Building in New

York and Dulles International Airport Terminal near Washington. Pelli was project designer for Saarinen's Trans World Airlines International Arrivals Building at New York's John F. Kennedy Airport. During the decade Pelli was with the firm, it grew from about 25 people to more than a hundred.

"Working for Eero was exciting," Pelli recalls, "because with each building you designed, you felt you were exploring a new form of architectural expression. Nothing was ever brought from one design to the next, so you could never reach a level of refinement. When you were constantly in pursuit of some new architectural approach, there were more chances to make a mistake. There were times when we would realize after several months on one design that it wouldn't work. At the last minute we had to pull something out of the back pocket.

"Eero tended to start with an overall vision of a building, then fit that to its purpose. I see myself proceeding in a more systematic way. I start with the building's function and a very thorough idea of its needs. Only then do I start to consider what are appropriate forms. Rarely, if ever, do I end up discarding three or four months' work."

Pelli remained with the firm for three years after Saarinen's death in 1961, finishing projects they had started. "I wanted to go out on my own," he says, "but it really wasn't an option. I didn't have the family or personal connections you need. I couldn't start by designing houses for my friends, because all my friends were architects." He was never a very socially gregarious person like Bruce Graham, the enormously successful rain-maker for the Chicago office of Skidmore, Owings & Merrill.

Pelli joined a Los Angeles architectural firm—Daniel, Mann, Johnson & Mendenhal—best known for cost-competitive engineering. It was an unexpectedly good career move. Pelli designed a hillside housing project that gave the developer a lot of rentable units while avoiding landslide problems and preserving most of the landscape. For this, Pelli won a 1966 Design Award from *Progressive Architecture*. He was beginning to establish an independent reputation.

By 1968, he was asked to become partner in charge of all architectural design at Gruen Associates, a large Los Angeles architecture and engineering firm. The following year, he headed a team which won first prize in a global competition to design the International Organizations Headquarters and Conference Center, Vienna. The design called for seven modular towers on a landfill island in the Danube. He remained with Gruen for eight years.

"Working for these larger, more demanding firms was wonderful training," says Pelli, "because it forced me to do things in two or three weeks which I would have spent several months on when I was with Eero. I discovered they were just as good, often better."

Perhaps his best-known design at Gruen was Pacific Design Center, a brilliant blue glass, six-story showroom for the interior design industry which dominates its surroundings yet harmonizes with them. "If you have ever been in an Italian fishing village," Pelli smiles, "when an ocean liner comes into the harbor, you can look down the street and see that it doesn't destroy the scale of the village. It's so different by nature that it strengthens the area. I wanted the Pacific Design Center to provide the same strength to an area which has cheaply built one- two-story buildings without any urban character."

Pelli loved the give-and-take of teaching architecture, and periodically he stepped away from his practice to do that: in 1960 at the University of Tucuman and the University of Cordoba; in 1972 and 1974 at Yale University; in 1975 and 1976 at the University of California, Los Angeles.

On January 1, 1977, after finishing a design for the Yale Music Center, Pelli was named dean of Yale University's School of Art & Architecture, where he was a popular lecturer. He enjoyed discussing architectural theory, and he thrived amidst the enthusiasm of students.

By the end of January, he was asked to design the renovation and expansion of the Museum of Modern Art in New York. This would include an adjacent 52–story condominium tower to generate income for the museum.

He took nine months setting up Cesar Pelli & Associates. His founding partner was Fred Clarke, an associate at Gruen. "Fred and I have a very similar temperament," Pelli says. "I can communicate with him in a kind of shorthand, faster than with almost anyone else." They hired 14 people. By October, Pelli was ready.

He devised an elegant design distinguished for its exterior, which uses 11 shades of white, blue and charcoal glass. But about a year and a half later, Arlen Realty, the developer, encountered financial problems, and the project was shelved. Suddenly, Pelli had to let almost everybody go. It was a discouraging, reflective time—during 1978, the only new commission he got was to renovate the U.S. Embassy in Havana.

Things began to look up in 1979, though. An Italian entrepreneur named Giorgio Borlenghi emigrated to Houston and asked Pelli to design two 40-story towers that would contain 400 condominiums and be called Four Leaf Towers. Then Borlenghi commissioned Pelli for Four Oaks Place—a 1.8-million-square-foot office complex. Pelli did designs for developers in Pittsburgh, Los Angeles and New York.

Late in 1979, the Museum of Modern Art project was revived with a new developer, Charles Shaw of Chicago. While it was great to have that going again, there were headaches aplenty. Art curators tangled with each other for more exhibition space. Many people were concerned that the condominium tower would encroach on the museum's sculpture garden. Before he got final approval, Pelli gave more than 200 presentations. He showed himself to be tactful and resilient.

In early December 1980, Pelli got a call from a man who identified himself as Ron Soskolne, vice president for development at Toronto-based Olympia & York. Would Pelli want to participate in an architectural competition for the proposed Battery Park City office complex? There wasn't much time, because plans had to be submitted within three weeks.

"The usual process is to hem and haw for a while," Soskolne explained to me. "You select an architect on the basis of qualifications, recent buildings and how comfortable you feel about working with each other. Then the architect spends a few months developing a design concept.

"Well, a competition—this was our first—might enable us to accelerate the whole process. We'd get architects working at a fever pitch, producing a range of concepts we'd never get from a single firm.

"I looked through recent architectural magazines, my eyes out for the kind of work we wanted. The size of this project and its location at the tip of Manhattan, on the Hudson River, gave us the potential to do the kind of thing which hasn't been attempted since Rockefeller Center was built during the 1930s."

Soskolne contacted a dozen major architects. Philip Johnson and his partner John Burgee were busy with Houston projects, so they declined. Kevin Roche was working on the new General Foods headquarters. Davis Brodie, a firm perhaps best known for housing, agreed to participate, as did Edward Larrabee Barnes, who designed the new IBM Building on Madison Avenue, New York; Mitchell/Giurgola; Kohn Pederson Fox; and Zimmer Gunsul Frasca.

What most fascinated Soskolne about Pelli was a design he had done for the recent Bunker Hill competition. At stake was the largest undeveloped tract in downtown Los Angeles, and it brought proposals from the top architects and developers in North America. Olympia & York participated. Cadillac Fairview won with a design by Vancouver architect Arthur Erickson. Pelli was part of an architectural team assembled by a Los Angeles developer named Robert Maguire.

All Pelli did was a single tall office building, but it was a striking idea: a granite jacket from which emerged a soaring glass-and-steel tower. It had a sleek, modern look, yet it evoked romance. It was widely published in architectural magazines. Something like that might help Battery Park City achieve distinction and spur leasing, Soskolne thought.

"Soskolne told us that to make the project pay, they needed 6 million square feet of leasable space," says Pelli. "Since, having analyzed the market, the Reichmanns believed Fortune 500 corporations were the most likely tenants, they wanted fairly large floors—most 30,000 to 40,000 square feet. They asked that some floors be as much as 60,000 square feet. They wanted the various office towers to be obviously part of a single, coherent project, yet offer a distinct identity for each lead tenant."

The site master plan, by urban planner Alex Cooper, specified more requirements that had to be fulfilled. Pelli couldn't design towers more than half the height of the nearby World Trade Center. There had to be setbacks. A certain proportion of space had to go for gardens and other public spaces, and the master plan specified they should be on several levels. The amount of retail space was specified in the master plan as well as service systems such as storm water drainage, private utilities, security and parking. These and dozens more details had to be observed.

There were more constraints. Subway tubes passed under part of the site, limiting the number of places where a building foundation could go. Further complicating things were five-foot-wide underground pipes that circulated water between the Hudson River and the World Trade Center cooling system. Also the project had to provide room for the planned Westway highway.

Since Pelli would be competing against some of the most successful architects, the odds were against him. Olympia & York offered to pay only $16,000 for his time, and the money didn't cover much overhead. "But we felt quite confident of winning," Pelli says, a little cocky, "because I knew we understood the issues better than anyone else."

It posed a monumental challenge which Pelli dreamed about. Very few architects ever had an opportunity to work on such a big project. The extraordinary location, furthermore, on the waterfront, near the tip of Manhattan—this would excite an architect's wildest fantasies.

If done right, the job would cap a career in grand style—like Cass Gilbert who designed the fabulous neogothic Woolworth Building in New York. Or William Van Alen, designer of the exuberant Art Deco Chrysler Building. Raymond Hood was remembered for his inspired shapes at Rockefeller Center. The sleek Seagram Building helped establish Mies van der Rohe's mighty reputation. Though many very tall buildings have gone up over the years, the Empire State remains among the most famous, earning lasting distinction for its designers: Richmond H. Shreve, William F. Lamb and Arthur L. Harmon have a secure place in architectural history. Cesar Pelli could enter this pantheon, too. He was 54.

The issue of designing tall buildings had preoccupied Pelli for years. He's a curious person, fascinated with philosophical questions. He ponders how office buildings came to look the way they do and how they should be designed in the future. This is a favorite subject, and he can talk about it for hours.

"The first very tall buildings appeared during the late nineteenth century," he explains, "when structural steel became available, and safe elevators were developed which enabled people to go up and down quickly. In that era, anything over 10 stories was considered a skyscraper. Being a decidedly vertical structure, it posed different issues than you encounter in most buildings which are horizontal. For ideas, designers turned to the classic proportions of the Italian Renaissance palazzo. There's a base, middle and top ending in a cornice. This was the basis for Louis Sullivan's buildings.

"The next major advance came with the slender Metropolitan Life Tower, which Napoleon LeBrun did in New York, 1910. It was a crazy idea, small offices, a stairway and a bell tower, modeled after the Campanile in St. Mark's Square, Venice. But LeBrun understood that very tall buildings have qualities which are in the nature of being tall. These qualities go beyond the function of a building.

"Though Cass Gilbert designed the Woolworth Building like a cathedral, which obviously has nothing to do with offices, he was also addressing the issue of height. Soon after that, architects began to see they could reinterpret past ideas in a new way. No more confusing a cathedral or campanile with an office building. No more toilets in the nave!

"What we think of as skyscraper style emerged during the late 1920s and early 1930s. I'm thinking of the American Radiator Building, McGraw-Hill, Empire State, RCA and especially the Chrysler Building. They expressed the exhilaration of height. They don't look like anything else—they're skyscrapers. As Louis Sullivan wrote, 'A skyscraper is a proud and soaring thing.'"

"Construction of big buildings virtually stopped with the Great Depression. It didn't resume until the 1950s. By that time, the architects who had developed the skyscraper style were all gone. The new generation wasn't much concerned about the meaning of height anymore. A break in the continuity of architectural ideas is rare, but it happened during that 20-year period from the 1930s to the 1950s.

"What emerged, of course, was the International Style, particularly as represented in the United States by Mies van der Rohe and his followers at Skidmore, Owings & Merrill. They have a strong ideology. Instead of being concerned about the public presentation of a building, its relationship to the ground and sky, Mies turned a building inward. He was concerned about its structure. The exterior should have a proper relationship to the function of a building. The result usually was a glass and steel box with a flat top. He advocated highrises rather than skyscrapers. Manhattan's World Trade Center, which Minoru Yamasaki designed, may be very tall, but I don't think it symbolizes a skyscraper for anybody.

"I concluded it's time for a new theory. First, it should incorporate the intelligence of International Style buildings. Mies established what is now standard practice of designing utility functions like elevators, plumbing, electrical cables, heating and so on to a building's core. Offices go around it. You have rectangular, subdividable, modular space, because you never know what's going to be done with it. This approach gives everybody maximum flexibility. You may be surprised to learn that other approaches were being tried as late as the 1950s—like putting elevators on the outside of a building. Mies transformed a custom into a standard, and it makes the most sense.

"Buildings have a public nature, and I believe design should be done with this in mind. A building should relate to things around it—each place has a distinctive character. A building should contribute to the vitality of a city. A building should be good for pedestrians. It should be a good citizen. We don't build for books where designs get published.

"Downtown Manhattan, especially with a project as large as Battery Park City, you should resonate with the feeling of skyscrapers from the 1930s. They are soaring things, buildings which express optimism. They celebrate their connection to the sky.

"You can combine these public qualities with function. On the one hand, you don't need to borrow past ideas as many architects are doing now. You can do a soaring top integrated with its structure rather than as an added-on flourish. It can have a simpler, clearer meaning—a place where mechanical equipment sits. Similarly, while the office grid maintains its modular character, the thickness of each element in the band may be varied, so the building looks more interesting."

Soon after agreeing to do plans for the competition, Pelli and his associates were on their hands and knees in the office. Using scissors and cardboard, they built experimental models, which helped determine the optimum number of towers. That was the first issue they faced. To get 6 million square feet in two towers would require huge buildings. On the other hand, five towers wouldn't fit very well on the site. Pelli decided that with the right design, they could minimize a bulky appearance. He opted for three buildings.

What material to use? Pelli thought about granite, the classiest exterior building material. It was solid, had a beautiful texture and offered a good choice of colors that were stable. Marble? Only white remained true. Since other kinds of marble faded under prolonged exposure to direct sunlight, it was suited only for interiors. Until recent years, any kind of stone was too expensive for exteriors, but with the automation of Italian quarries during the 1970s, it became economical. Very thin slices could be mounted on a frame and secured to the building. Philip Johnson's AT&T Building was among the first since the 1930s to break away from the glass-and-steel International Style and resume using stone. Pelli specified granite for his Battery Park City designs.

To minimize the feeling of bulk, he arrived at a design that got lighter in appearance the higher it went. As with the Bunker Hill competition, there would be a stone jacket out of which emerged a glass and steel structure. There would be four setbacks. On the lowest three floors, there would be more granite than glass. From there to the ninth floor, glass would occupy four feet of each 10-foot-wide exterior strip. Between the tenth and twenty-fifth floors, there would be six feet of glass per ten-foot strip. Above that, eight feet of glass. The very top floor of each building would be all-glass.

Each setback, incidentally, would break up wind patterns for the benefit of pedestrians below. By contrast, a straight-sided building without any setbacks—the World Trade Center, for instance—tends to catch winds from great heights and channel their fury straight down the building. Wind could reach ferocious velocities and slam people into the concrete benches.

Pelli was concerned about light and views from the office towers. He wanted to bring as much natural light as possible into the buildings, consistent with the needs of heating and cooling—this wasn't just a question of saving the developer money, because New York City regulations specify how much energy a building can use. The most basic challenge, of course, was that a square tower always had two sides primarily shaded and two sides with the most exposure to the sun.

"While you can't do much about that," Pelli explains, "you can influence how natural light strikes public places, parks and interior spaces. For instances, we designed two indoor parks where people can sit, eat and relax comfortably, even in winter. We rotated the southernmost tower and slid it back to allow more natural light into those spaces. One reason we designed setbacks on the upper floors of each tower is to allow more light into the courtyards below.

"We responded to the architectural tradition of downtown Manhattan. We gave each of the towers identifiable tops—a dome, pyramid, sliced-off pyramid and a stepped-top. The grayish-brown color of the buildings relates to the tonalities downtown. The setbacks where the proportion of granite and glass changes correspond with familiar building heights you see around lower Manhattan."

Pelli's entry in this competition was unusual, since his design went through very few changes. The basic ideas were developed early on, and they just had to be refined. Pelli's three proposed buildings were to be clustered north of Liberty Street and west of the proposed Westway. The two northern-most buildings would front on Vesey Street.

Then came the presentation models, about two feet high. The day before Christmas 1980, two of Pelli's chief designers, John Pickard and Ann-Marie Baranowski, drove through a snowstorm to deliver the plans together with the models to Olympia & York's office at 245 Park Avenue. "We were so excited about this thing," Pickard recalls, "but they weren't expecting us. The only person we saw was a secretary. We eagerly opened the box and explained why it was a great design."

Pelli was prepared for a long, anxious wait, because many developers take several months to weigh options and make a decision. Not the Reichmanns. Soskolne called the following week: Pelli was a finalist, along with Mitchell/Giurgola and Gunzel Frasca.

The Reichmanns anticipated that their most likely tenants would be financial services companies, so they believed it was crucial the project have a strong link to the financial district. This meant Liberty Street. The closest building to it couldn't be very close, because subway tubes got in the way. Pelli and the other finalists were asked to address that concern in the second-round competition. The Reichmanns funded each architect with more than $25,000.

Pelli pondered the site and the 6 million square feet of rentable space this project had to produce. Prompted by the Reichmanns, he considered adding a fourth building south of Liberty Street. Then maybe he could connect the two buildings on either side of Liberty Street with lighter structures that wouldn't require extensive foundations. Subway tubes wouldn't hinder these. Such structures might be designed as octagonal portals, a gateway from Liberty Street to Battery Park City. The more Pelli explored the implications of this idea, the better he liked it.

Then he had to reduce the size of the three original buildings, so those plus the fourth building would yield the desired number of

GRAND DESIGNS

square feet. "It was just a question of recomposing the volumes," Pelli told me. "I knew this would be more appealing financially, because four buildings mean a developer has the potential of signing four lead tenants instead of three."

A simple lean-to structure would have satisfied the city's design guidelines, but Pelli imagined better things. He pulled out his pen and planned the Wintergarden as perhaps the most magnificent gathering place in Manhattan—a great vaulted crystal palace that could accommodate 70-foot-high palm trees and offer panoramic river views. How well that upgraded the whole project was testimony to Pelli's genius.

After three weeks, Pelli submitted the second-round plans and models to Olympia & York. But because two long-dormant projects became active and required significant time from Pelli, suddenly he was overloaded. He told Soskolne, Paul and Albert Reichmann that he was submitting his revised design because he had agreed to, but even if he were selected, he couldn't handle the project. They were stunned, because they had virtually decided on Pelli. They were incredulous that anybody could walk away from such a fantastic commission.

"They insisted there must be a way to resolve the problem, and sure enough there was," Pelli recalls. "We arranged with other architects to help with design development. Jim Bagby of the Toronto firm Adams & Associates had worked with the Reichmanns before, and he provided invaluable assistance on the project. Then, too, we got ourselves mobilized faster than we anticipated. Walking away from the project would have been the stupidest thing I ever did!"

Critics raved. Ada Louise Huxtable, *New York Times:* "an apparently hopeless situation, which included near-default on Battery Park City bonds, has been turned around. If all goes according to schedule, New York will get a coordinated and architecturally first-rate urban complex of the standard, significance and size of Rockefeller Center that will add a spectacular new beauty to the New York skyline. There has been no large-scale development of comparable quality since the 1930s. This is just as important as it sounds for New York's economic and architectural health and style."

Now Pelli could get to work. Every detail—from the design of stairs, elevators and windows to the placement of pipes—required a drawing. Anything overlooked would leave somebody on the construction site guessing what to do. That would mean mistakes which had to be corrected at considerable expense.

The Reichmanns visited Pelli's offices once. "They're extraordinarily polite," he recalls. "They treat you with more respect than developers usually treat architects. They listen carefully and say little. They understand everything the first time around. They're just very smart." John Pickard adds, a little amused: "They found the place themselves in their rented Chevrolet."

As Pelli encountered problems, designs had to be modified. If certain materials weren't available when needed, substitutes had to be found. Their characteristics would differ from the original materials, and the implications had to be reflected in new drawings. "When you come out of architecture school," says Tom Morton, Pelli's project manager for Battery Park City, "you may imagine that buildings are designed by people sitting at drafting tables. Well, that's partially true. But a design isn't really finished until everything is installed.

"Take, for instance, the granite on our buildings. It's a natural material, so quality may vary. It's hard to predict. It isn't like producing sheets of glass where you can specify the color, grade and amount you want.

"We had picked a warm gray granite called polychrome from a quarry near Bagotville, Quebec. It's the top of a little mountain. After we had about a third of the granite we needed, the orange crystal which made it so warm started disappearing. The granite turned a cooler gray. No matter where the quarrymen dug, they couldn't find the crystal again.

"I flew to Montreal, chartered a plane to Olma and inspected the quarry for myself. I visited other quarries. Some could offer us better color, but the grain would be noticeably different if you had stone from different quarries on the same building. We had to make a decision fast, because many months pass from the time a block is cut until the finished panels were available.

"We met with Keith Roberts, who headed construction for Olympia & York, and Otto Blau, in charge of construction purchasing. The issue was resolved in typical Olympia & York style: fast. We flew to Italy and looked at about 30 kinds of granite. We decided to continue using granite from the original quarry, because the change in grain would be more evident than the changing tone. One of this company's great strengths is they're capable of a rational, quick decision."

Faster than anybody anticipated, the Reichmanns signed deals with major corporations to come into the project, which they renamed World Financial Center. Each wanted its own interior design, and sometimes this involved redesigning basic parts of the building systems like elevatoring, heating and plumbing. American Express wanted a cafeteria on the third floor. As a consequence, escalators had to be moved. These changes, moreover, had to be consistent with American Express's security plans for limiting access to various parts of the building. A lot of time was spent just coordinating details between Pelli and the American Express interior architect, Swanke, Hayden & Connell.

Merrill Lynch, which leased two buildings, had Skidmore, Owings & Merrill design their interiors. Merrill Lynch needed large trading rooms with double-height ceilings. Executives wanted an employee cafeteria. Moreover, since it was crucial for the firm's brokers to be at work when the financial markets opened, they needed six additional elevators to handle the heavy morning traffic. Pelli had to design these, figure out where to put mechanical systems which the new elevators displaced, then redesign the lobby, so it would handle the elevators.

Occasionally, there were jurisdictional disputes. For instance, who should design elevator cabs? They ran through the building and opened in the lobby, so they would seem to be Pelli's responsibility. On the other hand, the elevators opened into the tenant floors, and the other firms wanted a say. Pelli had the final word in three buildings, but Swanke, Hayden & Connell won in the American Express Building, since that was an outright purchase rather than a lease deal.

Pelli and his associates moved from grand conception to myriad practical details, and there was growing exhilaration. Where once a barren sandbar faced the Hudson River, visions existing only on blurred blueprints, immense steel frames now shot out of the ground. Each visit to the construction site revealed more floors up, more granite and glass in place. It was a stirring time for an architect who had labored on fine plans that never happened—dashed by a capricious developer, political pressures or tight money. Those who played a part in epic achievements like the Empire State Building or Rockefeller Center must have experienced similar feelings. Here were dreams you could touch.

IV

MONEY DEALS

8.

OTHER PEOPLE'S MONEY

THOUGH A REAL ESTATE PROJECT MAY BE IDENTIFIED WITH AN EN-trepreneur's name, it's never financed entirely out of pocket. Usually even those entrepreneurs who can afford to would rather reduce risks by relying on other people's money. Since real estate lenders are sel-dom willing to cover a project's entire cost, equity capital has to be raised. Real estate took a giant step forward with the emergence, during the late 1940s, of syndicates that enlist large numbers of peo-ple able to contribute modest sums.

So I arranged to interview the two men who pioneered real estate syndication: attorney Lawrence A. Wien and entrepreneur Harry Bracken Helmsley. Both have their offices in a stately old property they syndicated—the Lincoln Building, 60 East 42nd Street, New York, across from Grand Central Station.

Helmsley is better known, thanks largely to hotels which he devel-oped in recent years. Now at the crest of his career, he enjoys some visible pleasures like his rousing, cornball "I'm Just Wild About Harry" birthday parties.

Each March 4, Laurence Rockefeller, Walter Annenberg, Frank Sinatra, Gregory Peck, Claudette Colbert, Mike Wallace and a couple hundred other friends are invited to Manhattan's Park Lane Hotel. They celebrate Helmsley's birthday with an old-fashioned dinner dance regaled by a 16-piece orchestra, for Harry and Leona Helmsley love ballroom dancing and go whenever they can. Everyone wears a but-ton declaring "I'm Just Wild About Harry," and Helmsley's own button says simply, "I'm Harry." At midnight, "I'm Just Wild About Harry" balloons drop from the ballroom ceiling. There are party fa-vors to take home, like music boxes and T-shirts imprinted with Helmsley's baby picture. It's just the kind of sentimental shindig you might expect at a Des Moines Kiwanis Club.

For Leona Helmsley's July Fourth birthday, Harry has the Empire State Building lit up red, white and blue at night. This is his prerog-ative, since he heads a syndicate which controls and manages the famous landmark.

Harry Helmsley is a trim 6-foot-3-inch bespectacled man of 76 who's among the biggest U.S. landlords. Largely through syndicates, he controls an estimated 50,000 residential units and 50 million square feet of office space in 16 states. Most properties are in New York, including landmarks like the Graybar Building, Flatiron Building and Lincoln Building. From his office, Helmsley can see the Empire State Building. Around him are replicas of the Empire State Building, and more than 300 red-bound looseleaf books containing legal documents for the various properties where he has an interest.

Real estate observers believe his net worth qualifies him as a billionaire. "The best advice I ever got," he smiles, "was from my mother. She simply said, 'Buy real estate.' As a dutiful son, I bought and bought and continue to buy throughout the country."

Helmsley has his critics. Some tenants and competitors chide him for cost-cutting that compromises tenant comforts. He's seldom seen spending money to improve a property. Some investors, moreover, have accused him of padding expenses and self-dealing—selecting building services companies in which he has an interest. Real estate gadfly Bernard Gallagher attacked him as "Hungry Harry." Helmsley shrugs. "After a while, when you have enough irritants, no particular one bothers you."

Yet Helmsley is generally well-liked throughout the real estate business. He's a sage who, during a career which has spanned a half-century, anticipated most major turns in the New York real estate market. He was largely unscathed by the real estate crunch of 1973–75, which devastated so many other real estate entrepreneurs. Throughout his career, he has participated in industry functions and given generously to charities like the national Council to Combat Blindness and the Federation of Protestant Welfare Agencies.

Proof of Helmsley's celebrity status: An enterprising New Yorker marketed a pair of dolls dressed like Tarzan and Jane with faces that bore the unmistakable likenesses of Harry and Leona Helmsley.

To help support her family, Leona Mindy Rosenthal, third child of a Brooklyn milliner, tried showroom modeling when she was 16. She was rejected for being flat-chested, so she bought a bra and cotton balls at Woolworth's, appeared for another audition and got a job as Mindi Roberts.

While still a teenager, she married a lawyer, "because my parents thought I should." They had a son but were divorced in a few years, and in 1962 she ventured into real estate. For seven years, she sold co-op apartments for Pease & Elliman before starting the residential division of Sutton & Towne. Her commissions made her a millionaire.

In 1968, she was converting the 35 Park Avenue apartment building into a co-op when she met Helmsley's partner Leon Spear, who lived there. He told her he would buy his apartment if she agreed to meet Helmsley. She did, and he told an associate: "Whoever she is, get her." He gave her "a handsome base salary and a percentage in a building." She joined Helmsley's firm Brown, Harris, Stevens as a senior vice president in 1970.

She captivated Helmsley, and, like real estate entrepreneurs Gerald Hines and James Rouse, he divorced his wife of more than three decades. "Miss Roberts," Helmsley asked in 1971, "will you date me?"

"I don't think so," she said. "You're my boss, you're a Quaker, and I like honorable intentions."

Apparently he was convincing, for soon they spent evenings together. "Once I got onto a dance floor with him, we just fit," she said. Six months later, he proposed on his bended knee.

They were married in April 1972 in Helmsley's duplex suite on the forty-seventh floor of the Park Lane Hotel, which he had built the year before. "It's great," he says, "you have maid service, food, everything right there. Can't beat it."

They have a bedroom, two kitchens, a dining room, solarium, terraces and endless closets. They enjoy their custom-made Scalamandre rug, a sixteenth century bronze Buddha, a jade collection, Steuben glass collection and paintings by Dufy and Pissarro. Harry could stroll around the balcony and admire many of the buildings he owns.

Long a private man, Helmsley cuts a high profile with Leona. They nuzzle in public. They attend a few charity balls a week. She persuaded him to light up the tops of his most famous New York buildings. They fly to their Palm Beach apartment in his BAC-111 jet.

Leona is a familiar figure in advertisements for the 27 Helmsley Hotels she runs. "The Helmsley Palace is the only hotel where the Queen stands guard" purrs one headline. Though male executives are respected for being tough, aggressive leaders, she's criticized for the same qualities. Nobody faults her, though, for insisting on the highest standards of guest service.

Many people are put off by her publicly doting on Harry. "Look at the shape of his head," she told one interviewer, "You could see the brain just sits there. Beautiful head, darling. I love it." On another occasion, she gushed about his "gorgeous big feet."

"We've never been apart a night," he says, grinning. "Even when I went to the hospital for a hernia operation"—the result of lifting another woman on a dance floor—"by golly, if Leona didn't raise so much hell that they brought a cot into the room for her."

Part of this public affection, certainly, is because they have only each other. He has no children. Three years ago, her only son died of a heart ailment while a young man. When memories flash into her mind at unexpected moments, the pain brings tears to her eyes.

Every morning, Harry swims half a mile in their 22-foot enclosed pool, relaxes in a whirlpool, showers and catches up on news over breakfast. He heads for work by 9:30, usually with two briefcases. He's on the phone all day until he leaves the office at 5:00. From time to time, Leona surprises him by hiding in their limousine, on the floor of the back seat, waiting for him to appear.

Back at the Park Lane, he takes another swim and does some work while Leona answers letters from hotel guests. "What else would I do?" he asks. "Play golf and shoot 110? I'd rather think through various problems so I'll make another million. That's fun."

Weekends they like to spend at their secluded 26-acre, Greenwich, Connecticut estate, which Sotheby's had listed for $12 million. The Georgian style mansion has 28 rooms for the two of them. There's a dance floor atop their indoor swimming pool. Free of interruptions, they do crossword puzzles.

They're more wary than they used to be, since a robber wearing a gas mask stabbed them at their Palm Beach penthouse back in 1973. Harry's arm was gashed, and Leona, stabbed in the lung, was lucky to survive. Since then, full-time bodyguards help protect their peace.

Helmsley started his career in 1925 as a $12-a-week broker for the New York firm Dwight, Voorhis & Perry, one of several dozen firms he had approached about a job after graduating from Evander Childs High School. He pursued real estate because his grandfather had done well at it. He collected rents in rough neighborhoods like Hell's Kitchen on Manhattan's West Side. "They saw my sterling worth," he told me, "and soon they gave me a raise to $15 a week."

During the Great Depression, a broker might go for several years without making a single sale. The firm turned more to managing foreclosed properties.

He bought his first property in 1936. It was a deteriorating, money-losing 10-story office building which the previous owner was happy to unload for $1,000 down. All Helmsley had to do was take over the $100,000 mortgage. His unemployed father Henry Helmsley became building superintendent, and Helmsley hustled for new tenants. Soon the building was filled. He sold it a decade later for $165,000.

Poor eyesight kept him out of World War II, so he spent a lot of time at bankruptcy auctions, where good properties could be had cheaply. He remembers buying 5 East 57th Street, for instance, a

25-story office building with a $400,000 mortgage at 4 percent, only $16,000 down. If he brought in just one or two more tenants, the building could make money, and that's what he did.

Meanwhile, he bought more bargain buildings, cut their operating costs and brought in tenants. "The Depression wasn't a great time for real estate," he says, "but I had all kinds of tenants, and I could see their businesses weren't doing well, either. I decided to stick with what I knew."

His career took a momentous turn in June 1949 when, as a broker, he represented St. Louis University, which wanted to sell their two-story office building at 161 Columbus Avenue. The buyer was tall, erect Lawrence A. Wien, attorney for a syndicate. It wasn't a large syndicate—only a half-dozen investors—but it was a new kind of real estate deal that Wien had devised. It enabled small investors to band together and buy properties bigger than they could afford individually. After concluding the $165,000 deal, Helmsley asked if Wien might be interested in other properties.

Wien, then in his 40s, was the son of a prosperous New York silk manufacturer. The family moved to Paterson, New Jersey, where he attended high school before going to Columbia University. He earned his undergraduate and law degrees there. He specialized in residential property investments, because his father Joseph had done well with real estate.

"I thought up the syndication idea in the late 1940s," Wien said to me. "What I wanted to create was a vehicle which could achieve a yield of 12 percent while avoiding the high corporate income tax. I analyzed the tax statutes and realized that if I could create a partnership which isn't engaged in business but merely receives a fixed return on capital investment through a conduit, then the investor would have to pay only an individual income tax. Moreover, I could save half or more of the investor's return from any taxes because that part would be a return on capital."

After some legal research, he found an obscure Ohio case that covered a deal similar to what he had in mind. He discussed his ideas with two of the best tax lawyers in the United States—Roswell Magill, a senior partner in Cravath, Swain & Moore, and Randolph E. Paul of Paul, Weiss, Rifkind, Wharton & Garrison. Convinced that Wien's idea would work, they gave him legal opinions interpreting the statutes, and Wien contacted the Internal Revenue Service. After considerable argument, they accepted syndication as a legitimate financing technique.

Soon Wien was syndicating property. He enlisted about 200 investors to buy a $7 million office building at 25 Broad Street from

City Investing Company. For several years, most of Wien's syndications involved apartment buildings, often in Harlem. Though slack business meant a weak office market, people needed someplace to live, and apartment buildings did well for investors.

"When I met Harry at that Columbus Avenue closing," Wien recalls, "he struck me as one of the most astute people I ever met. He had a great power to evaluate real estate and its potential. He could dig up a great number of investment opportunities. I could see we would work together well. I'd provide the money. He'd bring the opportunities."

In each case, a partnership would buy a long-term lease on a building, then sublease it to Helmsley's management company. Investors fared better than if they had owned land, since land costs can't be depreciated against taxable income. Lease costs are. Helmsley slashed overhead and hiked rents to achieve at least a 12 percent annual yield.

The men didn't always agree on the properties they should syndicate. Helmsley was more interested in sheltering income, so he preferred properties that could be acquired for an unusually low down payment with a large mortgage. This meant more tax-deductible interest. As the money-raiser, Wien was more worried about losing money. He pushed for a bigger down payment, lower mortgage, less monthly interest cost and therefore a lower break-even point on the building. This way, there was more cushion in the event of vacancies.

Though the stock market boomed during the 1950s, there was a buoyant demand for good real estate deals, too, and Helmsley and Wien prospered. One Friday, for instance, they mailed prospectuses for their syndication of Manhattan's Plaza Hotel. These went only to people who had previously participated in their deals. By Monday, they had cash deposits for $11 million, more than was needed.

On a few occasions when a syndicate lost money, Helmsley and Wien dug into their own pockets to compensate investors. This happened, for example, when they leased the Taft Hotel to William Zeckendorf in one of his typical byzantine deals. Zeckendorf paid $4 million for the lease, then turned around and sublet it to New York real estate investor Sheldon Bar for $4.5 million and immediately reported a $500,000 profit to the stockholders of his public company, Webb & Knapp. But the hotel was a money-loser, and Bar quit the deal. Overextended, Zeckendorf couldn't absorb the losses, so he dropped the lease back on Helmsley and Wien who, when they decided they couldn't turn the situation around, let the insurance company take over the property. "Bill Zeckendorf was the greatest broker I ever met in creating a deal," Wien remembers, "but he was impractical in projecting costs. He counted on inflation to bail him out, and that didn't always happen."

Helmsley expanded into virtually every aspect of real estate. In 1938, he bought out his original broker-partners, and the firm became Dwight, Voorhis & Helmsley. Spear & Co., a respected old-line Manhattan brokerage firm was offered for sale in 1955, and Helmsley bought it, changing the name to Helmsley-Spear. In 1964, he acquired Charles F. Noyes Company, which manages buildings. To these holdings he added Owners' Maintenance Corporation, a cleaning service; Brown, Harris, Stevens, Inc., a firm managing co-op apartments; Deco Purchasing, which does purchasing for Helmsley's hotels; and Helmsley-Spear Hospitality Service Inc., which manages non-Helmsley hotels. Altogether, he has more than 500 employees, and not surprisingly, they're an important source of ideas for new Helmsley deals.

Meanwhile, in 1961 Wien and Helmsley made their biggest deal when Chicago financier Henry Crown decided that changing tax laws made it advantageous for him to sell his interest in the Empire State Building. Wien and Helmsley negotiated an $85 million price. To finance this, they took a $6 million mortgage from Crown, borrowed $3 million from New York shipping tycoon Daniel Ludwig and $20 million from Prudential Insurance Company of America, which actually bought the building.

Wien raised $33 million of equity capital from 3,300 investors who put in a minimum of $10,000 and were offered—not guaranteed—a 9 percent annual return, then considered a handsome return. Wien and Helmsley personally invested only $500,000 apiece. Their syndicate leased the Empire State Building for 114 years from Prudential. Then they subleased it to Wien and Helmsley, who would perform management services for half of any profits above 9 percent.

Upon closing this deal, Wien collected $1.1 million in legal fees, plus a $190,000-a-year retainer to represent investors and Helmsley's management company. Helmsley banked a $500,000 broker's fee as well as a $90,000-a-year management fee.

As he often did, Helmsley slashed costs. The bookkeeping staff, for instance, was cut from 28 people to 6. With a lower overhead and rent rolls climbing due to inflation, return to investors exceeded the most optimistic expectations. Two decades after the deal was put together, investors got $8 million of the $36 million gross. Share prices doubled—a little disappointing, since inflation tripled during the period. Helmsley and Wien collected $6.5 million annually, while Helmsley's companies got $5 million for cleaning, management and insurance.

Escalating real estate prices meant fewer bargains, so Helmsley built some new buildings including One Penn Plaza, 10 Hanover Square and 22 Cortland Street. He did these on his own, because this game was too risky for Wien. Helmsley, as might be expected, kept tight rein on the bottom line. "I think it's important that you have an architect who realizes you're a commercial developer," he told me. "In the final analysis, if a building doesn't make a profit the architect hasn't served you. I know many a building which is a monument to the architect but a disaster for the developer."

His best-known new property was the Palace Hotel, on Madison Avenue facing St. Patrick's Cathedral in New York. He invested $5 million of his own capital as general partner, bought five of the 23 limited partnership shares, which raised another $23 million, and financed the balance with a $50 million mortgage.

A splash of publicity brought reservations not only for Helmsley's $120-a-night palace, but also for the Palace, a Bowery flophouse that charged winos $2.85 a night. The name of the uptown extravaganza was changed to the Helmsley Palace.

Though Helmsley is developing buildings now, he remains far more conservative than his friend the late William Zeckendorf. "Whenever he got in financial trouble," Helmsley recalls, "Bill would ask me to take a ride in his limousine around Central Park, where we wouldn't be interrupted by telephones. We'd talk about properties he was putting on the market. I bought quite a few buildings that way. He was a great guy, but I could never take gambles like he did."

Not everything Harry did has turned out well. His biggest headache: rent-controlled apartments—chiefly, 2,700-unit Tudor City in Manhattan and 12,271-unit Parkchester complex in the Bronx. A lot of people thought he was foolish to buy them during the 1960s, but he figured the risks were reflected in bargain prices—the price tag on Parkchester, for instance, was $90 million. He doubted that rent control would last forever.

Two decades later, rent control is still around, suppressing the value of apartment buildings. It was virtually impossible to terminate a lease with a tenant in a rent-controlled building. Helmsley tried to build apartment towers on two lots near Tudor City, but tenants claimed the lots were parks, and nothing could go forward. "Nobody in their right mind would buy these properties," Helmsley groans. Though he sold Tudor City in early 1985, he was still stuck with Parkchester.

Wien continues syndicating properties, with or without Helmsley. He conducts his business from sedate mahogany-paneled offices of his firm Wien, Malkin & Bettex, a few floors below Helmsley. It's decorated with 18 watercolors of buildings he had syndicated.

He lives a more low-key life than Helmsley. He has remained married to the same woman, Mae Levy, for more than 50 years. They have two daughters, Enid W. Morse and Isabel W. Malkin, married to one of his partners. Wien's personal fortune is estimated at $150 million.

As an avocation, he enjoys needling corporate behemoths to benefit charities. He buys a hundred shares of stock in almost 500 corporations, then as a stockholder presses management to disclose the scope of their annual giving. In most cases, he argues that the percentage is too small and ought to be increased. He claims more than 400 corporations have done so.

Helmsley, in his 70s, has become more adventurous than ever. He uses less of other people's money and puts more of his own into projects. "It's crazy to take these risks," he cracks, "but I do it." He enjoys stirring a little controversy from time to time, as he did when he talked about building a giant new Manhattan skyscraper that would be the world's tallest—an ambition he shares with another Manhattan real estate entrepreneur, Donald Trump. Like Dallas entrepreneur Trammell Crow, Helmsley also hankers to build a movie studio. Clearly, business continues to invigorate him, and there's no telling what he might do next.

Despite the innovations of Wien and Helmsley, real estate syndication was in its infancy until the late 1960s. Then a new generation of financial wizards harnessed the marketing clout of major brokerage firms to sell syndications. The most successful syndicators were spawned in Chicago.

I went there and talked with the most successful of them all—Neil Bluhm, 49, a wry, restless deal-maker and president of JMB Realty Corporation, North America's largest syndicator, which manages an estimated $10 billion of real estate investments. JMB's net worth is estimated to be in excess of $1 billion. Bluhm owns 34 percent, while bearded Chairman Judd Malkin, an accountant who was Bluhm's classmate at Von Steuben High School and the University of Illinois, provides financial acumen and stability to the firm. He owns 34 percent. The balance of JMB stock is held by JMB's key executives.

JMB raises more than $1 billion of new equity capital a year. They have more than 250,000 limited partners. In recent years, JMB became one of the largest U.S. developers with office, hotel and retail projects across the country.

Bluhm, I learned, grew up hustling. His father, a liquor store merchant, abandoned the family when Bluhm was 13, and his mother went to work as a bookkeeper for a bar. "She was a bright, aggressive, typical Jewish mother," he told me. "Early on, I developed a burning desire to make a lot of money."

"Neil always wanted to be rich," reflects Jerry Reinsdorf, a former associate who became a competitor of Bluhm's. "He doesn't want the money so he can spend it and lead a decadent life. I think he believes that money is life's report card. I recall once when we were flying back from a Las Vegas convention, and Neil asked about my goals. I said I wanted to build a syndication company and sell it. His reply: 'I'll never sell.' "

Single-minded and tenacious, Bluhm is also a genial man noted for tripping over office rugs and spilling coffee during meetings. "If you're interested in having a hole burned in your sofa, invite Neil to dinner," says Malkin. Almost every day as he drives to work in his sunroof Mercedes, Bluhm talks with Malkin about deals over his car phone—occasionally passing his exit. Adds Lawrence Levy, a Chicago developer with whom JMB has collaborated on several projects: "Neil is part Bernard Baruch, part Inspector Clouseau," referring to the bumbling fictional gumshoe.

Neil and Barbara Bluhm enjoy the rewards of his risk-taking in a north Chicago suburb. They collect modern art by Picasso, Dubuffet, Leger, Calder, De Kooning and others. "I like art because it doesn't take a lot of time—I don't have yachts and things," he says. "With art prices being so high, I negotiate as hard as if I were buying a piece of real estate." The Bluhms give substantial sums to charity, particularly Chicago's Michael Reese Hospital and Jewish United Fund.

"I have no idea what my kids will do," he says. "I'd be delighted if one of them wanted to grow up buying companies, but I don't like situations where a rich father kicks his kids around." He and Barbara have three children: a 20-year-old daughter who has her eyes on becoming a lawyer; an 18-year-old son who loves football; and a 16-year-old daughter exploring all kinds of things.

JMB began in 1969 when Judd Malkin, a Midwest distributor of Toyota cars, realized that Toyota would acquire all their distributorships, putting him out of business. He searched for other opportunities. After deciding on real estate, he backed a friend, Robert A. Judelson with the Chicago real estate brokerage firm Baird & Warner, who opened an office as an independent broker. Judelson found a little strip shopping center in Mundelein, a Chicago suburb, and Malkin raised $100,000 to buy it.

To structure the deal, Malkin called on his friend Bluhm, who had earned a law degree at Northwestern University and become a real estate and tax attorney with the Chicago firm Mayer Brown & Platt. The deal succeeded, and soon Malkin brought Bluhm another deal, an Arizona mobile home park. Malkin grew confident of the possibilities in syndication, and he talked to Bluhm about becoming a partner.

"I had no idea there was anything like a real estate syndication industry," Bluhm reflects. "But I knew a lawyer could never be rich, especially in a big firm. I liked the intellectual aspect of putting together deals rather than being a lawyer and advising a client. After about six months of thinking about the possibilities, I decided to join Malkin and Judelson." They formed JMB Realty Corporation.

They got a boost from Jerry Reinsdorf, a friend of Bluhm's, who, as a tax lawyer, probably incorporated more Chicago doctors than anybody else. At that time forming a corporation was the only way a doctor could make pension contributions and thereby shelter income from punitive taxes. "I told Neil I heard good things about their syndications," he says, "and I'd love to have some real estate investments for my doctor-clients. Why not, I suggested, establish a real estate fund for my doctors."

This became Carlyle '71, a syndication offered in 1971 that raised $7 million. The idea was to provide equity funds for new developments, so investors would gain tax benefits during early years, have their equity leveraged with borrowings and realize long-term capital appreciation. There was an estimated annual yield of 14 percent.

As they raised syndication funds, they scouted the country for attractive properties to invest in. Bluhm recalls negotiating the first apartment deal at a Los Angeles lawyer's office. "We were hungry, so we went to Tony's, a nearby hot dog stand, about the only place open at 3 in the morning. We got so sick that they had to agree to the deal."

The most difficult trick was timing. Their limited partnership offerings closed on December 31. If funds were to go into a deal, JMB had to have them by that deadline. Property purchases had to be completed at the same time. As soon as it was known that a certain amount of money would be coming in, JMB people would race to find property with enough yield and other characteristics they were looking for.

Bluhm, Malkin and Judelson pitched stock brokerage firms to sell their syndications. While most brokers initially rejected the idea because investors were locked in for 5 to 10 years, there were always a few brokers who, noting the doldrums of the stock market, welcomed a new investment product. "Rather than have investors try to profit from short-term security trading," Bluhm argues. "Let them get the cash flow from real estate. Later we'll sell the property and distribute proceeds to the investors." Carlyle '72 raised $16 million.

It became clear that Reinsdorf's doctors represented only a small part of the market for real estate syndications. Reinsdorf realized that he was missing the big money, so he and Judelson sold their interest in JMB and launched their own company, Balcor, which became a major syndicator. They sold it to American Express in 1982.

During the 1970s, there was a wild boom of real estate investment trusts—aggressive lenders who often covered 100 percent of a developer's cost—but JMB played a conservative game. They got properties from publicly-held merchant builders who wanted to book a modest, quick profit and show immediate earnings rather than retain ownership for potential long-term gains. Furthermore, since JMB paid cash before buildings were completed—when developers were often stretched for cash—JMB negotiated more favorable deals than buyers who needed to extend payments. Before JMB would participate, builders had to guarantee not only completion of projects, but cash flow according to their own projections. "We never wanted to take the development risk," Bluhm notes.

In 1973, Merrill Lynch asked JMB to offer syndicated properties for their clients. Rather than give them a Carlyle fund, JMB and Merrill Lynch conceived a new series of syndications (JMB Income Properties Ltd.) which bought established properties. There would be no tax loss benefits, but because such properties were fully leased, they yielded immediate cash flow. Clients responded enthusiastically to brokers' inquiries, but when they got the intimidating prospectuses, which disclosed every imaginable risk, they canceled their orders. Stock buyers weren't accustomed to wading through legal documents.

Faced with the sudden prospect of failure, Bluhm and Malkin decided they'd have to educate Merrill Lynch brokers themselves. For four months, they traveled around the country, explaining how prudent long-term investing, rather than quick in-and-out trading, could yield profits in real estate. Gradually, the Merrill Lynch syndications caught on.

Though they offered tax benefits, JMB's main concern was to devise profitable investments that would make people want to invest again. "Tax deals are vulnerable two ways," Bluhm explains. "First, the more borrowed money, the higher the interest cost and less margin of error in the event vacancies cut income. Second, every year, there are new tax laws introduced. A tax deal is always vulnerable."

Inflation and recession devastated many real estate investment companies during the mid-1970s, but JMB prospered. While their cash flow dropped, they didn't experience any foreclosures, and none of their investors lost any money. JMB never stopped distributing profits. Their very survival marked Bluhm, Malkin and their associates as players to be reckoned with.

JMB became a good source of cash for developers around the

country, since their game is to do as much as possible with other people's money. In 1975, for instance, JMB was approached by urban visionary James Rouse, the pioneering shopping center developer who built the planned community of Columbia, Maryland. Having transformed Boston's decrepit, 150-year-old Quincy Market into the retailing success known as Faneuil Hall Marketplace, Rouse wanted to expand the project by renovating two adjacent market buildings. For this, he needed equity capital.

He laid out a sumptuous spread when Bluhm and his associate John Schreiber came calling. Rouse explained why he believed Faneuil Hall Marketplace would revitalize Boston and enrich investors.

Meanwhile, Judd Malkin inspected the two market buildings. He climbed ladders and peered into dusty corners. He was discouraged by the mess. The numbers weren't strong either: only about 22,000 of the 164,000 square feet in those buildings were preleased to conventional retail tenants. Financiers weren't comfortable with Rouse's eclectic mix.

Malkin was against the deal. But his partners were swayed by Rouse's vision, and they bought Faneuil Hall Marketplace for Carlyle '75. JMB purchased their interest for a $2.5 million cash investment and arranged $16.6 million of long-term financing. After the project became a robust success, Bluhm says, "We kidded Judd that his gut reaction about prospective properties wasn't very valuable."

Rouse offered JMB his next festive market, Harborplace, in Baltimore, but they couldn't see sleepy Baltimore emerging as a major tourist attraction. They passed, and Harborplace became an even bigger success than Faneuil Hall Marketplace. When Rouse announced that his company would develop South Street Seaport in New York, JMB cheerfully bought a 50 percent interest in it for approximately $10 million.

JMB boomed during the late 1970s as the company tailored syndications for growing numbers of middle income people who believed real estate was a sound investment. These syndications, many purchased for Individual Retirement Accounts, emphasized cash flow rather than tax benefits.

JMB's superior performance meant not only greater popularity among individual investors, but also a new appeal for institutional money managers who needed to diversify their holdings—almost exclusively stocks and bonds, which were dismal performers during the 1970s. Since 1981, spearheaded by lean, lively John Lillard, JMB has built a $1 billion business syndicating real estate for major pension funds.

As JMB raised more and more investment capital, they looked for

ever-bigger properties. This meant turning away from garden apartments, the staple for most syndicators, and going after commercial
buildings as well as major shopping centers, long the domain of insurance companies. Breaking into this market, JMB faced giant rivals
like Prudential, Equitable and Metropolitan.

Real estate executives at the insurance companies grumbled that
many syndicators, especially those who emphasized tax shelter deals,
were pushing property prices out of sight. "A real-estate syndicator
recently paid $58 million for a downtown office building in a major
Western city," reported *Investment Trendwatch,* published by Equitable. "The building's asking price had been $50 million. In another
transaction, a syndicator is investing hundreds of millions of dollars
in a mixed-use development that institutional bidders figure to be
worth almost one-third less than what is being paid.

Bluhm's reply: "I hope they're not referring to us, because Equitable's agents sell our syndications." Indeed, though syndicators like
JMB competed against the insurance companies for hot properties,
they do business together. Syndicators offer their products to insurance companies, buy their buildings and borrow long-term funds from
insurance company mortgage departments.

Noting the huge sums being made by syndicators, major insurance
companies began entering the market. In 1983, Prudential offered
its Prudential Acquisition Fund I, which pointedly excluded apartments and targeted commercial buildings.

JMB, meanwhile, continued to thrive. Bluhm talked with Albert
and Paul Reichmann of Olympia & York, shrewd financial men who
tapped more different money sources than any other developer. Syndicators elbowed each other to cut a deal with the Reichmanns. In
1983, they sold a Manhattan building—850 Third Avenue—to Peter
Morris, chairman of VMS Realty, a Chicago-based syndicator which
rivaled JMB. Tag: $101 million, more than four times what it had
cost the Reichmanns just six years before. During this period, its
annual cash flow had surged from $1.5 million to $8 million, providing a hint of just how lucrative a good building can be.

Like everybody else, Bluhm negotiated with the cagey Reichmanns in their offices, both in Toronto and New York. They were
tough, tenacious, thorough, exhausting. In May 1984, JMB raised
$124.3 million and acquired a 48.25 percent interest from the
Reichmanns in 245 Park Avenue, a 46-story, 1.6-million-square-foot
midtown Manhattan property known as the American Brands Building. It was the kind of prime property any syndicator, insurance
company or other financial institution would hunger to have in its
portfolio. This syndication was marketed as a private placement
through Merrill Lynch and Kidder Peabody.

Though it was difficult to negotiate an initial deal with the Reichmanns, things proceeded faster when they had confidence in somebody. Apparently, they liked Bluhm, for soon much more cash changed hands. JMB raised $168 million for a 46.5 percent interest in three New York buildings controlled by the Reichmanns: 237 Park Avenue, 1290 Avenue of the Americas and 2 Broadway. These properties are subject to a little over $1 billion of long-term financing.

JMB was generating a huge cash flow. What to do? "We wanted to invest in something," Bluhm muses, "but we didn't want to be in a conflict of interest with our publicly-syndicated funds. So we decided to begin developing ourselves."

Still conservative players, they entered into joint ventures with experienced developers. Metropolitan Structures, for instance, a Chicago giant headed by a professorial, pipe-smoking entrepreneur named Bernard Weissbourd. His office, decorated with reproductions of drawings by the German Renaissance artist Hans Holbein, looked more like a scholar's study than the office of a real estate tycoon. He had been attorney for Chicago developer Herbert Greenwald who was killed in a 1958 plane crash. Greenwald's partners asked Weissbourd to help finish his various projects, and suddenly he was in the real estate business.

During the early 1960s, Weissbourd envisioned gold in the eyesore Illinois Central Railroad tracks east of downtown Chicago, then bought a $50,000 option for air rights. They would give him the right to build office towers over the tracks and transform a wasteland into valuable real estate—much as had happened in Manhattan when ugly New York Central tracks were covered to make way for posh Park Avenue. It was a tedious negotiation, delayed a decade by lawsuits and political wrangling.

The result, though, was 83-acre, $2 billion Illinois Center, the city's most ambitious mixed-use project. Weissbourd cut a deal with the Pritzker family, which controlled Hyatt. With 2,033 rooms, the Chicago Hyatt Regency became the largest hotel in the Pritzkers' galaxy, and it pushed aside the aging Conrad Hilton Hotel as the city's dominant convention facility. Illinois Center includes residential towers housing more than 4,000 people and office towers for some 50,000 people. The first office tower was designed by modern master Mies van der Rohe. There are more than a hundred retail stores throughout the underground concourse that connect these buildings. JMB raised syndication capital for three of the Illinois Center office buildings.

More joint ventures followed. In 1982, JMB acquired participating interest in Federated Realty, a subsidiary of Federated Department Stores, which owns New York's Bloomingdale's, Filene's in

Boston, Rich's in Atlanta, Sanger-Harris in Dallas, Bullock's in Los Angeles and other retail properties. JMB had previously acquired shopping centers from Federated for their JMB Income Property Funds. With their collaboration, JMB develops shopping centers approved for a Federated store. It's a sweet deal for JMB, because the toughest part of any shopping center is obtaining a department store anchor. JMB concentrates its energies on fast-growing regions— Florida, Georgia, Texas and California. The firm manages a respectable 8 million square feet of malls.

Then in 1984, JMB began negotiating for Copley Place, a $500 million complex including posh stores, four office buildings, a Westin luxury hotel and Marriott convention facility in Boston's Back Bay. This was developed by Urban Investment & Development Corporation, the real estate subsidiary of ailing Aetna Life and Casualty. Urban was loaded with $1.2 billion of debt and in 1983 earned only $30.6 million on revenues of $773 million.

Carlyle XIII invested $80 million in cash for a half-interest, and it was a controversial deal. It was ill-advised from Urban's standpoint, according to Thomas Klutznik, who was one of its co-founders and its chief executive during the 1970s. "It doesn't make sense to take all the risks, sweat through seven years of development, then sell a year before the project opens," he told me.

But overbudget costs as well as depreciation depressed Aetna's accounting earnings. JMB, as a privately-held company, wasn't interested in accounting earnings. Bluhm and his partners were concerned about cash flow. Aetna guaranteed completion of the project, and so JMB got what most observers considered a tremendous property at an attractive price.

Aetna's troubles continued. During the first nine months of 1984, Urban posted an $8.3 million loss on revenues of $192 million. Cost-overruns were blamed.

Again JMB stepped up with the cash. At stake this time: Urban's remaining $1.4 billion real estate empire. Included were a crescent of huge shopping centers in Skokie, Oakbrook, Libertyville, Orland Park, Bloomingdale, Aurora and Calumet City, which dominated the suburban Chicago retail market. Urban had built Water Tower Place, an office-hotel-retail money-maker on North Michigan Avenue, the city's most lucrative retailing street. There were offices and hotels in Chicago, Philadelphia, Denver and Seattle.

Urban was the most daunting deal JMB had ever tackled, because each property had to be appraised individually. Moreover, it wasn't clear how the 1,500 Urban employees would be melded into JMB's lean, entrepreneurial organization.

Bluhm traveled around the country handling many of the negotiations himself. He flew to Vail, Colorado for one meeting which lasted just an hour. He negotiated in Chicago, New York and Hartford, Connecticut, where Aetna had its headquarters. When he was done, Aetna had booked a $100 million capital gain, and Bluhm had added 17 million square feet of space to his company's portfolio.

JMB emerged as a giant that could syndicate property, engage in joint ventures and develop for its own account. Observes Chicago developer Lawrence Levy: "JMB is a money machine that couldn't be turned off if they wanted to. Through the syndications they pioneered, Neil Bluhm and Judd Malkin opened real estate investment to the public, and they became like the New York Stock Exchange for real estate."

9.

CASH CRISIS

IF REAL ESTATE ENTREPRENEURS OFTEN HAVE VERY LITTLE OF THEIR own money in a deal, they still may face staggering risks. During bad times, partners are liable for their share of losses. They must come across with cash or be squeezed out as other partners contribute their share.

The worst nightmares are during recessions when losses may engulf many projects at once. This happened in 1970 and 1974–75. Although the economy is doing well now, there's a glut of office space, with average vacancies around 15 percent. Worst-hit are energy capitals like Houston, Denver and Oklahoma City—vacancies between 20 percent and 30 percent. Many real estate entrepreneurs have no other choice but to walk away from their empty buildings, which cost millions.

Perhaps the biggest, most dramatic brush with bankruptcy I know involved Trammell Crow. When recession hit him in 1974, at age 60, he was personally liable for $151 million of loans. He had contingent liabilities for another $433 million. On paper, he was bankrupt.

For quite a while Crow ignored the warning signs. Now and then, a partner would call asking for money—an advance to handle a temporary shortfall or money for a cost-overrun. The calls kept coming, though. When somebody in Crow's office voiced concern to him, he brushed them off. He wasn't angered by bad news. He just didn't seem to think that the person bearing it was very smart.

Crow had endured bad news before. Around 1960 there were rumors that the ambitious Dallas merchandise marts he was building—largest in the United States—had drained all his cash. Crow was a partner in Lincoln Property, an aggressive developer of apartment buildings which he had launched with an aggressive, 30-year-old Dallas broker named Mack Pogue in 1965. Lincoln Property faced $25 million of cost overruns in 1969, and many people doubted that Crow could survive. He did, of course, and naturally he'd survive whatever this new thing was about.

The Texan was a consummate deal-maker. He'd analyze growth patterns in local markets, size up real estate opportunities, facilitate financing and take a percentage. He never put much money in a deal. He wasn't concerned about the downside potential of all those percentages, because the value of his holdings almost always went up. Crow was just beginning to gain national recognition for his wizardry—in November 1973, *Fortune* had published a glowing profile of him titled "Trammell Crow Succeeds Because You Want Him To."

While some of Crow's deals were making money, altogether they had a $25 million a year negative cash flow. That was how much Crow needed to stay afloat. He didn't have it, because his cash was always plowed back into new deals, tied up in properties.

Crow wasn't alarmed, since he had experienced cash flow crises before, and they had taken care of themselves. "In real estate," he used to say, "it's hard to make a mistake, because you've got the stork on your side." He concentrated on generating new business, and that's what he would continue doing in this situation. Crow's deteriorating financial situation alarmed L. McDonald Williams, then 34, a trim, personable lawyer who had handled much of Crow's legal business before coming to work for Crow full-time. Williams, more perhaps than most partners, had Crow's ear.

Five years before, Williams was in an elevator when Crow remarked, "Oh, by the way, can you go to Hong Kong with me next week." Williams had never been out of the country. Crow was working on a complex Hong Kong deal with Sheraton and a Chinese company. They spent a couple weeks negotiating it. Several months later, the Chinese company reneged. Crow gave Williams general power of attorney, asking him to return and straighten things out. He was there three weeks.

"That Trammell would give a young lawyer power of attorney to handle his affairs 10,000 miles away shows you the extent to which he'd trust people," Williams told me. "I love law practice. Two other guys and I started our own firm with no business to speak of. We had over 35 lawyers when I left to join Trammell. I made the move because it was a uniquely appealing partnership."

Williams was the one who convinced Crow his cash flow problem wasn't going to take care of itself. It had to be faced. First task: understanding Crow's overall position. Nowhere was that summarized. Certainly his bookkeepers didn't know. They were confused and discouraged. Williams together with Ken Leventhal, a hefty Los Angeles accountant, began unscrambling all the partnerships. It wasn't easy, because there were an astonishing 604. Interlocking relationships numbered in the hundreds.

The key problem was some 30,000 acres of raw land. Crow believed in having a sizable inventory, so you could start building as soon as you were ready. He was also a radiant source of ideas, many of which weren't very good—par for the course with anybody. But some partners responded uncritically to his every word. Williams recalls: "If Trammell remarked, 'Buy all the land you can in northwest Austin,' a partner did that. Yet obviously that's not what Trammell meant. Somebody who had knowledge of a local market was expected to exercise their judgment. Well, they didn't. The situation was repeated often."

During the 1974 recession, interest rates skyrocketed, and Crow's raw land was a disaster. It was mostly financed by short-term borrowings, so the carrying charges became enormous. Meanwhile, there was no income from it. The land was a pure cash drain. The only way to generate income was to invest more money and build something, but that was unthinkable amidst a recession. "I thought we had a five-year supply," Crow conceded, "but with things going the way they were, it was more like a 10-year supply."

The most troubled partnership involved Willard Baker, an apartment developer. He had 6,400 acres of raw land with $60 million of carrying costs. Crow pumped $25 million into the deal before he was through.

This was just for openers, though. Crow had 5,475 garden apartments in Texas that lost money for two years. He had 350 condominiums that remained unsold in Atlanta.

Then there were international properties. Crow had partnerships in Switzerland, France, Belgium, Italy, Spain, Brazil and the South Pacific. Many were blowouts, conceived with little understanding of the local markets. A red-ink project in Belgium was located between two submarkets, the Flemish and Walloons, missing both. Crow agreed to a deal that put a $100 million office complex in the communist section of Paris, among the worst possible locations. It never rented.

Despite these crises, bankruptcy was something Crow never seriously considered, because it would have meant more humiliation than he could bear. He started in poverty, and he vowed never to know its bitter taste again. He had made a $100 million fortune; he dreamed of far bigger things in warehouses, office buildings, hotels and more. He mingled with the likes of President Gerald Ford and Secretary of State Henry Kissinger. Bankruptcy would mean joining the ranks of the failed, the has-beens, the crumpled wrecks of humanity who spend their declining days in hopelessness. Not Trammell Crow!

Obviously, many properties must be sold. That would take time. Meanwhile, Crow had to meet with his lenders and seek immediate relief. A meeting which brought them all together would have been the standard approach, so every banker and insurance company real estate officer would know what deals the others were getting. But this was impossible here. Crow had relationships with too many lenders. Leventhal joked that the meeting could only take place in a football stadium.

So Williams, Leventhal and Crow went on the road, explaining their position to small groups of lenders. Their position: They intended to pay every penny, but they couldn't sustain the carrying costs now. There would have to be a reduction or even moratorium of payments for a while. They'd begin the slow process of selling assets.

Some banks like First National Bank of Dallas accepted right away. So did Dallas mortgage banker Lomas and Nettleton. Partially, this was because they had long-standing relationships with Crow, and they trusted him. They also couldn't afford to see him fail. In 1975, Crow accounted for 13 percent of Lomas and Nettleton's mortgage portfolio. If he went belly up, they might, too.

Many lenders, of course, balked. To dramatize the case, Williams, Leventhal and Crow brought a big chart depicting all the partnerships and lender relationships. It was an awesome thing, frightening in its implications. The obvious meaning was that if Crow were allowed to fail, many institutions would be dragged down. One observer who soured on Crow recalls: "Crow's attitude was that he was too big to fail, and he was right. Nobody could afford it."

The lenders could see that forcing Crow into bankruptcy would tie up the properties for a decade or more. However, if lenders came to terms with him, there was a better than outside chance that he could resume scheduled payments in a couple years. A consortium of lenders advanced Crow $46 million of working capital loans.

Williams began monthly meetings with the 20 largest partners. The first was January 31, 1975, in the top floor of 2001 Bryan Tower, a slow-to-lease office building of bronze-tinted glass which Crow built in downtown Dallas. It was Crow's headquarters. In the windowless conference room, Crow stood up and explained his predicament. He needed their help. He passed around a sheet of paper which listed the partners' names and the amount of money each was expected to raise by selling assets. Crow would receive his percentage in cash. He would give a note for 75 percent of the balance—so they wouldn't be out the capital gains taxes on older properties. That there would be capital gains taxes due was a tribute to Crow's achievements.

All partners but one agreed to the deal. Many, like Williams, had only modest experience when Crow decided he trusted them and would take them into his circle. Most of Crow's partners became wealthy. If he failed, then he wouldn't be around to guarantee their loans anymore. They had to back him as best they could. They contributed half their combined net worth, raising almost $70 million.

The dissenter was Gillis Thomas, Crow's first partner. He had worked with Crow for 24 years. He ran the warehouses that were a big money-maker, and he believed it wasn't right for him to suffer the mistakes of others. Crow believed he had helped Thomas become wealthy, and he was shaken by Thomas's decision to stand apart. It shattered their friendship. Their partnership was dissolved.

During the turnaround, partnerships were terminated with those responsible for the worst misjudgments. Willard Baker was among those to go. Partners who carped about their misfortunes with Crow—out.

Mack Pogue had become rich with Crow's help, building an apartment empire worth over $600 million. Crow approached Pogue for help, but he had his own cash flow crunch to worry about, and he declined. Their partnership was dissolved, too.

It hurt when Crow had to sell part-interest in projects, because that meant surrendering future profits, which he was sure would come. Metropolitan bought a $7 million interest in his 2001 Bryan building. Equitable bought an interest in his warehouses for $35 million. Kuwaiti investors agreed to pay the $2 million of cost overruns in his Atlanta office-retail-hotel complex.

Altogether, Crow sold about $100 million of assets, and almost every one seemed to tear at his flesh. Crow wanted to amass tangible assets. He wasn't a trader whose primary goal was money in the bank, a rather abstract satisfaction. Nor was Crow's reward high living. He and his wife Margaret enjoyed a comfortable home in Highland Park, but his lifestyle didn't change much as he grew wealthy. He loved his projects. He took pride in seeing solid buildings rise from the ground. He saw jobs he helped create, communities that were prospering in part because of his efforts.

Crow hated to sell Allen Center which was to have become an office-retail-hotel complex in Houston. Metropolitan Life was his joint venture partner. But his first building went up during the early 1970s along with the Houston Hyatt Regency and the new Enterex Building being developed by Kenneth Schnitzer, the second biggest Houston developer after Gerald Hines. Those two buildings stood between Allen Center and the network of underground tunnels that enabled people to move among buildings without going out in the wilting heat and humidity. Since Schnitzer and Crow were competing for the same tenants, Schnitzer certainly wasn't going to approve a tunnel through his property to Crow's building that would make it more desirable. Consequently, it never got more than 60 percent leased, and it was a big loser for Crow. Rival Schnitzer eventually bought it.

With John Portman, Crow had developed two North Dallas buildings called Park Central. These were sold to Equitable Life Assurance Society for $21 million.

Crow and Portman were also partners in the $300 million Embarcadero Center, the San Francisco complex of office buildings with a Hyatt Regency hotel. They got the Security Pacific Building up, but as the market soured, prospective tenants demanded more in office finishes than was budgeted—a common occurrence during a buyer's market. Moreover, the Embarcadero Hyatt opened during this recession, and its miserable occupancies resulted in $7 million of losses over two years.

This was a sobering time when partners had to ante up more cash. Prudential covered their 50 percent. David Rockefeller contributed his percentage. Portman didn't have the money for his share of losses, but he couldn't be squeezed out, because he was the project master planner as well as architect. He was needed to complete the project. Crow, however, was squeezed out of his 8.3 percent, and he never forgot that. He had assembled the deal in the first place, gaining approval from the San Francisco Redevelopment Agency with Portman's designs. David Rockefeller bought Crow's interest for just $1 million.

To help preserve his peace of mind amidst these crises, Crow started having breakfast every other Monday morning with a group of nine friends, and they'd talk about nonbusiness things. Edward Cox, an oilman on the board of Southern Methodist University, attended these breakfasts. So did James Goodson, president of Southland Life. Oilman and real estate developer Herbert Hunt was there, along with Dallas contractor Henry Beck, attorney Charles Story, attorney Irium Worsham, investment banker James McCormick, utilities executive Louis Austin and commercial real estate broker Henry Miller. At each breakfast somebody would give a talk about a topic which interested them—the autobiography of J. Paul Getty, the art dealer Joseph Duveen, the situation in Iran or China. Crow wasn't a particularly religious person, but he closed each breakfast with a simple prayer.

He continued his brilliant, sometimes eccentric and mysterious ways. He appeared radiant at one breakfast. "Gentlemen," he said, "I've got it. The idea came to me last night. I've thought of a name for the big new hotel I'm planning here. The Anatole. Isn't it great?" Everybody sat there wondering what to say. He got the idea from some book.

Henry Miller told me that early one morning about 4 A.M. Crow called to talk about the name of his brokerage firm—Henry S. Miller & Company. It was getting to be a major national operation, and Crow thought it would sound more professional if the middle initial were dropped. The middle initial, he believed, made it seem like a small-town deal. Miller appreciated Crow's suggestion and retained the middle initial.

Crow emerged from his crisis considerably sobered. He was much more careful about selecting his partners. There was more central control, directed chiefly by Don Williams and Joel Peterson. They evolved a structure of 15 general and 41 limited partners in 38 cities. No partner, including Crow, was allowed to take more than a quarter of any deal. To help guide partners, Williams established balance sheet standards for liquidity and debt. He required minimum cash reserves to cover contingencies like rising interest rates. He set aside over $100 million of reserves. The performance of each partner was reviewed formally each year.

Crow's financial strategies are more conservative than they used to be. Only about 20 percent of construction costs are financed by loans, and construction loans are written to limit the liabilities of partners. About 60 percent of costs are financed by joint-venture deals. "Since Don took over," Crow says, "we have money in the bank."

Yet Crow extends as free a rein as ever to those he trusts. "Before I graduated from Harvard Business School a decade ago," chief financial officer Joel Peterson told me, "I wrote him a letter. I was looking for a job. He got back to me right away, saying he had a board meeting in Boston and he'd like to meet me. I visited him at the Ritz-Carlton Hotel. He was in his underwear, dressing while we talked. I'm sure he asked me about my objectives and other obvious things. Trammell was a charming person I took an immediate liking to. He invited me to Dallas.

"Somebody in the office insisted on giving me some fancy personality tests to see if I would fit the company. Trammell walked in.

"'Don't pay any attention to that baloney,' he said. 'They make me do that stuff. You got a job.'" Peterson played an important role helping Crow to regain his financial strength.

Perhaps the biggest change came when Crow, awed at the momentous turnaround Williams had led, stepped aside in 1977. Williams and the key partners, he believed, had earned the right to run the business according to their own lights.

It was as if the Godfather were gone. This was the Trammell Crow

Company. He was the dynamic dealmaker, father confessor, the chief whose desk was out there on the floor with everybody else. Key financial relationships were cultivated by Trammell Crow. He helped land big tenants, and he was always there to offer his advice. He would retain a 17.5 percent interest in the Trammell Crow Company whose assets were estimated at $4.5 billion. He'd still have his desk. He might spend some time there every week, but he directed most of his energies toward his family's business ventures.

As boyishly enthusiastic as ever, Trammell Crow poured his energies into building a new empire. He amassed $117 million worth of single-family houses, $704 million of apartments and condominiums. He plunged into movie production, developing a 140-acre studio complex in the northwest corner of Dallas. He built 7,000 hotel rooms. Cornerstone of his empire was the Dallas Market Center with 9.2 million square feet on 150 acres. He entered a joint venture to build the new Merchandise Mart near John Portman's giant Marriott Marquis Hotel on New York's Times Square.

"Don't sell your properties!" he growls, as confident as ever in the value of real estate. "Tough it out. You might build a hotel which loses money the first several years, but you should believe in it and hold on. Keep it, suffer the losses, stick with it, make it work!

"I'm a very lucky person. I was lucky to be born in Dallas. I was lucky to have married Margaret, an outstanding person. I was lucky to have my children. I was lucky to go through the Great Depression and come out of it. I was lucky to start my career as an accountant at the Mercantile Building. I was lucky to have met John Stemmons and become his real estate partner in the merchandise marts. Nothing can hurt me. I'm tempered. I've been through it. It seems that no matter where I go or what I do, what I'm involved in, something comes out of it. That's luck."

10.

HIGH FINANCE

REAL ESTATE IS A CONSUMMATE MONEY GAME. THIS IS BECAUSE real estate entrepreneurs rely so heavily on borrowed money; consequently, interest is among their highest operating costs. A fraction of a point on a big financing isn't chopped liver.

Unquestionably the greatest real estate financiers today are Albert and Paul Reichmann. Nobody else shops the world money markets as aggressively in search of the cheapest money. The Reichmanns borrow from conventional sources like banks and insurance companies only when they're competitive. They sell equity interest in buildings through syndicators such as JMB. They issue commercial paper through Merrill Lynch, Eurobonds through Morgan Stanley International and first commercial mortgage notes through Salomon Brothers. Kenneth Hubbard, a partner of Houston developer Gerald Hines—a detail maven—was astonished to discover that the Reichmanns would endure the trouble of a security registration just to save a quarter point interest. "A quarter point may not be important to everybody," Paul Reichmann says, "but it makes a big difference to us."

They're at once cautious and daring. They hedge their risks by being exceedingly thorough. Every move is deliberate. They're intellectually curious men who relish the pleasure of turning an idea over and around in their minds until they're convinced they have the best of it.

They exhaust those they negotiate with. Though a contract might run hundreds of pages, each issue seems to have equal priority for them. They won't be rushed. Nor do they hesitate to reconsider ideas other people think are settled. It's exasperating.

If the Reichmanns believe a proposed project is sound, they'll boldly go ahead and build it without any long-term commitment from lenders—as they did with their $1.5 billion World Financial Center in Manhattan. Very few real estate entrepreneurs are so daring. Often a building will be most of the way up with a major tenant or two signed on before the Reichmanns arrange long-term financing. By that time, the risks are less than a project starting from scratch, and they'll benefit from interest as much as three points below the prime rate—saving millions compared to most developers who pay perhaps a couple points above prime.

The Reichmanns see themselves as long-term players rather than quick in-and-out stock operators, but they can be as fast as anybody. Anticipating a real estate boom during the late 1970s, the Reichmanns eyed Trizec, a company originally created by the flamboyant tycoon William Zeckendorf. Trizec's holdings included 14.7 million square feet of office space and 72.7 million square feet of retail space. Trizec owned 100 percent of Ernest Hahn Co. and 20 percent of The Rouse Company—both premier retail developers. Liquor heirs Edward and Peter Brontman controlled Trizec with a 50.01 percent holding. The Reichmanns paid $156 million for English Property Corp. Ltd., Britain's third largest real estate investment company, which owned the other 49.99 percent of Trizec. If they didn't gain control, the Reichmanns had a nifty piece of a well-run company.

After their 1977 purchase of eight Manhattan office buildings had appreciated from $320 million to $2 billion, the Reichmanns invested part of their gains in the lower Manhattan sandbar that became the $1.5 billion World Financial Center, one of the most lucrative deals in the history of New York.

As they looked for ways to diversify some of their holdings out of real estate, they reviewed asset-based businesses, which have much in common with real estate. "We understood those," Paul explained to me, "whereas something like consumer products would be strange to us."

They became intrigued with Abitibi-Price, the world's largest newsprint producer. That market was weak in 1981, and the company was headed for a convulsive strike. Undeterred, the Reichmanns battled the wealthy Pathys shipping family of Montreal and the Thompson newspaper interests of Toronto. Five weeks of bids and counterbids resulted in the Reichmanns taking over Abitibi-Price. They paid $536 million for 88 percent of the shares. Later, they boosted their stake to 93 percent. They poured more than $150 million into improvements. The newsprint market recovered, and the value of the Reichmanns' Abitibi-Price stock almost doubled to more than $900 million.

To be sure, some of their moves seemed ill-timed. They diversified into oil, gas and mining when prices were near their peak. Their holdings included 7 percent of Bow Valley Industries Ltd., 11 percent of Hiram Walker Resources, 20 percent of MacMillan Bloedel

Ltd., 52 percent of Brinco Ltd. Some of these were slow to recover, and a couple remain duds. Hiram Walker fell from $35 a share in 1981 to $24 three years later. During the same period, Brinco plunged from $12 to $2.20.

In early June 1984, there was a flurry of speculation involving the stock of Cadillac Fairview, largest publicly-held North American real estate company controlled by liquor barons Charles and Edgar Bronfman. The company's shares were depressed because of its widely publicized troubles, which included an embarrassing cancellation of a New York land deal with Citibank and the subsequent loss of a $21 million deposit. Since then, Cadillac Fairview had cut overhead, pruned marginal operations and focused their resources on what they do best—office buildings.

Since the market hadn't yet recognized that a turnaround was in the making, the Bronfmans tried to buy back up to 15 million of their shares. When their $13.50 a share bid was topped at the last minute by unknown buyers who offered $13.75, the unknowns grabbed 16.2 million shares or 22 percent of Cadillac Fairview. The interlopers' outlay was $222.7 million. There weren't many people with that kind of spare change, and by June 6 the Reichmanns were identified as the new minority stockholders of Cadillac Fairview. Charles and Edgar Bronfmans' bitter rivals, their cousins Edward and Peter, must have had a good laugh.

While the Texas takeover king T. Boone Pickens was dueling for control of Gulf Oil, the Reichmanns faced off against Edward and Peter Bronfman again, all of whom coveted Gulf Canada Ltd. Many energy analysts believed it was the richest prize of the Canadian oil patch, because of its Hibernia field in eastern Canada and its discoveries in the Arctic. In March 1984, the Reichmanns bid $15 a share for the 60.23 percent of Gulf Canada controlled by Gulf Oil. Soon they upped it to $17.50. But at $2 below the current price, Gulf rebuffed the bid.

Meanwhile, to avoid Pickens, high-living Gulf executives agreed to be taken over by the more spartan crew at Chevron—it was a staggering $13.3 billion transaction. Gulf executives may have lost control, but the Reichmanns were still around. By May 23, 1985, they had proposed a deal with Chevron that would give them 112 million shares or 49.24 percent of Gulf Canada for $22.21 a share—$2.49 billion altogether. They negotiated an option to buy Chevron's remaining 11 percent holding for $526 million.

Apparently, they had wanted to sell Gulf's refining and marketing properties as soon as they bought, thus reducing their cash outlay. The most likely prospective buyer was Petro-Canada, but the deal was never closed. Observers believed that Prime Minister Brian Mulroney objected. On July 17, the Reichmanns announced they weren't going ahead with the Gulf takeover. They forfeited a $25 million deposit. Thornton Savage, a Chevron vice president, commented: "There isn't a chance of reviving the deal, because they withdrew, and I don't see any reason to revive it."

Yet just two weeks later, the deal was done. The Reichmanns would pay Chevron $2.31 billion for a 49.9 percent interest in Gulf Canada. They got options for another 10.3 percent. At the same time, Gulf Canada would pay $1.25 billion for 84 percent of Abitibi-Price Inc., 93 percent controlled by the Reichmanns. Furthermore, Gulf Canada would sell its refining and marketing properties through a partnership to cut Gulf Canada's tax bite from $80.5 million to $2.8 billion. Thus, they would control Gulf and, through it, Abitibi-Price. The Reichmanns flew to Switzerland for a much-needed vacation.

How do they find asset plays like this? They ponder the financial pages in the daily newspaper, especially commodities prices and capital market rates. They believe they anticipate economic cycles better than the money supply gyrations that many people follow. They have an exceptional ability—crucial for success as a financier—to recognize basic trends, unclouded by fear or greed. This may seem easy, but it's a rare talent.

The Reichmanns' thought processes were revealed dramatically as they prepared to raise a half-billion dollars during 1982. It was to help pay for buildings underway in a half-dozen cities, plus World Financial Center whose ground-breaking would be on October 6, 1982.

Borrowing a half-billion wasn't an attractive option, because fear of inflation kept interest rates high. Investors wanted equity in real estate, among the most popular inflation hedges. Accordingly, the Reichmanns explored some sort of equity financing that would involve the eight New York buildings bought from National Kinney and one from Penn Central. Neither Paul nor Albert Reichmann like giving up equity, but it was the least expensive way to go.

Then mid-August 1982, unexpected downticks in inflation brought interest down from between 16 and 17 percent to between 14 and 15 percent. This triggered a powerful rally in the bond market. The Reichmanns could raise a half-billion by borrowing money, and they could retain complete ownership in their buildings. The equity idea was dropped.

The Reichmanns considered a participating mortgage, a deal favored by many insurance company lenders. Usually this involves a low fixed-rate of interest plus a share of cash flow, commonly 50 percent. Upon sale of the building, the lender would get an agreed-on cut of the appreciation. "But many insurance executives impose so many restrictions on you that participating mortgages just aren't worthwhile," Paul says.

Even the biggest insurance companies, in any event, weren't big enough to provide all the money the Reichmanns needed. They were talking with giant Aetna about a $220-million, 20-year loan secured by their building at 245 Park Avenue, New York. It would be the largest single transaction Aetna ever handled, yet it was a fraction of what the Reichmanns were looking for. The way buildings were traditionally financed, Olympia & York was bigger than the market.

The Reichmanns had another concern. If they were to negotiate with the few insurance companies capable of loaning this kind of money, they would be at an obvious disadvantage. Insurance company negotiators sitting across the table would know the Reichmanns didn't have many alternatives. It's always the availability of alternatives that helps keep negotiations honest. The Reichmanns' need for alternatives was growing, because the more they analyzed Olympia & York's financial needs, the more convinced they became that they ought to go for a billion dollars.

As he wrestled with these issues, Paul Reichmann decided to seek the advice of an investment banker experienced at selling debt, particularly to savings and loans. It was a volatile market, but nobody knew it better than Salomon Brothers. The firm had been a minor player that had muscled its way to the elite of Wall Street, despite some well-publicized setbacks.

Salomon was run by blunt, brusque, cigar-smoking John Gutfreund, the son of a New York entrepreneur who had a trucking company and wholesale meat business. Rejected by Harvard, Gutfreund enrolled at Oberlin College, where he majored in English. He contemplated a career teaching literature. He had a yen for swimming, tennis, canoeing, jazz, classical music and the theater. But after an army hitch in Korea, he was hired by William R. "Billy" Salomon whose forebears Arthur, Percy and Herbert Salomon started the firm in 1910 by betting their $5,000 savings on a bond-trading venture.

When Gutfreund became a $45 a week trainee in 1953, Salomon Brothers was still primarily a bond trader. He blossomed at the firm's municipal bond desk and became a partner by age 34. He prodded the firm to expand into underwriting. The most prestigious companies relied on investment bankers they had used for years, but some business like public utility bonds were put up to auction. This gave other firms like Salomon Brothers a chance to bid for business. Salomon made enough winning bids to range farther afield. During the 1970s, volatile inflation, interest rates and financial markets put a premium on keen trading instincts honed at Salomon. Other investment banking firms found that long-established ties with major companies didn't count as much as they used to. Salomon Brothers bid aggressively for offerings and sold adroitly.

They concentrated on marketing pools of home mortgages. Best known were securities backed by the federally administered Government National Mortgage Association—so-called Ginnie Maes. Also offered were securities of the privately-managed Federal Home Loan Mortgage Corporation—Freddie Macs—and the Federal National Mortgage Association, or Fannie Maes. The result was a security as safe as a Treasury bill but offering about 2½ points higher interest.

During the 1970s, Salomon sold billions of dollars worth of these financial instruments, which helped bail out endangered savings and loan institutions. Their depositors had fled from low-paying passbook savings accounts for better returns elsewhere.

Salomon's guru of mortgage-backed financing was a 34-year-old Brooklyn-born Italian-American named Louis Ranieri. Rebuffed for lacking experience when he first sought a job at Salomon back in 1967, he told a recruiter: "What I'm applying for is to be a clerk on the night shift in the mailroom. How much experience do I need?" Because of his relentless drive, he was asked within a few years to set up the firm's computer operations. He learned how to trade utility bonds and became intrigued with mortgage-backed securities.

Mortgage-backed securities became the rage of Wall Street when housing boomed in 1977. They were handled by some 30 firms. But two years later, housing collapsed, and all but a few firms left the field. Only one—Salomon Brothers— actually strengthened its capabilities. When real estate revived in 1981, so did the market for mortgage-backed securities, and Salomon was ready. Ranieri's crew gained an astonishing 40 percent of the business, twice as much as its nearest competitor, First Boston Corporation. Other firms like Merrill Lynch, Paine Webber and Citibank were far behind.

With stunning successes like these, Salomon's capital mushroomed to $300 million. Gutfreund, who had guided orderly growth, was a star. When Billy Salomon retired in 1978, Gutfreund seemed the natural successor.

The firm made some horrendous trades, though, which suggested the risks the Reichmanns had to weigh. For example, IBM always had turned to Morgan Stanley for advice, but when IBM chairman Frank Carey decided the company would issue its first bonds in 1979, he startled the investment banking community by picking Salomon as the lead manager with Merrill Lynch as co-manager. It was a momentous $1 billion deal, which involved about $500 million in seven-year notes and about $500 million in 25-year debentures.

As investment banker, Salomon would be buying the securities from IBM, and naturally Big Blue wanted the most money possible. Salomon hoped to turn around and sell the securities quickly at a profit. If their yields were set too low, they wouldn't sell, and Salomon would be stuck with huge potential losses.

Interest rates were hiked five times during September 1979 when Gutfreund and his partners were pondering how to price the securities. Salomon canvassed its regular clients as well as 225 other firms that were part of a syndicate Salomon and Merrill Lynch had assembled. About 12:40 on the afternoon of Wednesday, October 3, Carey and top IBM financial executives agreed to offer a yield on the notes of seven basis points above Treasury bonds, a pricing standard because they were considered among the safest investments. The IBM debentures would be offered at 12 basis points above Treasury bonds. A basis point was a hundredth of a percent, the standard unit for pricing debt securities. Based on then-prevailing market conditions, IBM would pay 9.41 percent for the debentures and 9.62 percent for the notes.

Within hours after the terms were set, Treasury bond interest rates headed up five basis points, almost wiping out the original spread between them and the IBM notes. The next day, the Treasury auctioned $2.5 billion of four-year notes similar to the IBM issues—for 9.79 percent. Then the Federal Reserve announced steps to tighten the money supply, and interest rates jumped again. To offer equivalent yields, the IBM issues traded in the market for $5 less per $1,000 face value. With an unsold inventory around $350 million, the syndicate's losses were about $10 million.

Gutfreund's biggest bombshell was the announcement on October 1, 1981 that the Salomon Brothers partners had sold their interest in their firm to Phibro, one of the world's largest commodities traders and a publicly-held firm. Salomon's partners would get $254 million of Phibro stock at $27.78 a share, and Phibro would recapitalize the firm with $300 million. The total was about 2.5 times book value, the knockdown value of the firm's assets. It wasn't a great deal—Bache, a troubled brokerage house, had sold for two times book value to Prudential, and American Express bought Shearson Loeb Rhoades for 3.4 times book. But Salomon required its partners to keep most of their money in the firm, so the deal was attractive because it enabled them to cash out years earlier than they otherwise would have.

Soon afterward, oil prices plunged. Since oil was a big part of

Phibro's business, its earnings took a dive, and its stock dropped to $20. Salomon's business, however, was booming. In 1982, Salomon's pre-tax earnings hit $362 million. The partners resented not being compensated according to their contribution to the firm. By October 1983, Phibro-Salomon stock recovered to $36, and many Salomon partners sold their holdings, only to damn their timing when the stock hit $60 in mid-November. Gutfreund persuaded the board of directors to make him a co-chief executive with David Tendler, the Phibro boss. There was a boardroom confrontation August 6, 1984, and Gutfreund emerged the winner. Tendler resigned. So Salomon partners cashed out for millions, then regained control.

Back to the Reichmanns: by the spring of 1983, Paul Reichmann, Olympia & York vice presidents Bernard Baum, Ken Leong and Camille Jensen met almost weekly with Salomon Sales Manager J. Steven Manolis, Vice President Gregory White and Vice President Steven Roth at Olympia & York's 245 Park Avenue office. Considering the hundreds of millions of dollars at stake, this was a surprisingly young crew in their 20s and 30s.

On the Olympia & York side: Baum, a Canadian, and Leong, a Hong Kong Chinese, had an exceptional facility for numbers, and they spent their time working out the implications of deals being considered. Moreover, they had to make sure that any proposed agreements satisfied the Reichmanns' need for flexibility. They wouldn't permit a lender to have approval rights over tenants, building expenditures or other decisions, as long as the Reichmanns were meeting their obligations.

Jensen's job was to recommend ways of raising money at the least cost. Like a surprising number of executives at Olympia & York, she had studied city planning—at Harvard's School of Design and later in the office of Vancouver architect Arthur Erickson. Recognizing that architects tend to come onto a job after the most basic decisions are made about the site, overall plans and financing, she switched to the real estate financing division of Morgan Stanley, the investment banking firm. She joined Olympia & York in 1982 as the Reichmanns explored major financings. She did most of the day-to-day work on the Olympia & York side of this deal.

Salomon's blond, blue-eyed Manolis is credited with helping to conceive more than $5 billion of transactions. Hailing from Vermillion, South Dakota, he started at the firm as a bond salesman and later built the mortgage sales force before spearheading real estate operations. He's a premier presenter who delivers a powerful pitch without notes. He has a bold conceptual mind, commands vast knowledge of capital markets and speaks with intense, evangelical fervor. When a client gives the go-ahead for a deal, Manolis usually takes charge.

White, a lean man with black hair who handles many of the detailed negotiations on a deal, has lived in airplanes ever since he came to Salomon from Chase Manhattan's real estate department. He displays tremendous stamina as he defies jet lag to London for a client meeting, then catches the next flight to New York before seeing clients on the West Coast and elsewhere. He has perhaps the most intimate knowledge of a deal and the patient staying power essential to resolve endless intricacies which make a transaction possible.

While clients feel comfortable working with polished corporate front men such as Manolis and White, they depend on a shrewd trader like Roth to sell their securities advantageously on the trading floor. He has a brusque, incandescent manner, which he cultivated while promoting concerts for San Francisco rock impresario Bill Graham—Joan Baez, Joni Mitchell, Bob Marley, Boz Scaggs, Santana and the Grateful Dead are among the acts Roth remembers. He talks with his hands, and when the trading is fast, his expletives go off like sparklers. He has a towering ego given to oracular pronouncements about the kinds of deals that can and cannot be sold in the current market. He's wrong sometimes, of course, but he has an iron stomach needed to survive setbacks.

Paul Reichmann asked the Salomon people if they could do for him a deal like the recent $110 million participating mortgage sold as a public issue by Drexel Burnham, the maverick junk bond dealer. The offering was for Indianapolis shopping center developer Melvin Simon. It was a mixed-bag deal with first mortgages, second mortgages, leasehold interests and even an unfinished property, which wasn't generating any income. Investors were offered only 15 percent of cash flow above interest and 25 percent of the increase in final value. There was little information about what internal rate of return investors could expect. Yet it sold out at 10.95 percent, which almost any developer would envy. Since Olympia & York had first mortgages on established income-producing Manhattan office buildings, Paul Reichmann reasoned, he should be able to do even better.

As he requested, Salomon polled their clients. Results suggested the Melvin Simon deal was an inexplicable aberration. The low interest rate wouldn't be duplicated. Maybe it reflected lucky timing or Drexel's skillful marketing. Whatever happened, the factors that worked for this deal would surely fail if applied to a far larger, $1 billion deal.

Paul Reichmann asked about possible interest in what he termed a "real rate of return mortgage." This would be aimed at pension funds, a tempting market, because they had more than $1 trillion of funds under management. Since they were obliged to pay out a minimum return to retirees, they needed assurance of steady gains. Reichmann proposed offering investors an inflation-adjusted return. There would be a regular stream of payments plus incremental payments to compensate for depreciating purchasing power.

Sticking point: the frequency of those incremental payments. Reichmann wanted them to be due at long intervals—say, every decade. His reasoning was that inflation tended to run in cycles, and at long intervals they'd benefit from periods of low inflation. Salomon polled their clients and reported that incremental payments every one, two or three years might be acceptable. Five years, possibly. But ten years was out of the question. The performance of pension fund managers was typically judged by short-term standards.

By late 1983, Salomon people were confident that savings and loan institutions might be the answer. They lent money for 15 years, which was what the Reichmanns wanted. Savings and loans hadn't made loans for major commercial real estate before, but maybe an attractive deal could be devised.

S&Ls were squeezed, because deregulation meant they had to pay volatile, variable rates to attract depositors. Yet the bulk of their income continued to come from fixed-rate loans, because most homeowners were worried about inflation. They were wary of variable-rate mortgages, which could sear their wallets.

With the decisive independence that is their hallmark, the Reichmanns concluded inflation was in a cyclical downtrend, and it would not be a problem for some time. Therefore, they should switch from borrowing money at a fixed rate to borrowing at a variable rate. Rather than lock themselves into what could be a relatively high rate, they would take advantage of the downtrend they foresaw. According to this analysis, it would benefit Olympia & York to offer S&Ls a variable-rate debt instrument, so that any increase in interest they had to pay for deposits would be matched by increased revenue from the variable-rate debt instrument.

It would have been easy for the Reichmanns to let their emotions get in the way. The last time they loaded up on variable-rate borrowings, during the late 1970s, Olympia & York's margins were hammered as interest rates jolted toward 20 percent. They had bet on an interest rate decline and lost millions. It was an agonizing period. Most developers could still think of nothing but how to protect themselves against high interest rates.

The Reichmanns, by contrast, were actually worried about the risk of locking into a fixed rate. "Suppose you borrowed heavily at 14 percent," Paul explains. "You'd be locked in for 20 years or whatever the term is for your loan. Very seldom are lenders willing to give a prepayment privilege. If rates fell to, say, 7 percent, somebody who financed a building at that rate could lease space for less than you, and as leases in your building expire, you'd gradually lose tenants. There isn't much you could do to make your leases more competitive, because you're still paying 14 percent for your money."

Of course, Paul Reichmann wanted to protect against the risk of rising interest rates. He visualized a variable-rate borrowing with a cap, so they would know in advance the maximum rate they might have to pay.

He explained his thinking and told Manolis, White and Roth that he wanted to be in the market by September 1983. He was nervous about the financial outlook beyond then. On a billion dollar deal, if interest rates notched up a quarter-point, this increased the annual payments by $20 million. The higher the payments, the less money the Reichmanns could afford to borrow.

The Salomon people considered the uncertainties about marketing to savings and loan associations. Most worrisome was the inexperience of these institutions at assessing the risks of commercial properties. Furthermore, S&Ls were accustomed to lending only in their region. It would be hard to sell them on different kinds of properties hundreds or thousands of miles away from their offices.

Some commercial banks might be interested in a variable-rate borrowing, because demand for commercial loans declined during the 1982 recession. However, when commercial loan demand picked up again, commercial banks could be counted out, because commercial loans don't have interest rate caps. They're a more appealing alternative. Finally, commercial banks seldom make long-term loans.

Adrenalin was running strong at Salomon, because Olympia & York was a mighty name on Wall Street, and a successful offering for the Reichmanns would help boost the careers of Manolis, White, Roth and everybody else associated with it. Yet for one reason or another, most deals that people talk about never happen. This whole thing could fizzle.

All of Salomon's meetings with the Reichmanns—the analysis and advice provided—were without compensation. Salomon, like other investment bankers, was paid for successful results. Fees aren't figured by the hour as with lawyers. There would be a reward only if Salomon brought an offering to market and raised an agreed-on minimum amount of money.

Having agreed on broad terms, though, the Reichmanns retained Salomon as Olympia & York's exclusive investment banker for this transaction. Paul made it official with a simple three-page letter on October 7, 1983. Salomon's fee would be several million dollars.

Since there wasn't any one building that could secure a billion dollar borrowing, Paul Reichmann began considering some kind of deal that would involve pooling mortgages from several buildings. Despite the parallels with pools of home mortgages, there was no precedent involving commercial mortgages. Home mortgages in most pools were under $150,000. No one mortgage, were it to default, could have much impact on a pool with thousands. A security backed by several commercial buildings would be far riskier. If occupancies and cash flow tumbled at one building, the whole offering would be in jeopardy.

Which buildings to use as collateral for the notes? "The timing was right for three," Paul explains. "About 60 percent of the leases in the Sperry Building, at 1290 Avenue of the Americas, were expiring. They yielded $8 to $9 a square foot. New leases were for $37 to $38, so the building reached a new plateau of value, and it was an obvious choice for refinancing.

"The situation was similar at 2 Broadway, a 1.6-million-square-foot building in the financial district. About half the leases rolled over to rates three to four times higher than what they were before.

"During the late 1970s, we had bought 237 Park Avenue, stripped it down to the frame and rebuilt it around a 23-story-high atrium. This building was substantially leased at current market rates, so it, too, was suitable for refinancing."

These three buildings offered investors a diversified package—buildings downtown, on Park Avenue and at Rockefeller Center. Each was a distinctive office market.

Salomon began the tedious process of analyzing the cash flow from these buildings, so they could go to the S&Ls with an offering. There were more than 250 leases, and every one had to be examined. Since many tenants had expanded to available space on different floors, there were cases where a single tenant had a half-dozen leases. Each lease was different. One had 18 amendments, the eighteenth countering what was covered in the previous 17. Leases varied in the way office space was calculated—a factor determining the total rent due. The Reichmanns credited tenants with various expenses. How leases affected net income was crucial, for an office building was valued according to the net income it yielded.

There were excruciating negotiations over the terms of the offering between Olympia & York and Salomon. Paul Reichmann and his associates constantly pressed for terms favorable to them. The people at Salomon were concerned that the offering be salable—they didn't want another IBM debacle on their hands. "When you're going to the market for a billion dollars," says Manolis, "you've got to be right on almost every count."

Detail: Most lenders require that cash flow be about 1.1 times the debt service. This is a way lenders satisfy themselves that debt service could be handled. But what exactly was cash flow? Was it the cash flow resulting from the buildings as they were, with some vacancies? Or would you assume that the vacancies would gradually fill, and the cash flow would be higher? One way or another, lenders had to be presented with the equivalent of 100 percent leased buildings at the time of closing. After several months, Paul agreed to what was called a Master Cash Flow Agreement. It specified that Olympia & York would put up U.S. government securities to generate approximately the income which would have been provided by the available space if it were leased. Then, as new tenants signed leases, Olympia & York could withdraw securities.

Salomon retained the structural engineering firm Syska & Hennessey to examine the physical condition of the buildings. Two—1290 Avenue of the Americas and 2 Broadway—dated from the 1960s, so it was quite possible that mechanical systems needed costly repairs or even replacement. Their report confirmed the basic soundness of the structures.

Salomon retained Landauer Associates to do the appraisals. They monitored sales comparable to Olympia & York's properties. The leasehold on 1180 Avenue of the Americas, for instance, realized $39 million, or $133 a square foot, in May 1983; 909 Third Avenue sold for $31 million, or $100 a square foot, the same month; 711 Fifth Avenue, $57.6 million, or $205 a foot, in July. No building was in exactly the same condition or located at the same place, so analysis of these sales required experienced judgment.

To project cash flow for each of the Reichmanns' buildings over the next 10 to 15 years, Landauer also analyzed each lease to estimate the likelihood that a tenant would renew or vacate upon expiration. The firm projected building maintenance costs before arriving at the bottom line.

Salomon Brothers' attorneys at Cravath, Swain & Moore analyzed laws that govern the kinds of investments savings and loan institutions could make—specifics vary from state to state. The point was to help design a security that could be offered as widely as possible, at the very least, in all the major states.

How to price the offering? For a while, Salomon considered a spread over the National Cost of Funds Index, which is published monthly by the Federal Home Loan Bank. It's based on the cost of funds at member banks. But savings and loan institutions Salomon talked with reported that it didn't reflect their cost of funds accurately enough, and the idea was discarded.

Another idea was an index that tracked the cost of funds in California's Eleventh District, where the largest U.S. savings and loan associations were located. Those S&Ls used it to calculate rates for their loans both on single-family homes and commercial properties. Rates in the Eleventh District parallel rates elsewhere in the United States. But it would be difficult for the Reichmanns to hedge against notes based on this index. S&Ls were comfortable with notes based on Treasury bills, and these the Reichmanns could hedge against by going into the Treasury bills futures market.

How much of a spread? This depends on demand. Salomon polled savings and loans about their interest in notes offered at 1.50 points above average bond equivalent yields of three-month Treasury bills. Yields on the notes would be adjusted monthly. But this didn't generate enough of a response. At 1.75 points above Treasuries, the notes seemed likely to succeed, and that became the pricing.

Manolis, White and Roth prepared presentations to investors. They explained the offering. Then they talked about collateral—the market and the buildings. The first presentation was in New York, at the Grand Hyatt, before the firm's salespeople.

In November 1983, the Salomon trio took their road show to Boston, Atlanta, Miami, Chicago, Dallas, Houston, San Francisco and Los Angeles. Presentations were given in London and Amsterdam, though Salomon didn't expect many foreign investors to be interested—they seldom bought unrated deals, and this type of deal was so new, it wasn't rated by a major rating agency like Standard & Poor's. The overseas presentations were to educate foreign investors about mortgage-backed securities. Held in a hotel conference room over lunch or dinner, each presentation was attended by 25 to 75 local salespeople and prospective clients.

White was more involved than the others at Salomon, for he worked full time on the Olympia & York offering. After a session presenting his case to one S&L, he'd be asked to fly across the country and meet with another one. There were a half-dozen meetings with some S&Ls—their officers, lawyers and others who could help determine whether this was the kind of deal they should participate in. "There were quite a few months when I wasn't home very much," he recalls. "About all I ate were turkey sandwiches. Not very glamorous." Fortunately his wife, Mindy, a broker for A.G. Becker, understood.

"We were surprised that a lot of savings and loans were against investing in New York City," acknowledges Roth. "We who worked in New York knew what a buoyant real estate market it was, but investors in the Midwest especially didn't want any part of New York for a while."

On November 2, prospects were sent a term sheet—several pages that outlined the offering, described the buildings and Olympia & York. Then began an anxious waiting period, as investment committees met behind closed doors to decide whether they would take any of the Olympia & York notes. After several weeks, calls began to come in. The first one, from a midwestern savings and loan, expressed interest in $10 million of notes.

"But these weren't firm orders," notes White. "In the securities business, we have what's known as a circle. When an investor says 'I circle $10 million of those bonds,' that's a commitment. Real estate deals, though, tend to involve more documents that come later, and many investors cancel because details in the documents suggest the notes won't suit their needs. You never know whether somebody would actually buy the notes until they sign a binding purchase application. This may not go out until months later, shortly before the closing."

On December 12, prospects were sent a preliminary memorandum which contained more details about the offering. By January 1, there was interest in about a third of the offering. A month later, two thirds was spoken for.

But there was slippage, too. Soon after expressing interest in $25 million worth of notes, the investment officer of a midwestern bank announced his resignation. The bank notified Salomon that since nobody else had the man's real estate expertise, they didn't feel comfortable with the notes, so they were canceling. Altogether, about half the investors who expressed interest in the notes canceled. Salomon salespeople were constantly in touch with everybody who expressed interest until the deal closed, so they'd know who was wavering and who stood firm.

While Salomon sold the offering as hard as they could, top executives at American Savings & Loan, among the largest thrift institutions, approached the Reichmanns about making a loan. They had a worrisome rate of defaults on their home lending operations, so they welcomed the opportunity to buy into major downtown properties with a firm as strong as Olympia & York. Such notes would mean a definite strengthening of their portfolio. The more the Reichmanns thought about it, the more they realized a deal could be integrated with the floating rate offering.

What resulted was a $350 million loan with a fixed rate at 12.75 percent. This amount would help hedge the risks, so the entire loan amount wasn't floating.

The formal private placement memorandum went out to investors on February 6. It was 82 pages, surprisingly short as real estate deals go. Greg White was on the road almost continuously through January and February, answering questions that prospective investors had about the notes. More expressed a tentative commitment for notes. "We figured we were comfortably over the top," White told me, "when an eastern savings and loan told us they would take more than $30 million of the notes." About $50 million more came in after that. Altogether, there were 42 investors.

However, the exact amount of notes any investor bought depended on an agreed-on formula which involved the latest verified cash flow from the three Olympia & York buildings and the opening coupon rate for the notes on an agreed-on date about a month before closing, whenever that was set. This was delayed by continued negotiations over terms with the Reichmanns.

The cash flow from the buildings was about $110 million, a stable number since leases and maintenance costs changed little. But nobody had a crystal ball on interest rates.

Negotiations dragged into February, as Treasuries began to rise. They passed 10.99 percent—according to the terms of the security, that would have meant raising an even billion dollars. But rates edged higher. When the negotiations were finished, all the lawyers had to do was verify that there hadn't been any material changes in the condition of buildings since negotiations started. Pricing of the notes would be determined by interest rates as of February 22. Closing would be March 20. That number turned out to be 11.34 percent. They would fall short of their billion-dollar target, raising a still-record $970 million.

Salomon instructed investors to wire their money at specific times; Monday March 19 and Tuesday March 20. Held in escrow, the funds were invested on an overnight basis until the actual closing.

Work on the closing started Sunday afternoon, March 18 at the One New York Plaza offices of Fried, Frank, Harris, Shriver & Jacobson, Olympia & York's attorneys. They, together with Salomon's attorneys from Cravath, Swain & Moore, checked hundreds of pages of documents. There was the note itself. A master cash flow agreement. Mortgages, rent collateral agreements, estoppel certificates, title reports, mortgage tax recording papers, articles of incorporation and corporate resolutions—all had to be reviewed. Olympia & York Executive Vice President William Hay signed, and the deal was done.

More than 50 people had a hand in the proceedings—attorneys, officers from Olympia & York and Salomon. Title insurance people were there, and so were a few investors. The job was done by noon on March 20. Everybody toasted with a plastic glass of Dom Perignon champagne, then returned to work. Some of the lawyers went home to sleep.

Notably absent were the Reichmanns, busy with myriad other things. Paul did call Gutfreund, White, Roth and Manolis to express his thanks for their help. White got a paperweight enclosing a miniature "tombstone" notice, which announced the offering. He valued it almost as much an another paperweight which announced that "Mindy S. Geltzer has merged with Gregory White, April 30, 1983." It was a successful offering.

Camille Jensen had planned to wed corporate lawyer Peter Douglas, a merger specialist, the week after the closing. But since the closing was delayed, Jensen was honeymooning in the Grenadines when the deal was finally done. She learned of its success via ship-to-shore radio while they were cruising.

The Reichmanns did fine, too. They limited their risks by taking $650 million of Treasury bill futures contracts, which would generate higher income to help cover additional payments due on the notes in the event of a rate rise.

But rates fell about 150 basis points, and in the year after the offering, the Reichmanns saved about $15 million compared to what they would have paid if they had given in to the fear of rising interest and secured a fixed-rate deal.

The Reichmanns were lucky, for the window had largely closed at savings and loans. Within months after their offering, consumers began accepting variable rate home loans. Consequently, savings and loans didn't have the same need for the Olympia & York notes they had before. Commercial loan demand picked up, so even fewer commercial banks would be interested in a deal like this.

But by showing how to transform illiquid commercial mortgages into cash, the Reichmanns had a potentially tremendous impact on Wall Street. Salomon did similar deals turning commercial mortgages into liquid securities for American Motor Inns and Fluor Corporation. For American Express, Salomon raised $500 million—these notes were backed by the company's new headquarters, bought from the Reichmanns. Insurance companies like Massachusetts Mutual, Penn Mutual, Guardian Life and New England Mutual issued more than $2 billion of notes, which securitized properties in their investment portfolios.

Meanwhile, the Reichmanns could be counted on to devise more creative ways to satisfy the needs of a particular market and time. That's how you make chunks of money on Wall Street or anywhere else.

V

POWER PLAYS

11.

LAWSUITS AND STREET PROTESTS

REAL ESTATE DEVELOPMENT CAN BE AMONG THE MOST POLITI-cally risky of businesses. In a city like New York, San Francisco or Boston, a proposed project may need approval from a couple of dozen government agencies before it can proceed. It can be shot down practically anywhere along the way, with losses in the millions.

You might imagine that people would welcome an entrepreneur who proposes to inject new development into a deteriorating area and help turn it around. But this may unleash explosive controversies, as happened to John Portman when he wanted to build a hotel amidst the pimps, prostitutes and porn parlors in New York's Times Square.

Portman's hotel opened in October 1985, an incredible two decades after initial efforts to develop something on the site. It's a very large facility with 1,877 rooms. His hallmark atrium is a record 35 stories tall, substantially more than the Atlanta Hyatt Regency, which put him on the map a decade and a half before. The hotel has a 1,507-seat theater, making it among the biggest on Broadway. Plus, the hotel has more than 1,400 lounge and restaurant seats. Tagged at an estimated $400 million, this may be the most costly hotel ever.

The germ of the deal goes back to New York's Mayor John Lindsay and his midtown planning director, Jacquelin T. Robertson, who were among those concerned about sleeze taking over Times Square. It could mean the end of the fabled theater district, which attracted so many people to the Big Apple. Historically, Manhattan real estate development moved north and east, so it would take a tremendous effort—almost certainly a major project—to pull development west-ward where it might have a positive impact on Times Square.

Along came a shy, fastidious yet aggressive hotelier named Peter Sharp, owner of New York's plush Carlyle Hotel and other proper-ties, who had assembled a site west of Broadway between 45th and 46th streets. He figured it would be good for an office building. For architectural plans, he commissioned Emery Roth & Sons, a large commercial firm that probably had designed more glass-and-steel boxes around New York than anybody else.

In 1970, Robertson suggested Sharp use Philadelphia architect Robert Venturi to help assure a lively design. Impressed with all the bright signs at Times Square, Venturi recommended featuring signs prominently on the facade of Sharp's new building. However, the recession that year resulted in slack demand for office space, and the project was shelved.

Meanwhile, Robertson accompanied Sharp to Atlanta, so he could see the hugely successful Atlanta Hyatt Regency hotel. "Peter ran around like a monkey in a cage," Robertson says. "He loved that hotel. He stayed up most of the night just taking it in." Sharp decided he wanted architect-developer John Portman to design a hotel for his Times Square site and to joint-venture the development. Portman, who had talked with Robertson about developing a merchandise mart on the old Madison Square Garden site, saw the potential of reviving Times Square and accepted right away.

While Robert Venturi seemed to believe the essence of Times Square was neon, Portman insisted a dynamic environment was the key— 24-hour activity resulting from bringing several complementary uses together: offices, restaurants, shops, theaters and hotels. As with the Atlanta Hyatt Regency and hotels he designed since then, he conceived an atrium as the primary drawing card.

In 1973 he proposed a 2,000-room, 56-story hotel consisting of two towers linked together. The first 11 floors would contain shops, restaurants and other facilities. The hotel lobby would be on the twelfth floor, and that was where the atrium would begin. Portman negotiated with Western International Hotels, a division of United Airlines' parent UAL Inc., to become the hotel operator. Construction cost was pegged at $150 million. These ambitious ideas required more land, so Portman negotiated options on the old Piccadilly Hotel, and the Helen Hayes, Morosco and Bijou theaters.

Though these plans would require dozens of zoning variances, New York Mayor John Lindsay's backing augured well. But getting all the necessary approvals took a couple of years, and Sharp decided the project was too big for him. He sold his interest to Portman.

Soon Portman found himself facing a severe recession as well as New York's fiscal crisis. Then-Mayor Abraham Beame postponed plans for a $230 million New York Convention and Exhibition Center envisioned for the Hudson River waterfront west of Times Square. Consequently, Portman, who had raised $40 million in equity, couldn't secure mortgage commitments from any New York lenders. He canceled the project in December 1975, letting his options expire. "That was probably the worst time to build a convention hotel," he says. "There was really no interest in New York mortgages."

Portman's cancellation was just the latest setback for Times Square. Another was Manhattan Plaza, conceived as a middle and upper income housing development on 42nd Street West of Times Square but adapted for lower- and middle-income people. Meanwhile, the ailing retailer W. T. Grant Co. went bankrupt and vacated its offices at 1515 Broadway, across 45th Street from Portman's proposed site. That building was hemorrhaging red ink.

Three years later, New York City's economy had improved. Edward Koch, elected Mayor in 1977, encouraged Portman to try again. Times Square was as seedy as ever, and the need for a galvanizing project was great. City officials offered to help finance it by obtaining a second mortgage or an Urban Development Action Grant—the new federal program to subsidize central city projects when not enough private sector funds were available.

Having already spent $4 million on feasibility studies and plans, Portman agreed. He renewed his options on the theaters. He got permission from the Advisory Council on Historic Preservation to demolish the Helen Hayes, a grand Beaux-Arts style, 1,000-seat theater built in 1910. It was a gem with graceful terra cotta detailing, and it was listed in the National Register of Historic Places. Nobody made claims for the architecture of the 1,000-seat Morosco, though it suited intimate dramatic performances. The 300-seat Bijou Theater was a popular place for children's plays.

By 1979, Equitable Life Assurance Society was on board. They headed a consortium to raise $150 million of long-term loan money.

Then the project hit another snag: new investors who now owned the 54-year-old Piccadilly Hotel on West 45th Street refused to sell. They bought the property in 1977 after Portman's options expired. Without the Piccadilly, it was felt, Portman's hotel wouldn't have enough critical mass to survive in such an adverse environment as Times Square. If the new Piccadilly owners—Ulo Bared, Isaac Krakowski, Harry Krakowski and Robert Born—proved to be stubborn hold-outs, the cost of land could escalate well beyond the $32.8 million budgeted, and the project might become too risky. Efforts to seek mortgage financing were suspended.

The Piccadilly owners protested they weren't trying to hold out for an outrageous price. "This is how we make a living," Bared explained, "buying second-rate hotels and fixing them up without help from the city or federal government." He reported they had spent more than $1.5 million renovating the 550 rooms since acquiring the place. "This city needs more middle-class rooms," he continued.

"Not many people can afford luxury." The Piccadilly charged about $35 a room versus $80 to $100 which Portman estimated rooms at his proposed hotel would cost. *Fodor's* described the Piccadilly as "one of the best hotels in its area, with warmth, charm, and comfortable, adequate rooms."

Mayor Koch wanted to press ahead. He favored having the Piccadilly condemned and demolished only as a last resort. Its owners filed suit with the State Supreme Court to block this action. Koch wrote them emphasizing the high priority he placed on Times Square development. In December 1980, they reached an out-of-court settlement. Suits brought by Actors Equity, the theatrical union, to block the demolition of the three theaters as well as Café Ziegfield, a Piccadilly tenant, were withdrawn.

Thus, the way was cleared for New York City's Board of Estimate to consider recommending the project for a federal Urban Development Action Grant. Because so much time had elapsed, though, cost estimates were hiked to $261.5 million, and this would entail a grant of $21.5 million. If approved, it would have to compete in Washington with a multitude of applications from other cities.

Metropolitan Life Insurance Company, Equitable Life Assurance Society and the New York State Employees Retirement Fund would provide a $150 million first mortgage, believed to be the biggest of its kind in New York, and Manufacturers Hanover Trust agreed to finance a $30 million second mortgage. Portman would provide 11 percent of the $90 million equity.

Portman had been negotiating with Trusthouse Forte, a large British hotel chain, when he was approached by Marriott—anxious to establish a flagship property and penetrate the huge convention hotel market. Portman and J. (John) Willard Marriott Jr., 52, negotiated a deal for Marriott to be the operator and joint-venture partner with 89 percent interest.

Marriott is a spartan Mormon who works in a simple orange and green office decorated mainly with the American flag. His family's 22 percent stake in Marriott Corporation is worth about $530 million, but he and his wife Donna live in a modest Chevy Chase, Maryland brick home done in pink and green colonial style.

Marriott is as doggedly devoted to his properties as Portman is to architecture. Aloft—flying coach class—Marriott logs more than 125,000 miles a year, inspecting his properties, which include more than 59,000 hotel rooms, quadruple the number a decade ago. The Marriott empire includes more than 500 restaurants—Roy Rogers, Bob's Big Boys and Hot Shoppes. His $3.5 billion Washington-based company purveys food to more than 130 airlines and 210 food service outlets, which serve colleges, hospitals and businesses. During the past decade, Marriott's earnings grew at a sizzling compounded rate of 17.6 percent annually.

But the market his company traditionally served—roadside and airport inns—was becoming saturated. Downtowns were alive again after years of discouraging decline. Yet these are costly, difficult places to develop which must charge high rates to prosper. Only a hotel operator with a reputation for luxurious accommodations would be likely to attract enough business.

Marriott blamed himself for not seizing the opportunity much sooner. After the hugely successful Atlanta Hyatt Regency opened in 1967, the Pritzkers built snazzy, upscale hotels across the country and dominated the luxury market. "I had a chance to buy what became the Atlanta Hyatt Regency," Marriott says. "If I did, there wouldn't be a Hyatt chain today. Among other things, I didn't understand the importance of architecture back then."

So he welcomed the opportunity to buy into Portman's New York hotel, even though it would be the most expensive project he had ever undertaken. "When I was growing up," Marriott recalls, "Times Square was the world's biggest deal. It *was* New York." He dubbed this new property the Marriott Marquis Hotel.

By a 10 to 1 vote, the New York City Board of Estimate approved the application for the Marriott Marquis, and attorney Harold W. Suckenik, representing an informal group called New Yorkers to Preserve the Theater District, filed suit in United States District Court to block the Urban Development Action Grant. He contended the long-term financing wasn't in place as required. Moreover, he continued, an environmental-impact statement must be filed, and this wasn't done. As defendants, he named Moon Landrieu, Secretary of Housing and Urban Development, which must file an environmental-impact statement or delegate the task to a local agency; Alan Weiner, New York area director of HUD; Mayor Edward Koch; the New York City Board of Estimate; Edward V. Regan, New York state comptroller; the New York State Employees Retirement System, which hadn't yet closed long-term financing for Portman's hotel; the New York State Urban Development Corporation and Richard A. Kahan, its president.

On December 27, 1981, lawyers for Actors Equity and the Natural Resources Defense Council charged influence peddling. They filed sworn statements which claimed President Ronald Reagan's top political adviser, Lyn Nofziger, pressured the Advisory Council on Historic Preservation. He was described as insisting the Advisory Council reverse a November 17, 1981 decision to place the Morosco Theater

on the National Register of Historic Places, thereby approving demolition of the Morosco and Bijou theaters—or a White House order
would dismantle the Advisory Council on Historic Preservation.
Nofziger acknowledged calling council officials, but he denied applying pressure.

Secretary of the Interior James Watt reportedly insisted that the
November 17 decision was made without his permission, and he
issued an ultimatum that it be reversed. "Either the council had to
roll over in this matter or it would be out of business immediately,"
Jack L. Goldstein, an Advisory Council employee, recalled. He was
warned that disclosure of the behind-the-scenes maneuvering could
be damaging. The decision was reversed by November 20—a process
that usually takes weeks or months.

"I don't see anything bad about it," Alexander Aldrich, council
chairman, asserted. "This hotel project is most important for the
economy of New York City. And I have made it one of my causes
that bureaucratic delay not be part of the Council's process."

Glen Isaacson, Portman's project manager in New York, acknowledged: "It's true we exerted political influence" to take the Morosco
Theater off the National Register of Historic Places, so the hotel
could proceed. "Every day of delay is very expensive. There is a limit
beyond which we cannot go."

Judge Kevin Thomas Duffy of Federal District Court refused to
grant an injunction delaying demolition of the Helen Hayes and
Morosco theaters. But on January 6, 1982, he was directed to issue
it by the United States Court of Appeals for the Second Circuit. The
three-page ruling was written by judges Sterry R. Waterman, Leonard
P. Moore and Ellsworth A. Graafeiland. They noted Portman's claim
that "the project may be at stake because the financial package may
collapse," yet they contended that if demolition weren't delayed the
groups trying to save the theaters would be "deprived of all meaningful opportunity to litigate their remaining claim."

Three days later, New York State Supreme Court Acting Justice
Richard Price approved demolition of the theaters. He warned that
delay could imperil efforts to clean up Times Square, surrendering it
to the "purveyors of pornography and prostitution and the massage
parlors and sex shows that have marred its streets and avenues." He
recalled that Times Square "once was a vital and important area which
made New York City the entertainment capital of the world." Now,
he regretted, it was "one of the most blighted, tawdry and depressed
areas of Manhattan." He dismissed a complaint filed by the Natural
Resources Defense Council, while praising its intentions.

On January 12, the United States Court of Appeals approved

demolition of the Bijou Theater. Bulldozers moved in the next day. Across the street, theatrical producer Joseph Papp spearheaded a rally to save the remaining theaters. Actor Christopher Reeve wished he were Superman, so he could "catch the wrecking ball and tear it apart."

This raging controversy split the community. Against demolishing the theaters were the Actors Equity, American Federation of Television and Radio Artists, Screen Actors Guild, Society of Stage Directors and Choreographers, American Guild of Musical Artists, American Guild of Variety Artists, Theatrical Wardrobe Attendants Union and the Treasurers and Ticket Sellers Union. Favoring demolition and the Portman hotel: City of New York, League of New York Theaters and Producers, International Alliance of Theatrical Stage Employees and Moving Picture Machine Operators, Associated Musicians of Greater New York, Broadway Association, West Forty-Sixth Street Block Association and Eighth Avenue Community Association. At the Plymouth Theater, just before a performance of *Nicholas Nickleby,* the playwright David Mamet stalked up to Gerald Schoenfeld, chairman of the Shubert Organization and snapped: "You call yourself a producer, but you don't know how to create anything. All you know how to do is destroy."

Helen Hayes was anguished. After meeting with Mayor Koch in July 1980, she gave "two cheers for the Portman hotel." She explained: "I did tell the Actors Equity people I was not about to join their battle." By the fall of 1981, though, she switched positions, saying she hoped the theaters would be saved. She telegramed President Reagan. Later, she said, "I've been inundated with mail from both sides, and I'm torn between sentiment and good sense."

Meanwhile, critics began objecting to architectural plans— approved three years before by the Board of Estimate—which provided a two-block-long pedestrian mall, from 45th to 47th streets, which would mean closing Broadway at that point and diverting traffic to Seventh Avenue at 48th Street.

The mall was designed not by Portman but by Tippetts Abbett McCarthy Stratton together with the New York City Planning Department and its design consultant Paul Friedberg. Its estimated cost: $7.5 million, financed with $300,000 from New York State, $3.5 million from the Federal Urban Mass Transit Administration and the balance from New York City. To maintain the mall, the City would impose additional taxes on area property owners.

As delays over the project stretched into weeks, theater people became more vocal to save the Morosco and Helen Hayes theatres. A special marathon was announced for 12:30 March 4 at 45th Street West of Broadway, the Portman hotel site. Actors and actresses would read six Pulitzer Prize winning plays performed at the Morosco Theater: George Kelly's *Craig's Wife* (1926), Thornton Wilder's *Our Town* (1938), Arthur Miller's *Death of a Salesman* (1949), Tennessee Williams's *Cat on a Hot Tin Roof* (1955), Charles Gordone's *No Place to Be Somebody* (1970) and Michael Cristofer's *Shadow Box* (1977). Also read was Eugene O'Neill's *Long Day's Journey Into Night* (1956), which was performed at the Helen Hayes Theater. Among the readers were Arthur Miller, Lauren Bacall and Jason Robards. Lending their support were Jerry Ohrbach, who performed in the musical *42nd Street,* and John Rubenstein, star of *Children of a Lesser God.*

Not everybody in the theatrical community was against the project. "I hate to see those beautiful theaters go," lamented writer and director Garson Kanin. "But I've also seen the theater district deteriorate to a shameful degree. The hotel project has come in to rehabilitate the whole area."

Associate Supreme Court Justice Thurgood Marshall issued an order delaying demolition through the weekend. New York Court of Appeals Judge Jacob D. Fuchsberg delayed demolition until March 22. Producer Joseph Papp claimed a victory. Portman warned: "The determination of the courts to be very fair in listening to all sides now is causing all sorts of problems. We are in a dangerous situation in regard to keeping this project underway."

He was joined by Max Arons, president of Local 802 of the American Federation of Musicians. "As a union, we seek opportunities for employment. The Portman hotel will have seven ballrooms and a theater. If you look at the records of those antiquated theaters—the Morosco and Helen Hayes—you will find there were no musicians who played there at all."

Opponents pressed on. Washington attorney Bruce Terris, representing Save Our Broadway Committee and allied groups, announced he would ask the United States Supreme Court to consider the case if the appeals court didn't act by March 22. His aim: bring to the fore a plan, by architect Lee Pomeroy, in which the hotel would be built on top of the Morosco and Helen Hayes theaters. Portman's proposed new 1,500-seat theater and the pedestrian mall would be eliminated.

While this plan had the appearance of a compromise—the atrium and most of Portman's other principal ideas were included—it became a tactic for killing the whole project. Pomeroy acknowledged that redesigning the hotel would take at least nine months. Others estimated the process might take a year. Engineering drawings would have to be redone. New permits would have to be applied for. Almost certainly the financing would collapse as inflation tacked on perhaps another $25 million to construction costs. The latest estimates pegged the project at $292.5 million. The proposed package would require a $30 million tax abatement as well as a $21.5-million Urban Development and Action Grant. Portman declared he would abandon the project if required to redesign it.

John Cullinane, architect for the Federal Advisory Council on Historical Preservation, reported: "A design solution which would allow a clear span over both theaters isn't practical."

Lorna Goodman, assistant corporation counsel who represented New York City in this and eight other cases involving the Portman hotel, added: "One of the overriding principles of law is that you must challenge municipal decisions within months after they're made. Pomeroy went to the city and the Urban Development Corporation long after the city had decided to go ahead with its plans. And you don't have to be an engineer or an architect to know that his plan doesn't work."

Rumors began spreading that Portman's financial backers might withdraw. They were reportedly concerned about further delays in the project and weakening demand for New York hotel rooms.

Joseph Papp organized a nine-day demonstration beginning March 12 with a street performance of *Rodgers & Hart,* a musical presented at the Helen Hayes theater seven years before. Among the other performances scheduled: *Abie's Irish Rose, Perfectly Frank* and *Arsenic and Old Lace.* The demonstration would conclude March 22 with *Royal Family,* featuring Irene Worth and Estelle Parsons. By that day the New York State Court of Appeals was scheduled to decide whether to review the case of the theaters threatened with demolition.

The decision came six days earlier than expected: no case. Consequently, demolition could proceed. Joseph Papp fumed: "We will lie in front of the demolition equipment if necessary." He promised he would move into the Piccadilly Hotel, an effort to block its demolition. "We will have an honor guard of 50 people on duty at all times, so they won't be able to start demolition in the middle of the night."

In yet another legal maneuver, Producer Alexander H. Cohen, City Councilwoman Carol Greitzer, two members of Community Board 5 and the Project for Public Spaces Inc. filed a petition with New York State Supreme Court on March 18. The petition protested demolition of the theaters and motioned for delay until the proposed pedestrian mall could be further reviewed. If the mall could be killed, then possibly the hotel, so big that it would extend into the mall, would be killed, too. Acting Justice Richard L. Price took less than a minute the following day to deny the motion. Plaintiffs vowed they would take their petition to the Appellate Division.

Opponents of the pedestrian mall had a glimmering of hope, because required land-use hearings could easily last six months. The only way to avoid those was redesign the hotel so it remained within the boundaries of the existing block.

The last battle over the theaters ended around 10 A.M. March 22 when the United States Supreme Court lifted a temporary stay against demolishing the theaters. Nearly 1,000 demonstrators gathered at a rally in an empty lot next to the Bijou Theater. Some 170 people occupied the site to be demolished, and police carted them to the Midtown North precinct station house on West 54th Street. They were issued pink summonses for trespassing, then released until court appearances in April.

By 2 P.M. a mammoth hydraulic backhoe, emblazoned on its side with the name Godzilla, tore at the remaining wall of the Bijou Theater. Protesters shouted "Don't do it! Don't do it!" The wrecker punched a hole into the east wall of the Morosco. A brisk wind lashed demonstrators with brick dust. Somebody played a wailing bagpipe.

Many arrested demonstrators returned and, wearing summonses pinned to their hats or lapels, marched down Eighth Avenue to 45th Street, chanting "Shame on Koch!" Soon placards appeared: "Free the Morosco 200!" Performers played on a portable stage as wreckers proceeded with demolition.

There was gloom in the air. Colleen Dewhurst, who starred in the 1974 hit *A Moon for the Misbegotten* at the Morosco, recalled, "It was almost a perfect house. You could knit the whole audience into one person and hold them like a womb." Mia Dillon, who played in *Da* at the Morosco: "A performance is so immediate, and then it's gone. Having the theater where those words lived, having it gone too, is such a killing thing. I just have an incredible anger and frustration this could happen."

John Portman did halt demolition of the Helen Hayes Theater, so art works could be salvaged. Among them: terra cotta blocks which formed the facade above the theater marquee; three terra cotta panels which were above the doors; a galvanized iron cornice; profiles of Helen Hayes which were on two box seats and on the proscenium. Salvaging these and other items cost about $200,000 and took almost three weeks. Since this was a job requiring special skills, Portman retained Meadows/Woll, an architectural firm with expertise in historical structures. He hired a guard to protect the Helen Hayes Theater against vandals.

As a conciliatory gesture, he offered memorabilia to theater people. Joseph Papp got a thick piece of plastic swag with the name Morosco on it and two electrified signs which had hung above the Morosco. Helen Hayes got eight seats from the front row of the theater named after her, and they were moved to the television room in her Nyack, New York home. The New York State Museum, Albany, acquired the wood-paneled ticket office from the Helen Hayes Theater—it still had tickets from the last play performed there, *I Won't Dance*. The Shubert Archives wanted playbills and posters.

The pedestrian mall? City officials announced they wouldn't approve it. Portman specified a new configuration for the escalators and redesigned the hotel entrance, so it would take less room. The depth of the ground-floor theater stage was reduced, and a café that would have operated along the mall was eliminated. The hotel was built within the existing lot. Birkhead Rouse, who took over managing the Times Square project in 1981, shrugs: "John just wears down the opposition."

Around the corner would rise a new $400 million Merchandise Mart for computers, apparel and designer furniture. It would be built by Portman's former partner and now adversary, Trammell Crow. Those two titanic spirits found themselves together again.

12.

CITY COUNCIL WARS

RECENTLY I WAS WALKING OUT ALONG CHICAGO'S NAVY PIER, A majestic, crumbling 70-year-old pleasure palace which juts 3,040 feet into Lake Michigan northeast of downtown. It's on the National Register of Historic Places. From the end of Navy Pier, you have a sensational view of Lake Michigan and the Chicago skyline. If Navy Pier is out of the way for many people, the location suggests tantalizing possibilities for development.

Yet this is a place where political squabbling got so bad that nothing much ever happened. Efforts by some of the most successful real estate entrepreneurs proved futile. The city got a black eye.

In 1979, while Chicago's Mayor Jane Byrne was in Boston attending a mayor's conference, she saw firsthand how The Rouse Company's Faneuil Hall Marketplace energized a long-decrepit part of the city. She thought Chicago could benefit from something like that, so she contacted James Rouse, the company's founder and urban messiah. On October 5, she retained them to see what might be done with Navy Pier.

It had eluded solution for decades. When it opened in 1916, it was touted as the largest recreational pier in the world. Certainly it was bigger than the piers of Atlantic City. Throughout the 1920s, its golden age, it was an ongoing festival, with plays, concerts, carnival rides, art exhibits, excursion boats and other activities going from 8 in the morning until midnight. Mayor "Big Bill" Thompson sponsored "Pageants of Progress," which featured fireworks, marathon swims, firefighting demonstrations, pigeon, speedboat and airplane races at Navy Pier. For a while, each day's festivities climaxed with a fire dive by Jack "The Human Torch" Turner.

Navy Pier became part of Chicago's underworld lore during Prohibition, when bootlegger Bugs Moran lost some $75,000 of Canadian scotch there. He had used the pier as a drop-off point, but alerted Federal agents staged a lively raid. On another occasion, police charged that Navy Pier was "enlivened by the contortions of an uncommonly agile dancer."

Fewer ships came to Navy Pier as truck competition reduced the overall volume of shipping. Politicians proposed various schemes, but they ran out of money during the Great Depression. Nothing came of plans to build a $100,000 statue of a sailor.

One effort after another to revive Navy Pier fizzled. Promoters tried unsuccessfully to stage concerts and operas. The Navy used it to train new recruits during World War II, but all this ended afterward. The University of Illinois used it for classes—the place was dubbed "Harvard on the Rocks," and among its illustrious graduates are jazz musician Ramsay Lewis and Illinois Governor "Big Jim" Thompson. The place was abandoned once again when the university built its new Chicago campus.

After years of neglect, the East End of Navy Pier was restored for the Bicentennial. It's a splendid auditorium, glass all around, which can accommodate as many as 5,000 people. There are dramatic views of Lake Michigan and Chicago's skyline. But city officials—not exactly the most enterprising folks—did little more than rent the place for an occasional bar mitzvah, wedding or corporate seminar.

During the 1970s, Navy Pier was the scene of Chicago Fest, which started as weekend musical events appealing to children, teenagers and adults. Within a few years, this evolved into summertime hard rock festivals and lost much of the audience. So Chicago Fest folded. Navy Pier deteriorated as politicians talked about dreams which required a lot of money they didn't have.

As Mayor Byrne requested, Rouse Executive Vice President Michael Spear and Development Director Williams Fulton began exploring the potential of Navy Pier. They retained consultants whose fees the city agreed to pick up. The market for new retail shops had to be evaluated—what kind would complement Chicago's Michigan Avenue and State Street retail districts, how many shops made sense, how they would best be presented, what kind of sales volume they could reasonably expect, how much lease income might be generated. Since a hotel worked well in such a retail setting, Rouse people analyzed the Chicago hotel market, projected likely occupancies and rates. They considered how entertainment facilities and a marina might fit into the project.

Before any of these things could happen, the pier had to be renovated. New electrical lines, water lines and sanitation lines were required. Somehow Navy Pier had to be linked to the city's mass transit system, so crowds could be accommodated easily. There must be provision for at least a couple of thousand parking spaces.

Rouse people delivered a 79-page report to Mayor Byrne July 31, 1980. It proposed a 200,000-square-foot festive marketplace, with shops, restaurants, a hotel and 400-slip marina. This met with approval at City Hall, so the Rouse Company was asked to proceed and develop the financial implications.

There was talk of a project costing well over $300 million, with the city as landowner contributing $100 million to put the pier and buildings in structurally sound condition, link the project to Lake Shore Drive—the major north-south thoroughfare—and provide public transportation service. But $100 million was clearly more than the city could handle, so officials agreed on $60 million.

The Rouse Company submitted their 55-page financial report in February 1981. They would arrange $217 million of financing for costs of the marketplace, hotel, parking garage, children's play park, all common and service areas, promenade improvements, on-pier shuttle service and on-pier utilities. This, plus the city's $60 million, brought total estimated project cost to $277 million. Mayor Byrne asked her people to negotiate a Letter of Intent for The Rouse Company to develop Navy Pier as outlined in these reports.

Heading negotiations for the City of Chicago was the tall, graying, easygoing public works commissioner, Jerome R. Butler. After graduating from "Harvard on the Rocks," he started work as an assistant city architect in 1960. This was during the administration of legendary potentate Mayor Richard J. Daley. Butler helped design just about every kind of building the city put up, from libraries, courthouses, police stations, senior citizen centers and health facilities to O'Hare International Airport—he has a wall full of design awards. He was a city architect in 1979 when Mayor Byrne asked him to head the Public Works Department, which was responsible, among other things, for managing Navy Pier.

Most negotiations took place in Butler's cozy fourth floor conference room at City Hall. Trouble started right away, as Chicago officials played musical chairs. Rouse people shuttled to Chicago for a meeting with officials who inexplicably turned out to be someplace else. When they'd come prepared for four people, they'd find the conference room jammed with a couple of dozen. A law firm was brought in—reportedly a big contributor to Mayor Byrne's political campaign—which had little prior experience with real estate. Sometimes three of their attorneys would appear, sometimes one or two, and on many occasions there were none at all—though they presented the city with legal bills totaling $163,000. The city hired hotel consultants to call some shots. A traffic official got involved. A sewer official showed up to render his business opinions.

There was agonizing gridlock. Considerable time was lost briefing everybody in the parade. None of these officials had experience developing real estate, they became so cautious they were afraid to make key decisions that would move the project forward.

Although the city was contributing less than half the value of the deal, officials insisted that to sell it politically, they had to have a 50-50 split of any profits. The Rouse people agreed. Then officials wanted to be able to tell the public there would be ground rent. So Rouse proposed that the first $500,000 of cash flow go to the city, the second $500,000 to Rouse, the third $500,000 to the city and so on until each side had $2 million. Thereafter, cash flow would be split 50-50. This way, officials could cite the $2 million figure as ground rent.

To finance the project at an economical cost, Rouse needed an agreement that the city would subordinate its interest in the new pier buildings to the lender. This meant that in the event of default, a lender could seek to recover the money by taking over the buildings, and the city wouldn't interfere.

But city officials didn't want to lose control over the site. They were specifically afraid that it would end up being used for things they didn't approve of. After months of back and forth, language was worked out where the city recognized Rouse's need for subordinated interest, and Rouse recognized the city's need for assurance that the site wouldn't be used for unauthorized purposes.

By July 1982, negotiations were done on a nine-page Letter of Intent. So after a tedious 18 months, there wasn't even a binding document. Any entrepreneur would wonder whether this was a smart way to spend time. The Rouse people decided to persevere, since Navy Pier was such a fantastic location.

The Chicago City Council approved the Letter of Intent and gave Rouse and city negotiators another 18 months to agree on terms for a 30-year lease.

City officials became more and more fearful of risk. They worried that if the project were unprofitable, there wouldn't be any revenue for the city. That $2 million involved a formula for dividing cash flow, not a guarantee. So they began insisting on a minimum annual rent. Rouse agreed to a nominal $200,000.

Then officials agonized that by subordinating their interest to a lender, they would appear to be giving away the store. That little provision could be a political time bomb. So they pushed Rouse to eliminate it. Rouse countered that without subordinated interest, financing costs would be quite a few million dollars higher. If they had to swallow this, the money would have to be made back elsewhere in the project. Discussions continued, but the issue remained unresolved.

Any lease agreement needed approval by Chicago's City Council, and it wasn't likely to act unless there were widespread public support. So Butler, other city officials and the Rouse people talked about Navy Pier with whoever would listen. Butler spoke at the Chicago Chamber of Commerce, Union League Club, American Bar Association, American Institute of Architects, Merchandise Mart, University Club and Chicago Athletic Club. He argued that while many ideas for Navy Pier might be wonderful, the Rouse proposal was the only one on the horizon that had a prayer of being financed and getting done.

Opposition began building among merchants on North Michigan Avenue and State Street who feared new competition. State Street merchants were particularly hostile, since that once great retail district lost affluent shoppers to Michigan Avenue during the 1970s. Goldblatt's State Street department store closed. Sales volume at Marshall Field's nineteenth century State Street store ranked well behind their new Michigan Avenue store. Fashionable shops gave way to discounters catering to poor blacks. As far as State Street merchants were concerned, Navy Pier might be a death blow. These merchants made friends with wily Alderman Bernard Stone, who wanted Navy Pier to become a national park like Yosemite and Yellowstone.

During the two decades when "Hizzoner" Mayor Daley was around, he settled such controversies by knocking heads together. Chicago was known as a city that worked. Nobody since Daley has had that much power. Certainly Jane Byrne didn't. More than anything else, Navy Pier needed a nod from a personable, quick-witted man across the street from City Hall, holding court in a shabby fifth floor office at the Bismarck Hotel. His enemies called him Fast Eddie.

Edward R. Vrdolyak was alderman for Chicago's South Side Tenth Ward, and he headed the so-called 29 who controlled the city council. Once a pliable greased palm for Mayor Daley, the City Council had, under Vrdolyak's relentless prodding, acquired enough clout to make life impossible for anyone who stood in the way. That included the current mayor.

Vrdolyak's business was trading favors. When he wasn't on the phone, he was taking care of people who waited in his cream-colored outer office with a frayed green rug. Some people hoped for a job. Ward residents wanted local nuisances taken care of. Other people needed help out of a legal jam. For each favor he collected an IOU.

Despite being often surrounded by controversy, Vrdolyak did all right for himself. He had a comfortable home, a horse farm in Michigan and a vacation home on Marco Island, Florida where he liked to fish. "I don't know how to swim," he laughs. "Much to the chagrin of my enemies, I don't even know how to float."

He was controversial enough to feel the need for a half-dozen bodyguards, one of whom served as his chauffeur, driving a dark-blue bulletproof Fleetwood Cadillac. Once he inadvertently referred to it as a limousine, and that indiscreet suggestion of prosperity became a minor political flap.

A secret of Vrdolyak's popularity and power is his earthy touch. He's proud of his humble beginnings. His father Peter emigrated from Selo Slivno, Yugoslavia to the Minnesota iron mines. Peter Vrdolyak married, had four children and, after his wife died, returned to Selo Slivno where he married Matilda. They returned to the United States, settled in Chicago and had three children. Edward was the youngest.

Peter operated the South Chicago Beer Garden, a neighborhood bar. "There was a fortune teller next door and a gypsy downstairs," Vrdolyak recalls. The place was patronized by ironmongers, mill workers and seamen.

When Vrdolyak was 12, he opted for the priesthood, enrolling at St. Francis of Assisi Seminary in Westmont. He endured the rigorous self-denials for four years. "By the time I was 16," he says, "I didn't think I could go through with it." He finished his senior year at Mt. Carmel High School and earned money working in a Swift & Company packinghouse.

During his first year at the University of Chicago Law School, in 1960, he was indicted for murder. The charges were dismissed 10 months later, but meanwhile he was suspended from the law school and humiliated. "It teaches me not to believe what one person says about another," he says. "Especially if it's printed in the media."

While studying for his bar examination in 1963, he worked as a precinct captain serving Tenth ward alderman Emil Pacini, an acquaintance of his father. When votes were counted, Pacini lost the ward, but Vrdolyak helped carry the precinct by knocking on doors and offering to do people favors if they'd vote for his candidate. "I liked getting the job done," he says. "I liked it when somebody said 'I need a tree cut . . . a garbage can . . . an abandoned car towed away' and I could get it done."

For years, Vrdolyak scrambled. He married Denise Danaher, and they lived in what was described as a shack behind his father's bar. After he was sworn in as a lawyer in May 1963, Vrdolyak borrowed enough money from his father to start his practice at 91st Street and Commercial. He handled mostly personal injury cases, for which

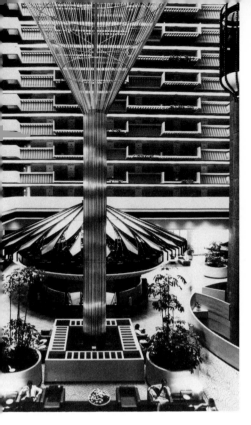

When it opened in 1967, the spectacular 22-story atrium of the Atlanta Hyatt Regency Hotel (*left*) helped secure fame for architect and entrepreneur John Portman (*seated below*). (Atrium photo credit: Atlanta Hyatt Regency Hotel; Portman photo credit: Portman Properties)

The most valuable property in Dallas—Trammell Crow's complex of merchandise marts and hotels. It is the city's greatest drawing card. (Dallas Market Center)

Trammell Crow

The Reichmann's World Financial Center, at Manhattan's southwestern tip, includes the 51-story tower here under construction, which will be the new headquarters of American Express. (Olympia & York Developments, Ltd.)

Vienna-born Albert, Paul and Ralph Reichmann (*left to right*) fled the Nazis to Tangier, then emigrated to Canada where they bought an aging tile company and parlayed it into Olympia & York, North America's largest real estate company. (The Globe and Mail, Toronto)

Architect Philip Johnson (*left*) helped introduce the International Style to America. In recent years, with his partner John Burgee (*right*), they have led a trend toward distinctive styles.

Downtown Houston skyline shaped by Gerald D. Hines. He commissioned I. M. Pei to design the tall, slender Texas Commerce Tower at far left. Philip Johnson and John Burgee designed the short, dark trapezoids of Pennzoil Place, as well as the spiked, Dutch-gabled Republic Bank Center immediately to its right. (Gerald D. Hines Interests)

Chinese architect I. M. Pei is among those who continue to pursue the spare, elegant geometry of modern architecture. (Evelyn Hofer)

Cesar Pelli is transforming a lower Manhattan sandbar into the greatest urban complex since Rockefeller Center a half century ago. (Cesar Pelli & Associates)

"Buy real estate!" Harry Helmsley's mother advised. So the would-be tycoon began buying used buildings at distress prices. Helmsley now controls an estimated $5 billion in real estate.

hicago attorney Neil Bluhm earned his fortune hitching real estate syndication to the marketing out of major brokerage houses during the 1970s. is JMB Realty Corporation is the largest ndicator, with $12 billion of property. (JMB ealty Corp.)

Superbroker Kenneth D. Laub chats with New York's Mayor Edward Koch about markers describing the historical significance of selected Manhattan locations. During his career, Laub has probably earned $50 million brokering Manhattan property. (Steve Friedman)

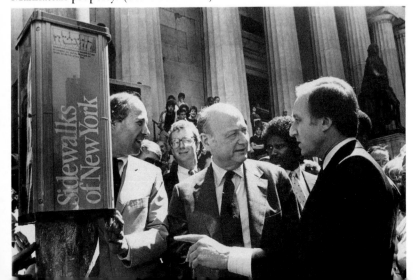

Manhattan's Donald Trump, 39, is wo
an estimated $400 million. Here he surv
his domain in the peach marble and bras
atrium of Trump Tower. (Don Hogan
Charles/New York Times)

Lobby of Hallmark's Kansas City Hyatt Regency Hotel, after two skywa
collapsed, killing 114 people and injuring 239.

Here you see the dramatic impact of construction managers who keep a job on schedule. The barren 600-acre Orlando, Florida site (*top*) cleared for construction of Disney's EPCOT Center. EPCOT Center (*above*) was ready for opening just two years later on October 1, 1982. (Tishman Realty & Construction)

Milton Gerstman, second from right, was the Tishman Company's construction boss responsible for building EPCOT Center. (Tishman Realty & Construction)

John Tishman invented construction management, and built such mammoth projects as Chicago's John Hancock Center, Detroit's Renaissance Center, and New York's World Trade Center. (Tishman Realty & Construction)

he was accused of ambulance chasing. "If you open a law office at 91st and Commercial," he snaps, "you do not get a lot of antitrust work."

Gradually, things began to look up, and he bought a building at 85th Street and Stony Island Boulevard where he moved his office. He seemed to thrive without a partner. "The harder I worked, the luckier I got," he grins.

In 1966, there was grumbling in his neighborhood about the incumbent alderman, John Buchanan. Vrdolyak decided to run against him. But Buchanan countered by proposing that if Vrdolyak agreed not to run, he'd back the young lawyer for committeeman. Vrdolyak accepted.

The incumbent committeeman, however, was a crony of Richard Daley. Vrdolyak donned his good suit and called on the Mayor. "I told him that if I succeeded, I would like to work within the system," Vrdolyak recalls. "I wanted to do a good job helping people in the ward, and the way to do that was to work within the system." Daley consolidated his power by working with just about everybody, so he welcomed Vrdolyak's initiative and respect for the established order. "You win your race, and I'll help," Daley reportedly said.

In June 1968, Vrdolyak won his race by 497 votes. It was the first time in half a century that an outsider had beaten a machine committeeman. "A tremendous victory," Vrdolyak exults. "You just don't go out and beat an incumbent committeeman."

Looking for an issue which would help further his ambitions, Vrdolyak found busing. "I had a child in public school then, and they were going to bus kids all over. I'm for neighborhood schools. You buy a home, you make an investment, and that's where your kids should go."

He formed the Tenth Ward Citizens Committee for Neighborhood Schools and declared that if the school board proceeded to bus kids, thousands of people from the South Side would stage protests. Within weeks, the busing scheme was abandoned. Vrdolyak was underway.

In 1970, according to the *Chicago Sun-Times,* "Vrdolyak charged that Alderman Buchanan spitefully held up approval of water mains in a development where his sister, Mrs. Henry R. Simmons, is building a home at 11445 S. Ewing. 'Because of this matter,' said Vrdolyak, 'I might very well run against him.' "

It was a nasty cat fight. When somebody wanted a tree removed, Vrdolyak would do them a favor and get the job done fast. The tree would appear in front of Alderman Buchanan's house. Vrdolyak would arrange to tow away an abandoned car, and that, too, would be deposited at Alderman Buchanan's house. Vrdolyak won the election by 2,500 votes.

Alderman Thomas Keane was imprisoned for crooked land deals, and Mayor Daley asked Vrdolyak to assume some of Keane's parliamentary responsibilities in the City Council. Vrdolyak ran for county assessor against Mayor Daley's candidate Thomas Tully and was clobbered, but the mayor still cultivated Vrdolyak's goodwill. In 1975, he was appointed chairman of the powerful, scandal-prone Buildings and Zoning Committee.

Mayor Daley died suddenly on December 20, 1976, triggering a power scramble. As president *pro tem* of the city council, Thirty-fourth Ward Alderman Wilson Frost declared that he was acting mayor. But he was black, and it was unheard of for Chicago to have a black mayor. So a deal was cut. Daley's favorite Michael Bilandic, alderman in Daley's Eleventh Ward and chairman of the finance committee, became acting mayor provided he pledge not to run for mayor in the next election. Frost became chairman of the finance committee, so the black community was mollified. Vrdolyak was named president *pro tem,* and he would occupy Bilandic's chair when Bilandic was away.

"What the deal did was make sure that the way we had been functioning would not change," Vrdolyak says. If this backroom maneuvering didn't make much of a stir at the time, it signaled that power in Chicago was shifting away from the mayor to the city council.

In the 1977 special election following Daley's death, Bilandic ignored his previous deal and decided to run for mayor. He won handily. Harold Washington, a 54-year-old state senator and newcomer to citywide elections, got 11 percent of the vote. He's an intense, charming man and charismatic speaker, the first black to make a serious bid as Chicago mayor.

As the 1979 election approached, Bilandic decided to run for reelection. Polls showed him favored by more than 80 percent of voters. Rival Jane Byrne, former city consumer affairs commissioner, had an 8 percent rating. Then came the blizzards. The city snarled with snow, and Bilandic seemed helpless. Vrdolyak's Tenth Ward, however, was clear, for he had arranged to use equipment belonging to U.S. Steel, Wisconsin Steel and Interlake, which had plants in the Ward. Vrdolyak's ward gave Bilandic the second-highest number of votes among all the city's wards, but Byrne won the election.

After campaigning as a reformer who would shake things up, she let Vrdolyak reorganize the city council. Lacking experience in aldermanic wars, apparently she wasn't eager for a fight with him. Vrdolyak became chairman of the Cook County Democratic Party, a post that was the cornerstone of Mayor Daley's power.

In turn, he supported her as she hiked taxes by $400 million and pushed spending up 40 percent to almost $2 billion. He agreed to help her promote the Rouse proposal on Navy Pier. If he and the other alderman had civic good in their hearts, they were also eyeing the potential goodies—legal work, engineering contracts, construction contracts, maintenance contracts and other enticing rewards for friends.

However, Navy Pier negotiations went nowhere. It didn't help that musical chairs continued, as a different cast of characters showed up at City Hall practically every week to try negotiating a lease agreement with Rouse.

City officials acknowledged that it would be difficult for them to come up with the $60 million Mayor Byrne promised to invest in Navy Pier. Rouse negotiators Michael Spear and Williams Fulton proposed so-called tax increment financing, used by many other cities to help finance urban development. This means tax revenues generated by development would become available as the city's capital contribution. The Rouse people estimated tax increment financing here could raise perhaps $40 million.

City officials grumbled that school districts would expect their customary cut, and there would be a furor if they didn't get it. The Rouse people countered that school districts never got anything from Navy Pier before, since nobody had figured out how to put it on a paying basis. How could they lose what they never had? The issue was unresolved.

Meanwhile, events at City Hall didn't bode well for Rouse. Though Mayor Byrne conceded power to Vrdolyak, she was a contentious person who didn't observe many niceties of Chicago's political stewpot. She appointed two white women and a white man to the Chicago Housing Authority, angering the black community. This and other swats at machine traditions multiplied her enemies.

In the primary for the 1983 election, she was challenged by Harold Washington, and this time people began to take him seriously. He blamed Mayor Byrne for the city losing jobs. Appearing with him on speakers' platforms was his fiancée Mary Ella Smith, the demure daughter of a Pullman porter who became an elementary schoolteacher.

With a booming voice, he appealed to blacks who were a majority in Chicago. "We've been giving white candidates our votes for years unstintingly," he thundered in black churches, "hoping they would include us in the political process, while knowing they probably wouldn't.

"We've been pushed, shoved, murdered, emasculated. Our families have been systematically disrupted. There's been an unfair distribution of goodies. We influence no institutions in this country except our own. We have no power. We have no land.

"But through all that struggle, we've stayed together. We've maintained our equanimity. We've become more courageous. We've become more tolerant. We've become more understanding. We are humanitarian. We have elevated Amazing Grace to the level of an art. Now it's our turn. When I'm elected, you won't have to fight City Hall. You will be City Hall."

Washington grew up in a brawling South Side neighborhood where he was a skilled hurdler and boxer. "I could pick up $5 to $15 boxing over a weekend," he recalls. "I never got hurt. I was a reasonably good second-rate amateur fighter."

Washington loved political intrigue. His father, Roy, was an attorney, police court prosecutor, assistant Chicago corporation counsel, Democratic precinct captain in the Third Ward and second-generation Methodist minister. His parents were divorced when Washington was young, and his father got custody. "For years, he was not only my father," Washington recalls, "he was my mother. So I knew who Santa Claus was. He came home every night, put his feet under the table and had dinner with me."

After three years as an Air Force engineer during World War II, he enrolled at Roosevelt College with financial help from the GI Bill. It was a 95 percent white institution, yet Washington displayed enough charm to get elected class president and president of the student senate. Then he earned a law degree at Northwestern University. He married during the mid-1940s but was divorced a decade later.

Though he inherited his father's law practice and became assistant corporation counsel after his father's death in 1953, Washington never made much money as an attorney. He couldn't always pay property taxes on a building his father bequeathed him. His toughest years were during the 1960s when he sometimes earned less than $10,000. For four years, he didn't bother to file income tax returns, and when the IRS caught up with him, he was jailed for 36 days and fined $1,036.

His financial situation didn't improve much during the seventies. The Illinois Supreme Court suspended his law license from 1970 to 1976, because he allegedly cheated a half-dozen clients. He admitted that he took their money and did no work.

He drifted into politics. During the 1960s, he ran Alderman Ralph Metcalfe's Third Ward political machine. He was elected state representative from the Twenty-sixth District in 1965. He served for 11 years, winning reelection by wide margins despite censure in the legal profession. Then he was elected a state senator. His fiery speeches were credited with influencing many votes. He made his first bid for the Chicago mayoralty in 1977. Four years later, he was elected Congressman from the First District.

He beat Jane Byrne in the 1982 Democratic primary. Soon he was huddling with Vrdolyak. Though the alderman promised his support, there was speculation that he favored the Republican candidate Bernard Epton, who was popular in Vrdolyak's ward. Washington enraged Democratic regulars by pledging to reform the patronage system and dismantle the political machine.

As might be expected, all of Washington's past mistakes were aired during the election—his failure to file tax returns, his fine, time in jail, and the loss of his law license. There were further allegations: that he was a deadbeat in Springfield and Chicago, with unpaid bills going back five years.

At the very least, he seemed disorganized. He was slow to make decisions about his campaign team. He invited opponents to a debate, then appeared 45 minutes late. Frequently he kept his own supporters waiting more than an hour for a speech. He didn't show up at all for an interview with Wally Phillips, a radio personality who had a million listeners.

Generally an adept politician, he made some inexplicable blunders. Among the most memorable was an appeal for votes among inmates at Cook County Jail, where he had spent time for income tax evasion. Local televisions gleefully displayed his mug shot.

Since politicians were preoccupied by the election, it was useless to try generating support for Navy Pier. But the negotiations always had dragged along so slowly that the election didn't make much difference. The Rouse people were losing their patience.

Washington's election was followed by a scramble for 900 patronage jobs. He axed a thousand city workers and angered labor unions. Business leaders didn't know what to expect, since he never talked much with them.

Rouse President Mathias DeVito and Executive Vice President Michael Spear met with Mayor Washington and briefed him on the Navy Pier project. He became decidedly supportive.

Jerome Butler continued as commissioner of public works, but Mayor Washington appointed University of Illinois economics professor Robert Mier as commissioner of economic development, and he became the chief point man on the Navy Pier project. The short and stocky Mier told Rouse people that since Mayor Washington had campaigned on a promise to revitalize neighborhoods rather than downtown, the Navy Pier project had to be linked in some way to neighborhoods. Approval for any Navy Pier lease required, among other things, that the Rouse Company agree to donate cash or expertise or both for some neighborhood project. The Rouse people agreed in principle, but the issue wasn't resolved.

Mayor Washington fired former Mayor Byrne's favored law firm, whose members wandered in and out of the Navy Pier negotiations. He brought in attorney Robert Newman from the Chicago firm Arvey, Hodes, Costello & Berman. Unlike the previous attorneys, Newman had plenty of real estate experience. He was also a partner of Mayor Washington's buddy, Corporation Counsel James Montgomery.

Nonetheless, negotiations stalled. The city officials Mayor Washington appointed were quick to say that the $60 million Mayor Byrne promised for Navy Pier was a pipedream. It never existed. Furthermore, the city's credit was definitely unavailable. Mayor Washington's officials were more willing to consider tax increment financing.

They demanded more upfront money: a $1 million minimum guaranteed annual rent instead of $200,000. They weren't willing to give up a percentage of any profits in return. The Rouse people balked.

There was mounting concern at City Hall about taking any financial risk. Officials wanted The Rouse Company to assume more of the project financing. To defer costs, officials proposed building new access ramps connecting Lake Shore Drive to Navy Pier a little at a time instead of all at once. The Rouse people objected that it was no way to do a project which would probably attract in excess of 16 million people a year.

Rouse people insisted that if the city couldn't provide convenient linkages to the mass transit system which met their exacting standards, The Rouse Company reserved the right to step in and do the job by private means, charging the cost to the city. Buses must run on a reliable, frequent schedule between Navy Pier and downtown hotels, the subways and train stations. The buses must be cleaned on a set schedule, and they must be safe. City officials responsible for Chicago's miserable bus system suspected they couldn't meet these standards, and they didn't want to be stuck with the tab. The point remained a loose end.

Seemingly small issues chewed up tremendous chunks of time. When city officials realized Navy Pier needed a place for buses to turn around and people to wait comfortably, they maintained it was part of Navy Pier—The Rouse Company should pay for it. Estimated price tag: several million dollars. Rouse people countered that since such a place was a bus station, it was properly part of the transit system, which the city should take care of.

If Mayor Washington intended to push Navy Pier, he soon became embroiled in ever more bitter battles with Vrdolyak. "The people in my ward knew Washington wasn't showing any friendship to me or the other committeemen," Vdrolyak explains. "He wouldn't come to a rally in our ward. He was appealing only to blacks. He had been convicted of income tax problems, and he had those problems with his law license. A black without those problems would have gotten a lot more white votes."

In the face-off that loomed with Vrdolyak, the mayor had formidable advantages. First of all, nobody in recent memory had won an important battle against a Chicago mayor—patronage plums, contracts and services to the wards helped consolidate considerable power. Washington was backed by 16 black aldermen and five white liberals. He was just five short of a city council majority.

His idea was to show he was a reformer. The Sunday after his election, he met with his strategists, and they agreed that Vrdolyak should be ousted as president *pro tem* and chairman of the Buildings and Zoning Committee.

Washington figured he could intimidate Vrdolyak. He told the alderman he was finished. Vrdolyak would have to give up both his prestigious posts. While Vrdolyak agreed to surrender as president *pro tem*, so the mayor could have his own man representing him when he was gone, giving up the chairmanship of Buildings and Zoning was out of the question. "It was a manhood thing," Vrdolyak insists. "He was trying to strip me of my manhood."

At this point, Washington's weaknesses began to show. He lacked city council experience. He didn't seem to have Vrdolyak's tenacity. The Cook County Democratic Party chairman was a street fighter who could appeal to the city council's white majority.

Vrdolyak's game was to obstruct the mayor wherever he could, and he pursued it with finesse. He got on the phone and persuaded 28 city council members that it was in their interest to vote as a bloc. Washington threatened them all, he argued, and they should sign an oath affirming their allegiance. Vrdolyak concluded with a convincing flourish: he would resign as chairman of Buildings and Zoning to demonstrate that he didn't seek the alliance for personal gain.

If Washington had cultivated their loyalty, some may have gone with him, but Washington didn't call. He wasn't wise to the crucial importance of stroking. "I wasn't going to kiss their asses," he told a reporter. Washington made overtures only after the aldermen had signed the oath with Vrdolyak. It was too late. The Oath of 29, as it was called, was hung with pride on many aldermanic office walls.

Vrdolyak enlisted sophisticated advice from attorney David Epstein who had counseled Washington. "I had done work for him in Springfield and helped him against Byrne," Epstein said. "When he got elected, I made four or five phone calls to him. Eddie asked me: 'Did he ever call you back?' I had to say no. So Eddie said: 'Give him until five o'clock. If he doesn't call you back, then you make your decision.'" Washington didn't respond, and Epstein became a Vrdolyak ally.

As long as Vrdolyak could control 26 votes, he'd have his way in the city council. Epstein and Vrdolyak plotted how to handle different situations as if they were planning D-Day. They concluded that the biggest blunder Washington could make would be to get angry and storm out of the city council chambers. That's what he did, and it solidified Vrdolyak's power.

Vrdolyak did more. He modeled his press operation after that of Earl Bush, who worked for Mayor Daley, assiduously building up his reputation among community newspapers. Vrdolyak hired a shrewd press agent named Joe Novak, who passed dirt about his opponents to reporters and generated a stream of positive stories for his man. At Novak's suggestion, Vrdolyak held a press conference where he proposed saving children's lives by requiring seat belts in school buses. Whatever the feasibility of the idea, it got ink about Vrdolyak's concern for children. By contrast, Mayor Washington's press aide Grayson Mitchell always seemed to be playing catch-up, reacting to events.

The sniping got worse. "Is Washington effective?" Vrdolyak asked. "No. Does he put the hours in? No. Can he make a decision? No. Does he know how to bring people together? Not yet. Can you trust him? I don't know. He never gave me his word except to say he was going to call me back once, and he never did. I don't think he's a bad man. He's 61, never been a businessman, never an effective legislator, and he has great difficulty with basic arithmetic, like filing his tax returns, and great difficulty doing work for the poor and indigent from whom he took legal fees. Now everybody expects him to change because he's mayor."

These battles looked to many observers as a clever ploy to show that each politician was fighting for his constituents. Under-the-table deals, it was expected, would still be cut. But the battles became dirtier.

Racism was a recurring issue. "In the bungalow wards, the wards where people might have already moved once or twice to get away from blacks," said an aide to Vrdolyak, "you're going to find real racism among people and their leaders. I'm not going to deny that racism plays a big part in what happens in this city. Aldermen reflect the concerns of their constituents.

"But as guilty as our side is of racism, the other side is just as guilty. Harold Washington gets up and exhorts his race to vote for him on the basis of race. The 29 are reflecting a few decades of frustration. When they say 'race,' it's racism. When Washington says 'race,' it's pride. I believe that the 29 do less race baiting than Harold Washington. They are tired of it, and they want him gone."

As the politicians raged at each other the 18-month deadline approached for concluding Navy Pier negotiations, but the Rouse people were losing interest. They were asked to assume all the risks politicians wanted to avoid, while paying more money upfront and reducing their potential profits. Despite Commissioner Mier's encouragement, Rouse and city officials were so far apart that further negotiations seemed pointless.

Even if a lease were negotiated, the fights between Vrdolyak and Mayor Washington doomed it in the city council. Everybody seemed to have different ideas about what should be done with Navy Pier, though nobody had money. Mayor Washington argued that developing it without retailing would be impractical. He claimed they could get their hands on federal dollars, so taxpayers around the country would help pay the city's part of the deal. Some aldermen favored housing rather than stores and a hotel on Navy Pier. Alderman Roman Pucinski had long wanted to turn Navy Pier into a municipal gambling casino whose revenues could help ease the city's financial strains. Unable to decide anything, the city council, on December 28, 1983, extended the deadline for Rouse negotiations until February 15, 1984.

Throughout these interminable disputes, Navy Pier was closed to the public. Yet minimum required maintenance was costing the city $450,000 a year. Frank Perry, one of the two janitors who did a little sweeping from time to time, reported life was rather dull.

On February 3, 1984, Mayor Washington asked the city council to again extend the deadline for reaching an agreement with Rouse until June 30. He pleaded for more time to convince opponents that what Rouse offered was "the best possible package." Washington claimed there was less opposition from merchants near Navy Pier, and it was appropriate to move ahead.

Butler and Mier testified that the city could raise its $60 million through tax revenues generated by the project. They doubted another developer could be found to mobilize $220 million needed for doing it. Butler asked that the deadline for negotiations with Rouse be extended to June 30. More negotiations would cost the city nothing, he argued. The city would have to spend $60 million to make the pier safe, whether or not Rouse developed it.

Mayor Washington reminded aldermen that in the event the city broke off negotiations, the original letter of intent required the city to compensate Rouse for up to $1 million of costs they incurred working on the plan. However, his negotiators persuaded Rouse to reduce the city's liability to $450,000.

Alderman Bernard Stone, chairman of the joint committee which ruled against the negotiations, said he didn't know of anything that would win votes in the city council. "Mier and Butler told me they were talking with Rouse, and I said, 'Go ahead and talk.' So far I'm not convinced I'm wrong, and no one has done anything to change my mind."

The Rouse plan was killed February 6 when a special joint Chicago City Council committee refused to extend the deadline. The 15 to 5 vote reflected the Vrdolyak-Washington split. Mayor Washington denounced the vote as "irresponsible, incomprehensible and clearly against the city's best interest." Vrdolyak declared: "The city's got a white elephant, and if you fixed it, that doesn't mean you wouldn't have a bigger white elephant."

The *Chicago Tribune* growled: "Of course, the very aldermen who are now so anxious to pull this project out from under Mayor Washington were propping it up under the last administration, when it was just another of the Byrne administration's extravagant side shows. The project then had no thought behind it, no financial plan and was an obvious threat to State Street and North Loop development. While Navy Pier remains far less important than the North Loop, if both can be done they should be."

Scott Ditch, Rouse vice president of public affairs, groans: "We're straight players. If the mayor is supposed to be in charge, we go to the mayor. We don't try to divine hidden meanings or hidden agendas. We have too much business in too many places to do it any other way."

Rouse Development Director Fulton took over a project called the Gallery at Harborplace, Baltimore—a $200-million office-hotel-retail project near that city's lovely Inner Harbor. "What a relief," he says, "to do business with somebody straightforward like Baltimore's Mayor Schaefer."

Executive Vice President Michael Spear was already involved with urban retail projects across the country: South Street Seaport in New York, Union Station in St. Louis, Bayside in Miami, Riverwalk in New Orleans, Riverfront in Jacksonville, Pioneer Place in Portland (Oregon), West Lake in Seattle and Yuerba Buena Gardens in San Francisco.

On February 18, Charles Swibel, a politically influential businessman who was former chairman of the Chicago Housing Authority under Mayor Byrne, proposed bringing Edward DeBartolo in to develop Navy Pier. Based in Youngston, Ohio, De Bartolo was the largest U.S. retail developer, with 52 shopping malls in 20 states. DeBartolo was known locally as a sportsman who tried to buy the Chicago White Sox, but Baseball Commissioner Bowie Kuhn nixed the deal because DeBartolo also owned several racetracks that offered parimutuel betting. Nothing ever came of this pipedream.

Mayor Washington suggested that the prospect of a deal with DeBartolo may have motivated the city council to kill the Rouse plan. "You have to put two and two together," said the mayor's deputy press secretary Chris Chandler. "It certainly appears that Vrdolyak is trying to get Rouse out and his group in."

In Mayor Washington's State of the City Address, delivered April 15, 1984, he reaffirmed his desire to turn the city away from "the old way of doing things, which relies upon political patronage and inside contracts." He advocated "merit and merit alone." It was a slap against Vrdolyak and his allies.

Alderman Edward Burke, an opponent of the mayor, charged: "The Mayor is more interested in politics than government." He claimed the City Council was ready to act, but it was waiting for the mayor to submit workable plans.

Bickering continued. Mayor Washington blocked a new soccer field for Vrdolyak's Tenth Ward and a new branch library for the Daley family's Eleventh Ward. Mayor Washington backed a plan for a movie studio in the Near West Side, but the city council buried it. Alderman Vrdolyak's brother Peter appealed his firing from his $47,000 a year job as a city inspector. He claimed the dismissal was politically motivated.

Few were surprised when Chicago lost its A bond rating. In March 1984, Moody's Investors Service downgraded the city to Baa. Moody's cited a "pattern of financial strain." The lower rating would cost the city hundreds of thousands of dollars in additional interest payments on borrowings, making it harder for the city to fulfill its end of the bargain on major projects like any future renovation of Navy Pier.

People everywhere became aware of the Washington-Vrdolyak brawl during the July 1984 Democratic National Convention. The night Walter Mondale was to be nominated, CBS correspondent Ed Bradley interviewed Washington on camera. Washington boasted that he could deliver Chicago voters for the Democratic ticket in November, and he challenged Alderman Vrdolyak to do as well. Since Vrdolyak was standing behind Bradley, the reporter said, "Let's ask him."

"Turn that camera off, and don't ever do that again," Washington snapped. He pointed his finger at Bradley, spun around and sat down. In a subsequent exchange, Washington branded Bradley as "totally and completely bad, and I'm surprised a man of your high caliber and moral standards would stoop to such a thing." Washington demanded an apology from CBS. Bradley replied that he didn't need the mayor's permission to talk with the alderman. "A perfect example of the problems that exist in the city of Chicago and Cook County," he told CBS anchor Dan Rather.

Vrdolyak got into an imbroglio, too, only his involved Republicans. In June he reportedly asked a Republican Congressman to arrange a secret Washington meeting with President Reagan's chief of staff James Baker and political honcho Edward Rollins. Vrdolyak was said to have expressed a desire to even a personal score against Mayor Washington and Walter Mondale by frustrating Democratic get-out-the-vote efforts. Word was that before he'd do that, he'd need a little folding green. Recalling Watergate, Reagan's lieutenants declined.

When the *Chicago Tribune* reported the rendezvous, Vrdolyak issued a denial. "Insane," he declared. "Absolutely and totally false. I wouldn't know those guys if they were standing right in front of me." Within eight hours, he acknowledged there was a meeting, but they discussed only Tenth Ward business. The White House, he seemed to suggest, was devoting time to street cleaning services and playground repairs in his neighborhood.

The revelations inspired gadfly Mike Royko in the *Chicago Sun-Times:* "Now, we all know that Chicago aldermen consider snatching, grabbing and filching to be a normal part of their public duty. Some consider it an almost sacred trust.

"But most of them have limited aspirations. They hustle small businessmen who don't want to be plagued by city inspectors, or contractors who need building permits. They hustle their patronage workers and job-seekers and anybody else who needs a favor.

"Those aldermen who also are lawyers—a menacing combination—have a broader range of hustles. They squeeze clients who come to them because they are presumed to have clout with judges, police and prosecutors.

"And a select few, such as the legendary Tom Keane, had the skill and vision to extend their hustles beyond mere ward matters or the corridors of City Hall. They rub wallets with the big bankers and builders of LaSalle Street.

"But none of them—not even such great pocket-stuffers as Keane, Paddy Bauler, Hinky Dink or Bathhouse John—ever did what Vrdolyak recently tried to do: hustle a United States President."

From time to time, Mayor Washington reaffirmed his support for the Rouse plan, even though negotiations had officially broken off. Chicago newspapers reported talk that Navy Pier was still being considered. But nothing happened.

The 29, however, continued to denounce Rouse and the mayor. Bernard Stone of the Fiftieth Ward insisted that the plan would turn the pier into a "ticky-tacky collection of souvenir shops." He accused the mayor of "beating a dead horse." Reportedly, he had never seen a Rouse project.

In late November 1984, former Illinois Governor Dan Walker announced a plan by a team of his, Pier Group, which would involve no city financing. It called for 1,000 apartment units, a 500-room hotel, 400-slip marina, 100,000-square-foot entertainment center and three movie theaters. Walker claimed the condos would be financed through First American Savings & Loan, owned by the Walker family. "Rouse just puts activities out there," Walker said. "We'd put a neighborhood there." Another pipedream.

With Rouse out of the picture and the city as broke as ever, the political fighting seemed destined to drag on for years. The only sure thing was that Navy Pier would continue to rust and rot.

To be sure, Mayor Washington commissioned a study called *Navy Pier, A Vision for the Future*. It talked about nice things like parks, exhibitions, cultural events and a marina. There would be very few shops. The study outlined an attempted compromise plan which eliminated controversial commercial, taxpaying components. "This report doesn't go into financing," Butler concedes. "Obviously, the things here would require some kind of subsidy. The city doesn't have money, and I really don't see any federal funding available." Yet another pipedream.

Where were Chicago's business leaders when a respected national company like Rouse was being pasted by politicians? "They were either co-opted or cut off at the knees by Mayor Daley a long time ago," said Janet Malone of TRUST, a forum on urban issues, "and they don't know where to begin."

To be sure, Navy Pier wasn't the only casualty of the political wars. There were further delays in a major North Loop project. Americana Hotels pulled out of partnership that was to have built a hotel downtown at Wacker and State Street. The city spent $10 million to acquire the old Goldblatt's store with the idea of converting it into a new central library—price tag estimated at $60 million—but there weren't any approved plans. City officials wanted to save the State Street Theater, but they didn't have the $16 million they claimed the theater was worth. In any case, theater owners Henry Plitt and Thomas Klutznik insisted on $32 million.

None of this helped Chicago in its bid for business. "Official indecision is the hardest thing to deal with," noted George Lovejoy of Meredith & Grew, among New England's largest real estate firms. "Cities like Boston and Chicago are going against Sun Belt cities, which have their acts together. I took one client to a Florida city, and the key state and local officials met us at a reception. The mayor told my client, 'Everybody you need to get your project through is in this room. We'll do whatever is necessary. How about it?'" At last, people reasoning together.

13.

OUTRAGE AND COMPROMISE

SOMETIMES PROPOSALS TO DEVELOP AN EMPTY SITE WILL EXCITE A firestorm of controversy. Suddenly what seemed like a reasonable business risk may become a dangerous cash drain as delays, unexpected development costs and legal bills spiral out of control. This happened in Boston. Some of the people I talked with there are still licking their wounds.

For two decades, a 9½-acre site in the city's Back Bay tantalized entrepreneurs. It was about as prime as they come. Located between Prudential Center and John Hancock Tower—a couple of blocks from Boston's upscale, trendy Newbury Street shopping district, near the Hynes Auditorium, which was Boston's convention center—this site was potentially one of the most valuable in the city.

Many people thought about how to make money with it over the years. Sears, Roebuck considered buying the land. The University of Massachusetts was interested. Western International wanted to locate a hotel there.

Despite its potential, the site had plenty of problems. It was a spaghetti of commuter railroad tracks, rapid transit tracks, water pipes, electrical cables and six-lane divided Interstate 90 whose exit ramps dispersed cars in three directions. To prepare the whole site for major development without disrupting these functions would cost a prohibitive sum of money, since the ground was landfill requiring special construction techniques—during Victorian times, Back Bay was a swampy delta washed by brackish waters.

Officials of the Massachusetts Turnpike Authority, which owned the site, didn't want to sell the largest parcel, at the southwest corner of Copley Square, because they feared it was the only bait that could motivate a developer to do something constructive with the whole site. Selling this, the "golden triangle," might doom the rest as a permanent blight. So they continued to wait.

The man most responsible for deciding how the site would be developed was John Driscoll, 49, chairman of the Massachusetts Turnpike Authority. He was a friend of John F. Kennedy, and his office walls were filled with Kennedy photographs. Senator Edward Kennedy had recommended that Driscoll become turnpike chairman in 1964 and has urged that he continue since then.

At 36, the ruggedly handsome K. Dun Gifford, formerly with the Boston developer Cabot, Cabot & Forbes, was a wheeler-dealer who went off on his own and had offices in Prudential Center overlooking the site. Also a Kennedy associate, Gifford was with Robert Kennedy the night he was assassinated in Los Angeles, 1968. The more Gifford pondered the site from his window, the more intrigued he became with the possibilities.

After talking with Driscoll about the kinds of projects he might approve, Gifford decided to try assembling a development team. He formed Great Bay Company as the corporate vehicle.

In Boston, more than almost any other city except San Francisco, the choice of an architect is critical. Boston, after all, is a tapestry of Americana. Downtown developers had to design their skyscrapers around the little red brick buildings which survive from Revolutionary War days. No developer would dare suggest tampering with a place like the nineteenth century Old Corner Bookstore—its owner published works by contemporaries like Henry David Thoreau, Oliver Wendell Holmes and Ralph Waldo Emerson. Back Bay is a treasure trove of brownstone Victoriana. In Boston, zealous community groups, historical associations and city officials all scrutinize a proposed building to see whether it will be harmonious with their heritage.

More often than not, Boston projects die on the drawing boards. People resist new development even though, by the 1970s, the downtown still hadn't recovered from the Great Depression. Shoe manufacturing, textiles and other heavy industries left for the Sun Belt. Boston's magnificent harbor, which made the city a trading power during the Revolution, lost its importance as fewer goods were moved by ship. During the 1940s, Boston's roisterous Mayor James Michael Curley—who became a folk hero for taking a civil service exam so a poor constituent could get a Post Office job—campaigned against the business community, and it virtually bowed out of Boston's affairs. Curley was against new development even in the porn district, as one tabloid reported: "Curley Bars New Erections In Scollay Square." Crime menaced. During the mid-1970s, City Hall stumbled toward bankruptcy. Professional people fled to the suburbs. Boston suffered from everything that was wrong with cities. To succeed against these obstacles, a developer needed an exceptionally savvy, sensitive local architect.

Gifford contacted the Cambridge architect Benjamin Thompson, who had finished designing the renovation of Faneuil Hall Marketplace for The Rouse Company. Collaboration with Gifford offered the Thompsons an opportunity to apply their ideas on a larger scale. Gifford moved into their offices in late 1976. Of course, they didn't fancy themselves as the possible developer of the Copley site, because the staggering complexities involved would require a bottomless bank account. But even designing part of such a project was something to stir the imagination.

What entrepreneur could shoulder the task? Not a retail developer alone, because a 9½-acre shopping center wouldn't be economical in central Boston. A developer who did office buildings only wouldn't work either. You certainly couldn't fill the entire site with a hotel.

Gifford thought of the $160-million Water Tower Place, a recently opened, hugely successful, 74-story hunk of beige marble on Chicago's North Michigan Avenue. If it isn't much to look at from the outside—a slab and a box—Water Tower Place is an awesome enterprise.

It includes the 400-room Ritz-Carlton Hotel, which is rated by many as the finest hotel in the United States. There are restaurants, medical offices, a legitimate theater, four movie theaters and 40 floors of condominiums selling for $135,000 to $257,000. It has a snazzy marble, chrome and glass seven-story mall with 100 shops around a central atrium, anchored by Lord & Taylor and Marshall Field's. The recently opened Marshall Field's store at Water Tower Place grosses more than its century-old downtown dowager. Gross revenues of just the hundred stores at Water Tower Place were approaching sales of all other stores along North Michigan Avenue, and that's a retailing hot spot. "I don't know of any other street in the world with such a concentration of retailing wealth," fashion designer Bill Blass remarked.

Entrepreneurs in Boston and elsewhere eyed Water Tower Place to see what might apply to their cities, for at that time it was among the few dramatic successes in a central city area. Like the Boston site, this 50,000-square-foot site was a long time in the making.

Chicago developer Philip Klutznik became interested in it during the early 1960s when it belonged to Canadian liquor baron Samuel Bronfman. The two men were active with some of the same Jewish charities like B'nai B'rith. Klutznik would start talking about Bronfman's Michigan Avenue property. The first price discussed was a million dollars. Each year Klutznik upped his offer a million dollars, and Bronfman always said he didn't want to sell. Finally, at a meeting in Bronfman's office atop the Seagram Building in Manhattan, Klutznik made one more try: $10 million. Bronfman said he'd take it. They wrote a simple agreement on a sheet of legal paper, and they closed for cash about 90 days later.

Born in Kansas City, Missouri, Klutznik was a bold attorney who began developing real estate on a large scale during the 1940s. He built the community of Park Forest, which became a south Chicago suburb of 30,000 people. In the 1950s, he shrewdly caught the trend toward shopping centers, building the biggest ones around Chicago—several over a million square feet. When he made his deal with Bronfman, he was consolidating his various development partnerships into a single company, Urban Investment & Development Corporation. In 1970, he sold this to Aetna Life & Casualty for more than $50 million.

He was a political animal whose interests always extended well beyond business. Presidents Roosevelt and Truman appointed him to the Federal Public Housing Authority. He performed foreign missions for President Johnson. President Ford appointed him to the Advisory Committee on Indo-Chinese Refugees, and he served as Secretary of Commerce under President Carter. He has had a hand in everything from Boy Scouts to the Chicago Lyric Opera to Israel and the National Aeronautics and Space Administration.

Klutznik was the right person for an ambitious project like Water Tower Place. The conventional wisdom of retailing is that malls more than two stories high don't work, because customers won't go up. Retailing has been largely a horizontal business, confined to the ground floor of a high rise. Yet Water Tower Place proposed to lure people up seven floors. Nobody had done that before in the United States. Whoever could pull off Water Tower Place, Dun Gifford thought, could make something of the Copley site.

Philip Klutznik retired from Urban in 1972 to pursue his political and charitable interests, and he was succeeded by his bearded son Thomas. They had worked together during the 1960s, so Thomas Klutznik wasn't a newcomer to real estate. He proved to be as daring and tenacious as his father. He was the one who saw Water Tower Place through to completion. Among other things, he had to buck Aetna executives who were alarmed at the escalating costs and urged that the project be cut short. Urban's assets were about $45 million when he took over, and a decade later he had parlayed these to $800 million.

The man who actually sold Thomas Klutznik on the Boston site was lean, intense 29-year-old Kenneth Himmel who had known Gifford a little when they were both at Cabot, Cabot & Forbes. Himmel is a native of Swampscott, Massachusetts, who graduated from Cornell University's School of Hotel Management. He worked for Colonial Williamsburg and Hilton before joining Cabot, Cabot & Forbes in 1973. A year later, because of his hotel experience, he was appointed project director for the firm's Ritz-Carlton Hotel at Water Tower Place. Cabot, Cabot & Forbes sold its interest in the hotel to Urban, and Himmel stayed on as project director.

Himmel and his wife Janet much preferred living in Boston, so when the shake-out phase of Water Tower Place was finished, Klutznik agreed Himmel should return to Boston and pursue a project there. He got off to a fast start. He loved restaurant operations—it was always his favorite aspect of real estate—so Gifford introduced him to Ben Thompson, who needed help with the troubled Harvest Restaurant in Cambridge. It reportedly lost $200,000 in 1976. Himmel jumped at the chance. "I became a managing partner and brought in a management team to turn the restaurant around," he told me. Gifford handled finances, and Thompson did the interior design. The trio became partners in three restaurants at Quincy Market: Thompson's Chowder House, the Landmark Cafe and Wild Goose.

All the while, Himmel dreamed of a big project he could call his own. He couldn't get Water Tower Place out of his mind. "No one had ever come in here with a crack team to accomplish anything like that," he says. "Boston isn't an outsider's town."

"Ken asked me to come see the site near Copley Square," Klutznik said to me. "We stood there on Huntington Avenue, looking down on nine and a half acres of railroad tracks, turnpike air rights, ingress/egress ramps and Ken saying to me, 'I think we should do a building here.' I looked at him and told him I thought he was out of his mind.

"We talked some more, and I asked if anybody had attempted development there before. Ken explained why each developer decided against going ahead. After about almost two hours, I said let's give it a shot. What I saw there were virtually the same dynamics which evolved on North Michigan Avenue." Klutznik approved marketing and engineering studies.

In 1977, Gifford introduced Himmel to John Driscoll at the Turnpike Authority about the time Himmel opened a Boston office for Urban. He and Klutznik began meeting with Driscoll, Massachusetts Governor Michael Dukakis and Frank Keefe, a high-ranking city planner in the Dukakis administration. To allay Urban's concerns about obstacles facing development, Dukakis and his associates emphasized that the state owned the Copley site, and they wanted something done there. Their priority was to stimulate Massachusetts' ailing economy.

Keefe, an impatient, aggressive man with red hair who was known as the "shadow governor" because of his influence on state urban policy, was willing to appoint Urban as the developer if the firm would tackle the whole site. He and Dukakis were mindful of the Park Plaza debacle.

That involved a Montreal-born prodigy named Mortimer Zuckerman. He had studied political science at McGill, Wharton and Harvard, then joined Cabot, Cabot & Forbes. He displayed a remarkable facility for real estate finance. He was a brash bachelor who emerged a millionaire by his early 30s.

Zuckerman established his own firm, Boston Properties, in 1970 and soon was competing for an ambitious development called Park Plaza. With an estimated cost of $300 million, it was to replace decrepit buildings around Boston's Park Square with a hotel, offices and residential units in five large towers containing 6 million square feet of space. Zuckerman won the city-sponsored competition against, among other firms, his former partners at Cabot, Cabot & Forbes.

He presented plans in a way which suggested they were an accomplished fact. City officials and local people felt they weren't being consulted, and there was stormy opposition. Everybody seemed to rebel against him. Community groups argued the development was too massive for the local cityscape. Horticulturists feared the towers would cast shadows on the Public Garden. Zuckerman's visible fury made opponents more determined. Boston newspapers questioned Zuckerman's friendship with then-Mayor Kevin White, and competing developers badmouthed Zuckerman as an unsavory outsider.

Though the project was approved by the Boston City Council and the Boston Redevelopment Authority, the Department of Community Affairs balked. Four times they rejected modified proposals. Park Plaza triggered bitter political infighting. Department of Community Affairs Commissioner Miles Mahoney was fired for his opposition. Boston Redevelopment Authority Director Robert Kennerly and Deputy Director Stewart Forbes lost their jobs, too. Many embroiled in the project called Zuckerman "the undertaker." Finally, he just had enough. After spending seven years and $1.9 million on the project, Zuckerman abandoned it.

He blamed R. Dun Gifford, presumably acting at the behest of Zuckerman's rival Cabot, Cabot & Forbes, for circulating a report which criticized the Park Plaza proposal. This helped seal the project's doom. Gifford's role enraged the mayor, who badly wanted Park Plaza to help spur the city's economic revival.

To bolster his standing in Boston, Zuckerman offered to donate his time and supervise construction of a $35 million sports arena near Boston's South Station. Mayor White and Governor Dukakis supported it, but hostile Beacon Hill legislators killed it, even though the work would be done by a public authority—so he wouldn't profit. The idea was portrayed as a public relations ploy. It was another bitter experience.

Though Keefe saw Urban's interest in the Copley site as an opportunity to demonstrate that Massachusetts and Boston were on the mend, he again encountered stiff opposition. The volatile Massachusetts Transportation Secretary Fred Salvucci wanted a competition among developers. He was against designating anybody. His aim was to keep developers under this thumb.

"If the developer is in the scene from the beginning," Salvucci argues, "he pressures the planning system. It results in a product that is biased toward heavy development, and that sacrifices environmental values. The process is more objective if the developer is not on the scene. With competitive bidding, the developer has no bitch because he knew what the rules of the game were to begin with.

"The next thing I heard about the site," Salvucci fumes, "was when Driscoll came in with Gifford. It was bullshit. Driscoll knew the approach I wanted. Here he had me boxed in. He had a live developer."

Though Driscoll took the initiative, Salvucci had more clout. Thanks to his urging, Dukakis refused to name Driscoll chairman of the Turnpike Authority. He was acting chairman. "I had the feeling that if Driscoll were sworn in for an eight-year term," Salvucci says, "we'd have gotten no cooperation."

Himmel declared that Urban wouldn't have anything to do with a competition. "One very important reason," he explains. "Whatever I come up with, I'll never be able to deliver, because I don't have enough time during the typical three-month competition period to understand the problems. The gorgeous drawings submitted, the economic analysis and so on would be worthless. It took us more than 12 months to understand enough about the site to have a shot at building something." Keefe recommended that Urban be designated, without a competition.

Himmel, Thompson and Gifford presented Dukakis, Keefe and Salvucci with models of a possible development. It featured low massing. Somebody leaked word of the meeting to the *Boston Herald American,* and this intensified pressure for Dukakis to decide how development should be handled. He wanted a monument to his administration, proof that he was a strong governor who could make things happen. He didn't want a Park Plaza hanging over his head.

He designated Urban as the developer with two provisos. First, there would be a citizens review committee to evaluate the developer's proposals independently. It would have its own budget. Second, the state wouldn't set a lease price for the site until a formal agreement specified just what would go on the site. The more ambitious the developer's plans, the more rent the state could negotiate for.

Accordingly, on April 15, 1977, the Turnpike Authority awarded Urban and the Great Bay Company an option on the site. It cost

$30,000. The state retained Professor Tunney Lee of the Massachusetts Institute of Technology's urban studies and planning department to take charge of the citizen review process. Lee had worked with Salvucci at the Boston Redevelopment Agency during the 1960s.

Lee formed a committee to review designs by choosing people from the Boston Redevelopment Authority, Boston Society of Architects, Boston Landmarks Commission, Back Bay Architectural Commission, Massachusetts Historical Commission, Ellis Neighborhood Association, South End Project Area Committee, Neighborhood Association of the Back Bay, Trinity Church, Massachusetts Bay Transportation Authority, Tent City Task Force, Back Bay Federation, St. Botolph Street Citizens Committee and the South End Historical Society. Lee described many participants as "veterans who had cut their teeth on Park Plaza."

Meetings covered everything from massing and materials on the exterior of buildings to their surface treatment, pedestrian access, energy saving, parking, neighborhood shopping, jobs, wind—this last was a sore point, because Boston gained unwelcomed notoriety when thousands of windows blew out of I. M. Pei's John Hancock Tower.

Himmel described the components of the project he was putting together. Included was a 750-room deluxe hotel, which would be operated by Western International. There would be 600,000 square feet of offices, parking facilities for 1,000 cars and 350,000 square feet of retail space, hopefully anchored by two department stores. The project was estimated to cost $275 million.

Wrangling began. Some people wanted to make sure Urban committed itself to developing Parcel C, a difficult little piece facing the Back Bay train station along Dartmouth Street.

Ben Thompson encountered vehement sessions which bewildered him. He was growing accustomed to congratulations about the success of Faneuil Hall Marketplace. Yet at the Copley hearings, people denounced him for being insensitive. They claimed he'd scatter buildings in the slots between turnpike ramps. He wouldn't specify any development for Parcel C. He'd build a blank wall to face the South End. When people demanded subsidized housing, he suggested basketball courts.

"I don't know if Ben was being restrained by Urban," recalls Lee, "but in the opportunities we had to meet with him he was very bad. He couldn't communicate."

Thompson complained later that Urban pressured him to exclude subsidized housing, ignore part of the site and design taller structures. Since his original presentations to Dukakis described low-rise structures, he was worried he might be accused of misleading the governor.

Himmel became exasperated with Thompson. "He spent all his time designing the buildings. He never wanted to hear about the problems below ground. Yet every time you came up with a solution to a problem above ground, you found you couldn't deal with what was going on below.

"The Back Bay, remember, was an old dumping ground. In some places, bedrock was 150 feet down. Soil analysis suggested we'd have to put down about 3,000 pre-cast concrete piles before we could even think about the foundation. The soil was so treacherous that by the time we were through, we put down 4,000 piles. They had to be driven by hand, because conventional methods would have caused vibrations which might damage the Boston Public Library across the street.

"Then there were the problems above ground. If you solved a problem in two dimensions, you found yourself with a ramp in your way. You encountered an elevation which didn't work. Or you were blocked by a utility line or railroad track.

"When we started to design the hotel, it was to go on a 38,000 square foot triangle of land. Then we found out what the hotel wanted in the way of lobby space, ballrooms and so on. The design extended beyond the triangle into a street. Squeezing the desired amount of hotel space within the site resulted in an ugly building. You had to start over again."

As anger swirled around him, Thompson decided to withdraw on February 28, 1978. Whatever this project needed, he didn't seem to have the touch, and he didn't want any more grief. In an anguished letter to Governor Dukakis, Thompson snarled that he "will not become a 'hired gun' for the developer in defending a design whose principles we cannot agree with."

It took a month for him and Himmel, now enemies, to separate their interests in the four restaurants. "It was an absolutely untenable partnership at that point," says Himmel.

To handle architectural responsibilities, Himmel tapped The Architect's Collaborative in Cambridge. "Since he was a founder, I guess that didn't make things work any smoother," Himmel concedes.

Complications continued to mount. State Environmental Protection Secretary Evelyn Murphy asserted that carbon monoxide levels in the area exceeded federal standards—nine parts per million during an eight-hour period—and that they would get worse if the project were built. The Massachusetts Bay Transportation Authority objected because proposed plans didn't provide a link to the Back Bay station. Congressman Mel King, who represented the poor South End community, announced his opposition, saying the project would drive up housing costs for poor people, and it would be visually offensive. Plans were redone continuously.

Gifford, who represented Urban at a number of meetings, was arousing distrust. He seemed to say what everyone wanted to hear. People got the feeling that Urban flaunted their Kennedy connections in the hopes of sliding through the process without conceding much.

The Citizens Review Committee, while it was only advisory, filed a report, and city planner Frank Keefe accepted most of it. On October 19, 1978, he wrote Himmel that Urban must put retail development on Parcel C, build a deck over Southwest Corridor railroad tracks and include public housing. Himmel protested that the state was changing the rules, imposing terms which weren't specified before. "Everyone was looking for the big developer to give up something," he grouses. He resisted development on Parcel C.

Housing became an explosive issue. Himmel and Tom Klutznik met with Keefe on November 14, 1978. Neighbors demanded that subsidized housing be built on part of the site. "Housing had no place in that project given the undeveloped land available for housing throughout the South End," Himmel snaps. Amid the shouting, Klutznik swore he would cancel the project if required to do housing.

But as they approached the expiration of Urban's option on the site, December 15, 1978, they signed a commitment to build 100 units of subsidized housing, make things easy for pedestrians around the project and develop alternatives for Parcel C. The state would help secure a favorable real estate tax agreement and needed government approvals.

Gifford's position at Urban became an issue. When his salary from Thompson's architectural firm was disclosed, the conflict of interest upset people. This plus distrust he seemed to engender and annoyance at the way he name-dropped about the Kennedys. When negotiations with the state were concluded, Urban would have to deal with Mayor Kevin White, and here Gifford would be a liability—the long shadow of Park Plaza again. He had to go. He did, gracefully, while denying that he had any problem with Mayor White.

Himmel and Gifford reportedly split a $500,000 development fee for helping to consummate the Copley deal. This widened the rift with Thompson, who says he lost $100,000 on the project.

Himmel, made a vice president of Urban, began to romance Kevin White—something the mayor apparently relished. He was given a tour of Water Tower Place, which illustrated the kind of quality he could expect for Boston.

Meanwhile, the end of Urban's option year was approaching again, and a lease had to be signed. One controversial issue was jobs. The state got Urban to agree that of the estimated 6,200 permanent jobs the project would generate, 30 percent would go to minorities, 17.2 percent to residents of the area affected by the project, 50 percent to women, 50 percent to Boston residents, and there would be good faith efforts to "offer appropriate job opportunities for handicapped persons." As another community gesture, Urban would reserve 20,000 square feet of below-market retail space for neighborhood-oriented goods, half of which must come from minority-owned firms.

Many people who had participated in the community review process were angered to discover that since their report was issued more than a year ago, Urban had expanded the size of the project by 1.3 million square feet. It was set up in a way that made it look as though it were participatory, but it was participatory only in the sense that people may say what they want without having much input in decisions. They urged officials to delay signing the lease, so terms could be reviewed more thoroughly.

However, Michael Dukakis had lost the Democratic primary to Edward J. King, and King had won the election. His position on the project wasn't known. Worried that the project could become lost amid the political changeover, and all the effort would end in fruitless indecision, officials pushed for quick signing of a lease with Urban.

The last negotiations were the most bitter. They were about money. Himmel didn't want to lose the deal, because Urban had paid almost $100,000 for options. Feasibility studies and architectural plans had cost millions. The complexity of the project and escalating costs steeled him to take a hard line on rent.

His initial proposal was for $10,000 annual rent, but state officials laughed. "A hell of a lot of imagination went into that," scoffed Norman Byrnes, an attorney for the Massachusetts Turnpike Authority.

They countered with $140,000 the first year rising to $920,000 in the tenth through fifteenth years, adjusted for inflation thereafter over the next 25 years. Himmel hammered at the tremendous development costs Urban was asked to bear.

The state wanted its rent payments to take precedence over all other claims, but Himmel refused. In the event additional funds had to be raised, he explained, creditors and lenders would want to be paid first.

Negotiations reached an impasse. Himmel announced Urban was pulling out of the whole deal. He packed his papers and headed for the door. Keefe warned him that if a lease weren't signed by December 22, advertisements would appear asking for new proposals, and

Urban would be excluded from consideration. Before Himmel left, the state extended the deadline a week.

During that time, lawyers huddled and tempers flared. "You had public officials taking prerogatives with our money, while neglecting constraints they imposed on us," Himmel says.

He conceded on rent, and the state agreed to give creditors and lenders first priority if Urban should seek additional financing. The lease was signed at 4 P.M., December 22. Work could proceed at last.

"One of the reasons we got the job," Himmel continues, "was the community review process. We brought everybody into it who potentially would disagree with us and fight. Not that we were going to win them over. But we were face to face, so we could address the issues.

"We opened ourselves up for public review. There were over 60 meetings which dealt with every imaginable issue. I've got scars on my tongue from biting it so many times over the years.

"I came to the Copley site when I was 29 years old, and I wanted more than anything else in the world to build this project. I was willing to pay the price. Not everybody was willing to work as hard as I. Real estate is with you seven days a week. It never leaves you."

VI

SQUARE-FOOT
PEDDLING

14.
BROKER DEALS

NEGOTIATING A COMMERCIAL LEASE IS ONE OF THE TRICKIEST TASKS in real estate, because it can be extraordinarily complex—running into the hundreds of pages. Many factors may easily exceed the impact of rent. Often critical lease terms influence a company's decision to stay at a present location or leave a city, remain in business or go bankrupt. So even Fortune 500 companies retain specialized brokers to negotiate their leases. The top brokers earn far more than most corporate chief executives.

Recently I talked with lean, feisty Kenneth D. Laub, one of the superbrokers who handle the bulk of major commercial real estate transactions in New York City. To Laub's credit: deals with rentals in excess of $15 billion for 20 million square feet of space. Kenneth D. Laub & Company's commissions average 2 percent to 3 percent. Real estate observers believe Laub has personally earned more than $50 million during his career.

Keenly attuned to current market conditions, Laub is a master of the complexities of lease negotiating. More often than not, he represents tenants rather than landlords, who traditionally pay brokers' commissions. "If you're a big corporation with a lease expiring," Laub asserts in his booming voice, "there aren't many places you can go. A landlord with, say, 300,000 feet of space available has you by the kumquat. He'll squeeze you, particularly with nonrent variables like taxes, energy and operating costs, which can easily exceed the rent."

Success enables the spirited bachelor, 46, to indulge his many pleasures. He lives on the forty-third floor of an exclusive Sutton Place co-op with a splendid view looking east, north and south. His suite includes a library, recording room, exercise room and steam room. The whole place is wired for rich stereo sound. Laub has a 1920 Louis XIV-style Steinway oak grand piano. He writes ballads, which he plays on his piano, and uses a DX-7 synthesizer and mixer. He enjoys fine cars, including his 1974 Maserati Bora, 1979 Rolls Royce convertible and 1985 Rolls Silver Sprint.

For cruising the Mediterranean, Laub has an 80-foot yacht called

Exocet—named after a French flying fish. He celebrated his parents' fiftieth wedding anniversary by hosting them and a couple hundred friends on a weekend cruise to Nassau. Highlight of that occasion was a two-hour musical revue he wrote and performed along with jazz pianist Billy Taylor, New York newscaster Roger Grimsby, actor Dick Shawn, Mitzi Hamilton of *A Chorus Line* and Linda Hart, who used to accompany Bette Midler.

Some of Laub's pleasures are public. He backed Broadway shows like *Break a Leg* and *The Second Greatest Entertainer in the Whole Wide World*. He funds a Municipal Arts Society project marking historic sites around New York with eight-sided signposts describing and illustrating what notable buildings were on a site before.

Now he's writing and producing a record of ballads that will poke fun at the real estate industry and celebrate the city where he made his fortune. The record will be called *Giving a Little Bit Back*.

He and his sister grew up in Cedarhurst, Long Island, where his father was a dentist. Since Laub loved animals, he thought he wanted to become a veterinarian, so he spent his summers working on poultry farms, grain farms and dairy farms. "My dad showed me two nice schools, Cornell and Princeton, and I fell in love with Cornell," Laub smiles. "But I can say without the slightest hesitation that I couldn't cut it as a prospective vet," Laub says. After two years, he transferred to New York University, where he switched to business.

Meanwhile, a national intercollegiate bowling champion, he began his deal-making career at age 20, canvassing fire departments, police departments, B'nai B'rith and other organizations to hold their tournaments at Viking Lanes, a Babylon, Long Island bowling alley built by actor Kirk Douglas from his earnings in the movie *Vikings*. Soon Laub was canvassing for five bowling alleys, each paying him $400 a week—$2,000 altogether. That canvassing was great preparation for real estate.

"After I got out of the Army," he says, "I went to work for Barchris Construction, which built bowling alleys—I thought there was a bright future in bowling. Less than a month after I started, they told me I'd have to relocate to Atlanta, which didn't interest me.

"I didn't know what to do. I spent the next 11 months interviewing people. Instead of going out and looking for a job, I tried to find out what different industries were about. I saw people in market research, advertising, insurance and real estate. I realized I didn't want to be a salaried person. I wanted to be at risk with the world as my oyster. I'd be in the sales industry, so the task was to identify the greatest opportunity."

He started as a 22-year-old trainee selling commercial real estate for a New York brokerage firm Collins, Tuttle & Company. He got a $35 a week draw against commissions. "While real estate brokerage offered tremendous potential," he says, "you were cut up like a piece of pie every time you made a deal. You got 30 percent of the commissions you generated. Senior people had overrides. Moreover, you were allowed a draw against commissions that was just enough to get you through the day. I guess it was good training for anybody to get raped by an employer. Even at 30 percent commission, though, my high five-figure income was more than any other sales person at the firm.

"Like most commercial brokers, I'd go into a building and take the elevator to the top floor. I'd go from office to office, asking to see the office manager, administrative vice president or whoever was responsible for leasing and willing to see me. I'd ask when their lease expired, how much space they needed, whether they anticipated much growth, what they planned to do. If they were cutting back people and needed less space, I'd offer to help sublet it.

"When I was canvassing the building at 285 Madison Avenue, I met a man named Gabe Carlin with the Haloid Corporation, and they were thinking about new offices for a national sales operation. I showed them a 650-square-foot-suite—about the size of my living room—in the old Union Carbide Building, 30 East 42nd Street. They took a five-year lease for $6 a square foot. My commission would have been $150.

"After the lease was signed, I got a call from a Haloid executive named Jack Rutledge, who said another broker had previously showed them different offices in the same building, and apparently the broker was angry that he didn't get the business. Rutledge asked me to split commissions, so they wouldn't get into litigation over the matter. I needed the $150, but I agreed to do it. He thanked me for being gracious and promised that his company would grow, and he might be able to throw more business my way. I settled for a $75.64 commission.

"About a year later, things started to happen. Haloid changed its name to Xerox. I started doing deals for them not just in New York, but in Rochester, where their corporate headquarters are located, and elsewhere around the country. Altogether, I've done 37 deals with Xerox.

"Unfortunately, I didn't really get the comprehensive education I wanted while I was with Collins, Tuttle. That's why I left. It scared me to think that I was making money by being persistent and lucking out. How would I fare against somebody who was good? In retrospect, if it were possible for me to work directly with the key people, Wylie Tuttle or Herb Papock, I might have stayed.

"I got the directory for the Real Estate Board of New York. I virtually memorized it and learned the cast of characters in the New York real estate community. I decided there were two large, diversified firms where I might have a chance to learn many aspects of the business: James Felt & Company and Tishman Realty & Construction Corporation.

"At Felt, I would have worked for Stanley Sultan, a broker who had done some highly creative consulting work. He was 56 years old, bit his nails to the quick and lived with his 86-year-old mother. His desk was piled with papers, which was common in the real estate business, except that he was the only person who could find anything. So while he was a very bright man, I didn't think I'd enjoy the association."

The Tishmans were among the oldest and most powerful New York real estate families, their fortune founded by Julius Tishman, who built tenement houses on Manhattan's Lower East Side. Son David, who joined the firm after his graduation from New York University Law School in 1909, pioneered apartment buildings north of 86th Street on the West Side. Tishman Realty & Construction became a publicly-held company in 1928.

"There were a lot of Tishmans," Laub recalls, "and I didn't know exactly what each one did, so I started at the beginning of the alphabet. I called Alan on the telephone.

"I said, 'This is Kenneth Laub, I work for Collins, Tuttle & Company.' I figured that would be good enough, because the Tishmans certainly knew Collins, Tuttle & Company. Sure enough, Alan picked up.

"Mr. Tishman,' I continued, 'I'd like to come and talk with you.' I expected he'd figure it was about some real estate deal. But I was wrong.

" 'Why, do you want a job?' he asked, without a moment's hesitation.

"I meant to say 'Yes,' " Laub laughs, "but it came out about three octaves higher than usual. 'Y-e-s.'

"I lucked out again, because Alan Tishman was in charge of leasing their buildings. I had started with the right person. He introduced me to Joe Gavron, then director of commercial leasing. Joe liked me, and I was hired as an assistant director of leasing. I accepted with one condition: that they not pay me a salary. I wanted to earn only commissions.

Soon the Tishmans established a subsidiary called Tishman Management Corporation, which handled leasing, advised corporations developing their own buildings, provided consulting and brokerage services to tenants. "Behind me, I had an organization with credibility in leasing, financing, management and construction. I spent seven wonderful years, from 1962 to 1969, learning the business."

The Tishmans were a family of talented, diverse, sometimes eccentric characters. David Tishman, in his 80s, was a reigning patriarch along with his brother Norman, who was reportedly a wild driver in his Rolls Royce. When David negotiated with somebody who didn't want to sell him a property, he'd turn off his hearing aid, so he could say he didn't hear the insistent noes. David's son Alan, a rugged and handsome man with olive complexion, seemed perfectly cast as an outgoing salesman, and he taught Laub how a sophisticated landlord approached lease negotiations. Tall, lean, soft-spoken Robert Tishman, Alan's older brother, was very much an operations man. His domain was finance.

Tough, gruff John Tishman made the firm into perhaps the most formidable force in the construction industry. So highly valued was his expertise that many times when he failed to win a job as general contractor, he was retained as a consultant to watch over a big project. He was to tackle such mammoth undertakings as Chicago's John Hancock Center, Detroit's Renaissance Center complex and the twin towers of New York's World Trade Center.

Laub had an irresistible urge to meet John Tishman, so he walked in to ask for advice. "I told him I had this 3,000-square-foot tenant," Laub says, "which was a big deal for me since I was new, but it was small potatoes to him at the top of his profession. I asked the value of the work letter, which specified how much allowance the landlord would give a tenant for building interior finishes to their specification.

" 'What's in the work letter?' he replied.

"I explained orally—nothing written down. This was very naive, because if you really want to know how much a work letter is worth, you turn it over to the construction department. They have the various jobs bid and give you back a meaningful answer.

"Well, John started making funny noises like an adding machine— bup-bup-bup-bup-bup-click-bup-bup-bup-bup-bup-click. Then he gave me a number.

"I thanked him and left, feeling rather stupid."

Even in this league, though, Laub was a dazzler. Interpublic, for instance, was a troubled advertising conglomerate with a tangle of leases which, if renegotiated, might realize substantial savings. Laub handled more than 30 transactions in five years, canceling leases, consolidating space, subletting space for more money. The value of these transactions was about $150 million, and in the process Laub earned Interpublic an estimated $10 million when they needed cash badly.

John Tishman earned an $11 million fee as construction consultant for the World Trade Center, while Laub was applying knowledge of a landlord's pressure points to get tenants into the World Trade Center. He was hammering competitors and earning personal compensation of more than a half-million dollars annually. The Tishmans feared they'd be charged with conflict of interest and jeopardize their consulting fee, so they asked Laub not to lease any more space in the World Trade Center.

In 1969, Laub went out on his own with the Tishmans' blessing. Two years later, the real estate market slumped. Things got even worse when recession, inflation and unemployment struck together during the mid-1970s. Unable to pay their bills, many landlords abandoned their buildings. Companies found they were using far less space than they had contracted for, and they were desperate to sublet it and relieve the rent burden. Laub became the New York sublet king, doing more business than almost anybody else, finding takers for space hard-hit companies no longer wanted to occupy.

One of the earliest tenants to approach him was IBM. The company couldn't expand anymore at its 77 Water Street building. They hired Laub to study the market and explore their options. They paid him $36,000 for the report, but they weren't obliged to use his brokerage services.

"I set up a 10-point standard," Lamb explains, "for evaluating rentable versus usable space, nonrent variables like taxes, electricity, occupancy tax which was a new subject in New York. We had to evaluate the construction of buildings we were considering. We evaluated heating systems. We compared escalation clauses from one building to another. We analyzed the market. We estimated their future needs and their landlord's attitude toward granting them more space on various options and leaseback possibilities. By today's standards, this analysis was simplistic, but it was state of the art then, and it gave IBM everything they needed to negotiate. The outcome was that they decided to stay in their present building and sign a 300,000-square-foot lease. So IBM paid us for the report but didn't go on to use my brokerage services."

If Laub was disappointed, the market analysis he did helped him develop a remarkably thorough profile of the Manhattan office market. He established a file on every business leasing over 4,000 square feet of space in Manhattan—their space needs, rental levels and lease expirations. What he learned in barbershop talk with a Fortune 500 executive might find its way to a file along with the results of systematic surveys.

Laub seemed to thrive amidst crisis. When real estate tycoon Sol Goldman defaulted on the Chrysler Building during the mid-1970s, it reverted to the long-term lender, Massachusetts Mutual, which turned to Cooper Union, a college that owned the land—about 70 percent of its endowment. Massachusetts Mutual wanted to invest $30 million in renovation, but for this to be feasible, the insurer needed lower ground rent. Laub was retained to negotiate a deal that would protect that endowment. Both the Chrysler Building and Cooper Union have thrived since then.

In 1979, the *New York Daily News* was on the verge of bankruptcy. Contributing to the crisis were losses from their headquarters building at 220 East 42nd Street, where International Paper leased 550,000 square feet of space. Laub's rival, Cushman & Wakefield, recommended that the *News* accept a lease renewal for $7.50 a square foot. Laub scoffed that the market was significantly above that—at least $11 a square foot—and he insisted the *News* had an excellent chance of generating desperately needed cash if they told International Paper to take a walk. This was a tough decision for *News* General Manager Joseph Barletta, for International Paper also supplied him with newsprint, and he wanted to continue a good relationship.

But he did tell International paper that $7.50 was unacceptable, and Laub proceeded to lease the space. Since it was an antiquated facility—three buildings patched together, with floors ranging from 6,000 to 60,000 square feet—it would be inefficient for large tenants. It made sense for International Paper only if it were cheap.

So International Paper dickered for space at Park Avenue Plaza, a glass tower which Manhattan developers Lawrence and Zachary Fisher were building 10 blocks north. Rent would be about $17 a square foot. But since it wouldn't be ready for occupancy until a year after the International Paper lease expired, they offered Laub $5 million if he would extend the lease. "I refused," he says, "because I believed the market was working in our favor, and I didn't want to run the risk of losing the opportunity."

Laub went on to lease space vacated by International Paper not for the estimated $11 a square foot, but for between $25 and $30. The building filled with a lot of small tenants. The resulting surge of cash helped save the *News*. Several years later, the *News* sold the building for a nifty $150 million profit. Laub's $9 million commission seemed like a bargain.

Curiously, though Laub gave International Paper a hard time at the *News* building, the company sought his help several years later.

Unable to wait for Park Avenue Plaza, it signed a 15-year lease (1980–95) to move into 1166 Avenue of the Americas, a 1.5 million-square-foot building that became Manhattan's most famous default case.

Back in 1967, Tishman Realty & Construction had joined with Edwin Glickman to assemble a site on the east side of the Avenue of the Americas—Sixth Avenue—between 45th and 46th streets. Broker Henry J. Kassis did well assembling parcels until he encountered Bernard Pravda who, with his brother Alfred, owned a five-story loft building at 56 West 46th Street. Pravda agreed to sell for $170,000. He reneged on this, agreed and reneged on many subsequent offers. The Tishmans, who had bought out Glickman, decided to modify their design so they could build around Pravda after he demanded $2,066,000. Their total costs for assembling the site exceeded $42 million, but time was even more critical.

Delay meant the building opened during the 1974–75 recession, and it sat empty for five years. Avon considered it, but they were afraid of being the only tenant. They moved into 9 West 57th Street, where they reportedly ended up suing the developer Sheldon H. Solow. GTE considered 1166 Avenue of the Americas, too, but crime—particularly a bomb that went off in their building—helped convince them to build a new headquarters in Stamford, Connecticut.

Awash with losses and unable to lease any space, the Tishmans defaulted—walking away from more than $20 million they had invested in the property. The building passed into the hands of the construction lenders headed by Citibank. They defaulted. Then the building became the property of Sol Goldman, who owned the land. He defaulted. Teachers Insurance & Annuity Association took it over.

Their top real estate man, Martin Cleary, together with Jack Collins of New York Telephone, decided to buy the building for $32.5 million, the balance on the outstanding mortgages. New York Telephone occupied lower floors for a total of about 700,000 square feet. Levitt leased the ground floor plus upper floors—800,000 square feet—to International Paper.

Chairman Edward Gee, a tall man with a commanding personality, decided to spend an extraordinary $65 million on office improvements, which included a highly sophisticated security system, private reception area with escalator, corporate library, corporate auditorium, training rooms, conference rooms, executive kitchen and dining room, special dining rooms, full-floor employee cafeteria and lavish interiors by acclaimed designer Marv Affrime, which was the envy of New York. This was before a new breed of aggressive corporate raiders targeted profligate chief executives.

As recession and declining commodity prices forced International

Paper to tighten their belts, management decided it would be a good idea to cut the number of people at headquarters and transfer many functions to offices elsewhere. But the way their lease was written, they were vulnerable. Staying in the building until expiration in 1995 would mean paying a market rent which could easily exceed $60 a square foot. They hadn't used their tremendous space commitment as leverage to gain protection for their $65 million of leasehold improvements. Nor, if they sublet space, did they have a right to enjoy the profits.

International Paper Chairman Gee asked Laub for advice. He approached John Somers, a vice president at Teachers, and proposed to split 50–50 any profits generated by subletting space. The lease called for $17 a square foot, but the market was around $40. Teachers nixed the deal.

"I could hit a grand-slam home run for you Ed," Laub said, "if you move out of the building. Then we'd buy the space from Teachers. They'd make a profit. You'd also make a substantial profit by turning around and leasing or selling the space. A buyer would gain mortgage interest deductions, depreciation and tax abatement."

"That's not something I want to do," Gee replied. They were talking about the House that Gee Built.

But in a few years Gee retired. An equally strong man named John Georges became chairman. He faced a tougher financial situation, and he didn't have the personal stake in the offices. He commissioned Laub to arrange the purchase as he had proposed. Consummated in November 1985, this deal was worth an estimated $150 million, and observers rated it the largest condominium deal ever. It was expected that Laub and International Paper could "flip" the building to buyers for $300 million.

Among the current tenants in space acquired by International Paper: Laub's rival, giant Cushman & Wakefield. Being in the right place, obviously, isn't enough to clinch a deal.

Though Laub became known as a tenant's broker, he does many of his biggest deals representing landlords. The innovative, litigious developer Sol Atlas, for instance. He was a white-haired man of medium height who lived in a palatial contemporary home at King's Point, Long Island, with immaculately maintained Japanese gardens and a splendid view of Long Island Sound.

He built first-class office buildings with many innovative operating systems which hadn't been used before. He gambled that he could get enough extra rent to cover their cost. An aggressive negotiator, he was among the first landlords to pass fuel costs, electricity, taxes and cost-of-living adjustments onto tenants. He was rough and stubborn, enraging tenants. Quite a few corporations refused to go into a Sol Atlas building, no matter how much a deal might be sweetened.

During the late 1960s, he and his partner John McGrath, chairman of East New York Savings Bank, started One and Two New York Plaza, an office complex built upon landfill off the southeast tip of Manhattan. Anticipating a windfall, they never bothered with long-term financing. They figured when they had some major tenants signed up, they could get long-term financing at more favorable rates.

Then interest rates went up. Moreover, when their first building, 2.1-million-square-foot One New York Plaza, was around 80 percent filled—just short of the breakeven point—leasing stalled as recession set in. Tall, bespectacled Richard Boyle, a loan officer at Chase Manhattan Bank, wanted long-term financing to pay off their $75 million short-term construction loan. But since the building was a money-loser, a new loan would be available only on steep terms. Losses mounted, and Chase sat on its construction loan for nine anxious years.

In another of their attempts to lease space, Atlas and McGrath turned to Laub. He noted that Chase had options on five floors where leases were expiring by 1979. If Chase waived their options, those floors plus other space in the building would be big enough to attract a major corporation and increase the rent roll. "I asked Boyle for a dozen concessions, and he agreed to four," Laub recalls. "Fortunately, they were the right four for me. Among other things, he waived the bank's options to lease five floors. He also agreed not to raise interest rates for six months. I offered my best efforts to deliver a tenant for the vacant space and obtain permanent financing."

Canvassing the marketplace, Laub discovered that investment banking firm First Boston needed room for expansion. He signed them to a 20-year lease for 260,000 square feet starting at $12.50 a square foot. First Boston plus other tenants he signed boosted the rent roll more than $3 million annually, enough to achieve black ink. This enabled Laub to negotiate a 32-year, $70-million mortgage at 8.75 percent with a tall, gray-haired real estate loan officer named Bill Frentz of the Equitable Life Assurance Society.

Two hours after First Boston signed the lease, Laub got a call from George Shinn, chairman of the firm. He reported an unexpected rebellion among his corporate finance executives. They didn't want to stay downtown. They were pressuring to get out of the lease and move to midtown.

"Why did you sign the lease?" Laub asked.

"We felt committed," Shinn replied. "How much will it cost to get us out of the lease?"

Laub pondered the question overnight. "Sol Atlas and John McGrath won't let you off," he said, "because the long-term financing is linked to it. But with the lease at a fixed rate, it's an attractive deal for other companies who might consider subletting the space. You're not due to start paying rent for a year, so there should be enough time to sublet the space and realize as much as a $6 million profit."

Shinn asked Laub to sublet the space. Soon he was talking with Walter Fried of the downtown law firm Fried, Frank, Harris, Shriver & Jacobson which for two years had shopped for new quarters in midtown.

"Walter," Laub said, "it will cost you $3 or $4 more per square foot per year to move midtown. By piggybacking on the deal I did with First Boston, you and your partners can save $20 million over the term of the lease." Fried Frank moved into the space vacated by First Boston at One New York Plaza. Laub collected a $1.6 million commission in addition to the $1.6 million he got for signing First Boston.

First Boston executives liked the way Laub turned First Boston's multimillion-dollar headache into a whopping profit, so they asked him to negotiate the move of their back office into 110,000 square feet at Five World Trade Center. In November 1985, Laub arranged for First Boston to take an additional 50,000 square feet of contiguous space there. So the crisis triggered by First Boston brought Laub unexpected commissions worth millions.

There's more. One of the tenants at One New York Plaza was a small institutional research firm named Faulkner Dawkins & Sullivan which was bought by Sanford Weill, an aggressive financial empire builder who had bought the bankrupt brokerage firm Hayden Stone. The Brooklyn-born Weill started his career as a runner at Bear Stearns, after Merrill Lynch had rejected him for its sales training program. By 1960, his apartment-house neighbor Arthur Carter was starting a brokerage firm, and Weill became a partner in Carter, Berlind, Potoma & Weill. Partners came and went, and the firm changed to Cogan, Berlind, Weill & Levitt. They were known on Wall Street by their acronym, corned beef with lettuce. They did considerable business with wheeler-dealers like Charles Bludhorn, who built the conglomerate Gulf & Western, and Saul Steinberg, who took over Reliance Insurance, parlaying that into a tidy empire.

In 1970, the slumping stock market hit brokerage firms hard, and this in turn precipitated a wave of mergers. Weill was making deals as fast as he could. The firm acquired the troubled Hayden Stone, cut costs and labored to turn that around. Then it went on to acquire Hentz & Company, a commodities firm, and Saul Lerner & Company, an options broker. Weill had vehement differences with his partners about how their rapid expansion should be handled. In the ensuing shoot-out, Weill emerged on top. Marshall Cogan left and eventually took over another company called General Felt.

Weill acquired still more companies, at a faster pace: Shearson Hammill, a major Wall Street firm which became the umbrella for all the firm's holdings. Lamson Brothers & Company, a midwestern broker, was acquired, as was another midwest firm, Reinholdt & Gardner; a California mortgage banker, Western Pacific Financial Corporation; Loeb Rhoades Hornblower, a Wall Street firm resulting from several prior consolidations; and Faulkner Dawkins & Sullivan, then a tenant at One New York Plaza.

Weill is said to be a tough, tight executive who insists on controlling every aspect of the firm. He doesn't delegate much. When underlings stray from the policies he establishes, they may be summoned to his offices for a tongue thrashing. He cuts costs, lets people go, then looks for more places to cut. He's as tough on brokers as anybody else, trying to minimize or altogether eliminate their commissions. He's a polite man with ice in his veins, as one associate puts it.

Weill wanted to cut back staff and consolidate Faulkner Dawkins with his firm's other holdings. "You say you're so good," he challenged Laub, "do something special for me. Get us out of the Faulkner Dawkins lease without a loss."

It was for $14 a square foot—an above-market rent then—and had 12 years to run. If Laub failed, he wouldn't get any commission at all. Laub took the bait.

"What Sandy didn't know," Laub recalls, "was that Salomon Brothers, on the floor below, needed expansion space. They could have rented space elsewhere for $10 a foot, but this was convenient, contiguous space, and in any event I wasn't representing Salomon. So I called Vincent Murphy of Salomon. They agreed to take the Faulkner Dawkins space at $14 plus a 50-cent-per-square-foot commission.

"I saved Sandy about $120,000 a year of potential write-down, more than $1.4 million altogether. He liked that very much and gave me the right to represent his latest acquisition, Shearson. They moved into 330,000 feet at the World Trade Center, and I earned a $1.6 million commission."

Meanwhile, Weill's Hayden Stone acquisition gave Atlas and

McGrath a nightmare at Two New York Plaza, because when it went bankrupt, it defaulted on a lease there. After some scrambling, Laub produced another tenant—the brokerage firm A. G. Becker. Atlas and Becker executive Paul Judy shook hands on a deal for 120,000 square feet. Legal documents were prepared.

The summer evening before they were to be signed, Laub learned Becker was simultaneously negotiating with the Uris brothers to move into their office tower at 55 Water Street. "It was imperative that Sol find out what was going on," Laub says. "I found somebody who gave me Sol's unlisted home phone number, and I called, but Sol and Edyth were out. I didn't know just when he left in the morning to inspect his construction sites, but it was early. My general counsel Murray Grodetsky and I drove to their house, arriving by about 6:30 A.M.

"Sol's maid answered the doorbell. From upstairs, he sent word that the maid was to make us comfortable, and she did. She prepared scrambled eggs, crisp bacon, toast and coffee, which we ate outdoors, enjoying the gorgeous view of Long Island Sound. Sol didn't ask why we had come until after we were finished. He took everything one step at a time."

After Laub left, Atlas got on the phone to Becker executives and lawyers. They wanted out of their lease because they were worried they'd be virtually alone in Atlas's white elephant building. Atlas threatened lawsuits if they didn't sign the lease as they had agreed.

Becker refused to sign. They moved into 55 Water Street. Atlas didn't sue. Laub lost the deal, but it proved fortuitous.

American Express, in cramped quarters at 65 Broadway, was looking for a new building with at least 600,000 square feet. There weren't many choices. The Tishmans' 1166 Avenue of the Americas was still empty, but it was in midtown Manhattan, and American Express Chairman Howard Clark had agreed, partly because of David Rockefeller's urging, that his company should stay downtown and help keep the financial district strong. The World Trade Center had plenty of vacant space, but being over there would be a turnoff, surrounded by so many time-in-grade government employees.

So American Express executives negotiated with Laub. Talks became deadlocked, though, because American Express wanted to buy the building, and Atlas was more interested in collecting rents. After all, having taken the risks of development, he wanted to enjoy the cash flow and hopefully a big capital gain later. He set a high price at which he'd be willing to sell, and American Express balked. Soon afterward, Atlas died.

Virtually empty, Two New York Plaza lost $500,000 a month.

Alarmed, John McGrath, Atlas's widow Edyth and daughter Sandy Atlas Bass were eager to get rid of the building for a lower price.

Laub got a timely opportunity to resume negotiations when he received a handwritten invitation from Howard Clark. It was to a little evening get-together at the American Museum of Natural History.

But after Laub arrived at the museum, checked his coat and reached the reception area, he discovered more than 300 people already there. Perhaps a third were competing brokers and building owners. Suddenly, he grasped Clark's clever ploy: Everyone in the brokerage community was chasing Clark, and he lured them here so they'd at least benefit the museum. The situation wasn't encouraging.

Laub was further disheartened when he learned that the crowd was going to break up into small groups, with everybody drawing a number to determine which room they'd go to. Laub might never get a chance to see Clark. Some people went to agronomy, others to archeology and so on. Laub drew ichthyology. It was a dreary basement room filled with bottles of fish in formaldehyde.

"It was absurd," Laub remembers, "standing around staring at bottles of dead fish. How fond could you get of the museum? This didn't strike me as a reason why you should make a donation unless they were going to modernize jars for the dead fish.

"But I lucked out, because Howard Clark was in my group, and I was the only broker there." Clark is a broad-shouldered, good-looking man with a strong jaw. He looks like a chairman of the board for a major corporation should, a formidable presence. Alan Tishman, having heard Clark was in ichthyology, tried to wander in nonchalantly, so he could pitch the virtues of 1166 Avenue of the Americas. But Clark just said hello and told him he belonged in paleontology.

Though the party lasted a couple of hours, Laub had less than three minutes of conversation with Clark. It was enough. "I told him I represented developer John P. McGrath and the estate of Sol Atlas who owned Two New York Plaza," Laub recalls, "and I handed him a letter of authorization. I explained the terms were more favorable than any other location in Manhattan. If I could meet with him and his associates, I could show why it might fill their needs. He told me to put the letter back and call Stevens L. Shea, the American Express executive in charge of real estate.

"That three-minute conversation was crucial, for if I hadn't actually met and talked with him, there would be no personal chemistry, no reason for him to believe me. I'd have been forever brushed aside by secretaries and assistants."

About 18 months later, the deal was done: American Express would buy the building for $32 million. Two New York Plaza would become the company's new headquarters, known as American Express Plaza.

In 1981, Clark's successor as chairman, James D. Robinson III, got out his bankroll and peeled off more than $1 billion for Shearson, and as a major partner in Shearson, Sanford Weill immediately was one of American Express's major stockholders. He became president of Shearson/American Express, Wall Street's second largest brokerage firm. The parent company was a $35 billion giant that needed ever more office space. Weill eyed the magnificent Battery Park City office complex being built on the Hudson River by the Reichmanns of Olympia & York.

Many times he asked Laub to serve as a consultant, but he never put enough money on the table. Laub passed.

The commissions would have been beyond a broker's wildest dreams, because the deal was a blockbuster. Concluded in March 1982, it called for American Express to occupy 80 percent of a 51-story, 2.3-million-square-foot tower at Battery Park City. Rent and other payments reportedly would exceed $2 billion during its 35-year term. With a financial services giant like American Express signed on, the Reichmanns renamed their Battery City project World Financial Center. Since American Express would be vacating its old building, they sold it to the Reichmanns for $240 million. The hefty capital gains would be sheltered by losses in American Express's bond-portfolio. American Express Plaza was renamed 125 Broad Street.

Curiously, though Weill led the negotiations, his Shearson/American Express would be the only division of American Express that wouldn't move. Laub had got such a bargain for them at World Trade Center that they couldn't afford to vacate it. That deal involved 330,000 square feet for 25 years, starting at $10 a square foot.

Within months, though, Weill insisted on renegotiating the World Financial Center deal, because Manhattan office rental rates fell, and the lease began looking more and more expensive. Moreover, the bond market rallied, reducing American Express's bond losses. Consequently, capital gains on the sale of American Express Plaza would be exposed to taxes.

A new agreement provided that the Reichmanns would buy American Express Plaza for only $160 million, reducing American Express's capital gain on it. Then instead of leasing space at World Financial Center, American Express would buy their building for a reported $600 million.

If the Reichmanns regretted giving up ownership in a premier property, it virtually assured them huge profits at World Financial Center. A tenant may always demand to renegotiate a lease or walk out of it, but a purchase is final. American Express's decision to buy a piece of the Reichmanns' project demonstrated as no lease could that World Financial Center is a location for the finest companies and would become a stupendous success.

The American Express deal made World Financial Center a more serious alternative for Merrill Lynch executives, who were considering a move into the World Trade Center. The brokerage giant had 12,000 employees spread among 10 buildings in addition to their 53-story headquarters, One Liberty Plaza. By August 1984, Merrill Lynch agreed to lease two towers at World Financial Center—about 4 million square feet altogether—for 25 years. Price tag was about $1 billion. Merrill Lynch would gain a 49 percent equity interest in the towers, and the Reichmanns would take One Liberty Plaza off their hands. This transaction, according to Merrill Lynch Executive Vice President Edmond N. Moriarty Jr., would not only consolidate their operations, but also shave occupancy costs 25 percent. It was a byzantine transaction whose lease documents filled five four-inch-thick volumes. It would also represent a good real estate investment if they elected to lease some of the space.

Curiously, this deal was negotiated not by Laub but by a ferocious West Coast competitor named John C. Cushman III. After losing a struggle for control of his family firm, Cushman & Wakefield, he moved to Los Angeles where he became a star, single-handedly leasing an incredible 40 percent to 70 percent of the downtown space there. He cut deals with heavy hitters across the country, including the wealthy Hunt and Bass families. At 44, Cushman enjoyed annual commissions estimated around $10 million. When he wasn't speeding to new deals in his four-engine Jetstar plane, he might be enjoying his 80-foot yacht, 550-acre Idaho ranch or three Rolls Royces. He was no stranger to World Financial Center, having negotiated the very first lease deal there—to City Investing Company. However, City executives decided to liquidate the company, and so it never moved in.

While Merrill Lynch was the biggest deal at World Financial Center, it didn't mean riches for Cushman. He served as a consultant, rather than a broker, and a consulting job pays a fraction as much as the 2 percent to 3 percent commission involved with brokering.

Representing the Reichmanns, Laub got more for brokering the deal that brought Dow Jones, publisher of *Barron's* and the *Wall Street Journal,* into World Financial Center. They were cramped at 22 Cortlandt Street, a building owned by Metropolitan Life and Harry Helmsley.

Laub surveyed the market. Dow Jones signed a 20-year lease for 300,000 square feet, a deal worth about $300 million. In October

1985, Laub negotiated for an additional 60,000 square feet. His commissions exceeded $4 million.

The very next month, he concluded a 550,000-square-foot joint venture/lease transaction which brought Oppenheimer & Company into World Financial Center. His cash register rang up another $4 million more.

The Reichmanns were delighted. Like owners everywhere, they try to avoid paying brokerage commissions. The only significant commissions they paid were to Laub. Several years before World Financial Center was finished, it was 92 percent leased. Observers expect the remainder to go shortly. This leasing success is a triumph for their foresight and daring, Laub's expertise and tenacity.

15.

RETAIL RIVALRY

THE MOST CRUCIAL, DESPERATE LEASING EFFORTS ARE FOR AN AN-
chor—a lead tenant with a presence big enough and well known
enough to help lure other tenants to a project. Few tenants relish the
risk of being first in a building, because if it doesn't lease well, they
may be in a largely empty place for a long time. It's almost impossible to make a major shopping center work without an anchor retailer
sure to draw large numbers of shoppers, so other retail tenants will
feel comfortable and sign on.

Leasing is particularly fierce when major competitors face off against
each other. I followed one recent battle as it escalated in Boston.

At opposite ends of that city, during the early 1980s, two giant
retail developers squared off. Downtown, the suave Marco Tonci Ottieri, son of an Italian diplomat, represented Mondev International,
a Montreal-based company building a $130-million retail-hotel com-
plex called Lafayette Place. It's on the Washington Street pedestrian
mall known as Downtown Crossing, Boston's most popular shopping district.

Since 1976, when he was 29, single-minded Ken Himmel, senior
vice president of Urban Investment & Development Company, Aetna
Life & Casualty's real estate subsidiary, had been responsible for Copley Place, the office-retail-hotel project located in fashionable Back
Bay. By the time it opened seven years later, costs had doubled to
over $500 million, so successful leasing was especially critical.

Ottieri directed his firm's leasing efforts from plush thirty-second
floor offices at One Boston Place. "We have the people," Ottieri
boasted, "100,000 shoppers a day who go into the Jordan Marsh
department store, which connects to Lafayette Place. At peak times,
50,000 shoppers an hour walk along Washington Street. By compar-
ison, Quincy Market may get 50,000 on their best days."

Ottieri cited a recent $40,000 study published by the Boston Re-
development Authority, *Downtown Crossing: An Economic Strategy Plan*.
It estimated that shops in Downtown Crossing did sales of $373
million in 1982—$213 per square foot, more than any major shop-

ping center around Boston. Very few shopping centers in the United States surpass this. The study went on to predict that because of an expanding work force, Downtown Crossing sales would grow 60 percent within a decade.

Ottieri extolled the design of Lafayette Place. "The interior will have the feeling of intimate European streets. Very narrow like Florence, Siena, Rome and Venice, where you can walk down the middle of the street and see shops easily on both sides, because you're so close.

"Lafayette Place will be a delightful experience. Our streets will be an aggregate of black and gray marble chips, good for easy walking. There will be a dark ceiling that seems to disappear. Most of the light will come from gleaming storefronts. We'll have an open square like a European piazza, where people can relax—there will be nine family-operated eating places."

Prospective tenants were shown a glowing 12-projector slide presentation which emphasized the century-old tradition of downtown retailing, anchored by Jordan Marsh and Filene's. Merwin Kaminstein, chairman of Filene's declared: "Downtown, the mix and number of people who pass by our door everyday is sensational." Dawn-Marie Driscoll, president of the Downtown Crossing Association: "If a retailer is looking for high sales, high traffic, high profit, this is the place."

Financial backers appeared in the presentation and expressed their confidence. "We believe in Boston and its future," said Benjamin D. Holloway, executive vice president of Equitable Life Assurance Society. "Lafayette Place represents the reality of that vision. We decided we wanted to play a major role in its development." F. L. Bryant Jr., senior vice president of Manufacturers Hanover Bank: "As our cities rebuild, projects such as Lafayette Place will lead the way."

The presentation hit hard on its primary selling points. Over a fifth of the people who pass Lafayette Place, the presentation asserted, earned incomes over $50,000. Boston residents shopped downtown seven times more frequently than in Back Bay. More than $3 was spent in Downtown Crossing for every $1 that's spent in Back Bay.

Born in Rome, Ottieri was trained as an architect. He moved to Boston with his father Count Francesco Tonci Ottieri, consul general at the Italian consulate. This was where he established his roots, designing low-income housing and commercial buildings. On a ski trip to Sugarbush, Vermont, he met Peter Howlett, a legal consultant with Mondev International, who persuaded him to join Mondev's ventures, which included Westmount Square, a high fashion shopping center in Montreal.

In 1977, when Ottieri was 33, friends at Sefrius, a Paris developer, made him an offer to manage Lafayette Place with Mondev as a 50 percent partner. They had projected a lavish project costing $220 million, yet they faced heavy start-up costs which would make it difficult to handle the financing. Moreover, while Lafayette Place's venerable neighbor Jordan Marsh might serve as an anchor to help draw people into the project, standard shopping center practice called for two anchors, and after three years' effort, Sefrius couldn't sign a second major retailer. They stalled.

Land accounted for a substantial chunk of the project's cost, and it was owned by Jordan Marsh. Benjamin Frank, vice president of Allied Stores, which owned the store, was a tough negotiator. Ottieri didn't see how Sefrius, as an outsider, could match his clout as landowner. So Ottieri enlisted the Boston Redevelopment Authority on his side. Lafayette Place would offer parking as a public amenity, he argued, so it would be appropriate for the city to acquire the land. The city could handle Frank. Subsequently, the asking price for the land went down to $3 million, and the city bought it.

Next, Ottieri decided that mounting costs of carrying the project required him to proceed without a second major retailer. "It takes two years to find an anchor, if you're lucky," he says. "Major retailers won't come into a project just because you have an appealing retail environment. They develop their new stores far in advance. It's extremely tough to find the right kind of store whose plans will mesh with yours. Even then, the chances are they'll negotiate you to death." Jordan Marsh, whom they had bested in the land negotiation, would have to serve as their only anchor.

He fired the architect who developed preliminary plans and hired Mitchell/Giurgola. They evolved a horseshoe design in which "fashion lanes" began at Jordan Marsh, led people past 164 small shops, then back to Jordan Marsh. Without a second anchor, the project could be done for millions less than what was originally conceived.

In January 1981, cash-strapped Boston officials announced they couldn't build the $22.1 million parking garage they had promised, so Mondev had to do it instead. The Massachusetts Industrial Finance Agency would float tax-free bonds to finance it, and there would be an $8 million Urban Development and Action Grant. Mondev leased the garage from the city for 40 years. They'd pay base rent of $344,000 a year or 50 percent of garage revenues, whichever was higher. Sefrius couldn't afford to stay with it, and Mondev bought them out, assuming the burden alone.

Mondev signed Inter-Continental Hotels to operate a planned 22-story, 500-room hotel which would be linked with the mall. The hotel would be decorated in restrained taste with mahogany paneling and American antiques, befitting Boston's heritage. "A little like the Harvard Club," Ottieri says.

Unlike Himmel, who lives and breathes financing negotiations, construction schedules and other aspects of the development business, Ottieri exudes a virile sophistication, which he hoped would help lure retailers to a project like Lafayette Place. He has raced a 43-foot sailboat in European regattas. He drives a souped-up Group II Sirocco Volkswagen in about a dozen annual events like the Grand Prix of Canada. He designs patented ski boots and lightweight fiberglass chairs. He designs and builds radio-controlled model airplanes—more than 50 thusfar.

Ottieri conceived a slick advertising campaign which he hoped would speed the leasing process. It ran in the *New Yorker,* the *New York Times, New York* magazine, *Boston* magazine, the *Washington Post, Vogue* and *Women's Wear Daily.* But the campaign seemed to be pleading for tenants with headlines like this: "Ann Taylor, Bottega Veneta, Brooks Brothers, Louis, Carroll Reed, Dunhill, Jaeger, Laura Ashley, La Ruche, Marimekko, Paul Stuart, Toby Turner, Talbots . . . Lafayette Place is being built for you." Ottieri seemed defensive when he acknowledged that none of these had signed—he was just naming the kinds of tenants he wanted.

He fueled speculation that all was not well by refusing to disclose the names of any tenants he signed. Some Boston observers believed he hadn't signed a single tenant.

The most likely reason for trouble at Lafayette Place was the one factor Ottieri could do little about. Two sides of Lafayette Place bordered the Combat Zone. "I don't believe the Combat Zone will turn people off," Ottieri shrugged. "They can get to the hotel without going through it, whether they walk or drive. The Combat Zone doesn't seem to bother the thousands who come here to shop.

"Besides, in a few years it will be cleaned up. When I first visited Boston, Scollay Square was just as bad, but that's gone, and now we have Government Center. Quincy Market was nothing when The Rouse Company turned that into a fantastically successful festive marketplace. The Opera House, Wilbur Theater and Shubert Theater are being restored. The amount of downtown construction underway is incredible—altogether, it's estimated that about a million square feet of office space will be added each year for the next decade.

"Copley Place," he charged, "has nothing in terms of people. They're trying to create a tenth of what we already have. But they can afford to take that risk, because they have an insurance company behind them. Whatever it takes, they will pay.

"We are fighting for the same stores, and they're buying them, which is great. They go to Gucci and say, 'We'll do everything for you. We'll subsidize your inventory. We'll pay your architect. We'll pay for construction. We'll pay for start-up. We'll pay your advertising. It's the only way they can do it. When they saw stores weren't leasing that well, they set up a budget and bought the stores. I know, because the stores come to us and say, 'What are you going to do for us?' We say, 'Zero.' They say, 'Copley Place is going to build me a store.' I reply, 'Then go there. We can deliver the shoppers. You choose.' "

Ottieri scoffed at the high cost of leasing in Copley Place—from $25 per square foot for about 6,000 square feet of retail space to $100 per square foot for a 700-square-foot bank office. Then there were maintenance charges, taxes and other factors, which tack an additional $16 per square foot to the annual tab. Although the basic lease cost was comparable at Lafayette Place, the additional charges were only $10 per square foot.

In his Back Bay office at Hancock Tower, Himmel smiled: "There has never been a single moment in the years I spent putting together this place that I ever believed Copley Place had any competition. Washington Street is a very important shopping district, but it has never been and never will be the fashion shopping center of this city. Back Bay is the undisputed fashion shopping center of Boston. The only people who question that are people who don't understand Boston."

Skeptics questioned the glamorous appeals made for both Lafayette Place and Copley Place. Often mentioned was the fact that Urban's Water Tower Place, once devoted almost exclusively to pricey merchandise, was forced to accommodate the great middle market. "I believe a lot of the high-priced stuff will go down the drain," ventured attorney Lawrence Sperber whose clients included many of Boston's most successful retailers. "Boston is a city with good fashion sense but not high style."

Himmel, unlike Ottieri, didn't have a retailer next door that could be linked to the project. Originally, he contemplated a project with three anchors, but there wasn't enough room on the site to handle the traffic properly. He decided to aim for two anchors.

There were several prospects. B. Altman thought about a Boston location, but, operated by a caretaker trust, they weren't prepared to make any commitments at the time. Bonwit Teller had a Back Bay store in a handsome little brick building which used to house a natural history museum, and they negotiated with Himmel for expanded quarters. They backed off when they concluded the configuration of the site wouldn't be quite right for their needs.

Bloomingdale's was at the top of Himmel's list, because it represented the high end of retailing and had a broad line of merchandise. Owned by Federated Department Stores, they had a 100,000-square-foot store in the affluent suburb of Chestnut Hill. But it was only about 15 minutes from Copley Place, and they were concerned that a store there would draw from the same market, and business at both locations would suffer. Talks broke down in February 1979.

The situation was desperate. Himmel had been working on Copley Place almost three years, and what with the roisterous public hearings, continuous reworkings of the design and massive regulatory paperwork, costs were soaring. Aetna executives were alarmed, and there was talk of canceling the project to stop the cash drain. Back in Chicago, Urban's Chairman Thomas Klutznik shielded Himmel from much of the home office recrimination, so he could go about his job.

Himmel's whole career seemed to depend on finding an anchor store. It became an obsession. Though they had Westin signed on for a luxury hotel, Westin wouldn't build without an adjoining retail complex. No little store would lease space unless there was an anchor to help draw an ample number of shoppers. Office buildings by themselves wouldn't be justified on the site. So Copley Place could fizzle without that anchor.

Himmel switched gears. Instead of betting all on two anchors, he decided to go after a single anchor and a second hotel. A convention hotel would make obvious sense, since Boston's Hynes Auditorium would be expanded a few blocks away. Plans were revised again.

For a couple years he and Klutznik had talked with Philip Hawley, president of Carter Hawley Hale Stores. Based in Los Angeles, Hawley managed a number of prestigious retailers including glitzy Neiman-Marcus. If he could ever find enough time, he'd see about a possible Boston site for Neiman's. Hawley had gone to school in Boston, so he had a feeling for it. He knew the city lacked really upscale retailing, and he believed that meant opportunity.

Location was the issue. Hawley pored over demographic studies done by his own people, and he explored sites himself in early March 1979. He certainly couldn't ignore the high volume of shopping at Downtown Crossing. He considered Chestnut Hill. He walked through Back Bay—the chic shops on Newbury Street, the department stores around Prudential Center. He tried to envision how Copley Place might help upgrade Copley Square, which was rather seedy at the time, since Boston officials didn't have money to maintain it properly.

Himmel and Klutznik accompanied Hawley to the top of the Prudential Building, so they could survey the whole area. They talked about where the city was going, what share of the retail market Copley Place might achieve. Urban's Water Tower Place was a factor in Hawley's thinking, because its success had spurred him to build a Neiman-Marcus store next door, and it was going well. By April 1979, Hawley announced his decision: Yes! There would be a three-level Neiman-Marcus at Copley Place.

"When I heard that," Himmel exults, "I knew we'd make it. Neiman-Marcus would prove to be the great catalyst which would enable us to lease the retail space, build the hotels and offices and make Copley Place a home run."

Assured that he had a powerful anchor, Himmel planned a sky-bridge connecting Copley Place with Prudential Center, a major complex of offices and stores. The skybridge made it easy for people at Copley Place to reach Saks Fifth Avenue and Lord & Taylor. With these, Himmel achieved the near-equivalent of two more anchors. He set the stage to pursue the hundred smaller stores he needed. This task he put aside for three years as he devoted his energies to public hearings about design, then monitored actual construction.

The most important category of merchandise in almost any shopping center is women's apparel—accounting for perhaps a third of total volume, often six times more than men's apparel—and a key name to lure that type store is Gucci. Promotion makes it a visible name. It is known for achieving standout sales with stylish merchandise.

Like many selling high-end goods, Gucci executives had their eye on Newbury Street. It, rather than Lafayette Place, was their most likely alternative to Copley Place. The choicest blocks on Newbury Street were at the east end between Arlington and Berkeley—with the Ritz-Carlton Hotel, Brooks Brothers and Burberry's. Seldom was a site available there. Further west, the number of fashionable stores declined, and there were more sites. Copley Place could be much better than those.

Gucci executives decided on Copley Place in early 1983. Since they were well aware of their influence on other retailers, they were tough negotiators. "They got our best deal, no question about it," concedes James Klutznik, who negotiated leases for many Copley Place tenant deals. "We paid more of their construction costs than anybody else's, though we didn't finance their inventory or pay advertising as some people suggest. We stayed in the real estate business and didn't get into retailing. While we did incur greater upfront outlays with a few key tenants like Gucci, we also received a percentage of profits, which enabled us to recover our investment if things went well, as is happening."

Before Gucci, Himmel, Klutznik and their associates had closed about 30 lease deals. In the following year, they closed another 50. Among the fashionable names who decided Copley Place was a logical location: Art Explosion, Benetton, Caswell-Massey, Charles Jourdan, Coffee Connection, Crate & Barrel, Enrico Celli, Godiva Chocolatier, The Limited, Louis Vuitton, Saint Laurent, Rive Gauche, Pappagallo and Williams-Sonoma.

A Ralph Lauren Polo store would be a powerful magnet for retailers selling to men, but he had an agreement to buy a brownstone on Newbury Street's most desirable block, which he planned to convert into a store. When Lauren unexpectedly backed out of the deal and announced he'd locate in Copley Place, the odds improved that Himmel would achieve the mix of stores needed for success.

Tiffany became interested in a full-line Boston store after the success of their downtown shop selling gift wares for executives. The Tiffany name meant magic around the world—the phrase "Tiffany location," derived from their Manhattan store at the pivotal carriage trade crossroads of Fifth Avenue and 57th Street, meant the finest, most valuable and coveted spot anywhere. The name conjured rarity not only because of the precious wares it sold but also because the company had expanded little. There were less than a dozen Tiffany stores. So when they announced a new one, it was an event. Their decision to locate in Copley Place accelerated the momentum.

It's always a good idea to attract respected local merchandisers, and Copley Place began signing some of those. For instance, Mark & Company, which sold women's sportswear; Georgette, offering bridal wear; Safer, men's clothing and accessories from Italy; and Au Bon Pain, a French-style bakery and café. Le Chapeau, a hat shop that started at Faneuil Hall Marketplace, leased a store at Copley Place. Durgin Park at Copley Place was an offshoot of the famous Boston eatery which moved into Faneuil Hall Marketplace. Seeking the comforts of controlled indoor atmosphere over Boston's sweltering hot summers and bitter-cold winters, Irresistibles actually moved from Newbury Street into Copley Place.

Whenever possible, Himmel sought retailers to reinforce the high-end image. Instead of a mass market-chain bookstore like Waldenbooks or B. Dalton, mainstay at so many suburban shopping centers, he signed Rizzoli. It's a culture experience where urban sophisticates may browse among sculptures, art books, foreign language books and classical records. The Eastern Newsstand, owned by New York's Restaurant Associates, offers a wide range of foreign language publications.

Himmel wanted movie theaters, because they'd bring people to Copley Place at night and keep it lively. Theaters would also help the hotels, since with 2,000 rooms, there would be many people looking for something to do at night. The largest theater operators could afford to bid for the most popular movies, so Himmel and his leasing agents negotiated with several major chains. He reached an agreement with Sack Theaters, which built a nine-screen cinema.

Copley Place opened on February 11, 1984, about 80 percent leased. A year later, it was 90 percent leased. Sales hit $300 a square foot, which would rank it among the most successful shopping centers in the United States.

Meanwhile, Lafayette Place was foundering. The general contractor, Blount Brothers of Montgomery, Alabama, fell a year behind with construction. In early 1983, Marco Ottieri announced it "will open in time for this year's Christmas shopping season." An October topping-out ceremony, on the occasion of the building's highest structural members being installed, turned to disaster. Ottieri had hired a nonunion caterer, and the construction unions refused to do the topping-out, infuriating Mayor Kevin White. Christmas came and went, the gray hulk of Lafayette Place still dark. Ottieri promised an opening on May 20, 1984—the governor designated it Lafayette Day. That date passed, too. Delays tacked about $20 million to the project's cost.

The hotel deal crumbled. Massachusetts Mutual Life, which had approved a $33 million mortgage for it, pulled out. Ottieri couldn't find any other institution willing to write an equivalent mortgage, but he did persuade Manufacturers Hanover to roll over their original two-year, $33 million construction loan into a 10-year mini-perm.

On July 31, 1984, Inter-Continental President Hans Sternik announced he was withdrawing from the project. Suddenly, Ottieri wasn't just having a hard time, he was being abandoned. It was humiliating. Everybody could see him going down. Newspapers described the empty hulk of a hotel as an "orphan." "Losing an international hotel of that caliber is a blot to the project," said a local observer, "but it's not panicsville."

Hotel bookings were canceled, though. Wells Shoemaker of Shippensburg, Pennsylvania reserved rooms and conference facilities for a meeting involving a hundred cell membrane researchers. When Inter-Continental notified him they wouldn't honor the reservations, he searched around and ended up at a Howard Johnson's. "We'd like to sue them if we can," he says, complaining about the extra expenses incurred. "I'd never touch them again with a 10-foot pole." Ottieri filed suit against Blount Brothers and Inter-Continental for damages.

Inter-Continental never explained why they walked. Some Inter-Continental sources suggested Mondev was running out of cash and cutting back on quality, which Inter-Continental didn't want to do. There also were complaints that Mondev didn't deliver the top-grade retail tenants which were promised. It was "more South Shore Mall than Fifth Avenue," according to one source. Mondev people denied that the company was hurting or compromising quality. They speculated Inter-Continental became nervous at the large number of new hotels opening in Boston—competition was more worrisome than when Inter-Continental signed onto the deal six years before.

Whatever the reasons, Ottieri got calls from executives at Ramada, Holiday Inns, Trust House Forte, KLM, Radisson and Hilton—all interested in the Lafayette Place hotel site. Donald Tofias, who represented Swissotel, a joint venture with Swissair and Nestle, was the most aggressive. He agreed to pay cash for half interest in what would be called The Lafayette Hotel.

At last, the retail component of Lafayette Place opened November 20, 1984. Ottieri had closed deals with 110 stores. While most were decidedly less glamorous names than those at Copley Place, they nonetheless included solid mass market retailers like Florsheim, Radio Shack, Waldenbooks and Consumer Value Stores. Some, such as shoe merchant Johnson & Murphy, aimed at more affluent buyers. Lafayette Place had a Chinese, Indian and American restaurant as well as fast food places like McDonald's, Incredible Spud, Villa Pizza and All-American Hero.

Perhaps surprisingly, after the publicized rivalry between Lafayette Place and Copley Place, some retailers became tenants in both projects. Among those are Pappagallo, Benetton, Casual Corner and Au Bon Pain.

Ottieri claimed about $400 annual sales per square foot. "Keep in mind," he says, "that we don't have a department store anchor, and a good one would probably do less than $200 a square foot. It tends to pull your average down. A good bookstore may do $250. A shoe store, much more. Fast food, even more—we have one place generating $600 a square foot."

The Lafayette Hotel opened March 9, 1985 with over $4 million of advance bookings. The hotel appealed to the corporate market for board meetings and specialty conferences rather than major conventions. It was booked for social functions like a New England Medical Center annual fundraiser and the Opera Guild's 25th Anniversary Ball.

The Lafayette got raves for its luxurious service. Restaurant reviewer John Mariani, for instance, wrote in *Esquire:* "If I had to give an award for 'best new restaurant of the year,' Le Marquis de Lafayette in the new Lafayette Hotel would win by at least three lengths . . . one of the best meals I have had anywhere."

Looking back, Ottieri says, "the summer of 1984 was an exciting time for me. I stopped racing cars to concentrate full time on making the project go. I started smoking again after eight years. I'm happy to report that I quit by November, when things came together."

Plans are afoot to develop Combat Zone property around Lafayette Place. Mondev owns an adjacent parking lot slated for more retail stores. There is an 18-story office building going up just off Chauncey Street. The old Paramount Theater will be refurbished as an entertainment complex. Most heartening: the wealthy Bass Brothers of Fort Worth bought a whole block, which they expect to develop for offices and stores.

Who won this leasing battle? In the retail leasing sweepstakes, Himmel and Copley Place certainly appeared to have finished on top. They got an anchor store which wasn't there before. They signed more stores faster. Their total volume seem to be higher. Yet as real estate investments, neither will turn a penny of profit for years, because the start-up costs were so high.

In December 1984, Aetna sold Urban Investment & Development Corporation to JMB Realty, the Chicago-based giant of real estate syndication. Thomas Klutznik departed to form a real estate company with husky Denver oilman Marvin Davis, owner of the 20th Century Fox Film Corporation, and Gerald Gray, chief financial officer of Davis Oil Company. Soon he was joined by Himmel, whose mission is to develop more projects in the East. Onward and upward to ever bigger deals.

16.

LOCAL CLOUT

DESPITE THE EMERGENCE OF GIANT ENTREPRENEURS WHO OPER-
ate across the continent, real estate remains a business fought on
local issues. What counts primarily is the convenience, comfort and
cost of a specific project. A respected local developer who tailors
deals quickly for the needs of prospective tenants can do very well
against a much bigger competitor.

In Dallas, for instance, Trammell Crow faced unprecedented competition from well-financed Canadian entrepreneurs. But Dallas is his
hometown. He knows the local market and is widely admired. His
pride on the line, he's determined to be faster, more flexible and
creative than anybody else. It's a dramatic story that I got from Crow
and his principal rivals.

The "Canadian invasion," as Dallas newspapers dubbed it, began
innocently enough with burly Michael Young, a Toronto-born investment banker who had done work for major Canadian real estate
companies. In 1970, he moved to Dallas, looking for opportunity.
"My feeling was that because the Canadian developers hadn't been
in Dallas yet," he told me, "what you needed to do was sell them on
the market, and deals would fall out of that. So I wrote an extensive
market analysis. Then I took it around the Canadian developers and
explained why they should consider Dallas."

If many Americans knew comparatively little about the Canadians,
the Canadians could tap considerable wealth. They were backed by
buccaneering financiers at Royal Trustco, Canadian Imperial Bank of
Commerce, Bank of Montreal, Bank of Nova Scotia and Toronto-
Dominion Bank. Often they were willing to take greater chances than
their counterparts in the United States. They made real estate loans
based on a company's creditworthiness and the strength of its balance sheets, often inflated by appraised property values. Unlike many
U.S. bankers, Canadian commercial bankers didn't insist on a more
conservative book value. Nor were they always much concerned about
the project a developer wanted to finance, even though failure could
have devastating consequences. U.S. bankers, by contrast, loaned

money project by project, each mortgage secured by a specific property which must meet the bankers' tests. As a result, Canadian developers could outbid U.S. developers and close deals fast.

Young approached a free-wheeling entrepreneur named Don Love, president of the $1.6 billion Oxford Development Group Ltd. He was eager for a chance to gain an advantage over his Canadian competitors. Young sold Love on buying a centrally-located downtown Dallas site. It appealed to Ben Carpenter, chief executive of Southland Life, who was interested in expanded quarters, and he became the lead tenant of what became a $110 million, 530,000-square-foot building.

"I was plenty anxious about that deal," Young says. "I remember sitting in Don Love's Edmonton office explaining that my fee would be between $500,000 and $2 million, depending on how he chose to structure the deal. He allowed as how it would be the biggest fee he ever paid. I was a little breathless, for I had never earned that kind of money before. I had just bounced a $162 check to stay at the Four Seasons Hotel.

"After this transaction with such a strong developer who pioneered many Canadian real estate deals in the United States, it was much easier for me to go after other Canadian developers. I had more credibility, and Dallas was a place nobody could afford to overlook." In Toronto, Young talked with dapper Jack Daniels, president of Cadillac Fairview—one observer described the experience as a little like dealing with Cary Grant. "Once he sensed that his competitors were heading for Dallas," Young recalls, "he wanted to move fast. He was from the napkin school of dealmaking—just dash a few numbers on a napkin and go! You don't do that today, and not many people did it then, but he did, and for a while he was successful. His Dallas deals were.

"During the 1970s, the Dallas market was site-driven. If you could acquire a site, it was comparatively easy to find tenants. Daniels and the other Canadians were terrific site buyers. Financed by Toronto-Dominion Bank, he gave me as a broker the go-ahead to acquire a full-block site at the east end of downtown—bounded by Pacific and Elm, Ervay and St. Paul." When First City Bank signed on as the lead tenant in a planned 50-story granite tower, shock waves were felt through Dallas. Many of the major Dallas real estate developers did business with that bank, so they believed they should have had that job.

Cadillac Fairview became a more formidable competitor when Michael Prentiss took over the company's Dallas operations in 1981. He was authorized to make his own leasing decisions. He didn't have to clear things with Toronto. He could speak to prospective tenants as a principal, and he could respond fast. His ambitions extended from downtown Dallas all along the major corporate corridors.

He needed the full force of his personality to maintain credibility in the eyes of his clients. During October 1982, it was announced that Cadillac Fairview was canceling a Manhattan deal and forfeiting a $21 million down payment. Daniels had been obsessed with making a hit in New York, and when Citicorp's choice Lexington Avenue site across the street from their new Citicorp Center went on the market, he bid an astonishing $1,900 a square foot—$105 million altogether. It would be hard to get rents covering that cost at any time, but during the 1982 recession, even Daniels conceded anything built would only worsen the loss. Cadillac Fairview, in any event, was overextended elsewhere. The calamity triggered a crisis of confidence about Cadillac Fairview in Dallas and everyplace else.

Daniels was fired, and Leo Kolber, a streetsmart deal-maker long associated with the Bronfmans, took over. He cut Cadillac Fairview's staff in half. He sold 70 percent of the company's properties, including 10,931 apartments and 4,700 acres of land. He sliced volatile floating-rate debt by $1 billion. Though he was turning the company around, people couldn't forget Daniels. His reputation provided a convenient target for Crow to sell against, since tenants are naturally concerned about the staying power of a landlord.

"The Citicorp walk seemed to make people forget about the good things we had done here," Prentiss says. "Overcoming adverse publicity is always difficult. But I'm a tenacious person, and with the crew I assembled here, we proceeded to build more than 8 million square feet of space—projects worth more than $400 million."

The boyish-looking, intense Ken Field, president of the $1 billion Toronto-based Bramalea, was another Canadian with lofty ambitions. Michael Young showed him a 10-acre property owned by the Murchison oil and real estate interests. Located at the west end of downtown, it was bounded by Elm on the north, Commerce on the south, Griffin on the east and Lamar on the west. Here, during the mid-1960s, Dallas millionaire Clint Murchison Jr. announced a $350 million cultural and office complex called Main Place. One Main Place, an office tower, was built. But nothing more happened. Equitable Life Assurance Society bought that building for $40.5 million in 1968. Field decided to spring for the site.

Young helped him land InterFirst Bank as a lead tenant, and the building, the tallest in Dallas, would be called InterFirst Plaza. This deal, too, threw the Dallas real estate community into a frenzy. Trammell Crow, for instance, used to sit on InterFirst's Board. The Canadians had grabbed another plum.

It was just beginning. N. B. Cook Corp. of Vancouver bought

3,145 acres of land around Dallas and Fort Worth. Rostland Corp., Toronto, built three office buildings in North Dallas. Cadillac Fairview bought 420 acres of North Dallas land.

One of the wildest, most unpredictable entrepreneurs to invade Dallas was the Ottawa-based French Canadian Robert Campeau. He reportedly presided over board meetings of his $1.4 billion empire wielding his shoe rather than a gavel. A high school dropout who started his career as a machinist, he was a combative man known for his emotional outbursts at Ottawa zoning hearings. He ignored a zoning regulation against buildings more than 150 feet high, tangled with Ottawa officials and built a 342 foot tower. To prevent Campeau from removing some fine trees from his property, Ottawa Mayor Charlotte Whitton shielded them with her body, but he drove a bulldozer straight at her. She moved, and so did the trees. When they met at a formal party, he stepped on the hem of her gown and ripped off the back of it. Embarrassed, she fled.

Campeau entered Dallas full of grand plans: a downtown skyscraper, an office complex and a $400 million condominium community north of Dallas. He seemed a powerful new force on the horizon. Yet Trammell Crow, angry at some of the Canadians whom he felt were brash and boastful, smelled trouble. He remembered his own painful recent brush with bankruptcy, the result, among other things, of buying too much raw land which added interest costs without yielding immediate income. Campeau bought a lot of raw land, and when inflation pushed land prices up, he went back to his bank and borrowed more money so he could buy still more land. He boosted his holdings 150% within a couple years. With interest rates at 17 percent, his floating rate debt doubled from $156 million to $397 million. Crow worked out the numbers and figured that Campeau must be "bent if not broke." In 1982, Campeau recognized his plight and abuptly canceled his projects and fired people, leaving hardly a trace.

Albert and Paul Reichmann of Olympia & York were a different breed altogether. They seemed larger than life because of their daring moves in New York. Michael Young approached them in 1978.

"Accustomed as I was to flashy real estate developers with stainless steel teeth," he recalls, "I was surprised and charmed by Albert and Paul Reichmann. They're calm, sober people. They get to the essence of a deal fast. Their style is to negotiate with you as a partner, rather than as an adversary. They're successful in large measure because of the degree to which they address the other person's interests.

"I didn't sell the Reichmanns anything when I met them in Toronto, but I got a call from Albert a couple months later. Somebody had showed them a site in downtown Dallas. Would I investigate it for them and recommend whether they should purchase it? That was an unusual call, because developers tend to prefer keeping brokers out of deals, so they can save the commissions. Here he was asking me in.

"The site, at the corner of Bryan and Harwood, was a super location—perhaps the 100 percent location in downtown Dallas. Yet it was a tight site, so it wasn't clear what to do with it and what an appropriate value might be. Parking, for instance, would be a problem. Albert figured those difficulties could be resolved, and he asked me to try closing a deal. The negotiation was difficult, because one of the owners was Vincent Carrozza, a Dallas developer, who dug in his heels. But we closed in a few months."

The Reichmanns built a 36-story, 706,768-square-foot notched tower of polished pearl-gray granite. Typical floors were 25,000 feet, about right for Dallas. The craftmanship, energy systems, elevators and other features were consistent with the quality the Reichmanns insisted on in their buildings. Instead of digging a deep hole for below-ground parking, which would have added considerable cost, the Lebanese-born Dallas architect David Habib designed the first six floors to accommodate 400 cars. The building, called Olympia & York Tower, opened in 1982. It was rich with promise. The Reichmanns asked Coldwell Banker, the real estate arm of Sears, Roebuck, to handle leasing.

Olympia & York Tower is directly across Harwood Street from the building where Trammell Crow had his headquarters—the 1-million-square-foot 2001 Bryan Tower, among the first downtown Dallas office buildings by a developer. Until it opened in 1972, big corporations like Republic Bank, Southwestern Bell, Dresser Industries, Southland Life and Mercantile Bank dominated the local skyline. Crow was not only establishing a presence for himself as an entrepreneur building skyscrapers, but he was almost single-handedly pulling the downtown core northeast when a number of knowledgeable observers like the Murchison interests expected it to go southeast. But Crow took tremendous pride in what he accomplished, and he wasn't going to be outdone by anybody, especially in his backyard.

He'd whip the Canadians. He was joined by his 31-year-old son Harlan. Like his father, the solid, impulsive Harlan is a workaholic. "Buildings are what I do for work and relaxation both," he says. He started his career with the company as everybody else did, in leasing. He was paid the standard $18,000 a year plus commissions on space he leased. He began wearing out shoe leather in Houston. "I didn't like it," he acknowledges, "but I gained an invaluable understanding of the market, what people care about, what they don't like. Our whole aim is to deliver the kind of space people want."

Satisfied with his son's performance in Houston, Trammell assigned him to build an 829,888-square-foot office tower in 1980, next to the Olympia & York site on Harwood Street. It was an awkward design, with sloped bronze-tinted windows, and Harlan regretted it later. But he learned the business, and the building leased.

The biggest tenant there is Diamond Shamrock, a Cleveland-based company antagonized by Mayor Dennis Kucinich—he made a name for himself by spending that city into default and denouncing opponents as "lunatics." Crow's primary competitor for Diamond Shamrock was Plaza of the Americas, an office-retail-hotel complex a couple of blocks east. When Trammell Crow Company President Don Williams and Harlan Crow approached Diamond Shamrock, they offered to put Diamond Shamrock's name over the door. But at the other place, "Plaza of the Americas" would be over the door. "They came here," says Harlan Crow. "Corporate ego figures in a lot of decisions, as you know. Their new 75,000-square-foot headquarters helped attract other tenants, and before long they were taking more space themselves."

Two blocks away, on the other side of Crow's seven-story parking garage, Harlan Crow was building San Jacinto Tower, three parallel concrete slabs that were to provide another 844,098 square feet of office space. That $45 million structure was slated to open in December 1981—about six months ahead of Olympia & York Tower, so the two buildings would be going head-to-head for tenants.

San Jacinto Tower was an outpost on the eastern edge of Dallas's downtown, and Crow realized they must establish leasing momentum early. They began talking with William Webster, managing partner of Arthur Young & Company. The Big Eight accounting firm had offices in the heart of downtown, in the old Republic Bank Building. Their offices were scattered through almost 20 small floors. Rent was good—only about $14 per square foot—but Webster wanted to consolidate offices on fewer floors so the firm could function more efficiently. The bank wasn't responding with any solutions.

He considered Olympia & York Tower, but space there was tagged at $22 per square foot, and the Reichmanns weren't budging. That would mean a tremendous hike in overhead, since Webster needed about 120,000 square feet. Crow struck with a $16 offer. Webster could have floors four, five, six and seven, which would be available for occupancy before the entire building was finished. The deal seemed reckless to real estate observers, since it was admittedly below Crow's pro forma—a rent level which would make the building successful. Webster signed with Crow: a 10-year lease for an estimated $19.2 million.

Marsh & McLennan brokered the bulk of insurance for Olympia & York's buildings, so Crow didn't have much of a chance when the firm announced it needed new quarters—their old building was being demolished for redevelopment. Nonetheless, Crow leasing agent Barry Henry introduced himself to Marsh & McClennan's Dallas principals, Philip North and Herbert Thomas. They got along, but Henry didn't make any headway, so strong was the pull toward Olympia & York Tower.

"Our only hope was to find something wrong with it," Henry recalls. "We were losing the deal until a new recruit of ours, a recently hired guy named Chet Edwards, got an idea. He was poring over the plans for Olympia & York Tower, which wasn't up yet. He began thinking about the exterior which alternated five feet of granite with five feet of window. Assuming standard office measurements, some executives would have a single window, while others got two, so the design could trigger resentment among jealous employees. There were potential conflicts with Marsh & McLennan's code which, like that of many large companies, specified the perks various executives were entitled to.

"To demonstrate the implications of Olympia & York's design, Harlan, leasing agent Greg Young and myself pushed our desks aside— we were in Diamond Shamrock Tower—and had workmen install a sheetrock mock-up of the Olympia & York exterior wall with possible ways of dividing the offices. Late one afternoon, we invited North and Thomas to see. Startled, they inspected the mock-up, then looked down at Olympia & York's site and concluded the building would introduce problems they'd rather avoid. By contrast, San Jacinto Tower had windows 3½ feet wide framed by nine inches of sheetrock, affording more flexibility in configuring offices. Executives were likely to be happier."

Crow shocked the Dallas real estate community when he signed Marsh & McLennan to 60,000 square feet at San Jacinto Tower. It was a $16.85-per-square-foot, 10-year, $10.1-million-dollar deal. They moved in May 1982. The Reichmanns didn't do anything wrong. They followed their normal, proper practices, but this wasn't a normal market. Crow was on the warpath.

Merrill Lynch was a good prospect, because it was under pressure to move from its cramped quarters at the old Metropolitan Savings Building. That Class C space was beginnning to hurt its reputation, since major competitors occupied flashier offices—Dean Witter, Kidder Peabody, Paine Webber and Goldman Sachs moved into the Interfirst Two Building, for instance. Merrill Lynch seemed destined for Olympia & York Tower, as the giant brokerage concern had offices in the Reichmanns' New York buildings. They knew the Reichmanns were among the best landlords anywhere. Furthermore, the final decision had to be approved by a corporate real estate man in New York.

Merrill Lynch executives were wined and dined by Crow's people. Fred McCommas, an outgoing white-maned sales manager in the Dallas office, got along well with Crow leasing agents Barry Henry and Greg Young, declaring: "I may have snow on my roof, but I've got fire in my boiler." Henry and Young ventured to Manhattan, dining corporate real estate boss Jeff Landers at Tavern on the Green. They paid four waiters $100 to sing "Happy Birthday," even though it wasn't Landers's birthday. "People have fun doing business with us," laughs Young.

By this time, the Reichmanns cut their quoted price to $17.50, but it was too late. Landers approved a 10-year, 40,000-square-foot deal at $16 a square foot—$6.4 million altogether. It was a good deal for Merrill Lynch. They moved in May 1982.

While in New York, Henry and Young made a cold call to Tony Vasile, the executive in charge of real estate for Banker's Trust. He happened to have a Dallas map on his desk. The bank had outgrown subleased space at Plaza of the Americas, and they couldn't get any more there. Why not move to San Jacinto Tower, just a couple of blocks away? First, Henry and Young would have to become acquainted with Tony Mazilla, the Banker's Trust executive in Dallas.

They drove him an hour and a half north to Ponder, Texas, a wink of a community noted for the Ranchman's Café. It would fulfill almost anyone's outsize vision of Texas. There were cowboys in dusty boots. The place served great, greasy pan-fried steaks with greasy fries. Weathered women baked goopy coconut cream pies, lemon meringue pies, pecan pies, chocolate pies. Banker's Trust became a tenant at San Jacinto Tower with a 10-year, 20,000-square-foot lease at $17.85. It wasn't Crow's biggest deal, but every $3.5 million helped.

"Those early deals should have had the Reichmanns' name on them," concedes Michael Young who took over leasing for Olympia & York Tower after Coldwell Banker was fired.

While San Jacinto Tower was under construction, Crow announced plans for 50-story LTV Center, a 1.1-million-square-foot building that would be built three blocks north on Harwood—Crow was forming a rectangular urban campus with Olympia & York Tower at one corner.

LTV, however would raise the stakes considerably. Unlike the other Crow skyscrapers, which are boxes built in much the same fashion as he built his warehouses (cheap and fast), LTV would respond to current trends favoring more dramatic design and luxurious materials. Architect Rick Keating, of Skidmore, Owings & Merrill's Houston office, conceived a design like a Renaissance bell tower. Its exterior would be polished pink granite. The rotunda would be lined with white Italian marble. Lobby walls of kevazingo and bubinga wood from Africa. Elevator cabs—gleaming bronze. Glass portals were inspired by Ghiberti's famed Florentine baptistry doors. Around the lobby would be 20 bronze figural sculptures by nineteenth century French artists like Maillol, Bourdelle and Rodin. LTV Center was built and filled rapidly, despite a growing surplus of office space in Dallas.

On the drawing boards was 2200 Ross Avenue, yet another Crow tower, which would offer more than a million square feet of space. Keating was commissioned for that design, too. "We're a market-driven company committed to maintaining space inventory for our customers," says Don Williams. "We're not investors with a single property."

Sanford Bilsky, responsible for Olympia & York's leasing around the United States: "Crow was an awesome competitor. Dallas, with all those Crow buildings, was the toughest market we faced. It would be like Mr. Crow building offices in New York, where we are so strong."

Crow's ongoing construction program figured in the signing of Central & Southwest Company, a public utility which needed 180,000 square feet. Crow didn't have that much space available. However, the law firm Seay Gwinn Mebus Crawford Blakeney was dissolving and wanted to cancel its lease in San Jacinto Tower. Crow agreed, gaining 30,000 square feet. With the law firm Jones, Day, Reavis & Pogue, he traded 90,000 square feet, which they leased in San Jacinto Tower for equivalent space in LTV Center. These deals made possible the Central & Southwest lease, believed to be worth $36 million.

Since Crow was based in Dallas, he could offer more inducements out-of-towners like the Reichmanns had a hard time matching. "We're a very big company," Harlan says. "We use a lot of accountants and lawyers. We don't do business with people who aren't in our buildings."

William Lawley, president of the Swearington real estate brokerage firm that brought Crow some deals, comments: "Crow has said publicly he'll get bloody. He'll build right along with the Canadians.

They say he's not invincible, but I do believe he changes his clothes in a phone booth like Superman."

Though Michael Young signed some leases for Olympia & York Tower, the biggest deals there were made by the Reichmanns themselves. They control more than 50 million square feet of office space across North America. They have a first-class reputation. Among the most astute real estate financiers, they don't give away equity in buildings to their lenders like Crow does, so they have it available if necessary to help land a tenant.

The Reichmanns signed Shearson/American Express to 28,300 square feet, Coopers & Lybrand to 75,800, Fireman's Fund to 83,400 and Arco to 98,800. Each involved equity participation in the building. It was based on a sliding scale—the more space rented, the greater the equity, up to 49 percent.

However, Crow had dealt his most devastating blows. Leasing at Olympia & York Tower stalled. San Jacinto Tower quickly filled 85 percent of its space, while the Reichmanns inched up to 50 percent, probably millions below break-even.

The building's drawbacks bothered potential tenants, and they signed elsewhere. Parking, for instance—an important issue since Dallas executives love their cars. San Jacinto Tower had a parking space for every 1,500 square feet of office space, Olympia & York Tower, a parking space for every 2,500 square feet. Naturally, a prospective tenant would prefer fewer employee complaints about inconvenience.

Missed opportunities to sign tenants became ever more costly, because in late 1983 the Dallas real estate market took a dive. The demand for office space slackened while more new space kept coming onto the market. The average vacancy rate approached 15 percent. Not only was there more pressure to cut quoted lease rates, but developers began bidding for tenants with free rent. Eight months to a year of free rent on a five-year lease was typical.

Tenants who signed deals during the early phase of this decline still paid pass-through costs like taxes and maintenance. The developer absorbed financing costs which rent would have covered. Then, as developers became more desperate to sign tenants, "free" came to mean waiving all payments. A tenant who got a year's free rent didn't pay a penny to the developer until the second year of the lease.

Dallas developers gained a little consolation by reminding themselves that the situation was worse in Houston, where tenants were routinely offered free rent for more than half the term of a typical lease. "Did you hear the latest Houston deal?" one Dallas broker jokes. "Six years' free rent on a five-year lease."

By early 1984, work letters were costing developers more. These specify the interior finishes a landlord gives to its tenant—ceilings, floors, walls, carpeting, lighting fixtures and electrical outlets. The standard Dallas work letter translated to an outlay of $12 to $15 per square foot, but when the race intensified to sign a big law firm, for instance, bids shot up to $30 per square foot.

How taxes, maintenance and utilities would be paid were subject to negotiation. Sometimes desperate developers offered to pay a new tenant's moving expenses. "We didn't offer free limousine service as some newspapers reported," Crow smiles, "but if a key tenant wanted that, I'd have done it, sure."

With some Dallas tenants, the impact of these negotiations was to drive down the effective lease rate to $9 or $10 a square foot from a quoted rate of $18 or $19. "Crow viewed us as foreigners threatening their kingdom," says Bilsky of Olympia & York. "Sometimes in Dallas logic went out the window, and the object was to make sure nobody took a tenant away from you, regardless of cost. On many deals I've seen, the owner wouldn't make any money for five years. You cannot compete with that. We backed off many potential deals, because we're not in business to lose money!"

After three years, San Jacinto Tower was virtually all leased, and LTV Center was 75 percent leased. Crow started leasing 2200 Ross Avenue before the foundation was dug.

Olympia & York Tower limped along with only 65 percent of its space leased. Months passed without any action at all. Mounting losses meant it would be quite a while before this building ever saw black ink.

The Reichmanns sat tight, hoping for a turnaround in the discouraging Dallas economy. When that happened, they'd have space which could be leased at current—presumably higher—rates. Meanwhile, their drubbing demonstrated the power of a stubborn entrenched local man against even the mightiest developers on the continent.

17.
GLAMOROUS PROMOTION

WHILE MANY REAL ESTATE ENTREPRENEURS ARE FLAMBOYANT PRO-moters, very few succeed at becoming a brand name which means much in a competitive marketplace. Manhattan's Donald John Trump, however, is undeniably a glamorous name like Gucci, Cartier and Rolls Royce.

It seems preposterous, but almost anything he does excites publicity. Trump is blond, trim and a shade over 6 feet 2 inches tall. His youth, bold ideas, remarkable track record and wealth capture the public imagination.

The very idea of somebody 38 years old building an empire which gushes $110 million annually—there's something quite appealing about that. Trump's net fortune is estimated at $400 million.

To be sure, Trump is far from being the biggest or most successful real estate entrepreneur in the United States—the Trump Organization has developed just four major buildings. That it generates so much money is a tribute to his relentless persistence, keen eye for bargains, resourcefulness at devising clever deals—and his phenomenal gift for promotion.

He hung a giant "Trump" banner on Grand Central Station while he was restoring its facade and building the Grand Hyatt next door—a miffed Mayor Edward Koch wanted him to remove it, but it remained. Later Trump had his name emblazoned in two-foot-high brass letters outside Trump Tower, his luxurious retail-office-condominium complex on Fifth Avenue. His name is chiseled in the limestone facade of Trump Plaza, a posh cooperative apartment building on Manhattan's East Side. There it is again, in flashing lights on his Atlantic City casino, Harrah's at Trump Plaza. In a blaze of stardust, he bought an Atlantic City project from Hilton and opened it as Trumps' Castle Hotel & Casino.

Of course, Trump doesn't get a hit every time. In 1983, he asked Philip Johnson and John Burgee to design a 60-story residential and office building he envisioned for a property at Madison Avenue and 60th Street. It would be called Trump Castle, complete with turrets, a moat and gate. Trump dropped the idea when it became clear that at the price Prudential Insurance Company was asking for the property—around $120 million—the project would be too risky.

Though most of Trump's press notices are favorable, he outrages people, too. A current case involves 100 Central Park South, a rent-controlled building he's trying to empty, so it can be demolished and make way for new development. Since rent control entitles tenants to pay less than their share on an open market, it naturally encourages demand, squeezes the profits that make adequate maintenance possible and penalizes construction of rental housing. Hence, the chronic shortage New Yorkers have endured since World War II. Tenants seldom want to leave their apartments, since they're a steal, and evictions are virtually impossible. The insiders—tenants—enjoy powerful advantages over outsiders seeking apartments as well as over landlords like Trump. His agent, Citadel Management, has spent three years trying to get people out, and still there's no end in sight. It's legal trench warfare.

The fortune Trump earned in real estate has enabled him to pursue his passion for football, and it has made him even more of a media figure. In October 1983, he bought the New Jersey Generals, one of 18 teams in the shaky new United States Football League, from Oklahoma oilman J. Walter Duncan. Price: $5 million. Then Trump aimed high as ever: he coaxed Hershel Walker, star running back from the University of Georgia, to join the Generals in a four-year, $6-million deal. He got quarterback Brian Sipe from the Cleveland Browns for $1.9 million.

Trump fired coach Chuck Fairbanks and wooed Miami Dolphins' Coach Don Shula, who has one of the most enviable records in pro football. A much-publicized romance faded, Trump suggested, when Shula asked for the ultimate—a condominium in Trump Tower. "That's something more valuable than money," he says. Shula's recollection is a little different. "All I did was listen to what Trump had to say. They approached me. I didn't approach them." Trump eventually hired Walt Michaels, former coach of the New York Jets, who later transformed the Generals from a losing team into a winner.

In December 1983, Trump tried to persuade Lawrence Taylor, star linebacker of the New York Giants, to join his Generals. He loaned Taylor $1 million. Taylor agreed to perform promotional services for the Trump Organization, and he signed to play with the Generals after his contract with the Giants expired in 1988. Awakened from their slumbers, the Giants decided they didn't want to lose Taylor, so they paid Trump $750,000 for the option. Taylor gave the $1 million back to Trump.

His deal with Doug Flutie from Boston College was the most spectacular. Trump took action while the National Football League was mired in rigid procedures and indecision. When Trump had lunch with Flutie—a tuna sandwich brought into Trump's offices—that made the *New York Times*. In January 1985, Trump announced the signing of a deal worth as much as $7.5 million to Flutie at the four-story pink marble Trump Tower atrium. The press conference was like a carnival, attracting sportswriters as well as journalists who normally cover business and political affairs. Trump sold 7,000 more season tickets in the two weeks after the Flutie signing.

Trump prides himself on challenges against startling odds, and the USFL is one of those. Team owners lost $100 million, and the number of teams shrank to 14. Trump spearheaded a move to a fall season, competing directly against the entrenched National Football League, which has all the lucrative television contracts. He is behind a $1.32 billion antitrust suit against the NFL.

But his biggest football battle, it appears, is to maintain the attention of fans whose interest in the fledgling league seems to be fading. Flutie had some fine moments on the field, but his performance as a professional lacked the excitement and consistency people expected. By the end of the 1985 season, the Generals had finished in third place, and Trump discussed merging the Generals with the Houston Gamblers, which were owned by Stephen M. Ross, another New York real estate entrepreneur. The Gamblers' star quarterback, Jim Kelly, would be the new starter. Flutie would likely be traded to another team if the merger goes ahead.

Another possibility is that the antitrust suit may be settled by merging the best USFL teams—which would certainly include the Generals—in the NFL. For Trump, this is a much more interesting way to fulfill his big league dreams than just buying an established franchise.

With football on his mind, he proposes to build on a Queens site which contains about 70 junkyards—an 82,000-seat, white-domed stadium estimated to cost $286 million. He hopes to have it ready by the 1989 football season. Half the seats would be sold to individual and season ticketholders. The other half would be sold for an average of $12,000 or leased at $2,400 annually. There would be 221 luxury boxes leased for an average $60,000 annually. And people who bought seats, he suggests, would still have to buy tickets to individual events! Among the recent precedents for this idea, used a century ago to finance European opera houses: Texas Stadium in Irving, Texas, where luxury boxes which sold originally for $50,000 were resold for up to $600,000.

In December 1985, New York State and New York City gave Trump the initial go-ahead. For condemnation of land and site improvements, the city and state would contribute $150 million upfront, which Trump would repay over 25 years. Trump must secure approvals from the State Urban Development Corporation, the city's Board of Estimate, city council and state legislature. An environmental impact statement must be filed. There are sure to be legal fights with the Willets Point Business Association, representing about a hundred businesses with 2,000 employees who would have to relocate. The plan is conditional on Trump being able to attract a National Football League team.

Meanwhile, Trump's flight with football already seems to have enriched his net worth. During 1984, he accumulated American Broadcasting Company stock as a possible lever against the network, which he believed was treating the USFL poorly. The 1985 takeover of ABC by Capital Cities turned his holdings into a windfall estimated at $47 million.

When he gives money away, Trump may choose a memorable occasion so everybody will remember his contribution. At the dedication of New York City's Vietnam Veterans Memorial, May 1985, Trump donated $1 million for vet job-training. "I feel deeply that the vets didn't get a fair shake when they returned," says Trump. The ceremonies featured fireworks, a parade, Miss New York State and, of course, Mayor Edward Koch.

In 1976, Trump met the trim, blonde, aggressive Ivana Winkelmayr at a New York party. A Montreal model, she had been an alternate on the 1972 Czechoslovak Olympic ski team. They were married about a year later, on April 9, 1977, at Marble Collegiate Church by Dr. Norman Vincent Peale, the Trump family minister.

Ivana Trump works 10 hours a day on interior design for their various projects. She watches over the Trump Tower atrium as well as Trump's Atlantic City casinos. She did the uniforms worn by the New Jersey Generals. She designed the interior of their two-story, 15-bedroom Georgian mansion in Greenwich, Connecticut, which Trump had bought for $3.7 million in 1982—$1.5 million below the asking price. The Trumps have three children, Donald John Jr., Ivanka and Eric. Ivana Trump returned to work within days after Eric's birth.

The family real estate empire began with Fred C. Trump, 80, a tall, trim man with slicked-back hair and a thin moustache. During the 1920s, he started as a carpenter, and soon became an entrepreneur, building nice little brick houses for $4,000 to $5,000. They were in Queens, a mostly middle-income suburban borough of New

York City. By the end of the decade, he was doing mansions in the posh Jamaica Estates section. When that market disappeared during the Great Depression, he plunged into FHA subsidized housing for low-income people. After World War II, he resumed building one- and two-family homes, while he continued doing large apartment complexes. He expanded into Staten Island and Brooklyn. By the 1970s, his empire included some 11,000 apartments. He operated through 60 partnerships and employed more than 1,000 people. His family was worth an estimated $40 million.

Early on, Fred Trump recognized the value of political connections in helping to gain approval for subsidized projects. He joined the Madison Club, where he could meet politicians in the Brooklyn Democratic Organization. He contributed to their candidates. During the 1940s, while selling a single-family house he built on Remsen Avenue, he met accountant Abraham Beame, who held many jobs as he moved around the city's bureaucracy. Fred Trump's lawyer was Abraham "Bunny" Lindenbaum, one of Beame's closest friends. For three decades, Fred Trump shared dinners and attended dances with party regulars like Beame and Lindenbaum.

In 1960, Lindenbaum urged Mayor Robert Wagner to see that the Urban Housing Foundation didn't get a tax abatement for a proposed luxury cooperative near Brooklyn's Ocean Parkway. Fred Trump attacked the tax abatement publicly: "Brooklyn taxpayers should not be asked to subsidize more luxurious housing than they themselves enjoy." Power broker Robert Moses suggested Fred Trump develop two thirds of the site, the Urban Housing Foundation the other third. That became the deal. Later Fred Trump applied for a tax abatement.

Two months after he got the go-ahead for the project, to be called Trump Village, Mayor Wagner appointed Lindenbaum to the City Planning Commission. He arranged a political fund raiser for 43 New York builders and landlords who had dealings with the city. All pledged contributions for Mayor Wagner's reelection campaign. Fred Trump's $2,500 was one of the biggest. The affair erupted into a scandal, and Lindenbaum quit his post. Mayor Wagner won the race anyway, and Abraham Beame was elected city comptroller.

In 1966, the State Investigations Commission conducted hearings on the way Fred Trump had handled $60 million of Mitchell-Lama subsidized mortgages. He got these to provide 90 percent financing for Trump Village, which had evolved into a complex of seven 23-story buildings with 3,800 cooperative apartments. Under law, he was allowed a 7.25 percent profit—$3.2 million. But this was calculated using an estimate investigators claimed was $6.6 million higher than construction costs, so he allegedly pocketed $598,000 more than he should have. Moreover, he bought the project's 40 acres of land for $1.2 million less than he reported. Fred Trump was ordered to return the $1.2 million to state housing officials.

He was criticized for paying some of his subsidized mortgage money to well-connected political figures. MacNeil Mitchell, the state senator who wrote the Mitchell-Lama bill, got $128,000 reportedly for helping to sell the co-ops. Lindenbaum got $520,000 in legal fees. Commission Chairman Jacob Grumet slammed Fred Trump and Lindenbaum as "grasping and greedy individuals."

Fred Trump was at the peak of his influence during the 1970s after Abraham Beame won election as Mayor in 1973. Hugh Carey, another politician who got his start in the Brooklyn Democratic Organization, was elected New York State governor the following year.

In a Jamaica Estates three-story brick mansion, Fred and Mary Trump raised two daughters and three sons. Besides Donald, there's Maryanne, who earned a law degree at Rutgers, became a federal judge and married Newark attorney John Barry; Elizabeth, who's an administrative assistant at Chase Manhattan Bank; Robert, executive vice president in Donald Trump's Trump Organization, concentrates on their Atlantic City operations. Donald's older brother, Fred Jr., died in 1981 after a long bout with alcohol. He was 42.

Donald is the only one who displayed an early interest in real estate. As a boy, he amassed wood blocks to build imaginary skyscrapers. He was brilliant, brash, strong-willed, demanding, and he loved to hang out at his father's office on 600 Avenue Z. Fred Trump sent him to New York Military Academy, Cornwall-on-Hudson, hopefully for some discipline. After graduation, he enrolled at Fordham University, but having had his fill of military rigor, he didn't care for the strict Jesuits. He transferred to the University of Pennsylvania, where he thrived at the Wharton School. As a student, he started negotiating small real estate deals including Philadelphia buildings which he renovated.

Trump was determined that everybody would know his name. He recalls a cold, rainy afternoon in November 1964 when, as an 18-year-old, he attended opening ceremonies for the $325 million, 6,690-foot Verrazano-Narrows Bridge, which connects Brooklyn and Staten Island. "All these politicians who opposed the bridge were being introduced and praised," he says. "Yet standing there in the rain was this 85-year-old engineer who came from Sweden, designed the bridge and poured his heart into it. Nobody even mentioned his name." It was Othmar Ammann.

One of Trump's heroes was William Zeckendorf, a name to be reckoned with even as his empire skidded to financial ruin. Trump admired Zeckendorf's audacious vision, financial creativity and high-stepping style. Publicity? Zeckendorf was a one-man whirlwind who swept across the front pages.

Following graduation from Wharton in 1968, Trump entered the family real estate business. He was restless at the prospect of working in the boroughs like his father, so he scouted around California, Maryland, Virginia and Washington, D.C. for people who needed to sell good properties and offered favorable terms. He preferred those with FHA mortgages 40 years out, 5½ percent interest. Trump put up very little cash.

No doubt about it, he had a gilded touch. He claimed that on one occasion he earned a $140,000 commission for about 20 minutes' work selling a friend's interest in a housing project. Though he concentrated his energies around New York, he boasted of making $14 million in California within two years.

He craves the limelight, and he knew he'd get it only if he established himself in Manhattan. That's where New York's most famous names in real estate operated—like Zeckendorf, Helmsley, Tisch. Dressed in flashy suits, Trump rode around in a chauffeured silver Cadillac with his initials, DJT, on the license plates.

He was among Manhattan's most eligible bachelors. He liked to squire slinky dates to fashionable night spots like Regine's, El Morocco, Le Club and Doubles. He lunched at The 21 Club, the most high-powered lunch spot in town. He was frequently seen at Madison Square Garden, where he had season tickets for Rangers and Knicks games.

At the Waldorf-Astoria Hotel, he was feted as Man of the Year by the National Jewish Hospital in Denver. "I'm not even Jewish," he laughs. "Most people think I'm Jewish because we own so many buildings in Brooklyn."

Despite his flamboyant life style, Trump runs a lean operation. In 1973, he made his move into Manhattan by taking a little office at 466 Lexington Avenue, a dilapidated building between 45th and 46th streets. He remained there five years.

He stalked Manhattan for a promising site and concluded that there were possibilities in several properties which belonged to the bankrupt Penn Central Railroad. In March 1975, he optioned two. The first was a nine-acre tract between 30th and 39th Streets west of Tenth Avenue. It included rail yards and old warehouses. The other was a rail yard which stretched from 59th Street to 72nd Street between West End Avenue and the Hudson River. With 76 acres, it was the largest undeveloped tract in Manhattan, and Trump imagined that with Hudson River views, it might work as a complex of luxury apartments—provided city officials would agree to a zoning change.

Trump negotiated a $62 million price with Penn Central liquidator Victor Palmieri. But Trump would pay only as the properties were developed. He wouldn't owe a penny until he got zoning changes and arranged financing. Penn Central had an option on 25 percent of any profits from his buildings.

If none of the other Manhattan real estate operators could see how to make those rail yards profitable, it was still a remarkable deal, which brought Trump to their attention. Apartment king Samuel LeFrak called Trump "bold, daring and swashbuckling." But Trump concluded the luxury apartment idea wouldn't work, and within a year, he quietly let his option on the 76-acre tract expire.

Trump, like his father, recognized that political connections would help him gain government approvals needed to do what he wanted with property like the Penn Central rail yards. He began mingling in New York Democratic circles. He was a generous donor to Mayor Abraham Beame. When Beame lost to Edward Koch in the 1977 election, Trump donated money to him. "He wishes he didn't have to give money to politicians," says his lawyer Roy Cohn, one of the best-connected New York attorneys, "but he knows it's part of the game. He doesn't try to get anything for it. He's just doing what a lot of people in the real estate business must do."

Trump met Louise Sunshine, the restless wife of a New Jersey physician. She dabbled in Democratic politics by working for Al Blumenthal in his bid for the mayoralty. He lost, but she raised $1 million. She was tapped to raise money for Hugh Carey in his $3.5 million 1974 gubernatorial compaign, and she began staging glitzy fund raisers at the Waldorf-Astoria and Lincoln Center with tickets priced at an unheard-of $2,500. The chain-smoking Sunshine cultivated everybody—politicians, entertainers, investment bankers. The Trumps helped her efforts with a $135,000 contribution. Only Hugh Carey's brother gave more.

"Donald described some pretty farfetched ideas which appealed to me," Sunshine recalls. "The more farfetched, the better. He asked how much money I'd need, and I said nothing. I just wanted to see what we could do together. That's how we began."

As Trump acquired properties and needed more political connections, Sunshine's role in the company grew. While she held a $17,000 a year post in Governor Carey's administration—with the New York State Thruway Authority—she had a salary around $100,000 a year from Trump.

Trump explored properties Penn Central owned around Grand

Central Station. These were mostly outdated hotels like the Commodore and Biltmore, which had tiny, dirty $20-a-night rooms. Occupancy rates were below 40 percent. Nearby, the Hotel Roosevelt wasn't doing much better. The whole area was on the skids. "The Chrysler Building had just defaulted on its mortgage," Trump recalls. "There was a flea market operating on the corner of Park Avenue. Many people predicted that East 42nd Street would go the way of West 42nd Street. But I watched thousands of people streaming in and out of Grand Central Station, and I thought it had to be a great site."

He negotiated with Palmieri for the 1,900-room Commodore. It was Penn Central's weakest hotel, with annual losses around $1.5 million. It owed the City $6 million in back taxes. In 1976, for $400,000, Trump took an option on it.

With New York City in desperate financial straits and office buildings losing money, this was no time to contemplate more offices. But a hotel might have a chance. Trump cast around for a hotel operator who might be interested, and soon he was talking with the Pritzkers of Chicago. They wanted to be in New York. They agreed to manage his proposed hotel for 4 percent of gross revenues, plus 20 percent of profits. There were subsequent clashes, though, over who'd pay for what. "We're not deeply in love with each other," says Jay Pritzker.

Making a hotel work here, however, required some resourcefulness, because steep taxes would suffocate almost any business. Giving outright tax breaks to private developers was a touchy affair, but there were possibilities if the city owned the Commodore.

Trump hit on this solution: buy the Commodore for $10 million, sell it to New York's Urban Development Corporation for $1 and lease it back for 99 years. Next, Mayor Abraham Beame got approval for New York's first commercial property tax-abatement program, and Trump was the first in line. There would be no taxes for 40 years. Since the Commodore's taxes were $4 million annually, this part of the deal was worth $160 million. Trump would pay only $250,000 a year in rent initially, and it would escalate to $2.7 million. The city would also get 10 percent of the first $500,000 net profits and 15 percent of profits over $1.5 million.

Since then taxes on comparable properties have risen to more than $9 million. With the hotel earning more than $12 million, the abatement obviously has a dramatic impact on profitability. Altogether, the deal could save Trump $200 million to $400 million in taxes.

It angered a lot of people. Councilman Henry Stern denounced it as "the tax deal of the century." While the city could ill afford to give up so much tax income, it needed a visible project which would help convince people things were on the upswing. Financier Preston Robert Tisch, president of Loews Corporation which owned Americana Hotels among other properties, objected. "The $250,000 rental the city gets is comparable to taxes on an Eighth Avenue motel," he says, "but the deal was right in what it did for that section of the city."

Despite the tax-abatement, Trump had some difficulty with construction financing. Commercial banks considered New York City a terrible place to loan money, so they got busy loaning billions to bankrupt banana republics instead. Trump borrowed $35 million from the Equitable Life Assurance Society and $45 million from the Bowery Savings Bank.

Anger abated as the hotel took shape. There were going to be fewer rooms—1,407—but they'd be decidedly bigger than before. Architect Der Scutt sheathed the Commodore's 30-story steel frame with mirrored glass. Boasting terraced beige Paradiso Italian marble pools and bronze lobby columns, the lobby exuded luxury. Scutt conceived a mirrored four-story atrium and the Sun Garden, a glass-enclosed cocktail lounge cantilevered over 42nd Street—visible proof seen from afar that good things were happening. The hotel was to be called the Grand Hyatt.

Even when the old Commodore was dark, closed, waiting for approvals before the project could proceed, Trump made money from it. Inside were beds, blankets, lighting fixtures, silver, glassware, chairs, tablecloths, bud vases, everything a hotel needed. Trump had it all appraised, and a few days after Christmas 1978, he opened the place for a gigantic sale. He charged a $5 admission fee. People were welcome to buy and cart away whatever they wanted. Lines extended down 42nd Street and up Lexington Avenue, several people deep—despite the bitter cold. People who met at the Commodore, honeymooned at the Commodore, saw their loved ones off to World War II there, made deals there or for any reason had fond memories of the place visited it again. It was nostalgia time, and the press had a field day. When the hotel was pretty much cleaned out several months later, Trump had grossed about $1.6 million.

So great was the demand for remembrances that Trump had walnut presentation boxes prepared for his friends. Each had a brass doorknob, iced-tea spoon, demitasse spoon, saltshaker and pepper shaker. Many of these were in mint condition, from boxes that were a half-century old but never opened.

Controlling construction cost of the Grand Hyatt required all of Trump's manic energy. Demolition posed the first challenge. "Under the Commodore," recalls Jeff Walker, who dealt with the contractors, "we had Grand Central Station, a number of retail stores, two public arcades, two subway stations and loop tracks which belonged to Conrail. Still deeper in the ground was a substation for Grand Central, and below that, power converters. I spent much time in the bowels of the earth, to make sure that what we were doing wouldn't cause problems."

A couple hotel residents refused to leave, even after the place closed. Except for the tumultuous sale, it was empty. "I remember one lady," says Walker, "who lived in a dark, dreary, roach-infested room without a telephone or anything, yet she insisted that the hotel be left alone. She went for daily walks and spent a lot of time at the public library several blocks away. Trump arranged a freshly painted, nicely furnished, sunny clean room at the Biltmore, but she didn't want to hear about it. I tried taking her to lunch. When finally I got her to look at the Biltmore room, she loved it. Next day, I had a truck move her things. Several months later, I ran into her at the Pan Am Building. She was grateful for my help moving her. She reached into her handbag and tried to give me a $2 tip."

Saving the old Commodore's frame as well as selected other parts of the building was much more complicated than just demolishing it and starting from scratch. "You could put your finger through some of the steel girders, rusted from 60 years of standing water," says Walker. "We got the original building plans from City Hall, but what we found was often quite different, because somebody forgot to update the plans. Walls which were supposed to be solid weren't, for instance. We discovered that concrete on upper floors was mixed with cinders from the days when the railroad had steam engines. There wasn't any blasting on this site—everything had to be taken apart by hand. It was a slow, tedious, dusty process.

"Then there were design changes. With the invention of the change came the change order, and it was the bane of my existence. If you made a little change in structural steel over here, that required a change in the sheet rock over there, which meant changes elsewhere. A minor change may cost $50 in a bathroom, but when you have 1,407 rooms, that minor change became quite a number. Changes could tack millions of dollars onto a project like this. As it was, the hotel cost $110 million."

Trump was tough with the contractors. "He's an unbelievable negotiator," recalls Irving Fisher of HRH Construction Company. "I don't worship at the shrine of Donald Trump, but our company gave up trying to negotiate costs with him. We just said 'Tell us what you want, you're going to get it anyway.' "

The Grand Hyatt opened September 5, 1980, and it was well received. "This is the most spectacular large convention hotel New York has seen in more than a generation," wrote Paul Goldberger, architectural critic of the *New York Times:* "A building that thrusts aside the banality and triviality of the designs of structures like the New York Hilton and the Sheraton Centre in favor of a kind of glittery, cosmopolitan elegance New York has not seen in a big new hotel building since the Waldorf-Astoria."

Trump's timing made him look like a genius. As the Grand Hyatt was being built, New York City's economy rebounded. Hotel occupancies and rates climbed steeply. So did property values. Trump and the Pritzkers refinanced the project and cashed out. Trump garnered 80 percent of the profits. With occupancy around 90 percent, the Grand Hyatt is among the most successful New York hotels.

"Trump is almost a throwback to the nineteenth century as a promoter," said Victor Palmieri admiringly, after the Grand Hyatt was finished. "He is larger than life. Whether he's charming his way through or bulling his way through, he makes things move in an almost impossible environment."

Meanwhile, Trump persuaded officials, who wanted a site for a proposed New York City Convention Center, to use one of the rail yards he had bought from Penn Central—nine acres between 30th and 39th streets west of 10th Avenue. In March 1978, Mayor Koch and Governor Carey announced that the project would proceed. They estimated its cost at $257 million, but soon it was skyrocketing past $500 million. Trump brokered the property to the Urban Development Corporation for $12 million.

Trump asked for a $4.4 million broker's commission, but he offered to waive this if the project were named the Fred J. Trump Convention Center. Trump settled for a $500,000 commission, and it wasn't named after his father. Rather, honoring a popular New York senator, it became known as the Jacob Javits Convention Center. Trump wasn't selected to develop it.

"What really got me," says Peter J. Solomon, former deputy mayor for economic development, "was his bravado. I think it was fantastic. It was unbelievable. He almost got us to name the convention center after his father in return for something he never really had to give away. I guess he just thought we would never read the fine print or, by the time we did, the deal to name the building after his father would have been set."

Trump coveted the 12-story, 1930 Bonwit Teller building on the east side of Fifth Avenue just north of 56th Street, next door to Tiffany's. A taller structure would be worth much more—if anybody could build the site. Trump learned that Equitable Life Assurance

Society owned the land, and they wouldn't sell. That wasn't necessarily an obstacle, if he could acquire the leasehold held by the Nashville-based Genesco, which owned Bonwit's.

Flexibility proved to be a major asset for Trump. "He was one of many who approached us," recalls George Peacock, senior vice president of Equitable Real Estate Group. "He proposed that we join him in redeveloping the property if he got the leasehold. We liked the idea even though, at that point, we didn't know exactly what we would build. We agreed on a handshake basis that The Equitable would join him in whatever he could arrange."

Genesco was the key. Their Fifth Avenue lease had 28 years to go. For five years, Trump called just to see whether they might be interested in considering a deal.

In a business magazine, Trump read that Genesco was thinking about selling the Bonwit's chain and the lease for their Fifth Avenue store. Eventually Genesco sold Bonwit's to Allied Stores. Trump bought the lease from Genesco, paying more than $10 million. Bonwit's, in turn, got a sweetheart lease for 80,000 square feet on four floors in Trump's new building—$2.5 million annually. He didn't pay anything out of pocket for this deal, because Chase Manhattan Bank had previously agreed to finance his acquisition of various rights needed for a project there.

Since Fifth Avenue is a prime retail street, Trump visualized some retail in a new building. Probably several floors—Water Tower Place in Chicago demonstrated that a seven-story downtown retailing center could work. Trump would need something else besides retail to make really big money. The most conservative strategy might be condominiums, since they'd return his investment the fastest, if they sold. Anything which yielded only rent would take years to return his investment. Trump knew he could charge top prices provided he could build condominiums high enough for residents to gain panoramic views of Central Park and the rest of the city.

The Bonwit site had 115 feet of frontage on Fifth Avenue, and it extended back 175 feet along 56th Street—20,125 square feet altogether. The 1961 New York City Zoning Resolution limited the square footage of a structure to 15 times that of the site—what were referred to as floor area ratios. In this case, 301,875 square feet. There was no way a new structure could be economical there.

How to enlarge it? Trump inquired about a 50-foot-deep, 15,000-square-foot site on 57th Street, which connected to Bonwit's. It was available, and he bought it. He flanked Tiffany's on the east as well as the south sides. Still, this wasn't enough.

Since Tiffany's was an 11-story building, much smaller than the zoning laws allowed on their 10,000-square-foot lot, Trump wondered about the unused portion of their air rights. It was a landmark building, designed by McKim, Mead & White in 1906, so Tiffany's wouldn't contemplate demolishing it for a new structure. Air rights could be transferred only to neighboring sites, and he was the neighbor. Walter Hoving, chairman of Tiffany's, sold Trump the air rights for $5 million. It found money to him.

With air rights to a site exceeding 45,000 square feet, Trump could qualify for bonus square footage provided by the Special Fifth Avenue Zoning District. This was created during the early 1970s, in an effort to halt the invasion by banks and airline ticket offices which bid rents higher than retailers could afford. Stores were moving to Madison Avenue, Lexington Avenue near Bloomingdale's and out into the suburbs. If Trump agreed to build 61,000 square feet of shops, bonuses would enable him to boost his allowed square footage 20 percent. He'd gain another 20 percent if he provided public space open seven days a week, from 8 A.M. to 10 P.M.

With Der Scutt, designer of the Grand Hyatt, Trump explored a building which would provide all the square footage he was allowed. This would have entailed a box with a section cantilevered over Tiffany's. Trump decided that solution wouldn't look appealing. He needed something dramatic to attract people who'd pay steep prices. The design which Scutt evolved had 24 vertical facets and a cascading base. The height was the equivalent of 70 stories.

"My God, son," Fred Trump reportedly exclaimed, "what are you doing? I've never built anything with more than four corners." Trump explained how much more condominiums were worth with two views apiece.

Trump's proposal cut a striking profile, but it violated several provisions of the zoning code, so Trump needed variances. The formal urban land use review process would take six months. Regulations specified that if it weren't finished in that period, everything must be started over. Because the site was among the most prominent in the city, the proposal excited tremendous attention. A lot of people felt any large structure was out of keeping with the graceful old low-scale structures on Fifth Avenue, and they opposed Trump. Some zoning officials wanted to reduce the size of the building Trump proposed. Yet they realized he was entitled to more square footage than he was proposing.

The last day of the six-month review period, city planners approved two fewer floors than he wanted but otherwise gave him the go-ahead. They approved Trump's proposed linkage to the IBM Building next door. Approval by the City's Board of Estimate followed, and Trump was on his way. He could build a six-story atrium lined with shops—160,000 square feet altogether—plus 13 floors of office space and 263 condominium units above that. "Basically, we used the office space to get the condominiums up higher," laughs Louise Sunshine.

Trump wanted to bill Trump Tower as a 68-story building, though it had only 58 stories. He argued that while the atrium was six stories, its unusual height was equal to quite a few more conventional floors. Trump, of course, had condominium marketing in mind when he requested this nomenclature, which he got.

Trump's eagerness to move ahead cost him the glow of glamorous publicity he had cultivated. As crews were preparing to demolish the Bonwit Teller Building, preservationists began protesting that two intricate Art Deco bas relief sculptures ought to be saved. He had promised that the Metropolitan Museum of Art could have them, if the cost and problems of removing them were reasonable. But he figured delay would entail an additional $250,000 of interest, $150,000 of real estate taxes and at least $100,000 of tenant lease income lost.

Trump gave the demolition order. The Landmarks Commission and other civic organizations were enraged. The *New York Times* denounced Trump's action as "a memorable version of cash-flow calculations outweighing public sensibilities." The New York Landmarks Conservancy snorted that Trump wasn't "one of the more enlightened developers." Trump dismissed the sculptures as "junk." He protested: "My biggest concern was the safety of the people on the street below. If one of those stones had slipped, people could have been killed."

Gradually, resentment of his impulsive demolition faded somewhat as people could see what was rising from the rubble. "It has not been difficult to presume that Trump Tower would be silly, pretentious and not a little vulgar," wrote Paul Goldberger in the *New York Times*. "But if overbearing publicity and overdressed guards do not a good building make, neither do they a good building deny. For the fact of the matter is that Trump Tower . . . is turning out to be a much more positive addition to the cityscape than the architectural oddsmakers would have had it. In fact, the atrium of Trump Tower may well be the most pleasant interior public space to be completed in New York in some years. It is warm, luxurious and even exhilarating. . . ."

Donald and Ivana Trump are sticklers for detail. Ivana spent a week at an Italian quarry examining and approving slabs of the peach-rose-and-pink Breccia Perniche marble which went into the Trump Tower atrium. When it was discovered the trim in an elevator cab didn't quite meet the elevator wall, the whole cab was replaced. It cost Trump $75,000 to truck 40-foot, 300-pound ficus trees from Florida into Trump Tower. They were brought in through a specially built tunnel, so they'd be protected from frost damage. Trump wasn't satisfied with the way they looked after they were installed. When workmen refused to take them out, he ordered the trees felled with a chain saw.

Trump had excited so much publicity that when the time came to market the building, he played hard to get. There were no model condominiums or advertisements in the *New York Times*. If you were interested, you could stop by and see a slide presentation, which was modest compared to what other developers like Houston's Gerald Hines were doing.

Trump knows what the wealthy want. Before he sold a single condominium, he announced a price increase. He still hadn't sold a condominium when he announced another price increase, then another. He hiked prices five times in six weeks. Nobody could remember such aggressive tactics. By the time Trump was through, prices ranged from $500,000 to $12 million.

Trump Tower cost $150 million, and half the condominiums had binding offers before the building opened in February 1984. People bought sight-unseen. Trump sold more than $275 million worth. Buyers included celebrities like Johnny Carson, Steven Spielberg, Paul Anka and Sophia Loren. The Trumps moved into a top-floor triplex. Somehow rumors spread that Prince Charles and Princess Di might be taking a condominium, though they were never sighted.

That wasn't all. The offices command among the highest rates anywhere, up to $70 a square foot. Perhaps nobody charges more for retail space—as much as $450 per square foot. Trump landed exclusive names like Asprey, Martha, Harry Winston, Cartier and Buccellati. Altogether, the commercial space in Trump Tower brings in $150 million annually, almost pure profit.

In July 1984, Trump got still another windfall. He had applied for a 10-year tax abatement on Trump Tower. Twice, New York City Commissioner of Housing Preservation and Development Anthony B. Gliedman denied the request.

Trump argued he qualified because of a 1971 statute, Section 421 of the New York State Real Property Law, which applied to dwellings built on sites which are "vacant, predominantly vacant or underutilized." While the statute didn't define "underutilized," the old Bonwit Teller building used only 66 percent of the allowable floor area and 60 percent of the total square footage. The statute didn't exclude a luxury residential development from the tax abatement, and many projects like Olympic Tower, 800 Fifth Avenue, the Galleria and Museum of Modern Art Tower got tax abatements. "If the city objects to the abatement," Trump says, "the answer is to repeal it. Meanwhile, it's there."

Gliedman's ruling was reversed twice in lower courts and upheld by the Appellate Division of the State Supreme Court. At last, the New York Court of Appeals ruled in Trump's favor. "The Legislature," wrote Judge Judith S. Kaye, "did not choose to restrict availability of this exemption to construction of low and middle-income housing." The tax abatement was worth about $50 million to Trump.

"I either had the insight or the foolishness to start investing heavily in Manhattan back in 1975," Trump says. "The city was a disaster, and it was supposed to get worse. The time New York started taking off was when I opened the Grand Hyatt. So I owned all this property around Manhattan and, leveraged with bank loans, the value of my investments doubled in six months. Soon they quintupled. Suddenly, this property goes up and up."

While condominiums in Trump Tower were leasing, Trump had his eye on St. James Tower—the new $35-million, 35-story condominium building at 54th Street and Sutton Place. An eccentric Englishman named Michael Stevens bought the site from New York's leading apartment entrepreneur Sam LeFrak and developed it with Blanche Sprague, an effusive high voltage divorced mother with one young son. Though she never built anything before, she did a good deal of the development work on St. James Tower, for Stevens was usually aboard his yacht somewhere on the other side of the Atlantic. His father had amassed a fortune in textiles, and he made a pile of his own as an investment banker with the London office of Lazard Freres. He spent a lot of time unwinding. Meanwhile, Sprague sold almost all the units at St. James Tower within a year. It was an impressive performance for two novice developers.

Sprague got a Saturday evening call from her friend Jon Tisch, son of Loews Hotel president Preston Robert Tisch. They had just attended a tennis match with the Trumps, and Trump talked about building a $40 million luxury cooperative at 165 East 61st Street. It's in an affluent residential neighborhood and an easy walk from Bloomingdale's. Since Stevens didn't have any other projects in mind, Jon Tisch urged her to have breakfast with Trump the next morning. But Sprague had a brunch date, which she wasn't about to cancel for Trump or anybody.

When they met, Trump wanted to know how such a terrible building as St. James Place—every competitor seemed terrible in his eyes—could sell for so much money. Condominiums there brought half as much as Trump Tower, and that was remarkable. Despite his arrogance, he exuded great charm, and he convinced her to sell Trump Plaza, his planned cooperative.

The site, with a three-story commercial building, belonged to a thin, courtly-looking 70ish man named Donald Ruth. He refused to sell, because he wanted to leave it to his children Barbara and Philip. But he was willing to negotiate a lease agreement with Trump. Consequently, the project had to be a coop rather than a condominium, which in New York City required ownership of the underlying land.

Trump retained architect Philip Birnbaum to design a 37-story, 340,000 square foot, Y-shaped building. There would be five apartments on each floor above the ground-floor concourse. Trump Plaza would have 190 units altogether.

Like Trump's other projects, Trump Plaza was for the wealthy. The two-story-high lobby, with Italian Quarella marble, was marked with rich blacks and earth tones. Living quarters would have herringbone pattern parquet floors, marble tub-surrounds and 34-foot-wide living rooms with wall-to-wall windows. There would be little private ground-level gardens outside. Prices would range from $285,000 for a low one-bedroom apartment to $1 million for a three-bedroom apartment on an upper floor.

Trump faced competition from other residential developers. Three blocks north on Third Avenue, Paul Milstein and Robert Olnick proposed a 51-story cooperative building with 504 cooperative apartments. They needed a zoning change, which Trump tried unsuccessfully to block. The building is still under construction.

Trump was startled to discover a rival using his own design. Though Birnbaum's contract provided that he wouldn't design a building like Trump Plaza for anybody else, he proceeded to do just that at 60th Street and Third Avenue. The client was developer Morton Olshan, and the 43-story Trump clone would be called the Savoy. It would have 235 units. Trump sued for $60 million and sought an injunction to stop construction. The dispute was settled when glass rather than limestone was used on the exterior, but the building hasn't opened yet.

Trump Plaza opened in March 1984, and Sprague billed it as a homey place, and in short order she sold most of it. Among those who moved in were Mobil Oil Chairman Raleigh Warner, Avon Chairman Hicks Waldron, television producer Dick Clark and tennis star Martina Navratilova.

"Donald is a character," Sprague says. "He is like a child with an erector set, playing monopoly. He demands perfection. He is brilliant, almost frightening. Yet you cannot help be lifted by his overwhelming enthusiasm. He's like seltzer. Everyday is a new show." It's easy to see how she could sell all those apartments.

Trump's $220 million, 39-story, 614-room Atlantic City hotel/ casino is his most profitable property. Since opening in May 1984, it muscled its way to a 10 percent share of that market, and profits are estimated at around $8 million *a month*.

Trump had spent several years negotiating 27 acquisitions to form a seven-acre site on Mississippi Avenue, next to the Atlantic City Convention Center, where he would build. His hotel/casino would be linked to it via a skybridge. By the time he finished the assemblage, many big players had taken their places on the boardwalk. "I wanted the best site," Trump says, "and I didn't mind waiting while the others made their mistakes."

The number of people going to Atlantic City slowed to a trickle during the winter of 1980–81 due to inflation and high fuel prices. So Trump didn't push the project ahead. He waited while the New Jersey Gaming Commission examined his qualifications for a gaming license.

Trump himself wasn't suspect, but he leased one of the parcels on the site from SSG Enterprises. One of its principals was Kenneth Shapiro, a developer named in a recent federal indictment for channeling bribes from a Philadelphia organized crime family to Michael Matthews, mayor of Atlantic City. Matthews was voted out of office by a recall election held just before he was charged with extortion. Shapiro, granted immunity, testified before the grand jury which indicted Matthews.

Another principal in SSG was Daniel J. Sullivan, a teamster arrested on a 1975 weapons charge and a suspect in the mysterious disappearance of a teamster lawyer back in 1966. New Jersey's gaming enforcement division produced an 11-page report on Sullivan and his dealings with Trump. They had met while negotiating the Atlantic City lease, and later Trump asked his help in negotiating a labor dispute at the Grand Hyatt. Trump referred Sullivan to his banker at Chase Manhattan about a $3.5 million loan. Chase would O.K. it if Trump would guarantee it. He wouldn't.

The controversy threatened costly delays. Trump by himself would qualify for a gaming license, but it was questionable whether the landowners would be approved. Moreover, the issue was tainting him with unseemly associations. He bought out SSG Enterprises for $8 million. "I didn't want to be in the position," Trump says, "where we put up a $200 million structure and some of the people owning a little land beneath the building couldn't get a license." His license was issued in March 1982. Construction crews were at work by June.

Trump said he was prepared to operate the hotel/casino himself, but about six months after construction was underway, he was approached by Mike Rose, chairman of Holiday Inns, which owns Harrah's—perhaps the top name in the gaming business, having operated Lake Tahoe, Reno and Las Vegas casinos for 47 years. Harrah's already had an Atlantic City property, the marina which opened in 1980. It's viewed as among the most successful casinos there. But Rose couldn't resist Trump's location. He offered Trump $50 million cash to become his partner. Harrah's would guarantee the $170 million of mortgages and any operating losses incurred during the next five years.

"Construction was up to the third floor," Trump remembers. "I said to myself, 'Why should I own 100 percent and have perhaps $250 million of my own money in the deal when I can own 50 percent and have nothing in the deal—plus if the casino ever loses money, they guarantee it.' So I own 50 percent for zero money in and substantial money out. That's infinite return."

Atlantic City projects were plagued with mistakes and cost overruns, and Trump was determined it wouldn't happen to him. His brother Robert was in Atlantic City all the way through the project. "We brought professional development and construction disciplines to a market where they had been in short supply," Robert says, "and we proved you can build a high-quality product within original cost parameters and on time."

Donald Trump gloats: "Take the top 10 office buildings built in New York during the past five years, add them up, and they will make substantially less money than my hotel casino in Atlantic City." Still, his heart is in Manhattan. "It's the hottest piece of real estate outside Atlantic City."

In early 1985, Trump took advantage of Hilton's troubles in Atlantic City. The hotelier was denied a gaming license for its unopened 634-room hotel near the marina, because of alleged organized crime connections. Exasperated, Hilton executives decided to sell their property. Disposing of it was widely interpreted as a way to discourage Golden Nugget boss Stephen Wynn's takeover assault on Hilton Hotels. The company's two Las Vegas gambling properties generated an incredible 39 percent of total profits, and their Atlantic City property had comparable promise. Hilton's Atlantic City property had cost an estimated $308 million to build. Trump bought it for a reported $320 million.

He must have wanted that deal badly, for it was one of the very few he paid for in cash. "I got a castle for my thirty-ninth birthday," he smiles. He renamed the former Hilton property Trump's Castle Hotel & Casino.

Less than two weeks after the deal closed, Bear, Stearns & Co. sold a $300 million private placement mortgage bond backed by Trump's Castle Hotel & Casino. He got his cash back and still controls the casino.

However, now Harrah's is suing him for competing with Harrah's at Trump Plaza. They've spent millions promoting the Trump name, and many people will end up at Trump's Castle Hotel & Casino. "I'm honored," Trump says. "The name clearly created value." He adds that his contract with Harrah's doesn't restrict him from using his name, which figures in all his ventures.

One of Trump's ambitions is to emblazon his name on the world's tallest building. In July 1984, Trump proposed to build this on a 26-acre underwater site near South Street Seaport along Manhattan's East River. It would be part of a 110-acre redevelopment project abandoned during New York City's fiscal crisis in the 1970s.

The building would soar 150 stories to 1,940 feet and have offices or apartments totaling some 5 million square feet of space. The whole idea depended on Trump becoming the developer designated by New York's Public Development Corporation. The *Chicago Tribune* architectural critic Paul Gapp ridiculed this as "one of the silliest things anyone could inflict on New York or any other city." Trump slapped a $500 million libel suit against Gapp and the *Tribune*.

In December 1984, Trump paid $90 million for the 76-acre West Side yards which extend from 59th Street to 72nd Street in Manhattan. This is the same property Trump had optioned a decade before from bankrupt Penn Central, then let go. Later Argentinian businessman Francisco Macri and parking lot tycoon Abraham Hirschfeld optioned it, proposing a scheme to be called Lincoln West, which would include 19 buildings with 4,300 apartments and 10 million square feet of space, but lack of adequate financing killed their scheme.

On November 18, 1985, Trump proposed another idea for the world's tallest building—this time, on the West Side yards. There would be a waterfront promenade, parks, waterfalls, shops and six towers, the prelude to a 150-story tower with a triangular top reaching 1,670 feet—216 higher than Chicago's Sears Tower. Dubbed Television City, the project would include some 3.5 million square feet of offices and facilities for broadcasting companies. Altogether, there would be 18.5 million square feet of space, 7,900 luxury condominiums, apartments for some 20,000 people and offices for 40,000. The designer: Chicago's maverick Helmut Jahn, among the hottest architects now, known for flamboyant gestures and bright colors.

Trump timed his announcement exquisitely: a week after the National Broadcasting Company unit of RCA Corporation, now at Rockefeller Center, announced they would seek larger, improved quarters elsewhere—their present facilities would cost "hundreds of millions of dollars to modernize." Trump's announcement also came a day after Mike Wallace profiled him on *60 Minutes*.

If Television City survives review by the City Planning Commission, Community Board 7 and the Board of Estimate, Trump hopes for a groundbreaking in 1987. The project would keep him on the front pages well into the 1990s.

Oh yes, the price tag? Trump won't go far enough out on a limb to say, but other Manhattan developers figure it could be more than $6 billion—40 times more than his peach-marbled mecca, Trump Tower.

Meanwhile, oil was discovered beneath those West Side yards. "Isn't it amazing," Trump says. "It's a classic major oil find in Manhattan." New York state environmental officials believed it was No. 2 diesel oil for locomotives, which had leaked out of underground tanks. They guessed there might be 100,000 gallons of the stuff. Property owners in similar situations were able to sell the oil for 80 percent or 90 percent of the price realized by the Organization of Petroleum Exporting Countries. Not exactly a fortune, but it was what people came to expect of Trump.

Trump, these days, is seeking splendor along Florida's Gold Coast. In November 1985, he negotiated to buy Mar-a-Lago, the 118-room mansion which belonged to cereal heiress Marjorie Merriweather Post. In glorious days past, the rich chased little white balls across the nine-hole golf course on this 17.5-acre estate next to the exclusive Palm Beach Tennis Club. The place is on the south end of Palm Beach—Rose Kennedy's spread is on the north end. Assuming the deal goes through, Trump is expected to build perhaps nine baronial homes, each fetching several million dollars. He'll surely reserve one for himself.

The asking price for Mar-a-Lago was about $19 million, but Trump will reportedly pay only $10 million to $15 million. Characteristically, Trump seems to be taking advantage of a depressed market—in this case, because many foreign millionaires are selling their posh vacation villas.

Meanwhile, back in Trump's panoramic Trump Tower suite, 7-year-old Donny Jr. is just like his Dad—playing with wooden blocks. Who knows, in a few years, he may be playing with polished granite.

VII

END GAME

18.

FAST TRACK

HIGH, VOLATILE INTEREST RATES MAKE THE RISKS OF REAL ESTATE development greater than ever before. To save financing costs, probably more entrepreneurs than ever are fast-tracking their projects—starting construction before all the drawings are finished. This calls for sophisticated professionals who think ahead and anticipate thousands of details, so work can proceed with as few snafus as possible.

To see just what's involved with a fast-track project, I donned a hard hat and observed the construction of World Financial Center, which Albert and Paul Reichmann are building at Manhattan's southwestern tip. It's one of the most ambitious urban construction jobs attempted in years. Certainly it's the biggest deal New Yorkers have seen since Rockefeller Center during the 1930s.

World Financial Center has four office towers which will provide more than 6 million square feet of office space. Two gatehouses are nine stories high. Complicating the construction job are plans for more than 200,000 square feet of shops, plus 150,000 square feet of outdoor plazas and the Wintergarden. This will be a 120-foot-high glass-domed, palm-filled conservatory.

World Financial Center is on a tricky landfill site, created with soil displaced almost two decades ago by the World Trade Center. Subsurface soil conditions vary from place to place around the site. Moreover, the site is crisscrossed with subway tubes, cooling lines and utility lines. Furthermore, the Reichmanns had to use construction methods compatible with Westway, a controversial proposed thoroughfare.

Most major projects are done in stages over many years, but the Reichmanns committed themselves to work on all the buildings simultaneously. The project was due to be finished 4½ years from October 4, 1982, when the first spade was turned. The Reichmanns hired nine consultants, and more than 150 people at Olympia & York spent full time on World Financial Center. I talked with quite a few.

Before the project was half finished, the Reichmanns secured agreements to move in from coveted blue chips like Dow Jones, American Express and Merrill Lynch. Each, with specific needs, ordered major changes—more than $60 million worth—which put brutal pressure on the Reichmanns' construction people. Somehow they had to accommodate these companies and meet the originally agreed-on deadlines, so money would begin to flow in. This was crucial, because the Reichmanns provided $50 million of guarantees for the right to develop the site, and before they were through, the total project cost would climb to $1.5 billion.

The man in charge of Olympia & York's construction is Keith Roberts, a tall pipe-smoking, golf-crazy Englishman in his 60s. He's partially deaf in one ear, a reminder of military service in Palestine when, while trying to dismantle a terrorist bomb, it exploded in his face. He built military installations, factories and breweries throughout England before emigrating to Canada, where he joined William Zeckendorf's Toronto development office. After doing just one high-rise building, in 1963, he realized Zeckendorf's real estate empire was tottering toward bankruptcy.

"I was aware of the Reichmanns," Roberts says, "because they were doing a lot of one- and two-story industrial buildings around Canada. I called on Albert unannounced to see what the job prospects might be. They had less than 10 people and were reluctant to hire anybody else. I lowered my sights a bit, offering to start at $10,000. I talked for a while with Albert and Paul in their office kitchen. They liked me and here I am."

Soon afterward, he supervised design, purchasing and construction of the Reichmanns' first office building, the 14-story Toronto headquarters for the International Order of Foresters. Ever since, the Reichmanns have concentrated on office buildings.

"It was not until the early 1970s when I realized what a staggering amount of time and money was lost building a high-rise structure," Roberts says. "As you approach 70 stories, workers may be performing assigned tasks for only about 4½ hours of an 8-hour shift."

With these sobering thoughts in mind, Roberts and the Reichmanns analyzed the risks of the proposed white marble First Canadian Place, the most ambitious undertaking that they ever attempted. With 5 million square feet of office space and a retail concourse in two towers, it would boost Toronto's downtown office space about 10 percent. If successful, it could catapult them to the forefront of North American developers. But it was also clear that such a project would invite waste on a large scale, and this could ruin them.

Roberts visited construction sites in Canada and the United States to evaluate current methods being used by other companies. "We invested more that $3 million to develop systems which would move workers and materials better," Albert Reichmann says with evident pride. "We built elevators for fork lifts, so they could unload materials from trucks, then go direct to the floor where the materials were needed. We devised a conveyor belt which delivered concrete to the floors much faster than conventional buckets. As a result of these various measures, we saved over a million man-hours and cut our construction time 40 percent. Our first tenant, the Bank of Montreal, moved into their lower floor offices before the roof was up."

There was a recession when First Canadian Place opened, and it wasn't fully leased for an anxious four years. The cash drain during the first year alone exceeded $20 million. Yet because Roberts and the Reichmanns were relentless in their pursuit of savings, they were able to hang on until the building hit black ink. Practices introduced at First Canadian Place were applied wherever possible to subsequent projects of Olympia & York.

By the time they began preparing for World Financial Center, they had projects going not only in Canada but across the United States. Roberts needed a new construction manager, and he tapped a gruff, husky Englishman named John Norris. He was born in Alexandria, Egypt and educated in England where, with a gleaming silver helmet, red tunic and long saber, he was among Royal Guards who preceded Queen Elizabeth on ceremonial occasions. He got a job with Token Construction Company in London, which developed highrise office buildings and hotels in England.

As he began to think about who might handle strategic planning for World Financial Center, Norris recalled Peter Payne, an affable Londoner he worked with more than a decade before. Payne planned projects in France, Belgium, West Germany, Switzerland, Sweden, Egypt and Iran. Though he had built offices, residential buildings and hospitals, he became best-known for hotels. "The greatest appeal of doing a hotel as far as I was concerned," Payne said, "was I could buy everything down to the last knife and fork. The objective was to open that building on time. The hotel operator based financial plans on getting guests checked in by a specific date. Convention reservations were made as much as 18 months ahead."

Often working in remote regions where many things were hard to obtain, he learned to anticipate just about every conceivable emergency. "I remember building the Barbados Hilton," he says, "and we had to ship absolutely all we needed except for some coral limestone, which we cut out of the ground. If we had forgotten a simple screw or bolt, we couldn't have got it on time. The building was done in just 22 months."

Payne started his career as a structural engineer. "I realized I wasn't that brilliant in mathematics," he says. "I got out of structural engineering and into reinforced concrete contracting, a simple sideways step. Instead of designing reinforced concrete buildings, I built them.

"The secret of getting a building done on time is to do the jobs in proper sequence. Often you'll see a tall building where the entire frame is up, but it has only a few floors of exterior wall. That tells you something's wrong.

"I recall driving to inspect an apartment building near London with Len Mottram, one of my supervisors. Soon as we got a glimpse of the building several miles away, he said to me: 'There's no point going any further. The job's all right.'

"'How do you know?' I asked, incredulous. He said, 'Because I can see the building is in sequence.'

"A building in sequence has got the exterior wall right up to where the structural steel or reinforced concrete is being erected. Behind that exterior wall you should have the finishing trades, the mechanical trades, all close up behind one another. Construction is a continuous battle to keep things in sequence."

The first task in planning the construction of World Financial Center was to assess the site. "We had to consider the landfill, subway tubes going through the site and access to it," Norris explains. "The buildings were to be anchored on concrete piles as much as 70 feet deep, the last 25 feet socketed in bedrock.

"Then we addressed the buildings themselves—their design, the number of floors and so on. Here we drew on our experience with other tall buildings. The situation may vary from city to city, so we were particularly mindful of our recent Manhattan experience building 347 Park Avenue."

They developed a general understanding about the best ways to tackle the job. They decided where cranes would have to be positioned, where hoists would go, where steel, concrete and pre-cast concrete and material for interior finishes would be picked up. They worked out the best ways to handle the flow of workers and trucks.

Norris put jobs out to bid, and he considered all reasonable contractors who came in with a low price. But he, Payne and their associates challenged contractors to demonstrate just how they would do a quality job on time.

"We ask to see the proposed game plan," says Norris. "What's your approach? How long is that job going to take? What's your labor force? How many cranes have you got? Where are you going to put them? Why have you got only three hoists when you need four? We may agree to a contractor's price, provided we're satisfied that logistically and methodwise, the job is being approached correctly. Or we may not. We may be quite satisfied and say yes, we see the logic of that, it's good, go! So we get a pooling of industry and our thoughts. By the time we're through, we're pretty clear which is the best way to go under the circumstances.

"Before we accepted a bid for the steel frame, we wanted to know the contractor's proposed schedule. For Building A, Ermco of New York submitted a bid which involved using four derricks. For Building C, though, Canron of Toronto recommended three climbing cranes. These could do the job as well as derricks, so it was just a question of which equipment did a contractor happen to have. If a contractor could prove their particular approach would get the job done quicker than another approach, terrific.

"On Building D, Canron recommended using two tower cranes, and that's what their price was based on. How much more would it cost, we asked, and how much overall would be saved if they added a third crane which would help finish the job sooner? We told them that they might lose the job with just two cranes, because they'd take too long.

"They had also planned on positioning the cranes at certain points around the building. We said you can't put it there, because they'd interfere with mechanical systems at the top and electrical at the bottom. The cranes would have to be located at points which would cost us more money. Always there were trade-offs."

Payne is alert to the general practice among subcontractors of putting high prices on jobs they expect to do first and low prices on jobs which come later. This accelerates cash flow to the subcontractors, helping their financial position. But if Olympia & York insists on low-paying jobs being done first, a subcontractor may be squeezed for cash and the job shortchanged.

"Probably you'll see warning signs," Payne says. "Generally, there's a work slowdown. The subcontractor can't afford to meet Thursday paydays, so he cuts back the number of people on the job. On Building D, we had a steel erector who experienced financial problems, and he cut back to a bare minimum number of workers. I noticed on the schedule that a lot of steel was erected, but about 80 percent of the 150,000 bolts still had to be put in. He was making more money from erecting than bolting, because bolting was so much more labor intensive.

"Bankruptcy among subcontractors is common, so we could easily spend 60 percent of the money budgeted for a job and wind up with the subcontractor gone, the job still unfinished. We've faced this situation a couple times on World Financial Center. A Pottstown, Pennsylvania elevator subcontractor called Williamsburg went bankrupt with five out of 58 elevators unfinished. We had to pay the liquidator for those, find somebody else who'd complete the job and adapt the drawings to their way of making elevators. We faced a bigger problem when Weaver, a Pittsburgh subcontractor who handled structural steel on Building D, went belly up. They didn't get above the ground floor.

"Recently, I noticed that a heating, ventilating and air-conditioning contractor priced a job too low. He priced his equipment correctly, but I thought his estimated labor cost didn't seem to provide for some complications he'd face on the job. It involved installing equipment in the basement of a building. You might think this was easy, except you need a crane and a hole to lower the equipment through. It was partially blocked by existing structures. Fortunately, we caught this situation in time, and the contractor is O.K."

Since construction requires a team effort, it's critical to assess the individuals involved. "I want to know who the project manager is going to be," Norris says. "What's their record? Who's the superintendent in the field? We check to see if they have a good reputation in the industry, or if there are some strikes against them. Have they built tall buildings before? This is crucial, because when you start going above 20 stories, fitting components together precisely tends to become more difficult, and somebody who's experienced knows what to look for. We want people with drive, initiative, flexibility.

"We have a clause which says if we don't feel comfortable with somebody, we can change them. If we didn't have that in, they could put a junior on the job who never built a high-rise, and we would almost certainly have trouble, because they'd be learning on the job. I don't want to see any jackhammers on the job—that means somebody didn't know what they were doing, and work had to be undone."

Obtaining good, experienced workers for a job as big as World Financial Center isn't easy. Olympia & York needed 122 subcontractors and as many as 4,000 workers on the job site at one time: operating engineers, cement masons, structural iron workers, ornamental iron workers, metal lathers, bricklayers, steamfitters, boilermakers, electricians, elevator constructors, carpenters, plumbers, plasterers, painters, glaziers, roofers, teamsters.

There was a considerable amount of construction going on around New York, and many of the best subcontractors were already committed to other projects. "Before we started work," Norris says, "I called a meeting with the New York Trades Council and discussed what we intended to do. The consensus was that it would be very tough to get the people we wanted.

"We asked how much labor a subtrade had available, and we tried to get the best ones. We'd ask what other jobs a subcontractor is doing now. Where's your labor going? How would you provide enough workers for us? Would they be getting workers from the union? Have they performed for you before? Or are they new people you have little experience with? We want to know what we're buying, because it's tough finding people who can do a good job on time."

Many aspects of Cesar Pelli's imaginative architectural design required especially skilled workers. He specified distinctively shaped tops rather than a conventional flat top. "Anybody can build a flat top," Norris says, "but manipulating large sheets of copper for a dome, 51 stories up, with the wind and everything—we must have people who know what they're doing up there."

Some workers were unusually difficult to find. Marble fitters, for instance, needed to finish the lobbies at World Financial Center. Until recent years, there wasn't much call for marble in buildings, and most of the old craftsmen have died or drifted into other trades. It's a dirty, wet, unappealing business. Few remain who know the special techniques of grinding marble, cleaning it, fitting and joining it. Technically, bricklayers might be able to do it, but that's a different union.

"With labor, it's all communication," Norris says. "We deal with the unions direct. I have found them all approachable. At World Financial Center, they've been most cooperative."

He met with union officials to determine if they had any objections to the way Olympia & York anticipated handling the job— sometimes they affect plans. "We could sit back and say 'that's how we're going to do it' without considering their problems," Norris says, "but it isn't out approach."

At the time, there was a jurisdictional dispute between the iron workers and riggers unions. As a consequence, Olympia & York couldn't use cranes for different jobs during a shift. It could lift steel all day, and, when the steel men were finished work, another operator could use it to lift pre-cast concrete. Olympia & York had to plan deliveries accordingly.

"Most strikes," Norris says, "occur because one side or the other is stupid about some terms which should have been worked out. I have always found that provided we keep within the union-negotiated contracts and don't vary, and they keep within the union-negotiated contracts and don't vary, you'll get along."

Federal and state investigations showed, however, that in New York, union-negotiated contracts involve extortion. Unions are well aware that on a project as big as World Financial Center, financing costs exceeded $100,000 per working day, so Olympia & York was understandably anxious to keep the peace and avoid job actions.

As a consequence, unions demanded and got some astonishing concessions. One of the most notorious on New York construction sites was the so-called "working teamster foreman," designated by Local 282 of the International Brotherhood of Teamsters. Their base salary was $75,000 a year, and they were eligible for unlimited overtime, yet they weren't required to show up for work. In its ongoing probe of labor union featherbedding, the New York State Commission of Investigation identified some 150 "working teamster foremen" around various New York job sites.

George A. Morrison of Blauvelt, New York, was the biggest beneficiary of teamster extortion at World Financial Center. He was an operating engineer—somebody who ran heavy construction equipment like cranes and temporary elevators—whose normal compensation was about $60,000 a year. But in 1983, Olympia & York had to pay him $198,481 in wages and $76,980 in fringe benefits. During 1984, he did even better, pocketing $308,651 in wages, $96,441 in fringes.

According to payroll records, he was such a diligent teamster that he actually worked more than 24 hours a day for 221 of the 332 workdays in 1984. His average weekly compensation was $6,000—almost six times higher than his legitimate job afforded. Miraculously, according to credit card and telephone records, he spent much of this time in Europe, South Carolina, Acapulco, Mexico and St. Martin in the Caribbean. In this, union-grubbing at its finest, Morrison hit the jackpot—he was rated the highest-paid construction worker in all of New York.

A key to staying on schedule at World Financial Center is maintaining an orderly flow of men and materials. Chaos is easy with 400 trucks a day coming onto the site.

Olympia & York people designed roadways and established checkpoints to help monitor traffic to the right loading docks. At each building, there's one for steel, another for concrete, yet another for finishing materials and so on. Traffic managers don't seem like much, but they represent additional cost, and Olympia & York is among the few developers who incur it, believing that it pays off with a decidedly faster construction schedule.

The biggest bottleneck is the hoist. A truck can't be unloaded until a hoist is available. While waiting, a truck may impede other vehicles trying to move around the site. Not knowing when they'd be called to help unload, workers on an upper floor would be subject to sudden interruption. They'd leave half-finished tasks, and often important details would be forgotten by the time they finished unloading and returned to the job site. This may mean incompletely secured windows, for instance, which would develop leaks.

Olympia & York began computerized scheduling of hoist time. "It's like an airline reservation system," Payne explains. "Subcontractors book time four weeks in advance, confirm it 24 hours before and pay for it—$100 per hour—whether they use it or not.

"When you have no charge, the guy says I want the hoist four hours, that's mine. You can't get it back. But if he's paying for it, even though it's a nominal figure which covers the cost of operator and equipment, it's a different situation. He'll work a little harder or figure out some way he can get away with less lift time.

"Everyone said, 'You'll never do it in New York,' because of the union rules and congested traffic. But we enforced it. If a truck is more than about 15 minutes late, it loses its place and has to reschedule delivery another time. We refuse to let a latecomer throw off everybody else who plans on timely arrival of their shipments.

"When drivers see that their promptness really is rewarded with immediate unloading, they arrive promptly. Whether this means leaving earlier, not stopping for a cup of coffee—whatever they have to do, they do it.

"Materials move immediately from the truck up the building. You won't see any queues of trucks on our site. Or workers waiting idly because they lack materials to work with. Nor do we need trailers for storing materials. Drivers are better off, the contractors save money, and we get the job done faster. If you get rid of the logistical problems, you'd be amazed how many other problems disappear.

"Logistics affects morale. If some workers see others idle, they wonder why they're working so hard, and they begin to slack off. Idleness snowballs. It's a major cause of missed deadlines and cost overruns. A tremendous amount of this occurs simply because some workers don't have the materials they need to do their jobs."

When workers and materials flow properly, weather is less of a problem. More work will be done before winter when many things take longer and more work days were lost.

The toughest part of many construction jobs is the foundation— you never know what obstacles you may encounter below ground. So it's commonplace to fall behind right away, and this happened at World Financial Center.

After groundbreaking, work began on Building A, excavating soil down to a depth of about 10 feet. Men with churn drills moved in. These formidable machines have tungsten carbide bits which hammered a 30-inch-wide hole more than 60 feet straight down to bedrock.

Then the job got tough. A socket 15 to 25 feet deep had to be cut into bedrock, so a pile would gain secure footing. Bedrock is often some kind of granite, among the most stubborn, unrelenting rocks. The churn drills would grind and grunt a couple feet a day if they were lucky. But many days they pushed only inches further. Some of these holes took a couple tedious months to finish.

Into each hole went a steel tube known as a caisson. It was followed by a remote-control television camera, to check the socket. if no more drilling was required, steel bars were inserted through the caisson and concrete poured around it. Years later, after the steel tube rusted away, the concrete would still protect the steel bars and assure steady support for the building above.

Caissons were fashioned in clusters of four, 30 feet apart. Each cluster supported a concrete pad on which workers erected a structural column, beginning their upward climb.

Buildings B and C flanked the proposed Westway. One of the schemes New York officials contemplated would involve a thoroughfare 40 feet below ground level. In this event, soil would be excavated away from caissons supporting the World Financial Center buildings. Gradually, they'd rock into the void, and who knows what might happen.

This called for a variation known as battered caissons which stood at about a 45 degree angle. They wouldn't be affected by the removal of soil for Westway. However, they're often agonizingly difficult to accomplish. Many times bedrock sloped at an angle similar to the churn drill, and it repeatedly slipped off the rock. For days, workers couldn't get a purchase on it. Since there were 64 battered caissons, these delays set the project back more than a month.

Norris, Payne and their associates eyed the calendar, ticking off days until the winter of 1982 set in, when bad weather would cost them precious work days. The situation was so discouraging with Building B that they decided to abandon the battered caissons there.

Instead, they'd excavate all the way down to bedrock and build a basement. It would be secured with an 18-inch-thick concrete pad on bedrock. No caissons needed. Though far more expensive than laying caissons—when that was possible—a basement had the advantage of creating about 250,000 square feet of space which could be leased.

For a basement as deep as what was contemplated here, something different was needed. You couldn't just dig a 70-foot hole, because earth at the edges would continuously collapse, and the hole would become enormous, interfering with work elsewhere on the site. Some Italian contractors devised an ingenious solution during the 1950s, a technique known as slurry wall. This is a wall built in the ground.

A special machine with long tongs and baskets at the end dug a trench about three feet wide—the width of the planned foundation walls. Earth removed was replaced with slurry, a brownish-grayish-pinkish powder suspended in water. It had a remarkable ability to prevent earth from collapsing into the trench, yet as a fluid it could be penetrated easily—much like you'd push your finger into container of mercury.

The depth of the trench was monitored with graduated steel rods, which served as giant yardsticks. When the trench hit bedrock, the churn drills pushed through the slurry to dig a socket. Then concrete was poured into the trench. It sunk to the bottom, displacing slurry. Only after the trench was filled and the concrete set did the excavators move in to dig a hole for the basement.

But they had to proceed in stages, because the wall was supported by earth on both sides. If one side were removed, the wall would be vulnerable to collapse. So with every 10 feet of depth, holes were drilled in the concrete, and steel ties were pushed through at a 45 degree angle to bedrock. These ties would rust away in several years, but by that time, of course, the walls would be braced by beams in the building. The Building B slurry wall was finished in September 1984.

Since architect Cesar Pelli had specified granite for the exterior of World Financial Center, Norris had to contend with this fickle stone. Like a diamond, each block of granite is a puzzle. Its color might be a little different from the last block quarried in the same spot, and it could fracture inexplicably during the cutting process.

A shy, self-effacing Rumanian immigrant named Otto Blau was in charge of efforts to master the granite. He tries to drive away interviewers like me by emphasizing his mistakes, but he's a savvy buyer, intensely loyal to Olympia & York.

The Reichmanns began using granite extensively for exterior walls around 1970, and Blau made himself an expert on the subject. He turned to Quebec quarries—which had about 20 colors of granite—after an architect specified Caledonia brown from Riviere a Pierre, north of Quebec City.

However, the Canadians weren't able to assure precise cuts. "It's like slicing roast beef," Blau explains. "If you order a 1½-inch slice, some would be an inch, others 2 inches. North American granite-cutting equipment could achieve a quarter-inch tolerance—never quite straight.

Since the 1960s, Italians had the edge with techniques, which enabled them to maintain a one-sixteenth-inch tolerance. What they did was adapt marble-cutting equipment for granite. Italian labor costs were also cheaper than Canadian.

So Blau had granite quarried in Quebec, shipped to Italy where it was cut to 1¼-inch-thick panels, then shipped back to the building site for installation. The cost was $4 per square foot versus $4.50, the best price for doing the whole job in Canada—a substantial saving when hundreds of thousands of square feet are involved.

For World Financial Center, Pelli wanted Polychrome, a gray granite quarried near Bagotville in the Saguenay Valley, Quebec. The project would use 1.4 million square feet of granite, enough to consume a small mountain. To help assure cost and quality control, Blau helped set up Granicor, a Quebec-based venture to cut, then polish their granite. It operated as a partnership among Olympia & York, National Granite, which quarried the blocks, and Campologhi, the experienced Italian stone-cutting firm. Finished granite panels would be shipped to Fei Ltd., a firm near Dublin, Ireland which mounted them on steel frames. These would be secured to the exterior of the buildings.

Several sizes were needed, ranging from five by four feet which were mainly for lower walls and ten by two feet for upper walls. Unfortunately, the granite baffled the cutters at Granicor. They were plagued with frequent fractures, especially when trying to cut large panels. While they were able to cut smaller panels from a ruined large stone, the result was a shortage of large panels, which were needed right away. The small panels piled up uselessly, since they couldn't be installed until workers reached the upper walls.

In the fall of 1983, Blau decided he had to act. Granite blocks were shipped to Italy where Campologhi's more experienced stonecutters could do the job. Not only did they manage to reduce the number of fractures, but since they had more than twice as many stone saws, they could accelerate production.

Construction would have been a lot easier if the Reichmanns didn't have the good fortune to make deals for entire buildings. In a building with many tenants, only a limited number of changes are made. But American Express and Merrill Lynch ordered drastic alterations, which intensified pressures to get the buildings opened on time.

Biggest alteration: the order in which buildings were built. The first leases—City Investing and Dow Jones—were signed for Building A, so it was scheduled to be the first one open, in April 1985. Work on the basement of Building D would go on simultaneously, since it housed the cooling plant for the whole complex. Building B would begin next, then Building C and the above-ground structure of Building D.

However, in 1983 American Express executives decided they wanted to buy Building C. They retained Olympia & York as contractor, and the building was to be ready for occupancy June 6, 1984—after

Building A and the basement of Building D, with Building B and the above-ground portion of D to follow.

American Express had a number of specific changes. First, they wanted elevators serving the upper floors switched from the east to the north side of the building, so the floor layouts would better suit their needs. American Express executives reached their decision just days before caissons were to be put in. They're virtually impossible to remove.

American Express wanted a cafeteria on the third floor. Since the company would occupy the entire building, they wanted security systems for limiting access to outsiders. Floor load capacity was increased to accommodate massive vaults.

After the acquisition of Lehman Brothers in April 1984, American Express executives decided to make substantial interior alterations to accommodate the special needs of that investment banking firm. Before they were through, they made further changes, tearing apart 18 floors and doing them over.

American Express executives didn't want to work surrounded by unfinished construction. So they insisted that frames which would hold glass over the Wintergarden, flanking one side of the building, be substantially done before they moved in. This created further complications, because Norris had planned on using the Wintergarden site for cranes which would install the exterior wall on Building B. But it wasn't possible if the Wintergarden had to be finished with the American Express Building, before Building B. A new construction road was built for trucks to the crane in a new position near Building B. The cost of all American Express's changes was in the tens of millions.

The way this job was handled probably had as much of an impact on subsequent leasing as anything else, for it obviously wasn't just another speculative office building. Satisfying the intricate demands of a major corporation for its headquarters was far more difficult than building a standard steel box. Olympia & York did substantially what it contracted to do, and this really made people believe that the Battery Park City sandbar would be a choice spot.

By August 1984, structural steel on Building D was up to the second floor when Merrill Lynch leased both Buildings B and D. Building B wasn't started yet. They decided they wanted D finished first, and they ordered extensive alterations.

Among the first things Merrill Lynch ordered was a new loading dock, because more than 6 million pieces of mail flowed in and out of their downtown operations, which were being consolidated at World Financial Center. Loading docks required 17 feet headroom instead of 12 feet 6 inches as originally designed. To do this, a parking floor was removed and space was evened out among the remaining floors. As a result, the load of the slurry wall is supported by four floors instead of five as originally contemplated. Engineers had to double-check whether the slurry wall had enough support.

Merrill Lynch changed the elevator schemes. They wanted four elevator banks rather than three in Building D, to handle freight. In Building B, they eliminated elevators serving the first nine floors from the main core. Then they added elevators in their gatehouse to serve those floors.

Large trading rooms were needed. Each would occupy half a floor and would be two stories high, because it would ease the noise from all the boisterous brokers. Accordingly, plans were made to eliminate half the fifth and seventh floors.

Changes continued to pour in. Merrill Lynch wanted a cafeteria, small dining rooms and an auditorium on the third floor, and these required an escalator system from the main floor. To assure that computers wouldn't go down even in the event of a power system failure, Merrill Lynch would install two 4,000 pound turbine generators for emergency power.

All these changes meant the load on the building would be more than 150% greater than originally planned. Norris and his people huddled with Skidmore, Owings & Merrill, the architectural firm working with Merrill Lynch. They decided that in the worst case scenario, the building load would be 100 pounds per square foot. Accordingly, they began installing additional structural steel to strengthen the frame. These changes required by Merrill Lynch surely added tens of millions to the cost of the buildings.

There were setbacks. One April evening in 1984, there was an unusually high tide. In a century, high tide had reached six feet only once, so four feet of sandbags seemed enough protection. But the tide poured over and flooded the basement of Building D. It ruined five 40,000 pound GTE 15,000 volt air-cooled transformers. Removing and replacing them cost several million dollars plus weeks of lost time.

Norris, Payne and their associates were nervous knots of energy until steel workers built the frame all the way up to the roof. "You don't necessarily need the exterior wall up," Norris says, "but you must get at the roof. The faster you get the frame up, the faster you can get concrete floors done. The faster you do that, the faster electricians, carpenters, glaziers, heating contractors and everybody else can come in behind. Opening a building on time is a function of how fast you reach the roof."

Usually elevator machinery is installed there, and without elevators, the movement of workers and materials would be impeded. Without a roof, the building might absorb so much moisture that it would take months to dry out.

Tenants can't move into a building—nor would payments begin—until service elevators were finished. These took about nine months to assemble. Work started as soon as the roof was up.

In the spring of 1984, Norris and Payne could see that because of delays resulting from the reluctant caissons and granite, the winter of 1984 would be approaching without a roof on the American Express building. Exposed to winter wind, rain and ice, few workers would go up to the top of the building. "If we didn't get a roof on," says Payne, "we could lose a staggering amount of time."

But if, as anticipated, all the structural steel wasn't up until onset of winter, then there wouldn't be time to build the reinforced concrete roof originally planned. It would be exceedingly slow to cure, and the building wouldn't be waterproofed.

"We had to get rid of the concrete and replace it with something else," Payne says. "After nine months of testing various things, what we came up with was industrial siding—aluminum sheets which had an epoxy coating. From the architect's point of view, people would see a copper exterior. It would be copper on something, but nobody would see the something. Aesthetically, it didn't make any difference if the something was reinforced concrete or aluminum siding.

"We had to convince ourselves and American Express that our proposed substitute roof would withstand the powerful winds you'd get 51 stories up—they can generate more than 70 pounds of pressure per square foot. On the ground, we built a 20-foot roof section with all the corners, flushings and drains it would actually have. We had it rebuilt four times until we were satisfied. Then we loaded it with concrete blocks. To simulate sucking power, we turned the roof upside down and loaded it with concrete blocks again. We determined that it could withstand as much as 200 pounds per square foot with only minor deflections.

"We began putting it up soon after the structural steel was finished on October 25, 1984. The building would be waterproofed, and all the interior work could proceed. Then in the spring, we added the copper sheathing on top of the aluminum siding, which is what you see now. Some improvised solutions on this job worked perfectly, and that was one."

Though it's crucial to reach the roof as fast as possible, steel work tends to slow down alarmingly on the last few floors on a good many jobs. There's a saying in the construction industry that a lot of people can build, but very few can finish. "It's the hardest job in the world!" Payne says.

Often steel workers approaching the roof level anticipated being out of work, and they started looking for another job. There was chronic absenteeism, which brought seemingly endless, exasperating delays.

"It helped that we were building four buildings instead of just one," Payne says. "The structural steel subcontractor, Canron, was approaching completion of Building C in October when Weaver, scheduled to do structural steel on Building D, went bankrupt. We turned to Canron and asked if they wanted to bid on Building D. Canron got the job, and one result was they actually accelerated work on Building C. We finished about five weeks ahead of schedule largely, I believe, because of the psychological factor—workers knew there was another job waiting for them."

Meanwhile, Building A was ready for occupancy, and Dow Jones began its move in May 1985. This triggered the first monthly payment believed to be well over $500,000. Like the moves for American Express and Merrill Lynch, Dow Jones would take about six months—it was a little like planning the Normandy invasion.

D-Day, June 6, 1985, loomed for American Express. Having the building ready for occupancy by that date would trigger the first monthly check, which industry observers estimate to exceed $3 million. Men were pulled off Building A and shifted to Building C. They accelerated the installation of exterior wall and windows.

Then there were subcontractors who fell behind schedule. The American Express contract provided that the cooling plant had to be working at least three weeks before June 6. It consists of seven chillers with 1,750 tons of capacity, each capable of heating more than 400 single-family homes. The cooling plant is about 250 feet long and 90 feet wide.

Courter, the contractor, started work May 1984 and promised the job would be done in about six months. But the anticipated completion date slipped by, and there was a little yelling. Courter had worked on power stations, so they showed they could handle big jobs.

"Many of the contractors were experienced with tall buildings," Payne says. "They were used to lifting equipment up the outside of a building and taking it through an open floor. But they had little experience working below grade. You have a concrete wall rather instead of an open floor. You have to lower everything through holes, and there aren't many of those. We sweated that power plant. Finally, it was done in mid-April 1985, three weeks before the contract deadline."

The American Express contract required Olympia & York to finish the north pedestrian walkway which connected Building C to the World Trade Center. This was a huge 350-foot-long, 48-foot-wide covered structure—big enough to comply with codes for road bridges. Some 27 government agencies had to give their approval. Cesar Pelli had specified a costly structural design which would result in huge windows and an exterior look harmonious with the buildings. This job, too, came in before D-Day.

What's it like working under these pressures? "The younger you are, the more you take it out in your stomach," Payne says. "I got a lot of gray hair when I built the Barbados Hilton. I decided I wasn't going to lose sleep anymore. I discovered that often, because somebody panicked and did their job, the problem had gone away the next day."

There was jubilation when it became clear the American Express deadline would be made. But there was sadness, too, because the end of a job means a team will be breaking up, and many people would be out of work. They'll have to scramble for jobs elsewhere. Already, at the end, thousands of workers had already gone as their tasks are finished.

That's why public celebrations with the inevitable politicians are always at groundbreaking and topping out of structural steel. The end of a project is a private, thoughtful time. So for those at Olympia & York who remain on the job, everybody's minds are leaping ahead to Merrill Lynch and beyond.

19.

DEADLY OVERSIGHT

AN ALARMING NUMBER OF WALLS, BRIDGES, BUILDINGS AND OTHER structures collapse every year, reminding us that we can't take safety for granted. It remains a major risk of real estate development. People are killed despite all the professionals who are supposed to guard against design and construction errors. I was amazed to discover how things can go wrong when I went to Kansas City and investigated the deadliest building disaster in U.S. history.

At an evening tea dance, the Steve Miller band played Duke Ellington's classic "Satin Doll." Then, as one shocked witness recalled, there was "a small snapping sound." In seconds it became an ominous rumble followed by explosions, as two 120-foot-long concrete-and-steel skywalks started to collapse. Weighing 71,000 pounds each, they spanned the magnificent five-story atrium of the Hyatt Regency, Kansas City's newest hotel. The fourth-floor skywalk hit the second-floor skywalk directly below, and rubble rained on the people below—as many as 2,500.

This was July 17, 1981. At 7:08 P.M., Kansas City fire dispatcher Phillip Wall picked up the phone and heard an anguished woman cry: "Please come to the Hyatt Regency. Three of our skybridges have fallen."

"Three what?" he asked.

"Yes," the woman screamed, "and hurt people. Could you come over right away?"

"Are you talking about the elevators?" Wall asked.

"No, three skybridges," she said.

Wall: "We'll be right there."

The first ambulances arrived in less than 10 minutes, as calls flooded into the police and fire departments. Some were garbled, but their tragic meaning was becoming understood. "At the Hyatt! At the Hyatt!"

Rescue workers reported finding two dead by 7:53 P.M. Within hours, the death toll passed a hundred. A doctor of emergency medicine asked fireman Moen L. Phillips to cut through the torso of a dying man with a chain saw, so a less seriously injured man could be saved. Phillips did, then went berserk. He went after his wife and children with a chain saw. Fortunately, they escaped. Phillips landed in a psychiatric ward.

There were intestines and smashed brains on the concrete. "I couldn't believe the amount of blood everywhere," recalled Phillip Wall, who worked with a thousand volunteers pulling victims out of the rubble. "There were pools of blood down on the hotel floor. You could smell it—a real stagnant kind of pungent smell, just hanging in the air."

The collapse, which left 113 dead and 239 injured, didn't discriminate. Ruth and Bill Sigler were crushed—they had formed the Young at Hearts Club, the senior citizens group of St. Gabriel Church.

There was Rudolph Zatezalo, a former chiropractor and vice president of Civic Plaza National Bank, once accused of trying to bribe a public official. He had turned to selling steel plates, racks and shelving.

Gone, too, was Dr. Jerold Rau, a personable 42-year-old dermatologist who co-founded a neighborhood association. He is survived by his wife Jacqueline.

After her husband was shot by three youths who broke into their home, Ann Terry established a new life for herself, working as a secretary for the Visiting Nurses Association. She was among the dead at the Hyatt.

Susan Moberg, 46, was a psychic reader and spiritual healer who liked to meet people at the Hyatt Regency tea dances. She worked for the Kansas City Convention Bureau and is survived by a daughter and two sons.

Buzz Detrick remembers his father Calvin, president of a company which manufactured rubber rolls for the printing industry. Calvin loved big-band music, and he looked forward to tea dances at the Hyatt. He was killed there.

Jeff Durham, a young realtor who tended bar nights, usually met his friends at the New Stanley Tavern in Westport, a Kansas City suburb. This evening, though, he decided to go straight to the Hyatt and see them later. He never did.

The skywalk collapse shocked the proud Hall family who built and owns the Kansas City Hyatt Regency, part of their $500 million Crown Center. Buoyant, decisive Joyce Hall was the legendary co-founder and chairman of Hallmark who pioneered high-quality greeting cards. He was a poor Nebraska boy who arrived at the Kansas City YMCA in 1910. He cultivated quality and kept his inventory under the bed. During the 1930s, Hall introduced Walt Disney's characters on greeting cards. Later, he commissioned designs by Norman Rockwell and Charles Schulz. In 1949, he scored a coup by signing Britain's wartime Prime Minister Sir Winston Churchill, who painted cheerful landscapes. Hall sponsored TV's *Hallmark Hall of Fame* whose dramatic productions garnered 49 Emmy Awards, probably more than anybody else. Halls's famous slogan: "When you care enough to send the very best."

If Hall was a supersalesman of sentiment, he was also a shrewd real estate operator. He began buying Kansas City property in the Great Depression when it was cheap. He did a lot of building as Hallmark became among the largest privately-held U.S. companies— sales over \$1 billion with 14,000 employees. He was a fanatic about detail. A friend reportedly remarked that nobody was as serious about religion as Hall was about making money.

He had largely withdrawn from Hallmark's day-to-day affairs before the Hyatt was built; he was 90 when the skywalks collapsed. The man in charge was Hall's only son Donald, then 54 and Hallmark president since 1966. It was difficult following in the footsteps of an authentic American genius. He was less autocratic than his father, preferring to work on decisions quietly through his management hierarchy. The company's prior project, Crown Center, was a concern, because it had gone millions over budget, and Hallmark executives were determined that the Hyatt be completed within budget.

There was speculation aplenty amidst the carnage. James Stratta, a Menlo Park, California structural engineer who had analyzed the recent collapse of the Kansas City Civic Arena, was summoned back to Kansas City. "The first thing you have to do," he explained, "is determine whether something let go or broke. Then, if possible, to determine whether onlookers on the skybridges contributed to the collapse by swaying or dancing."

One of the most interested in the findings was Jack Gillum, the reddish-haired president of Gillum-Colaco Consulting Structural Engineers Inc., responsible for structural engineering at the Hyatt. Based in St. Louis, Gillum flew to Kansas City Friday night after the disaster and met with officials concerned about avoiding further problems. After reviewing the design documents, he "found everything to be correct."

Robert A. Babcock, attorney for the general contractor, Eldridge & Son Construction Company, ventured no explanation for the collapse.

Fred Havens, president of Havens Steel Co., acknowledged his firm supplied structural steel for the Hyatt, adding: "We made the steel in accordance with the specifications supplied by the architects."

The architects were Patty Berkebile Nelson Duncan Monroe Lefebvre Architects Planners Inc. of Kansas City. "Our standard design process includes constant rechecking," said Robert J. Berkebile, a thin, balding man. He noted that the skywalks met weight requirements in city building codes, and accordingly there were no posted limits to the number of people who could be there.

Hyatt President Patrick Foley flew in from Chicago and held a news conference on Saturday, the day after the skywalk collapse. "The architects, building contractors and subcontractors had ensured the structural integrity of this building," he declared. Many people wondered about atriums, which were the focal point of other Hyatt Regency hotels. "This was the only design of its kind," Foley said. He added that the Hyatt Regency at Chicago's O'Hare International Airport had a skywalk, too, but it was shorter than the three 60-foot skywalks in Kansas City.

City building inspectors? One of them, Jack Pullman, said: "I just believed those spans were designed to withstand anything. It's just incredible. The only explanation is that there must have been a serious design defect somewhere."

Supervisors rated as "above average" the city's officials who actually checked Hyatt construction documents: Robert Coffman Jr., 39, rated a senior professional engineer, and Bill Blauvelt, 38, a professional engineer. Coffman graduated from the University of Missouri, while Blauvelt got his training at Kansas City Junior College as well as the University of Missouri-Kansas City. "All an inspector can say," reflected William Bullard, planning director for Independence, Missouri, "is that a building went in according to this set of plans. But whether the elaborate set of calculations are correct, he would have no way of knowing."

Myron Caulkins, Kansas City public works director, affirmed that city officials did their job. "We checked the plans to see if they could withstand 100 pounds per square foot. A permit would not have been issued unless the plan checkers, in reviewing the plans, had found that to be so."

There was speculation that dancing on the skywalks may have contributed to their collapse. Certainly, structural engineer Gillum asserted, the skywalks weren't designed for dancing. "They were intended as walkways, and that was the extent of use. I would have approached it much differently had I known it was going to be used as a dance floor." The skywalks, he noted, were designed to carry "a static load" of 100 pounds per square foot, but if the load was dynamic, the figure was meaningless.

It sounded plausible that dancing could have contributed to the collapse, as George Hauck, a professor of structural engineering at the University of Missouri, Kansas City, explained: "Every structure has a natural frequency at which it tends to vibrate when put into motion." If waves of motion are reinforced—as by people dancing in rhythm—they may become violent and trigger a collapse.

On July 20, investigators examining design records discovered a critical change in the design of the skywalks. The original plan specified three 1¼-inch-thick, 46-foot-long rods which, anchored in the ceiling, would connect to each side of the fourth-floor skywalk and pass through to the second-floor skywalk. Thus, a total of six continuous rods would support both skywalks, and weight was to be distributed throughout the design.

Somehow this was changed, and there wasn't a single set of continuous rods. Instead, three rods extended 31 feet 3 inches from the ceiling to box beams on each side of the fourth-floor skywalk. Three different rods connected to each of those box beams and supported the second-floor skywalk 15 feet 11 inches below. As a consequence, stress doubled on the fourth-floor box beams, which were pulled up by the upper rods and down by the lower rods. Apparently, this wasn't considered a design change, for City Hall records don't show who ordered or approved the change in plans—a written report of changes isn't required.

Wayne Lischka, an engineer retained by the *Kansas City Star* to help the investigation, stated that, after his preliminary analysis, the design change was a significant factor in the collapse. The dancing? "That was a very significant factor—the loading of the people."

Gillum, the Hyatt's structural engineer of record, distanced himself from the design change. "I can't speak for the architect," he said, "but we don't know where it came from. It's not in any of our records. It's not in any of our design notes. It's not on any of our drawings."

Shoddy construction was thought to be a contributing factor, after experts examined support rods from the ceiling. There was a nut on each rod which connected to the fourth-floor skywalk. But one rod was missing its washer. Experts speculated that it may never have been installed. Such an oversight would have increased stress on the connection.

Construction documents drafted by Hyatt architects and engineers specified "full-development" welds to the skywalk beams. Such welds go as deep as the metal itself being welded. Yet experts who examined close-up photographs of the beams stated the welds were inadequate. "The tearing is so clean that it is obvious a proper, full penetration weld did not exist," said structural engineer Lischka. Another engineer cracked: "This is nothing more than a glue job."

People on the site during construction recalled that walkway bolts pulled loose in 1979 when concrete around them cracked. "It was obvious," recalled Don Ranville, a pipefitter on the hotel project, "the steel was pulling away from the concrete." Construction workers were ordered not to move heavy materials across the skywalks for several weeks until repairs were made.

Construction workers recalled that part of the atrium roof—about 2,500 square feet—had collapsed on October 14, 1979, fortunately a Sunday, when nobody was around. The atrium was barricaded and rebuilt. Workers weren't sure why the roof collapsed, and, after the skywalks collapsed, officials wouldn't speculate what happened with the roof.

After the collapse, the *Kansas City Times* retained Thomas J. Browne, an electrical engineer, who examined the hotel and reported 35 violations of the city's electrical code. He claimed that these violations, which included bare live wires, could pose a danger of fire or electrocution. Browne is a professor of electrical engineering at the University of Missouri-Columbia. Crown Center Redevelopment officials said the hotel wouldn't be reopened until these and the structural problems were remedied, the hotel declared safe.

Mayor Richard E. Berkley asked the National Bureau of Standards, Washington, D.C., the undisputed authority in the analysis of such accidents, to investigate the skywalk collapse. Accordingly, Edward Pfrang and Richard Marshall were soon on the scene. While they would seek to determine why the skywalks collapsed, they wouldn't fix blame.

It seemed that everybody had an opinion about this collapse. "The truth normally comes out," grumbled Neal FitzSimons, chairman of the American Society of Civil Engineers' Committee on Damaged and Failed Structures. "But it just takes so long. It's not that the truth is so hard to perceive, but sometimes it's molded to suit the different clients' views."

Bernard Ross, president of Failure Analysis Associates, Palo Alto, California, warned that since so many adversaries were involved, their various investigations would probably be secretive. Nonetheless, he said, if the analysis were competent, the conclusions should be similar. Only the National Bureau of Standards promised to make its findings public.

Paul Niewald, attorney for Occidental Fire & Casualty Company which provided liability insurance for the hotel, acknowledged: "Experts who have examined the debris already feel very strongly they know what happened. They still have work to do, sure, but because of the litigation it presents very severe legal problems to influence the public view in advance of the discovery process.

"We don't even necessarily want our experts to write reports. We want them to use their field notes and their opinions to deliver their conclusions in depositions." There isn't any legal requirement that such depositions, transcribed by court reporters, must be released to the public. Witnesses as well as attorneys want to keep potentially embarrassing disclosures private.

One of the first analysts to voice conclusions was Bogdan O. Kuzmanovic, a professor of civil and structural engineering at the University of Kansas. He faulted the design for its apparent lack of redundancy, meaning adequate backup support. "The failing of one beam," he said, "took the others like dominoes."

While these investigations got underway, Kansas City reporters examined city records to see just what the building inspectors were doing when the Hyatt Regency was being designed and built. They checked mileage logs which inspectors submit for reimbursement. The logs showed that though the project cost $50 million and had 40 floors, building inspectors devoted an average of 8½ minutes a week to the project—its foundation, structure, concrete and steel. During the 28-month construction period, inspectors made 37 on-site visits for a total of 18 hours and 20 minutes. Two visits lasted five minutes. Six were for 10 minutes.

It isn't easy to track down city building inspectors. According to investigators, logs showed that Jack Pullman spent the most time on-site—15 hours and 45 minutes during 29 visits, mostly within the first couple months after construction started. Yet in an interview after the skywalks collapsed, he said: "Actually, I was in there only a few times. I came in about a month to six weeks before it was completed. I coordinated all the final inspections and life safety tests." Dominic Serrone spent two hours and 30 minutes looking at structural concrete forms, according to the logs. He refused to talk. Fred Leive reportedly stopped at the site for five minutes.

In October 1979—the same month the atrium roof collapsed—a beam fell and killed an ironworker. The Occupational Safety and Health Administration investigated and fined contractors thousands of dollars for safety violations. But no city building inspector visited the construction site between August 15 and November 28. Apparently building inspectors weren't aware the atrium roof had collapsed.

City records apparently showed that other city inspectors were on the site: Pressure vessel inspectors spent 141 hours there; heating and air-conditioning inspectors, 77 hours; plumbing inspectors, 69 hours; electrical inspectors, 14⅓ hours. Kansas City Manager Robert A. Kipp admitted that building inspectors only "spot check" work in progress. Supervisors rated eight Hyatt inspectors as "above average," 11 "average" and one "unsatisfactory."

These revelations unleashed a barrage of charges. Inspectors Pullman and Serrone were added to the list of defendants for having "failed to spend sufficient time" checking the hotel. One inspector was found to have made false statements about his education on a job application. Another was fired after going to a drug-abuse center and failing to appear at work. Yet another allegedly filed reports claiming he'd inspected elevators at a building which had been demolished.

The Hyatt was rebuilt with a more conventional design that wouldn't invite further doubt—no skywalks suspended from the ceiling. A second-floor walkway was supported by columns anchored in bedrock. A new 120-foot-long steel truss added extra strength to the roof. The cost of all this work exceeded $5 million.

Subjected to national scrutiny, the hotel was scrupulously inspected by a technical task force assembled by the Chamber of Commerce of Greater Kansas City. Syska & Hennessy and Weidlinger Associates, engineering firms retained by Crown Center Redevelopment, satisfied themselves about the safety of the renovation. There was a quiet reopening on October 1, 1981. Edward O. Pfrang, the tall, articulate, gray-haired administrator who headed National Bureau of Standards' investigation, remarked: "The Hyatt is probably one of the safest hotels in the world right now."

Meanwhile, litigation promised to be a tremendous tangle. Within a couple months after the collapse, some 225 lawsuits were filed for over $3 billion. Of this, more than $2 billion was for punitive damages which required attorneys to demonstrate that defendants knew or should have known the skywalks were unsafe.

The amount of claims dwarfed available insurance funds. Hallmark, Crown Center, and Hyatt together had $302 million. The seven firms involved with design and construction of the hotel had about $30 million. One of these, structural engineer Gillum, had $1.5 million and reported a negative net worth.

Insurance companies developed their strategy quickly. Says Hallmark's associate general counsel Judith Whittaker: "No one doubted that if the cases went to a jury, the owner [Crown Center] or operator [Hyatt] of the hotel would be found at least 1 percent liable. In such event, under then Missouri law, the insurance carriers for Hyatt and Crown Center would be required to pay 100 percent of the compensatory damages, and they could try to recover 99 percent of the amount paid from the likely empty pockets of the construction defendants whose small amount of insurance would have been used in their defense. So, from the beginning, the carriers for Hyatt, Crown Center and Hallmark, reluctant realists, tried to settle cases and save defense costs."

Some cases were settled. Patricia Botman and her four children were awarded $600,000 for the wrongful death of her husband Henry. They had sought $10 million. Thomas A. Vance got $45,000 for the wrongful death of his sister Louise O'Connor. By mid-November, another 25 death and personal injury cases were settled for $564,000. Plaintiffs paid attorneys about a third of their awards.

Kansas City attorney Robert C. Gordon, a specialist in anti-trust and corporate fraud cases at Gordon & Whitaker, believed that the most equitable way to resolve all the claims was through a class action. "The liability issues were the same," he explains, "yet in Missouri the outcome of one case would have no bearing on any other. Consequently, if all the potential Hyatt plaintiffs went to trial, evidence establishing liability would have to be presented in each case—thousands of times. Plaintiffs would be waiting on the courthouse steps well into the next century. There's no justice that way."

There might be big punitive damages, yet their purpose is to punish defendants, not destroy them. So they aren't hit with punitive damages over and over again for the same wrongful act. Only the first few plaintiffs who win the race to the courthouse are likely to collect. Obviously, this isn't reasonable.

Gordon's idea was to resolve at once all liability issues which the cases had in common. Moreover, a class action would distribute punitive damages to every victim, including those who hadn't yet filed suit. Then plaintiffs would be free to pursue separate suits to determine the amount of their individual compensatory damages, since they'd vary.

Missouri state judges were inexperienced with class action cases, and Gordon had spent his career practicing in federal courts, so he prepared a class action for the U.S. District Court of Kansas City. Gordon sought one of the most formidable litigators in the country, Edward Bennett Williams of the Washington, D.C. firm, Williams & Connally, to be the victims' chief trial attorney. But Williams was battling cancer, so his associate Irving Younger became Gordon's co-counsel.

The class needed a representative who had a minimum $10,000 claim and didn't live in a state where defendants were based—Missouri, Illinois or Texas. Molly Riley, a Kansas resident who suffered cuts, lacerations and a sprained neck, was referred to Gordon.

On September 1, 1981, he filed a motion to certify a class action with her as representative.

U.S. District Judge Scott O. Wright was assigned to consider this, and during November hearings he acknowledged: "I thought it was the craziest thing I ever heard of." But he came to agree it would be the most effective way of assuring timely and equitable resolution of this mass disaster litigation.

Defendants opposed a class action, as Hallmark attorney Whittaker explains: "We didn't want to go to trial first on punitive damages and try this highly emotional tragedy to a jury which could only award punitive damages and was bound not to let the pathetic victims leave empty-handed."

In a curious twist, defense attorneys found themselves allying with many plaintiffs' attorneys who opposed the class action, including the so-called Whiplash Willy personal injury specialists who filed their suits in Jackson County Circuit Court. They'd be displaced by federal class attorneys whom Judge Wright would appoint—quite possibly Gordon and Younger, since they had initiated the federal class action. Lantz Welch, one of Kansas City's leading personal injury attorneys, represented 25 plaintiffs, and he definitely wasn't happy about a federal class action: "I told those carpetbaggers we'd run Irving Younger out of town on a rail. They're doing this to grab control of our cases."

At stake were gigantic fees. Personal injury attorneys like Welch could anticipate collecting a third or more of each recovery. Yet the arguments for liability and punitive damages need be prepared only once. This done, the arguments can be presented again and again, as many times as there are cases involving the same accident. Only the specifics of an individual plaintiff's damages had to be prepared anew.

There are no percentage fees in a class action. Fees are based on the amount of time actually spent preparing a case and the quality of work done, as determined by an impartial federal judge. So if the federal class action were upheld, the personal injury attorneys stood to lose millions.

How to destroy the class? Defense attorneys realized that Henry Rogers, whose HR Inspection Company had inspected the Hyatt roof collapse, was incorporated in Kansas. Nobody had thought of suing him, since his company had a net worth around $70,000, and he didn't have liability insurance. Defense attorneys insisted that he be included as a defendant to the class action suit, although they didn't bother to cross-claim against his company. Judge Wright decided that everybody involved with designing and building the Hyatt should be part of the class action. Consequently, since Molly Riley lived in the same state where defendant HR Inspection was incorporated, she was disqualified as class representative, and the class would be destroyed unless somebody else qualified to be representative.

To assure destruction of the class, defense attorneys proposed generous settlements for out-of-state plaintiffs, so there wouldn't be anybody left who could qualify as class representative. About a half-dozen plaintiffs did settle.

In one instance, defense attorneys called a Houston attorney named Robert Collins, who represented plaintiff Shirley Stover of Davenport, Iowa. He had asked $200,000 for her, but she was offered a reported $400,000. Collins wondered to what he owed this good fortune.

Then he got a phone call from Judge Wright. As a matter of courtesy, Judge Wright asked if Collins' client would mind serving as class representative, since this entailed some extra trouble if a class action were created.

Quite curious now, Collins called Kansas City personal injury attorney Max W. Foust who, like Lantz Welch, represented a number of Hyatt plaintiffs in state court. Immediately, he recognized that Judge Wright's phone call suggested bias for a class action and could be cited as grounds for an appeal against it. Judges rarely communicate with lawyers out of court, and when they do, it's common for copies of a letter, for instance, to be distributed among all the attorneys.

On January 25, 1982, Judge Wright certified a mandatory class action which would include every potential plaintiff, whether they filed suit in federal court, state court or even if they hadn't filed at all. Judge Wright designated Gordon and Younger as the federal class attorneys. Named defendants were Hallmark Cards Inc., Crown Center Redevelopment Corporation, Hyatt Corp., Eldridge & Son Construction Company and Patty Berkebile Nelson Duncan Monroe Lefebvre Architects Planners Inc. These agreed to pool their insurance funds.

Foust, Welch and other personal injury attorneys filed a motion with a three-judge panel on the Eighth Circuit Court of Appeals to cancel the class because of Judge Wright's phone call to plaintiff attorney Collins. At the same time, they argued that he had no right to force them from state court into a federal class action.

As the Eighth Circuit Court judges pondered the motion, they ordered defense attorneys to proceed taking depositions from their executives and producing documents requested by plaintiffs' attorneys. Judge Wright concurred. But Hallmark attorneys refused until the Eighth Circuit Court judges rendered their opinion. The Hallmark attorneys decided to cooperate after Judge Wright threatened them with a contempt of court citation and jail.

On June 7, 1982 the Eighth Circuit Court ruled that the class was invalid because Judge Wright lacked authority to force state-court plaintiffs' attorneys into federal court. The Eighth Circuit disregarded the bias motion against him.

Triumphant, state-court plaintiffs' attorneys resumed taking depositions. For 112 days, 52 witnesses were deposed. Their testimony filled 28,000 pages of transcript. All aspects of the Hyatt's design and construction were covered.

Meanwhile, defense attorneys settled with federal class representative Shirley Stover for a sum believed to be well into seven figures. The class action idea seemed to be dead.

In the midst of all this, along came Debby Jackson. She was a heavy-set Utah woman who suffered smoke inhalation in the 1980 MGM Hotel fire, Las Vegas—she settled for $38,000. She had the bad luck to be in the lobby of the Kansas City Hyatt when the skywalks collapsed, and she was traumatized. She consulted a Salt Lake City attorney who consulted Kansas City personal injury attorney Art Stoup.

His decisive contribution was encouraging Jackson to volunteer as class representative. This she did on September 19th. Four days later, Judge Wright issued an order to show cause why she shouldn't qualify.

On October 29, 1982, Judge Wright certified a voluntary "opt-out" federal class action—plaintiffs' attorneys could leave it. He set the trial date for January 10, 1983. He warned: "The risks of opting out are very great. Those who opt out of the class and proceed to separate individual trials face the strong possibility that any punitive damage award which they might receive will be diminished by the amount of a prior award or disallowed in its entirety."

What should the state-court plaintiffs' attorneys do? If they left it, they couldn't get a trial date before March 14. So the federal class action would likely win a decision first and gain all the punitive damages.

Clever defense attorneys took advantage of the rivalry between state and federal plaintiffs' attorneys. If the state-court plaintiffs' attorneys would form their own class action, then defense attorneys could negotiate a settlement before the federal class action trial. The alternative was receiving no punitive damages.

On December 6, 1982, state-court plaintiffs' attorneys and defendants' attorneys asked Jackson County Circuit Court Judge Timothy O'Leary to certify a state-court class. He did, and more than 300 plaintiffs left the federal class to join it. In the ensuing settlement, defendants would provide as much as $20 million, though the amount would be reduced by settlements. In the end, only about $7 million was paid to plaintiffs from this settlement. It was dubbed a "settlement fund" rather than punitive damages, thus avoiding any implication of wrongdoing by the defendants. Most of this money went to plaintiffs represented by Welch, Foust and another Kansas City attorney, Patrick McLarney.

Several firms involved in construction of the Hyatt hoped to remain on the sidelines, but they found themselves targets of plaintiffs suits. Structural engineer Jack Gillum and Havens Steel Co., for instance, maintained that the plaintiffs were already compensated. When Jackson County Circuit Court Judge Forest W. Hanna rejected the argument, Gillum and Havens Steel Co. decided not to oppose the class action. So did WRW Engineering, which prepared shop drawings for Havens; General Testing Laboratories, which tested the structural soundness of the hotel; Concordia Project Management, which coordinated construction work; and Marshall & Brown Inc., which inspected the hotel.

This left only 24 plaintiffs in the federal class action, all of whom were with minor physical injuries, so it was seriously undermined. Going for a knockout blow, defense attorneys proposed including federal class plaintiffs in the same settlement negotiated with state-court plaintiffs.

Younger thought it was better to receive some money rather than risk going away empty-handed. Gordon was adamant against a settlement, since it would leave the liability issues unresolved.

Younger went ahead and negotiated a settlement which was accepted by Judge Wright. A $150 million fund would be established to cover compensatory damages. As a "healing gesture," Hallmark would donate $6.5 million to the Red Cross, United Way, Truman Medical Center, Kansas City Board of Trust, Children's Mercy Hospital, Salvation Army and Kansas City Zoo.

As part of this agreement, defense attorneys advertised $1,000 damage awards to those who suffered emotional and mental anguish but little physical injury from the disaster. Thousands of people, far more than were in the Hyatt, appeared at the insurance office—lines stretched around the block. After the most obvious frauds were screened out, 1,592 people accepted their checks and released defendants from further claims.

In return, defense attorneys could claim innocence: "'Hallmark believes that it has no exposure for damages if this litigation were to go to trial, and these contributions are neither an admission of fault, nor a punishment."

Gordon was outraged at the prospect that Hallmark would slip off the hook. "The owner," he says, "is the only one who can and must take overall responsibility. It's Hall's building. He wanted it. He created it. And because of the way he split responsibility among so many architects, engineers, contractors and others, he was in the best position to assure a safe building. Hall was the one who failed to be sure that the skywalks were adequately built, tested and inspected. The evidence proved that the owner knew there was a problem with those skywalks long before the tea dance. Hallmark rolled the dice, and the victims lost."

He went on to say that defense attorney Hank Handlesman admitted that plaintiffs "have a case worth somewhere between $400 million and $600 million." Gordon accused Younger of selling out "for a penny on the dollar." Gordon was most outraged that the issue of responsibility for the disaster would remain unresolved.

He split with Younger, who left Williams & Connally afterward. Now Younger teaches law in Minnesota.

Gordon donated his $550,000 class action legal fee to individual victims and a proposed Kansas City park memorializing the dead. Now he and law professor James Jeans are representing fireman Moen Phillips who went berserk after using a chain saw to cut through the torso of a dying man, so another man could be rescued from the Hyatt rubble.

"Hallmark is a first-rate company," says Judge Wright. "They should have built a first-rate hotel."

Meanwhile, the most seriously injured plaintiffs sued for compensatory damages, unleashing powerful emotions. But because the liability issues were resolved by the class action against Hallmark, these trials concerned only the individual victim's damages. They were over in days rather than months. Kay Kenton, 28, was caught in the Hyatt collapse, her neck broken and spinal cord damaged. She was unable to continue at the University of Missouri-Kansas City Law School after two years. "I saw dead people lying all around and people screaming and yelling and blood all over," she testified. "It was hysteria." The jury awarded her $4 million, which Judge Hanna scaled back to a still-hefty $3.75 million.

Sally Firestone, 36, suffered a crushed spine which left her a total and permanent quadriplegic. Rehabilitation specialist Dr. Harry Robert Hahn testified that she would never again be able to fend for herself. She had serviced computers for IBM. She was awarded an incredible $15 million. This was reduced by the judge to $12.75 million, then reinstated by the Missouri Supreme Court.

Out-of-court settlements continued. Four-year-old Joshua Lee Henson shared $2.25 million for the wrongful death of his parents Thomas and Romelia Henson. Five children by Thomas Henson's first marriage were also part of the settlement. Harry Wilber and his two daughters got $2.275 million for the wrongful death of his wife Kathleen.

After these lawsuits were virtually all resolved—for about $150 million—Hyatt filed suit and later won a settlement against the hotel's designers and builders. The amount of the settlement wasn't disclosed, but Hyatt received less than the $4 million they sought as compensation for their injured reputation, plus business lost while the hotel was closed for renovation. "Hyatt's position as a victim of this tragedy has been established," says the company's attorney Thomas Deacy Jr.

Alas, none of the litigation determined who was accountable for the Hyatt disaster. Plaintiffs' attorneys were primarily concerned with seeking the biggest possible awards for their clients and themselves. "I know there are several of these plaintiffs' lawyers who opposed the class and became millionaires out of the Hyatt case," says Judge Wright. Kansas City personal injury attorney Max Foust reportedly pocketed in excess of $8 million. Lantz Welch, as much as $14 million. Altogether, plaintiffs' attorneys reportedly gained $30 million.

To be sure, the litigation produced over a million documents, perhaps 1,250,000 pages altogether. Much of this was stored in a depository, then returned to defendants after cases were resolved.

The National Bureau of Standards released its 349-page analysis of the skywalk collapse at a press conference on February 25, 1982, seven months after the collapse. The press conference was attended by representatives from 102 countries—the Hyatt disaster was the number one news story during 1981, according to the Associated Press. The National Bureau's conclusion: the skywalks collapsed because of the design change in the way they were suspended from the ceiling.

"It is true that the change doubled the load on that critical connection," reported Edward O. Pfrang. "Collapse occurred under the action of loads that were substantially less than the design loads specified by the Kansas City building code."

Tests showed the design as built could handle only 26 percent of the loads the city building code required such structures to withstand. Instead of 68,000 pounds, the skywalks could carry only 18,200 pounds. With a dancing crowd on the skywalk, the National Bureau estimated the actual load at 21,400 pounds maximum. "Had anyone known how weak they were," he said, "they wouldn't have let a janitor sweep on them."

Pfrang noted that the original design didn't meet code, either. It was capable of supporting up to 24,200 pounds. While Pfrang didn't believe skywalks built according to the original design would have collapsed, he said the design change "further aggravated an already critical situation."

As for the inspectors, Pfrang acknowledged there may be thousands of changes in a project as big as the Hyatt. It was impractical for inspectors to check every one.

Neither the quality of materials or worksmanship were believed a significant factor. Washers were missing from the ends of two suspension rods, but Pfrang reported evidence they had been installed. He concluded they were destroyed during the skywalk collapse.

Pfrang went on to criticize the welds that joined components of the box beams, a critical part of the skywalk suspension system. He observed that surfaces of these welds didn't conform to standards set by the American Welding Society. However, he said the welds met building code requirements.

Without actually pointing a finger at anybody, Pfrang said: "The engineer gets into that [structural design]. We have got to treat even the smallest details just as seriously as we do the major details of our buildings."

There was exultation at Havens Steel Company, which issued drawings where the critical design change first appeared. "We don't have any design responsibility," said Richard W. Miller, the firm's attorney. The general contractor, Eldridge & Son, which had gone bankrupt, appeared to be off the hook, too, though it, together with Patty Berkebile Nelson Duncan Monroe Lefebvre Architects Planners Inc., Crown Center Redevelopment and Hyatt, was still embroiled with the litigation.

Many observers were impatient, since nobody was found responsible for the disaster. "I'll bet the engineers didn't even calculate the design change," said Neal FitzSimons of the American Society of Structural Engineers Committee on Building Failures. "We've got a system where a lot of building inspectors pass certification tests easily because standards are too low, where architects try to practice engineering when they're insufficiently trained to understand how stress acts on a building. We have a construction industry that's highly unregulated. And the building codes people—where is their responsibility? None of this was answered in the National Bureau of Standards report."

Bogdan O. Kuzmanovic, a structural engineer retained by the *Kansas City Star*, snapped: "If responsibility for construction wasn't split up among so many specialists, this would never happen. Any dirty little country in Europe is more careful than that."

Stung by the report, Kansas City officials scrambled to assure better compliance with building codes. Councilman Emanuel Cleaver:

"It's obvious something needs to be beefed up. An idiot would be able to see that something clearly has gone awry in the inspection process. This is thoroughly embarrassing."

Who was responsible? The Missouri Board for Architects, Professional Engineers and Land Surveyors decided to pursue this simmering issue. During what newspapers described as a 30-month investigation, there was considerable speculation about who would be named in the ensuing official complaint.

The answer came on February 3, 1984. Missouri Attorney General John Ashcroft held a press conference to announce that engineers Jack Gillum and Daniel Duncan were charged with three counts of gross negligence, incompetence and unprofessional conduct. The complaint argued that the Hyatt's skywalks were badly designed, and calculations weren't checked.

Soon after the press conference, Ashcroft, a boyish born-again Christian, announced he was running as a Republican candidate for governor. With the Hyatt disaster on many people's minds, Ashcroft waged what was to be a successful campaign on his record of prosecuting wrongdoers.

However, he didn't actually handle this case against Gillum and Duncan. That task was assigned to Assistant Attorney General Paul M. Spinden, a serious young attorney with a modest build and thinning hair.

Apparently, Ashcroft's political ambitions may have caused him to announce the complaint prematurely, for the attorney general's office wasn't ready to pursue it. They filed for several months' delay, which Gillum protested. He wanted to get on with the proceedings.

The attorney general took the unusual step of retaining an outside attorney, a soft-spoken Irishman named Patrick McLarney. Since he represented a number of state-court plaintiffs, he had sat through many of the depositions and was familiar with the issues. He became the attorney general's chief litigator. A year later, annual licensing fees for Missouri architects and engineers were hiked from $30 to $50, perhaps to help defray McLarney's legal fee, which reportedly exceeded $300,000.

The case would be heard by Judge James B. Deutsch of the Missouri Administrative Hearing Commission. He's a methodical, patient man who struggled to master the byzantine complexities of this case. If he upheld the complaint, the engineers could lose their licenses to practice in Missouri. This could cause other states to revoke their professional licenses.

"We were shocked and deeply disappointed with both the complaint and the manner in which it was publicly disclosed," Gillum said after the attorney general's action was announced. "We attempted on numerous occasions and through various channels to meet with the Board for Architects, Professional Engineers and Land Surveyors to provide them with information which the complaint shows they clearly did not have."

Just who was Gillum? He was a business-getter rather than a pencil-pushing draftsman. He brought in the business for his firm. "A sharp dresser," recalls attorney Robert Gordon, "he created a good impression, wearing a blue blazer, regimental tie, gray wool slacks and Gucci shoes. He had that Bing Crosby kind of casual elegance."

Born in Wichita, Kansas, Gillum is a likable man over 6 feet tall who seems a qualified structural engineer. His father was a manufacturer of hydraulic hoses, and their family was close. Gillum attended Wichita State University, then transferred to the University of Kansas, where he received a Bachelor of Science degree in architectural engineering. He spent 22 months in the Army, including the Corps of Engineers. He married Alice Reese, an Army nurse, and they had a daughter Traci, and four sons, Jack Jr., Tim, Rick and Chuck.

After his hitch, Gillum gathered his family and headed for Colorado, because they loved to ski. He worked for four Colorado firms before forming Jack D. Gillum & Associates in Boulder, 1956. The firm grew to about 20 people.

When Alice died of a heart attack in 1971—she was just 45—Gillum transferred his children to Christian Science schools in St. Louis where he also became licensed to practice as a structural engineer. In 1973, he married Judith Hoffman. She has a son Chris from her previous marriage.

Gillum seemed to be in all the right professional organizations—National Society of Professional Engineers, Consulting Engineers Council, American Concrete Institute, American Society of Civil Engineers, Structural Engineers Association of Illinois and the Structural Engineers Association of California.

He was among the first structural engineers to use computers. "He could analyze structures from an overall point of view, not just component by component as many engineers do," says Hyatt architect Robert Berkebile, "and that's an important reason why we chose Jack. I know a lot of his other clients found his sophisticated computer analysis valuable, too."

Gillum's engineering practice boomed throughout Missouri. Among his Kansas City projects were the Mercantile Bank, Mutual Benefit Life, Westin Crown Center Hotel and a 373-bed wing of Shawnee Mission Medical Center. He was licensed to practice engineering in 28 states, and his firm grew, partially through acquisitions, to have one of the largest structural engineering practices in the United States.

Duncan, a little shorter and more muscular than Gillum, comes across like a well-scrubbed choirboy. He's clean-cut, with a neat brown moustache.

The son of a coal miner, he was raised in Millstadt, Illinois, a small German farm town. After graduating from Belleville Area College in 1963 as an Associate in Science, Duncan enrolled in the University of Illinois, where he got a Bachelor of Architecture degree. He went on there to get a Master's in Architectural Engineering. He was elected to Gargoyle, the national honorary society for architects, and Sigma Tau, the national engineering society. He and his wife Patricia, who was an art student at the University of Illinois, have two sons, Aaron and Mathew, and a daughter Alison.

Duncan worked for major architectural firms such as Skidmore, Owings & Merrill and Hellmuth, Obata & Kassabaum. Among the projects he worked on were the Psychology Building at the University of Illinois, the Northern Illinois University Library and One Shell Plaza—the Houston tower developed by Gerald Hines. Duncan joined Gillum's firm in 1972.

Judge Deutsch's hearings began in Clayton, Missouri, July 16, 1984—almost three years to the day since the Hyatt skywalks collapsed. They continued through July 27, then adjourned until August 20 when they resumed through September 10. There was a final day of hearings on September 17.

Testimony by Gillum, Duncan and others involved with the Kansas City Hyatt revealed how, through the whole design and construction process, responsibility was passed from the owner to the architect to the structural engineer to one steel fabricator, then to another steel fabricator until responsibility was lost. Lethal weaknesses in the Hyatt skywalks were overlooked because, incredibly, it didn't seem to be anybody's explicit task to check all the details. Each person assumed someone else would do the job, but nobody had time during this complex, fast-tract project.

The point of fast-tracking is to save an owner/developer money, so leasing or rental rates can be competitive. With the Hyatt's financing costs around $15,000 a day, executives at Hallmark Cards and their subsidiary Crown Center Redevelopment Inc. felt considerable pressure to push the project forward. Whether or not there was a day's delay, they still owed the banks $15,000. So construction began before all drawings were finished.

While Hallmark bore ultimate responsibility for the Hyatt, they weren't design experts, so they relied on their chosen architects, Patty Berkebile Nelson Duncan Monroe Lefebvre Architects Planners, Inc.

For aesthetic reasons, the architects reportedly wanted an "unobtrusive" suspension system for the skywalks. "The hotel has three components," Berkebile explains. "First, a 40-story-high tower with guest rooms. Second, a meeting center, which includes ballrooms, banquet halls, exhibition rooms, restaurants and bars. Third, an atrium, which connected the guest tower and meeting center.

"Since many of the meeting rooms are on the first four floors, we believed it made sense to connect them directly with the guest tower. Otherwise, you'd have to, say, take an elevator from your room down to the first floor, then go across the lobby and wait for an elevator in the meeting center. With sky bridges, you could walk directly between the guest tower and the meeting center without going through the lobby.

"Next, we considered the aesthetic issues. Should the sky bridges be an important visual element? Or is something else more important? We decided that primary activity was in the guest tower and meeting center, and these should be emphasized—not the sky bridges. The sky bridges should play a secondary role.

"We considered several alternatives. The engineers came up with this suspended bridge. Conceptually, we believed it was valid, and the owner did as well. It was a simple type of structure."

Since the architects weren't structural engineers, they delegated responsibility. Accordingly, on April 4, 1978, Gillum-Colaco was hired to provide "all structural engineering services for a 750-room hotel project located at 2345 McGee Street in Kansas City, Missouri," Architect Herbert Duncan testified: "I was assured this was a simple way of constructing the skywalks. I had total faith in the Gillum firm."

Probably the greatest pressure was on the structural engineers, since their drawings had to be finished first. Drawings for electrical, heating, air conditioning, ventilating and elevator systems, drawings which showed the exterior wall or interior finishes—all these could come later. Construction was held up until the structural engineers had analyzed loads and determined where supports should go. Engineers work with the lurking worry that an owner may sue them for damages if they cause any delay in the project.

Contract documents didn't seem to assign Gillum responsibility for designing the structural connections. That's the conclusion of Don Ostrower, an attorney who represents the Consulting Engineers Association of New York. He reviewed the contract documents after the tragedy. He didn't testify at the hearings. Responsibility for connections was assigned to the steel fabricator, Havens Steel, in accordance with industry custom and practice. "All agree," Gillum asserted, "that structural engineers design members and show their arrangements, and fabricators develop connections."

Supporting Gillum's position was Lev Zetlin, a tough, stubborn Russian Jew in his late 60s who had worked for British intelligence during World War II and helped untold refugees make it to Israel. A structural engineer based in New York, he was called to present his expert opinion in many cases of structural collapse. He explained that "as technology developed, alternative methods of connecting steel members were developed in the form of friction bolts, bearing bolts, high strength bolts, new welding techniques and other fasteners. Steel fabricators developed preferred methods of fabricating connections, based upon the capabilities of their fabrication shop and preferred types of connections for ease of erection by their field erection crews."

Edward Becker, a fabricator's engineer from Bethlehem, Pennsylvania, continued: "Steel fabricators soon learned that the type of steel-to-steel connections suggested by the structural engineer of record in the bid set of design drawings often did not conform to the particular preferences of that fabricator, which put that fabricator at a competitive disadvantage unless he could prevail on the structural engineer to change the projected type of connection. Steel fabricators gradually asked for and assumed responsibility for the design, by their in-house engineers, of steel-to-steel connections."

Gillum: "As this custom and practice became established, the in-house engineers employed by steel fabricators became skilled and experienced in the design of such connections. Design of connections became a specialty in which fabricators often had greater skill and understanding of connection design than did the structural engineer of record, who was primarily concerned with forces, loads and the design of the primary structural members that framed the building."

Becker: "Structural engineers, in the preparation of their design drawings, routinely showed the arrangement of structural members but not the connection details, and left the detailed design of the connections to the steel fabricators."

Gillum: "By virtue of this custom and practice, steel fabricators knew and understood, in reviewing the structural engineers' design drawings that did not show the complete design details for steel-to-steel connections, that the steel fabricators' in-house engineers were expected to design such connections.

"I thought he had an excellent grasp of the practice of designing steel-to-steel connections," said Gillum, referring to Havens' vice president and chief engineer William Richey—a man with 28 years' experience designing steel-to-steel connections. "They can design connections a lot better than we can," Gillum continued. "The consulting engineer is involved in many more things than just designing connections. The fabricator has engineers on his staff who design connections day in and day out, 365 days a year."

Altogether, Gillum-Colaco produced 60 structural design drawings for the Hyatt. After examining these and other documents, structural engineers Stanley Lindsey, Richard Ferguson and Edward Becker disputed Gillum's claim that his people didn't design connections. Two of Gillum's drawings—S405.1, sections 10 and 11—showed the original design of the box beam and hanger rod construction that failed to meet Kansas City's building code.

A skeptical Judge Deutsch: "One wonders why an engineer would even bother to prepare steel section detail drawings like S405.1 if the fabricator/detailer is going to completely design (or redesign) every connection and why there would be any need of shop drawing review."

Gillum denied that S405.1 was "a complete design." Rather, it was a "design concept" that showed the spatial relationship among structural members. Sections 10 and 11 "did not show a detailed design." Nothing could be built until all the specifics were resolved, and that was what the shop and erection drawings showed. Gillum: "We don't call out the weld sizes. We don't call out the plate sizes. We don't call out the washer sizes. We don't call out the nut size." Therefore, Gillum insisted, his drawings didn't fail to meet the building code. The problem was with the specifics developed by Havens Steel.

However, William Richey proved to be a formidable adversary. He was a balding, heavy-set man with an appealing, forceful manner. He was not only articulate, but he was obviously well-prepared by his attorneys, and he stuck to his version of events.

He asserted that S405.1 was a design which "gives us everything we need to make that particular detail. [It] indicates two miscellaneous channels 8″ deep, 8½ pounds per foot. It indicates a rod of 1¼″ diameter. It indicates a beam framing into it, and indicates a nut and washer on the underside of the rod." So Richey termed the shop and erection drawings a "refinement of the design" provided by Gillum. Welds, plates, washers and nuts involved "selection" rather than design, he maintained. Therefore, he argued, Havens had no responsibility for design, because Gillum had already designed the connections.

Walter Moore, an engaging, curly-haired Houston structural engineer with a national reputation: "We have basically been in business for 53 years, and I don't know when we have had to tell the fabricator that he was responsible for designing the connection. They just do it and submit the shop drawings."

Richey conceded that his company designed all the more than a hundred connections in the Hyatt atrium—except the connections that linked the skywalks to the ceiling.

"Doesn't that strike you as unusual?" asked Reeder Fox, an imposing Philadelphia attorney for Gillum seeking to undermine Havens' credibility.

"No, sir," said Richey.

Having argued that Gillum and Duncan designed the skywalk suspension system, litigators for the assistant attorney general argued that Gillum and Duncan failed to provide enough information so that their drawings could be detailed properly. At sections 10 and 11, the hanger rod is called out as a "1¼" Ø STL. ROD." There's no mention of high-strength steel. Consequently, the rods were built of "ASTM-A 36," a regular strength steel, thus failing to meet Kansas City's building code. If a high strength steel like ASTM-A325 were specified, the rods would have met code.

Gillum's attorneys countered that although Gillum's drawing S405.1 didn't specify high-strength steel, it was called for in Gillum's specifications:

"Section 2.2b2. Bolt field connections, except where welded connections or other connections are indicated. Provide high-strength threaded fasteners for all bolted connections.

"High-strength Bolted Construction: Install high-strength threaded fasteners in accordance with AISC 'Specifications for Structural Joints Using ASTM A 325 or A 490 Bolts.'"

Richey admitted: "[The drawing] does not indicate the grade of steel on this particular detail, so we would refer back to the general notes or specifications for grade of material."

Licensing board lawyers laughed at the idea of 20 and 40-foot-long "bolts." They suggested Gillum was playing word games to cover his oversight. But engineer Lev Zetlin testified: "As you will see in this drawing S405.1, they show clearly that the rod has a thread at the bottom, and has a nut at the bottom. Therefore, it's a bolt. So everything falls into place in accordance with accepted practice."

Gillum's attorneys introduced as an exhibit a 10-foot-long steel rod they claim they bought off-the-shelf and described as a "bolt." It was threaded and had a washer and nut at the end.

The attorney general's chief litigator, Patrick McLarney, objected: "All they've got there is a piece of material. That's not a bolt."

"I don't know whether that is a bolt or not," said the puzzled Judge Deutsch. But after some deliberation, he accepted the item as an exhibit.

Also introduced as exhibits: a "325 high-strength" steel nut and high-strength carbon steel washer like those used on the suspension rods. Since, Gillum maintained, these high-strength steel parts would customarily be used only on a high-strength steel rod, and Havens used them, Havens must have realized the rods were to be high-strength steel, too—even if they didn't consult the specifications. "It would be a waste of money," Ducan added, "to put a high-strength steel nut on a normal-strength steel rod."

Yet Havens didn't use high-strength rods. So, Gillum argued, they should be blamed for the resulting code violations. Debate on nuts and bolts dragged on for three days, as the hearings approached September.

Not only did Havens fabricate rods with inadequate lower-grade steel, Gillum went on, but they also misread their own weld symbols and used partial-penetration welds which bonded components of the box beams which the rods were bolted to. When those beams pulled apart, there wasn't anything else to avert collapse.

Edward O. Pfrang of the National Bureau of Standards conceded that when analyzing causes of the skywalk collapse, federal investigators disagreed whether the symbols meant partial or full-penetration welds. They decided to analyze a design with partial-penetration welds. A full-penetration weld meant a stronger connection, which, Gillum contended, wouldn't have collapsed. "Had we interpreted the symbols to be full-penetration welds," says Pfrang, "we would have had to conclude that welding contributed to the initiation of the collapse."

Gillum didn't do shop drawing 30 and erection drawing E3, which detailed the design change to the disastrous fourth floor skywalk connections. Because Havens Steel was overwhelmed with work, Richey subcontracted Kenneth Warner of WRW Engineering—he had 34 years' experience with steel-to-steel connections—to do 42 shop and erection drawings including the critical ones. The job was assigned to detailer Larry Robinson, who started it on January 12, 1979. Richey admitted that he never told Gillum or anybody else on the project that Havens wasn't preparing all the shop and erection drawings.

Thus, the potentially treacherous situation: Gillum was held responsible for the accuracy of drawings by a fabricator he didn't hire or have any contractual relationship with. Ultimately, Gillum was responsible for somebody he said he never heard of. At the very least, all this multiplied the possibilities for poor communication.

At WRW, Robinson asked Warner about an apparent contradiction between framing plans S303 and S305, and the steel erection detail on S405.1, sections 10 and 11. Moreover, since Robinson doubted the continuous-rod suspension system could be erected as designed, he asked Warner about modifying the design. To resolve this question, Warner called Richey who, after reviewing the drawings, didn't know the answer, either.

Richey testified that he asked Daniel Duncan who approved switching from continuous rods to double rods connecting at the fourth-floor skywalk box beams. Architect Herbert Duncan recalled receiving a phone call from Daniel Duncan, who reported the change and provided assurances that it was structurally sound. Daniel Duncan denied these phone conversations, testifying that he knew about the change from conversations with an unnamed architect and steel detailer.

During Judge Deutsch's hearings, Daniel Duncan testified that after he learned about the proposed switch to double rods, he performed a web shear calculation to determine whether double rods would be sound. Though it's customary to keep records of all such calculations, Duncan couldn't produce these for Judge Deutsch, claiming they were gone from his company's files. In any event, web shear wasn't the only stress involved. To evaluate the soundness of the connection required additional calculations such as web crippling and bending.

After purportedly gaining approval for the switch, Richey called Warner and gave his order: "offset the rods." Thus, the fateful decision to adopt a double-rod scheme. On February 7, WRW completed the shop and erection drawings. Warner approved Drawing 30 which showed a double-rod scheme. These drawings went out to Havens two days later.

Meanwhile, around February 5, 1979, Carl Bennett, the materials buyer for Havens Steel, told Richey that the connection design depicted in drawing S405.1 couldn't be built, because it called for unobtainable 1¼-inch round, 46-foot-long suspension rods. Since a total of only six rods were needed, Havens had to make do with what was available in steel warehouses. The 46-foot lengths could be achieved by splicing together pieces from 20-foot rods.

On February 7, Richey told Bennett to buy the steel rods in 20-foot lengths. The next day, Richey told Dell Olsen, who managed Havens' Drafting Department, to "inform WRW they need to show 1¼" Ø rods spliced as noted, 100 percent F.P. [full penetration weld] x-ray. This is critical."

Gillum and Daniel Duncan asserted that the switch to double rods was an unauthorized design change for which they shouldn't be held responsible. Warner and Richey claimed the switch was merely a "clarification," however deadly, for which they should be blameless.

Admittedly without checking Shop Drawing 30, Richey initialed all the shop and erection drawings, then forwarded these to the general contractor. According to the Havens *Quality Assurance Manual,* Richey was responsible for seeing that Havens' drawings contained "structurally-sound" connections. Richey testified that he assumed all work by Warner and others at WRW would be done according to acceptable engineering practice, since it was a reputable firm.

On Friday, February 16, Gillum and Daniel Duncan received 42 completed Havens/WRW structural steel drawings for the Kansas City Hyatt Regency atrium. These were approved and returned to Havens Steel seven business days later, on Monday, February 26. The drawings had the Gillum drawing review stamp.

Gillum's stamp meant only that the drawings were spot-checked. Contract documents required these to be checked "only for conformance with the design concept of the project." He argued further that spot-checking was standard engineering practice. He added that more lengthy checking wasn't feasible, since there were some 600 structural connections of all types at the Hyatt.

"When shop drawings came into the office," Gillum explained, "they would be logged in and dated, then given to the shop drawing team or technician checking that particular set of shop drawings.

"The technician then would review those shop drawings for conformance with the design concept shown on our drawings, which means he would look at it to see that they had members shown, that the member size was correct; and the strength of the structural steel was called out.

"He would take those shop drawings to the project engineer or project designer who would review them. In this case, the project designer would spot-check the simple details. He would make a detailed check of any very special conditions and satisfy himself they were performed consistent with good detailing practice. Then the drawings would be sent back to the fabricator."

Apparently, the technician Gillum referred to was Edward C. Jantosik. The Missouri Board for Architects, Professional Engineers and Land Surveyors revealed that he had failed to pass a Missouri engineer's license test. Yet he was the one who supposedly reviewed the deadly drawings.

Duncan admitted that neither he, nor Gillum, while allegedly spot-checking the drawings, performed calculations to check whether the suspension rods met the Kansas City building code. Nor were drawings of the connections checked. Nor did Gillum or Duncan ask anybody else to check the work.

Since, Duncan argued, S405.1 showed only a design concept and not a finished design, there was nothing for him to verify. As far as Havens' shop and erection drawings were concerned, Duncan asserted that a structural engineer doesn't assume responsibility for connections designed by a steel fabricator. "Each member of the design team and each member of the construction team is to be responsible for his own work."

"And you never asked anybody if he prepared any calculations?" asked McLarney.

"That's correct," Duncan said.

"So until July 17, 1981, you had no idea how the skywalks were being supported?"

Duncan: "There was no reason for us to. It wasn't part of our contract."

Gillum: "We didn't do the calculations. I don't know who did. The design of the connection between the rods and the walkways was a responsibility of the steel fabricator and its engineering subcontractor and not the structural engineer. We stand by the work we did at the Hyatt, but we cannot take responsibility for the integrity of work performed by others."

Gillum's tall, rangy St. Louis attorney Lawrence Grebel argued that it would be absurd to hold the structural engineer responsible for the work of structural engineering subcontractors. "When a design is approved by the owner, a set of design drawings are prepared and sealed, and those drawings then are part of the bid documents sent out to prospective contractors for purposes of obtaining bids. At the time the engineer seals his design drawings, he normally does not know the identity of the contractors who will be the successful bidders. To say that an engineer who places a seal on a design drawing that is used to obtain bids is therefore responsible, by virtue of that seal, for persons and organizations whose identity, professional qualifications and past performance were then totally unknown to him and not subject to his control is totally unfair and unreasonable."

Then Grebel noted the contract specifically stated that Gillum's approval "does not relieve the contractor from errors or omissions in the shop drawings." Nor did approval "indicate approval of an assembly in which the item functions."

Who should have checked the drawings? "Between the structural engineers, the general contractor and the steel fabricator," said Thomas J. Leittem, an attorney for the architects, "the determination would have to be made whether such calculations should be made and who should make them. But it wouldn't be the responsibility of the architects."

Gillum's attorneys insisted Havens Steel Company and its subcontractor WRW Engineering were contractually obligated to produce structurally sound skywalks. The attorneys cited the deficient shop drawings prepared by WRW.

Havens' brief claimed that they "relied on the structural engineer to make the necessary calculations. Havens was never provided with information regarding the design criteria or the load requirements of the walkways and thus could not and did not perform any engineering calculations on the hanger rod connections on the walkways."

Richey also argued that according to custom and practice, steel fabricators prepared detailed drawings, while structural engineers checked them. The engineers, he said, not steel fabricators, bore ultimate responsibility for accuracy.

In court, Richey traded boilerplate jargon with Gillum, reading from Hyatt construction documents that supported his position: "The engineer of record has a final and total responsibility for the adequacy and safety of a structure, and is the only individual who has all the information necessary to evaluate the total impact of the connection details on the structural design."

Kenneth Warner of WRW Engineering—the "R" refers to Richey of Havens Steel—is a short, quiet gray-haired man who testified that his firm was responsible only for determining that a structure could be built. Somebody else, he said, had to do the calculations that would show whether a structure would stand up. He was neither ordered to perform calculations nor paid for them.

Gillum's attorney Reeder Fox snapped: "You could have checked the connection, so the failure wouldn't occur."

"No, sir," Warner said, "I didn't have the load"—knowledge of weight which the connections would have to support.

Gillum admitted it was his responsibility to check the drawings his subcontractors did. He further admitted that he checked only a few. Wasn't more thorough checking prudent? Gillum: "The structural engineer, by virtue of the time pressures and substantial quantity of shop drawings inherent in a fast-tract project, can only spot-check connections."

On the witness stand, Gillum's attorney, Fox, asked Kenneth Balk, a St. Louis structural engineer whom they called as an expert witness: "In all those 25 years, have you ever known of any rule of the State of Missouri that makes you as a structural engineer responsible for checking in the course of your shop drawing review process the adequacy of each and every connection designed by a licensed professional engineer employed by the steel fabricators?"

"I am not aware of any such rule," he replied.

Structural engineer Walter Moore from Houston: "In my opinion, the structural engineer of record is not responsible for errors and omissions of either the fabricator or the erector or the general contractor.

"We try, however, as professionals, to do our best to catch as many errors as we can when we review shop drawings or when we go out in the field. But we are not responsible for things we didn't do or review."

Structural engineers shouldn't be expected to check details more thoroughly, asserted structural engineer John Tanner of Dallas. "That's practice, and we cannot afford timewise, or compensationwise, to go to the extent that we would accept the responsibility for any errors made on the shop drawings."

Assistant Attorney General Paul Spinden challenged Gillum's underlying assumption that the box beam hanger rod connection was simple and therefore needed only a spot-check. Rather, he maintained, it was an unusual configuration which had to withstand a concentration of loads in a public place. Despite this, the connections had no backup. If even a single box beam hanger and rod connection failed, there was nothing to prevent the skywalk from crashing into the lobby—as happened. Structural engineer Edward Becker testified for the state that the connections were "quite unusual and something that a fabricator would not see in his normal experience."

Structural engineer Stanley Lindsey, another expert witness brought in by the state, testified that the loads acting on the connection were complex and couldn't be predicted by routine inspection. The National Bureau of Standards reported that without an analytical model, there was no way of assessing the load capacity of the connection with reasonable certainty. Nobody on this job developed such a model or did more than the most basic analysis of stresses the connection would have to withstand.

Judge Deutsch became exasperated through the weeks of testimony as he heard so many witnesses duck responsibility. "The structural engineer drew a picture, and you didn't have to check it. Then you do something and draw another picture, and he doesn't have to check it. Where is it that anybody is ever sure somebody tested the load on it?"

It would be bad enough if failure to check structural drawings was the only blunder at the Kansas City Hyatt Regency. But there were many more.

From the outset, much testimony suggested, safety wasn't an overriding priority. Herbert Duncan Jr., Hyatt project manager for the architect, didn't want a full-time inspector on the construction site— he believed this was unnecessary. Wayne Beveridge, respresentative for Concordia Project Management, which managed the construction job, opposed a full-time inspector, too. The general contractor, Eldridge & Son, didn't have a safety-assurance plan, according to testimony. Ernest Brown, Gillum-Colaco's manager of construction services, reported seeing gaps in poured concrete, uneven walls and faulty inspection procedures.

Crown Center Redevelopment retained General Testing Laboratories Inc. to examine steel and concrete work as it was done. One of the inspectors was Daniel H. Hafley, a 20-year-old with a month's training on this, his first full-time job. His daily written reports were useless, but Hafley testified nobody from General Testing showed him what to do. He didn't inspect skywalk suspension rod connections or welds. He did, though, inspect steel connections that linked a roof beam to the north concrete wall. He missed the weaknesses that allowed the atrium roof to collapse on October 14, 1979.

The architects' representative on the construction site was Jerome W. Sifers who, while he had 17 years' experience in construction, failed Missouri's architectural licensing exam three times and didn't belong to any professional organization. According to federal class action attorney Gordon, Sifers couldn't remember what college he claimed to have attended. One of Sifers' jobs was to supervise Hafley.

The atrium roof collapse should have demonstrated to everyone on the job that something could be seriously wrong, and other drawings as well as construction practices ought to be checked. But this seemingly obvious opportunity was missed.

Consider the warnings of potential trouble. On October 8, Bob Webb, who worked for the general contractor, notified Duncan that the atrium sunscreen had pulled its expansion bolts out of the concrete atrium wall. Duncan checked the sunscreen on October 10 and ordered it shored up.

After the atrium roof collapse, Crown Center disqualified General Testing for further work on its projects, including the Hyatt. H. R. Inspection was hired to do the inspection work. Since Gillum-Colaco attributed the atrium roof collapse to a faulty steel-concrete connection, H. R. Inspection was instructed to look especially hard at similar connections.

The owner retained the Kansas City structural engineering firm Seiden & Page to determine why the Hyatt's atrium roof collapsed, and they found no design problems in the atrium roof. However, Charles Page testified later, "we had a very narrow and specific contract to perform, and we performed that fully and completely, but I made no negative observations about the skywalks, because they weren't on my mind any more than a stair, for example. . . . I wasn't supposed to, and I didn't pay any attention to the hanging rods."

Architect Robert Berkebile asked Gillum and Duncan to perform their own investigation. "We asked that they look at the rest of it [the atrium]," he said, "and review the design and review what was built and give us their evaluation."

Keith Kelley, the owner's representative on this project, stated: "Mr. Gillum assured me that he was going to check every detail in that hotel to be sure it was safe and met good engineering practice. . . . Mr. Gillum also assured me he would personally look at every connection in the hotel."

Gillum and Duncan concluded that the atrium roof collapse was caused by bad workmanship. Expansion bolts were inadequate. They had been forced into torch-cut holes which didn't allow enough movement.

Gillum and Duncan discovered that the fourth floor skywalk rested on two inches of bearing rather than four inches as specified in the drawings. Since this deficiency could result in collapse, Gillum and Duncan had the skywalk shored up.

"Our concern increased with each new discovery," Berkebile remembered. "We asked Jack to look at the design and the construction of the atrium as it stood at the moment and tell us if there were any other problems, and, if so, how would those problems be solved."

On October 20, 1979, Gillum sent a preliminary report to the owner. In his cover letter, Gillum wrote that he was proceeding with "a thorough design check of all members comprising the atrium roof." He went on to say he was examining the steel shop drawings.

Duncan's report followed on November 5. "This report," he noted, "is a culmination of *a design check of the structural steel framing in the atrium as per the request of Crown Center*. Due to the nature of a fast track schedule certain assumptions of loads must be made in the initial design of structural elements. *For this reason we not only checked the structural design for the original assumed design loads but also for recalculated loads that we now know will be present*. . . . Concurrently, with this design check a field inspection of actual site conditions was being made. Although this report addresses only the design check, some field conditions will also be referred to as it affects the design. A later report will be made addressing all field conditions. . . . *We then checked the suspended bridges and found them to be satisfactory*." [emphasis added]

At a meeting with the owner, architect and others on November 13, Gillum and Duncan discussed causes of the atrium roof collapse. "Now, after we submitted this report here," Gillum said then, "then we decided at this point in time that two things were necessary in concurrence with your offices. And one was for us to run a detailed, thorough reanalysis of all of the structure. And to determine if there were any other areas that were critical or had any kind of a design deficiency or detail deficiency. . . ."

Gillum introduced Duncan who reported: *"We went back, myself and another engineer, and checked all the atrium steel.* . . . Everything works as we originally anticipated . . . *Everything in the atrium checked out very well,* except when we got to the sunscreen on the west side." [emphasis added]

On December 12, Hallmark President Donald Hall told his key people on the project that he didn't want any loss of life associated with his name. "My intent at that meeting," the minutes recorded, "was to have someone identify those critical parts—points of the ho-tel that could cause loss of life or bodily harm—and have . . . [a] system of viewing and a system of inspection for the future." Ac-cordingly, Gillum identified six "critical areas" that had to be exam-ined and double-checked. These, according to the notes of Steve Byers, Hallmark's representative on the construction site, didn't include sus-pension rod and/or box beam supports which failed in July 1981. Yet Jack Gillum gave Hall assurances about the soundness of "every connection in the atrium, both steel to steel and steel to concrete."

Questioning Duncan about his assurances that the whole atrium was checked, state litigator McLarney asked: "That's not correct?"

"Yes," Duncan admitted, "it turned out Greg Luth didn't check every member in the walkway.

"You're saying you didn't know what Mr. Luth was doing?"

"I misunderstood what he had done."

Why, McLarney wanted to know?

"Unfortunately," Duncan said, "Mr. Gillum is above me, and when he tells Mr. Luth what to do, he does it."

Gillum said that after the October 14 collapse of the atrium roof, "it never occurred to us to check the walkways." The apparent cause of that collapse—bad workmanship—didn't suggest any problem with design of the skywalk connections.

In a December 1979 letter, Havens Steel attorney Richard W. Miller advised Hallmark attorney Judith Whittaker: "There appears to be structural problems throughout the entire structure which indicates to us the existence of design deficiencies."

Sure enough, there were warning signs, all apparently ignored amid the haste to finish this job. Among them:

• Seven weeks before the Hyatt opened in July 1980, a construction worker alerted architects' representative Sifers that the skywalks seemed to be sagging as much as three quarters of an inch. No one ever followed up.

• James R. Goheen, attorney for Eldridge & Sons Construction Company, reported: "At least from the date of full dead loading of the fourth and second-floor bridges, which occurred on the night before the opening of the hotel on July 1, 1980, the box beams began to distort and such distortion was visible to the naked eye."

• Six weeks after opening, on August 15, 1980, a memo detailed some 130 incomplete jobs. While this is a common enough situation, the memo raised a disturbing question: "Why isn't [hand] rail height [for the skywalks] the same?" Apparently this warning sign of stress was discounted.

• In February 1981, while covering skywalk box beams with drywall, John E. Holmes of Morford Dry Wall Inc., a Kansas City firm, noticed that one of the box beams was bending. He didn't think anything of it at the time, because not being a structural engineer, he didn't realize that the bending was a sign of excessive stress.

Assistant Attorney General Paul Spinden declared: "It was Gillum's engineering seal that appeared on the structural engineering drawings. It was Gillum and Duncan who had a contractual duty to review and approve shop drawings, and it was Gillum's stamp that appeared on those shop drawings. Neither Richey nor Warner placed their seal or their stamp on any document or drawing. It was Gillum and Duncan who the owner and architects turned to after the atrium roof collapse, not Richey or Warner. It was Gillum and Duncan who met with members of the construction and design teams in October, November and December 1979 to, among other things, discuss the design of steel-to-steel connections. Richey and Warner were not present at those meetings, nor were they asked to evaluate any of the structural design following the atrium roof collapse.

"Gillum and Duncan are telling the people of Missouri that 'we are big, we are important, and we do not have the time to design safe buildings.' Second, they do not attempt to justify or explain why the original design of the box beam hanger rod connection as used on the second and third floor walkways or the design of the 1¼ inch hanger rod was inadequate. Instead, they shrug off these inexcusable design errors by stating that the third floor walkway did not collapse and the hanger rods did not fail. They are saying that it is okay to practice unacceptable engineering in the State of Missouri as long as you do not kill or injure anyone on a particular day.

"Havens Steel, as the fabricator and erector, had responsibility for materials and such workmanship considerations as erectability, general fit-up of parts and dimensioning. Havens Steel, Richey's employer, fulfilled these responsibilities. The National Bureau of Standards report found that neither the quality of materials or worksmanship contributed to the collapse of the box beam hanger rod connection. That's why they aren't being charged with negligence. Gillum and Duncan had the responsibility to determine whether their structural design was adequate, and they cannot run from that responsibility by pointing their finger at everyone but themselves.

"Gillum is a busy man. In addition to being the engineer in charge, he is the corporate head and chief promoter of his firm. He makes a big deal of that. Gillum didn't have time to be looking over every aspect of the engineering project, as the statute requires. That's a sad situation. Gillum's priorities were misplaced. The legislature is concerned that the engineer in charge be reliable, someone the people can look to as its protector against the design of unsafe buildings.

"Gillum may well decide that he does not want to supervise an engineering task or that he does not have time for it, but he does so at peril. Perhaps, he should have passed designation as the engineer in charge on to someone else who did have the inclination or the time, but there is no provision anywhere for his delegating responsibility once he accepts it. He, and only he, is the person the people of this state will look to as their protector."

For a year and a half, Judge Deutsch plowed through the 5,200 pages of hearing transcripts and more than 450 exhibits. He took much longer than expected to render his decision, because virtually every issue was contested, and there were uncertainties in Missouri's licensing laws.

On November 15, 1985, Judge Deutsch issued a 442-page decision. "I don't know whether my decision is right or wrong," he says, "I just hope it enables the next judge to understand a little better what I was looking at."

He noted the arguments of Gillum and Duncan that everybody should be responsible for their own work. This sounds plausible, particularly in as complex a project as this. Yet, he noted, "successful completion of the plan by the team, as a team, does not enter in because there is no one who bears the ultimate responsibility for success or failure." This idea, Judge Deutsch continued, seems "concerned more with tracing responsibility after a failure than with preventing it in the first instance."

Because there was a team without a leader at the Kansas City Hyatt Regency, Judge Deutsch says: "We ultimately conclude from the evidence that *no one,* in an engineering sense, designed the box beam hanger rod connection shown at S405.1, section 10 and 11, on Shop Drawing 30 in its 'as built' condition. No licensed professional engineer, nor even an unlicensed steel detailer, ever undertook to analyze and test the structural soundness of the box beam hanger rod connections."

He ruled: "The structural engineer is, in fact and in law, the team leader bearing overall responsibility for structural design." Gillum and Duncan weren't relieved of their responsibilities, Judge Deutsch insisted, because the skywalk suspension design was changed from a continuous rod to double rod. Such a change is irrelevant.

Nor does it matter how many professionals may be involved on a project or who has contracts with whom. Nor is it relevant whether a contractor happens to have a staff engineer. A structural engineer has all the control needed to assure quality and safety: simply refuse to approve any drawings which, upon being checked, don't meet the standards.

Judge Deutsch blamed much of the Hyatt tragedy on a simple failure to communicate. Which building materials should be used, for instance. Or who actually reviewed the drawings and inspected the structures.

He scored Gillum and Duncan for a position "based upon their analysis of costs and benefits, convenience to themselves in their practice, and personal opinions of what engineers should 'reasonably' be expected to do in light of economic pressures . . . They appear to assert that the statute must be construed so as to make it harmonious with the business practices of the engineering profession . . . The purpose of the statute is protection of the public. It is not to facilitate the personal convenience of the members of the engineering profession."

He found Gillum and Duncan guilty of gross negligence. Duncan, Judge Deutsch concluded, was guilty of "a conscious indifference to his professional duties as the Hyatt project engineer who was primarily responsible for the preparation of design drawings and review of shop drawings for that project." Deutsch faulted Duncan for misleading architects on the adequacy of the box-beam connections.

Gillum, Judge Deutsch continued, should have supervised Duncan's work more carefully to assure safety. Not doing this represented "a conscious indifference to his professional duties as an engineer of record." Judge Deutsch recommended that the Missouri Board for Architects, Professional Engineers and Land Surveyors discipline the engineers.

The case isn't over. The Missouri Board for Architects, Professional Engineers and Land Surveyors must schedule hearings, and their decision may be appealed. The case could drag on for years.

The whole Hyatt experience remains a hot topic in the construction industry as people debate who should bear what responsibility and how it should be handled. Industry practice has changed a little. Fewer structural engineers perform a nebulous spot-check "approval" of shop erection drawings that they didn't prepare. More fabricators are required to have their own engineers seal their drawings and assume explicit responsibility for their accuracy.

"It's a double-check," say Darrel McGehee, manager of design and construction for AT&T Resource Management Corporation, which adopted this policy with its new 38-story Kansas City office building. "Obviously, the Hyatt proceedings have affected our perception as to what should be done."

But there are dissenters. If fabricators have to be responsible for drawings they prepare, warns Vernon K. Huso, a vice president of Paper Calmenson & Co., a St. Paul fabricator, builders "won't get the right kind of price." The National Bureau of Standards' Pfrang grumbles about engineers who approve drawings with stamps that bear slicker, more evasive disclaimers.

Washington, D.C. attorney Gerald W. Farquhar, an expert on construction litigation, is skeptical about new ways to prevent construction disasters from recurring. He notes that for years the American Institute of Architects' standard contract required written approval for any design changes. Yet the deadly change at the Hyatt was conveyed over the phone, if at all. Nobody claimed the change was ever written down. This made it easy for a design checker to miss. "Everything was already in place to prevent that disaster," Farquhar says. "You have to understand there's a problem of human nature here."

Gillum and Duncan are visibly shaken. They're cursed by anguished, bitter survivors who lost loved ones at the Hyatt—it is taboo for them to work in Kansas City again. They're considered an embarrassment to the Missouri engineering profession. For them, as for so many, the Hyatt disaster is a pall that may never go away.

Gillum's firm, which had employed over a hundred people at the time of the Hyatt disaster, had only about 60 when he was targeted by the attorney general's investigation. Its effect was to virtually shut off further business for Gillum. Earnings vanished. He was almost out of insurance money. In 1984, he sold his firm's remaining assets to KKB&A, an engineering firm based in Denver, and he joined them as a principal. He lost a small fortune, and, in his mid-50s, it was late to start over.

Gillum relies more than ever on his family and his Christian Science faith. During the proceedings, his wife as well as their children provided moral support from the courtroom gallery.

Sometimes Gillum also seeks to revive his spirits in the wilderness, fishing for trout around Missouri, Colorado or Wyoming. "It helps me put all the pressures out of my mind for a little while," he reflects.

He's proud that major clients like Aetna, Merck, McDonnell-Douglas, Exxon and McDonald's continue to have confidence in his abilities. Missouri Assistant Attorney General Paul Spinden ventures: "Because of this experience, I imagine Gillum's shop may turn out the most carefully checked drawings you'll find anywhere."

Duncan moved with Gillum to KKB&A. Since he still practices structural engineering and seals drawings, he's worried about losing his license and his livelihood. "My mission now," he says, "is to help prevent the kind of snafus which may result in unsafe buildings—I speak before groups of engineers whenever I can.

"The days following that disaster were the worst for me," he remembers, "the shock of so much human loss. If I hear about a plane crash, earthquake or other tragedy, it throws me back to the horror in Kansas City."

Clearly, Gillum and Duncan are at fault. If their responsibility meant anything, it included calculating the capacity of the structural system, regardless of who actually designed it. Moreover, they're on record as having assured the owner, architects and others that they checked the structural system—which they didn't. Or if they did perform the checks, as they maintain, obviously they botched the job.

Yet there seems plenty of guilt to go around. Hallmark is a sophisticated owner who calls the shots. WRW Engineering produced shop and erection drawings with deadly mistakes. Richey and others at Havens Steel were in a position to catch the mistakes, but they didn't. The Hyatt construction site was crawling with licensed structural engineers. The industry's customary practice, if that's what everybody actually followed—was inadequate. And how do you exonerate city building inspectors as well as inspectors retained by the owner who somehow missed apparent signs of potential disaster? The hell with all of them.

20.

CONSTRUCTION BOSS

WHAT DOES IT TAKE TO MAINTAIN CONTROL OF A BIG CONSTRUC-
tion job, achieve quality on time within budget? How do you avoid
a disaster like Kansas City? I'll tell you about the most formidable
construction boss I ever met.

He's a gangly, gray-haired man named Milton Gerstman who, at
64, works for Tishman Realty & Construction Company, Inc., an
industry pioneer. Gerstman managed construction on some of the
largest, most daunting projects, like the first phase of Detroit's Renaissance Center, a $284 million complex of four 39-story office towers
and a 73-story Westin luxury hotel. Gerstman managed construction
of the 110-story twin towers of Manhattan's World Trade Center.
He was construction boss, too, for EPCOT Center, Disney's $800
million extravaganza of technology and pop culture, which illumi-
nates 600 acres near Orlando, Florida.

When Gerstman corrected a subcontractor who had misspelled his
name, the man retorted: "Oh, I thought you spelled it G-O-D." Later,
explaining the exchange to me, Gerstman laughs: "Many people on
a construction site call me 'Emperor.' I take that as a compliment,
because they want somebody strong, a father figure in charge who
knows what he wants."

I was lucky to catch Gerstman between jobs in October 1985. He
just finished construction of Trump's Castle Hotel & Casino in Atlantic
City, and I talked with him in the dusty white trailer that serves as
his field office there. He had time to reflect on his experiences.

Gerstman is the heartbeat of a project. He eats construction drawings until he knows a job as well as anybody. He's responsible for
devising an intricate schedule that will enable thousands of workers
to perform their tasks and stay out of each other's way. Often when
workers encounter problems, he devises solutions on the spot.

He's a pile driver. "You can't just hand contractors a schedule," he
explains, "because nobody reads it. You'll hear all kinds of reasons
why contractors don't have time to look at their schedule or transmit
it to the appropriate people. So you must be on top of people con-

tinuously. You must see there's no question about who is supposed to do what when."

Gerstman is a fiercely loyal company man who downplays his importance, emphasizing that he's not a unique person at Tishman. But he loves being the toast of banquets that celebrate the successful completion of buildings where he's the boss. He relishes the engraved desk sets and bear hugs he gets from grateful chief executives.

From the time he was an immigrants' son growing up on Manhattan's Lower East Side, Gerstman dreamed about getting into construction. "During the Depression," he recalled, "I saw a newsreel which showed construction workers making as much as $50 a week— a tremendous sum back then. I didn't say I wanted to be an engineer or superintendent, just construction. Any part of it was fine with me. Those were days when, if you had a penny in your pocket, you could choose from a tremendous amount of candy."

His father Samuel had traveled steerage class from Austria around the turn of the century and found work operating a sewing machine in a raincoat factory. There he met Yetta Karp, a seamstress from Russian Poland. They married, took a two-bedroom flat at 9 Avenue D and had three boys—Frank, Sidney and Milton, all delivered by a midwife. In the kitchen were gaslights, an icebox and bathtub. A toilet down the hall was shared with neighbors.

"When I went to high school," Gerstman remembered, "I liked math and science. A lot of my friends were out playing ball, but I would do my homework. While my brothers became truck drivers, I went to City College, which didn't charge tuition, and I studied civil engineering."

After a hitch in the Army, Gerstman got a job with the New York City Housing Authority as a pile inspector—a junior engineer who checks the quality of foundation work. A year later—1947—he married Edith Dubrow, a buoyant bank clerk. Her parents were Russian immigrants working in a New York garment factory.

From foundations, Gerstman advanced to overall responsibility on construction sites. Among the jobs he inspected were the Carver Houses being built by Paul Tishman, a rather aristocratic renegade who left his family business, Tishman Realty & Construction Company, to strike out on his own. Paul Tishman Co. Inc., general contractor, was expanding, and he needed more supervisory people on his out-of-town projects. Gerstman's unusual thoroughness caught Tishman's eye. So in 1955 Gerstman, with soiled working clothes, was summoned to 21 East 70th Street, a mansion converted into Tishman's opulent dark-paneled offices.

"I talked with my wife about the prospects," Gerstman said. "Since

we had both come of age during the Depression, we valued the security of a civil service job. At the Housing Authority, I was earning
about $5,500 annually. Not so many years before, I would have taken
$2,500 for life if anybody had offered that much. We both agreed
that if I stayed in civil service, I'd end up with a modest pension but
never know what I could have done. We decided I should discover
the possibilities while we were still young. I took the job."

Paul Tishman was one of the most memorable characters Gerstman
ever met. An immaculate dresser, always in a conservative suit, he
stood almost 6 feet tall. He had graduated from the Massachusetts
Institute of Technology and had deep knowledge of the construction
business. He had a low-key insistent manner that seemed to intimidate many around him.

"He maintained some distance from all his people," Gerstman remembered. "During the 13 years I worked for him, it was always
'Mr. Tishman.' Never 'Paul.' The first time I ever called him 'Paul'
was after he retired, and I invited him to my son Ned's bar mitzvah."

With wide-ranging interests, Tishman exuded tremendous charm.
He bred German shepherds. At his East Hampton house he had
assembled an array of power tools that would have been the envy of
a respectable millwork shop—he made his own colonial-style hard-
wood furniture. He amassed a formidable collection of primitive art
from Africa.

Paul Tishman was a master at the treacherous business of estimating a bid. Before you can bid on a job, as a general contractor you
have to solicit bids from responsible subcontractors. You don't want
to accept bids from those who underprice a job, because they may
go bankrupt before it is complete. If that happened, the job would
be disrupted, and as general contractor, at a minimum, your expenses
would go up because you have to find somebody else. In the event a
bankrupt subcontractor isn't bonded, the general contractor like
Tishman is liable for the subcontractor's unpaid bills.

"Yet even if you were to take just the lowest bids and add them
up without including a penny of profit," Gerstman explains, "you
would not get the job. Absolutely not. Because subs give different
people different prices. A cash-short sub may pack more profit into
their bid. On the other hand, if you have a good relationship with a
sub, they may give you a lower bid. Or you may get a lower bid
because a sub wants to expand into your area, and they're anxious
for the business.

"When all the subcontractor bids came in," Gerstman remembers,
"several of us would gather in Mr. Tishman's office. He'd raise some
numbers, lower others. He might say, 'Our bids for the electrical

work range from $1 million to $2 million. Can the $1 million be responsible? We know the guy who bid $2 million is capable. Maybe we can get electrical done for $1.6 million.' After Mr. Tishman was through, he added up the numbers, and the total became his bid."

There were light moments. Once when Gerstman was drawing a sketch for Tishman's architect, he flipped the paper over and continued on the back. "Oh, I see you're an engineer," the architect observed.

"How do you know?" Gerstman asked.

"You write on both sides of the paper. Architects use only one."

It was while working for Paul Tishman that Gerstman really gained self assurance. "After I became a vice president for construction," Gerstman says, "I used to meet with Mr. Tishman every Friday, and we would discuss each job. He'd point out everything he believed was wrong—there were too many laborers on this job, that job was taking too long, on and on. All that criticism was tough to take.

"I thought about quitting, but I realized I couldn't, because I really liked being a boss. I thrived as a person in charge of a job. Then to help motivate myself, I adopted this as my credo: *I am doing the best I can, and nobody can do any better!*

"The next time I met with Mr. Tishman, he began by telling me I should cut back the number of workers on a particular job from five to three. 'No, Mr. Tishman, you can't do the job properly with fewer than five workers. And I believe it will take another four weeks to finish.'

"Much to my surprise, Mr. Tishman said, 'Well, O.K., if that's the way it has to be, Milt, but you just watch it.'

"I learned from Mr. Tishman that one of your primary responsibilities as boss is to provide a good work environment where people can perform their tasks without getting in each other's way. That's what scheduling is all about. You've got to do it yourself. You consult others around you who have more expertise with the various trades, but you don't leave scheduling up to a committee. When I'm alone, I pore over the drawings. Sometimes it takes a while for me to see how best to approach a complex job, but eventually the ideas come—I imagine it's like a composer writing a musical score."

When Paul Tishman decided to retire and dissolve his company in 1968, he arranged with his nephew John Tishman, who headed Tishman Realty & Construction, for key people to join that company if they were interested. This assured their continued employment, facilitated expansion of that company—and saved him the cost of severance.

John Tishman had started his career teaching high school math and physics. He speaks slowly and softly—bluster, a common currency in the construction business, isn't his style. He has penetrating eyes. He's personable with clients and associates, preferring from the outset that Gerstman and other people working with him call him John.

An engineering graduate from the University of Michigan, he was, in 1948, persuaded by his uncles to join the business that his iron-willed grandfather, Julius Tishman, started in 1898—he built Lower East Side tenement houses. Later, reflecting on his growing prosperity, he built luxury housing on the Upper East Side. He took his company public when the stock market was aboil in 1928. Since John Tishman's father, Louis, had died when he was a youngster, he didn't have an elder to promote his interests in the company. He prospered because he took it upon himself to become as knowledgeable as anybody about construction.

John Tishman makes it his business to know firsthand what's going on at his job sites. He walks around the perimeter of a property, for instance, to scope out logistics. He notes whether equipment might obstruct traffic. He scrambles up ladders to see whether work is organized, concrete is in properly and structural members are plumb.

Yet in some respects he seems distant from the dusty din of his business. He lives in a spacious contemporary home in Bedford, New York with four splendid Irish setters. From a family proud of their real estate tradition, Tishman doesn't seem bothered that neither of his children will follow him—daughter Katherine creates art pottery, while son Daniel teaches high school and college students under the auspices of the Audubon Society.

Tishman certainly could have joined New York's tony philanthropic establishment, but as a spirited entrepreneur, he prefers building something. His primary philanthropic interest is limited to medical research and to educational institutions like the New School for Social Research, where he serves on the educational policy committee so he can help it become a major intellectual center in New York.

He relishes adventure. He has roamed the Peruvian Andes and photographed wild game in East Africa and bizarre creatures in the Galapagos Islands. He is an avid pilot who loves to invite friends aboard his twin-engine Navajo so they can fly to Martha's Vineyard or Southampton for lunch.

During the 1960s, the Tishmans were among the busiest builders in New York. Since they built only buildings they would own, they were more attentive to detail than many entrepreneurs who built for quick sale. While they naturally wanted to bring a building in on time and within budget, they had a direct stake in a quality job.

The architectural firm Skidmore, Owings & Merrill asked John Tishman for advice on the new Regenstein Library at the University of Chicago. "The budget was $13 million," he recalls, "of which the Regenstein family would contribute $10 million, and the balance would come from federal funds. Well, when Skidmore's design was bid, the total was more than $18 million. The project would have lost its federal funding. Our people suggested less expensive ways of building the structure without affecting aesthetics. The job came in at $13 million."

This experience gave Tishman an idea that revolutionized the business: construction management, an independent professional service to help owners control their projects and keep a rein on contractors. His firm would provide management expertise, not concrete, steel, carpentry or any other work.

"Part of my idea," he says, "is that as construction manager, from the very beginning of a job we would review all bids—including bids which subcontractors give the general contractor."

He would be compensated with an agreed-on fixed fee—2.5 percent to 4 percent of the original budget. Thus, he doesn't stand to gain by pushing through extra expenses. Nor, since he isn't at risk in the event costs went up, would he be under pressure to compromise quality. "This puts us in a very different position than general contractors," Tishman explains, "who are an owner's natural adversary. Their incentive is to offer the lowest possible bid, then make back some money by cutting corners and charging retail prices on change orders.

"Competitive lump sum bidding at the general contractor level is like motherhood. The idea is to let the general contractor worry about subcontractor pricing. But actually this approach creates opportunities for more hanky-panky than you can imagine. Subcontractors may get together and decide who would be the low bidder on which job. The action is on the subcontractor level, and that's where we believe a construction manager must become aggressively involved in the bidding process."

Tishman is a restless innovator who, more than almost any other single individual in the construction industry, helped pioneer new building technologies. His people developed more efficient construction techniques such as a drywall system capable of withstanding extraordinary pressures in elevator cores. This system replaces slow-drying plasterwork, saving several months and potentially millions of dollars on a big job. Tishman, in partnership with United Technologies, helped devise energy-saving systems like Infracon (R), now a widely used technology which turns lights on automatically when somebody enters an office and off minutes after they leave. This cuts lighting energy consumption an estimated 50 percent.

Tishman pioneered "intelligent" buildings. The Hilton he developed at Walt Disney World Village was the first to incorporate a technology like the Five Star hotel telecommunications system. It enables a guest, through the telephone, to control the television set, room heating and air conditioning, as well as to gain more convenient telecommunications functions like a hold button and message memory. Moreover, this system, developed with United Technologies, is linked to smoke alarms, so they automatically notify security people where a fire is located.

Although Tishman's isn't the largest construction firm around, he's known for his ability to handle many of the biggest jobs. He directed the construction team for three of the world's tallest buildings—the 100-story John Hancock Center in Chicago and the twin towers of New York's World Trade Center. Although he didn't build the very tallest building—Sears Tower—he hired Irwin Miller, the man who did. After finishing Sears Tower, Miller became president of Tishman Construction Corp. of New York, a unit of Tishman Realty & Construction.

John Tishman made Milton Gerstman the project executive for the World Trade Center, an immense project which demanded all his logistical wizardry. Excavation for the World Trade Center's tight 16-acre site involved moving 1.2 billion cubic yards of debris. Since there was no staging area, delivery trucks had to be programmed precisely, so materials could flow direct to the floors where they would be used. Assignments had to be scheduled for some 4,000 workers across 230 acres of tower space.

Gerstman attended to other things, too. "I remember one evening when I found a handwritten letter from a fifth grader in New Jersey. The class had some kind of project about the World Trade Center. He wanted to know how we get those climbing cranes, used to erect structural steel, off the building once they reach the top. Well, weary though I was, I explained how one crane disassembled and lowered the other three, a derrick lowered the fourth crane, and the derrick itself was lowered through an elevator shaft. I wrote longhand, enclosing some sketches."

In May 1973, when tenants were moving into both towers, Gerstman left the World Trade Center for the next job. He seldom looked back, but he was obviously proud of the towering, tangible result. "The World Trade Center will be there forever, and everybody will see it," he says.

Among other Tishman assignments following the World Trade Center, he directed construction of an office building for Inland Steel in Washington, D.C., then was off to Detroit to work on Renaissance Center for Henry Ford II. "Early on," Gerstman recalls, "we made it clear to all concerned that we were directly responsible to the owner for controlling the construction job, and we were. It was a small site like the World Trade Center, where work on two tall buildings had to be coordinated both horizontally and vertically."

Gerstman lived near the Renaissance Center construction site during the week and commuted back to New York Friday nights so he could spend weekends with his wife Edie at their house in Cedarhurst, Long Island. As work became increasingly complicated, Gerstman would be away from home several weeks at a time. "I was the only guest at the Westin," he says. "I had to use my walkie-talkie to summon an elevator!"

In August 1976, Tishman, Gerstman and other key people at the firm were invited to an unmarked off-white two-story concrete building in Glendale, California—offices of WED (Walter E. Disney) Enterprises, which develops shows and rides for Disney's theme parks. Disney executives, who often dress in Mickey Mouse polo shirts, wanted to talk about constructing EPCOT Center (the Experimental Prototype Community of Tomorrow), a proposed expansion of Walt Disney World in Florida.

The man in charge was chief executive E. Cardon Walker, a tall, husky Idaho-born Mormon who started working for Walt Disney as a messenger during the 1930s. He worshipped Walt and devoted his life to fulfilling Walt's vision of wholesome family entertainment. He was a powerful man around Disney offices, as righteous and wrathful as an Old Testament patriarch.

Also present was Richard Nunis, a former football player at the University of Southern California who started out operating Disneyland rides in 1955 and became president of outdoor entertainment, which includes Disneyland and Walt Disney World. An operations man, he's responsible for seeing that his people generate the excitement of opening day everyday for visitors who come just to be entertained. He's a Wizard of Oz, who gets the place clean and makes sure rides work, restaurants are appealing and everything but everything is up to Disney standards. Disney people seem to view him with awe, respect and fear, because he demands accountability.

Another key executive of EPCOT was Howard Roland, a former New York University basketball player who administers Disney's construction contracts. Shrewd and resourceful, he started his career more than two decades ago with Restaurant Associates, where he had a hand in opening posh New York restaurants like La Fonda del Sol, Forum of the Twelve Caesars and Four Seasons, which Philip Johnson designed. Later Roland monitored construction of Sheraton hotels, then came to Walt Disney World in 1969. Besides construction contracts, he handled purchasing—everything from German beer to Moroccan tiles and American kitchen equipment.

Carl Bongirno, a stocky square-jawed man with curly grayish hair, is vice president of Walt Disney World. Later he became president of WED. Bongirno works well with "imagineers," who create new shows and rides. He's a strong executive, who guided the rapid, orderly expansion of WED from about 600 people to 2,000 within a couple years to build EPCOT.

EPCOT? Walt Disney conceived this project in 1958, three years after Disneyland opened in Anaheim, California. Seven years later, he revealed that he had acquired 43 square miles of central Florida wilderness, where he would build Walt Disney World and EPCOT.

Before he died of cancer on December 15, 1966, he narrated a 20-minute promotional film that outlined his vision of EPCOT. "I don't believe there's a challenge anywhere in the world more important to people everywhere than finding solutions to problems in our cities," he asserted. "But where do we begin? Well, we're convinced that we must start with the public need. And the need is not just for curing the old ills of old cities. We think the need is for starting from scratch on virgin land and building a community that will be the prototype of the future.

"Our Experimental Prototype Community of Tomorrow will always be in a state of becoming. It will never cease to be a blueprint of the future, where people actually live a life they can't find anywhere else today."

Disney proposed to create a clean, safe, efficient, satisfying community of about 20,000. He would rely on the wonders of technology more than most utopians, but otherwise these ideas paralleled contemporaries like James Rouse, who was preparing to build Columbia, Maryland.

From Walt's notes and sketches, his brother Roy, the practical man who scrambled to finance nearly a half-century of wild ideas, developed plans for EPCOT. They involved concentric circles—residences around the outside, a hotel, convention center, stores, theaters and other facilities at the core. People would glide along a convenient monorail between home and work. Pedestrian and vehicular traffic would be separated. Homes, schools, shops and work places would be integrated, so people wouldn't have to commute. People could spend more time with their families.

Walt Disney had more in mind than a community, though. He seemed to imagine that EPCOT would provide an ongoing forum where scientists, artists, industrialists and governments could explore new ideas. Emerging technologies would be displayed at Future World Theme Center. There would be three pavilions—Community, Communications & Arts and the science pavilion—where people could see the latest in everything from energy to sanitation systems.

EPCOT would also provide a permanent world's fair, where visitors could learn about different countries and have a chance to buy native wares. Perhaps as many as 35 countries would participate.

Nobody really knew what EPCOT would look like, but the company's plans for Walt Disney World seemed to suggest a bonanza bigger than Disneyland. Investors loaded up on Disney stock during the 1960s. It became one of the so-called Nifty Fifty favorites of Wall Street money managers, selling for as much as 82 times anticipated annual earnings. You didn't analyze the Disney company, you bought like you found religion.

Disney executives turned their attention to EPCOT after Walt Disney World opened in 1971. Soon the most visionary idea involving a permanent community was scrapped because of potential legal snags: There were bound to be residents who would object to Disney exercising total control over the community. Yet without this, Disney people couldn't be sure of maintaining rigorous high quality and excluding ideas that didn't meet their standards.

On May 15, 1974, Cardon Walker announced that the company was pursuing EPCOT—a "permanent showcase, industrial park and experimental housing center" that would be linked to Walt Disney World about three and a half miles away. He noted: "We do not seek the commitment of individuals or families to permanent residence. To the contrary, EPCOT's residents will primarily be visitors." In deference to Walt, the EPCOT name would be retained, even though there wouldn't actually be any experimental prototype community of tomorrow.

"We believe EPCOT will serve as a unique new horizon for the world," Walker continued, recalling Walt's glowing idealism, "an optimistic voice that, with international cooperation, says solutions to the great challenges we face are indeed possible. We seek the participation, the talents, and the skills of people around the world to make Walt Disney's greatest dream a reality."

Walker figured EPCOT would cost $250 million to $300 million—versus $700 million invested in Walt Disney World. But Disney planned on asking sponsors to share the cost. "We'd ask a company or country for whatever capital it takes to build the exhibit. We'll design and create it—at their expense—and we expect them to operate it. We'd probably charge some kind of overall admission price to visitors."

EPCOT signaled a new direction for Disney. It would appeal mainly to adults. While EPCOT had to be entertaining, it would address serious themes such as energy, food, communications and transportation. Alcoholic drinks would be served in some of the eateries—a Disney first.

As imagineers at WED developed ideas for EPCOT, the project loomed ever more important, because the company's theme parks were maturing. Attendance at Disneyland was flat at about 10 million annually, while Walt Disney World inched up from 10 million during its first full year to 13 million. During the 1974–75 recession, Disney World let go about 750 employees. Nonetheless, total income from the parks multiplied fivefold through the mid-1970s. Operating profit margins held steady above 18 percent.

Meanwhile, the creative spark seemed to flicker out at Walt Disney Productions, which made movies. From their 45-acre Burbank campus of stucco studios and manicured lawns came predictable sugary plots like those featuring Herbie the Volkswagen. Gone were movies that evoked strong emotions. Disney hadn't had a hit since *Mary Poppins* in 1964. Ratings sagged for Disney's hour-long Sunday television show. "I don't know what it is," Walker said. "We don't cut costs. Based on the quality of people involved in the film making, I would just have to say that we do our best."

As a result of this flagging performance, classics like *Snow White*, *Bambi*, *Dumbo*, *Pinocchio* and *Fantasia* contributed half of Disney's annual movie revenue. The company lived off their vaults, which contained 25 full-length animated features, 119 live-action features and some 500 other movies, primarily shorts.

Total film income accounted for only about 30 percent of revenues. Theme parks generated 70 percent. Disney had become a theme park company that also produced a few movies, a dramatic turnabout from Walt's days.

During the early 1970s, Disney executives tried to rebuild the company's long-neglected capabilities for animation. But in a few years, Don Bluth, one of their most highly regarded animators, walked out with 16 associates, and they started their own shop so they could be free of what they viewed as misguided restrictions at Disney.

Disney executives bemoaned what they saw as the passing of the market for family fare. The market is still there, but it requires more imagination to satisfy than Disney had. It didn't help that Disney had a reputation for paying less than other studios. Blockbusters like

Star Wars, The Empire Strikes Back, Return of the Jedi, E.T., the Extra-terrestial, Raiders of the Lost Ark and *The Black Stallion* demonstrated that a rousing tale could still excite huge audiences.

Though the company missed Walt Disney's creative genius, it prospered as a crack marketing operation. Total revenues climbed through the 1970s—there were a dozen straight years of record profits. Annual cash flow exceeded $100 million, and Disney had hardly any debt. It enjoyed a $200 million credit line. Observers guessed that the company could probably finance EPCOT on its own if necessary.

Nonetheless, by the mid-1970s, Disney's stock tumbled to around 20 times earnings—still respectable, to be sure, but no longer a high flier that investors bought on faith.

Changing fortunes precipitated a bitter struggle that rocked the company. On one side was Ronald W. Miller, a former football star at the University of Southern California who played with the Los Angeles Rams before marrying Walt Disney's elder daughter, Diane. He joined the company as an assistant producer during the 1950s and rose through the executive ranks. He was credited with being a genial man who could administer the company in whatever direction it seemed to go. This meant a greater reliance on theme parks. Chairman Walker allied with Miller.

Pitted against them: Roy Disney, son of Walt Disney's brother Roy. A Disney writer, cameraman and movie editor for 23 years, young Roy was a major stockholder who believed the company was being mismanaged. His Disney holdings had plunged about 50 percent from a peak of $96 million. Roy insisted it was urgent to make the company a movie star again. From movies, he argued, came new characters, which were the company's lifeblood. They helped keep the company in the public eye, and they generated new possibilities for the theme parks. Largely ignored by Miller and Walker, he quit in 1977 to strike out on his own. A half-dozen years later, he would muscle his way back into the company and help force Miller out.

Disney had become a very cautious company. The executives were traditionally conservative heirs who didn't stomach the kinds of risks that Walt took on. He mortgaged his home and borrowed against life insurance to finance many productions. If in 1937 he had lost the $1.5 million he staked on *Snow White and the Seven Dwarfs,* his company surely would have gone under. "He absolutely scared us all to death by betting the company's future on a full-length animated film," recalls Walker.

Disney executives had no intention of risking their future on EPCOT, important though it was. Construction was a major worry, since they'd had a bad experience building Walt Disney World. They relied on a contractor who lost control amidst logistical snarls, and the project soared beyond its original budget. After firing the contractor, Disney executives had to form their own construction company to finish the job. They were hit with subcontractor claims that cost millions to resolve. Disney, like any owner with deep pockets, was an inviting target for cash-strapped subcontractors, whether claims were legitimate or not. When Walt Disney World opened, the company had annual revenues around $125 million and a $400 million investment in that project, so success required a delicate financial balancing act.

By 1977, after 18 months of interviewing general contractors, estimators and architects who declared they could handle construction, the Disney executives decided they were most comfortable with John Tishman's people. They liked Tishman's idea of construction management and were reassured by the way his people commanded mammoth jobs like the World Trade Center and Renaissance Center. Tishman got the nod. Gerstman would be the top man.

But amidst the energy crunch and recession, Disney "marketeers" were unable to sign corporate sponsors for EPCOT pavilions—they probably pitched most of the Fortune 500. Walker single-handedly ordered all development work halted on EPCOT. He was the only one who had enough power to send such a shock wave through the company.

Meanwhile, to keep Tishman interested and to test his company's capabilities, Walker offered Tishman a $9.1 million, 144-room expansion of Polynesian Village, a resort hotel at Walt Disney World. Tishman seldom handled such comparatively small jobs. Tishman was also concerned that if they took this job and made little mistakes, they would jeopardize their chance to build EPCOT. "Imagine if somebody leaned against a railing which fell over, or there was a terrible accident like the Kansas City Hyatt," Tishman says. "Well, that would be the end of us, as far as Disney was concerned." But Tishman didn't want to tell Walker no. They went ahead.

Devotion to quality became apparent early on. Gerstman, for instance, saw mud where workers prepared to pour footings— steel-reinforced concrete blocks about eight feet long, five feet wide and three feet thick that sit on the soil and are fundamental supports for everything above. Apparently it had rained since Disney's inspectors approved the pour. "A footing like that may be capable of supporting 120 tons," Gerstman explains, "but if concrete were poured on top of this fine, slick mud, it would settle later, creating structural problems. I ordered the glop cleaned out and the preparation done over.

"Fortunately on that job," Gerstman says, "we came a few dollars under budget. We did it in 12 months, about a month ahead of schedule. The expansion, called Oahu, opened April 1978. We got along well with Disney."

Next, Gerstman was Tishman's project executive on the Golden Nugget, a glittery Atlantic City casino built for the charismatic 38-year-old gaming wizard Stephen Wynn. That $180 million job came in on time, too.

While the Disney people marshalled their forces for EPCOT, John Tishman and other family members wrestled with the real estate recession of the mid-1970s. The Tishmans' speculative office tower at 1166 Avenue of the Americas stood empty, racking up tremendous losses. Yet their company had a $14 million annual cash flow, and their various properties were worth about $30 a share—considerably more than they cost. But accounting conventions made Tishman look like an ailing company, since their buildings were depreciated to the point where financial statements showed a negative net worth. As a public company, Tishman wasn't allowed to pay a dividend. Consequently, the stock was battered down to $11.

In 1978, Tishman Realty & Construction Company decided to go private, so their assets would be evaluated more according to cash flow rather than fluctuations in the securities markets. It was dissolved and 17 properties were sold to Equitable Life Assurance Society for $107.5 million. Lazard Realty Inc. paid $78.5 million when it acquired several more Tishman properties. The 3,000 stockholders fared well, pocketing $30 a share—nearly triple what it had traded for.

The Tishman family went their separate ways. John's older cousin Alan had spent his career leasing and managing buildings, so he set up a new company to do that. Cousin Robert joined his son-in-law Jerry Speyer to develop new properties, and later they allied themselves with Equitable, which served as a money partner.

Most of the Tishman employees—about 275 altogether—were on the construction side of the company. John Tishman wanted to keep his team together, but news of the company's liquidation threatened to kill business prospects. So in 1978 he arranged a quick sale of his construction unit to Rockefeller Center Inc. for $7.5 million. He managed this as the Rockefeller's in-house real estate construction firm, reporting enviable pre-tax profits around 30 percent.

Tishman longed to develop property for himself again. However, this clashed with objectives of the Rockefellers. In 1980, he offered to buy the company back for $6.5 million, and the Rockefellers accepted.

As all this was going on, Card Walker was reconsidering whether to proceed with EPCOT, for on December 30, 1977, General Motors agreed to sponsor the World of Motion pavilion. It appeared that other corporations would sponsor pavilions, too.

Though soaring inflation and interest rates pushed EPCOT's likely price tag to around $800 million, there wasn't really any question whether the company could handle a project as big as EPCOT. The success of Walt Disney World showed they could fly on their own after Walt. Rather, Walker wanted to satisfy himself that Walt would be proud of EPCOT as they adapted the revered founder's original idea to current realities. At last, Walker gave EPCOT his blessing. On October 26, 1978, the construction management agreement was signed with Tishman. At the 1978 International Chamber of Commerce convention, Walker revealed that EPCOT was go.

There he announced opening day for 9:02 A.M., Friday, October 1, 1982. That date never changed. It would be the eleventh anniversary for Walt Disney World. More important, October was a slow season, which would give the 3,000 members of Disney's "cast"—as their employees are called—time to work into their jobs, resolve any problems with the shows and rides before the busy Thanksgiving weekend. They should be at peak performance well before the heavy travel season started in February. Finally, Disney's fiscal year begins on October 1, and if that deadline slipped by, the company would miss an estimated $60 million of investment tax credits.

Walker asked John Tishman if he really believed EPCOT could be finished by the deadline. "No problem with October first," Tishman quipped, "the only question is which year."

Authorizing EPCOT expenditures was agonizing for Walker, because he feared overruns. They could scare away potential sponsors asked to bear a hefty share of construction costs, and EPCOT could become a financial fiasco. Walker wanted to delay construction work until drawings were further along. On more than one occasion, John Tishman stepped in with his reassuring manner: "Card, we have only a few sketches on some of these proposed pavilions, it's true. But we will do everything possible to limit the risk of having to rework designs. If we don't move ahead now, the risk will be greater that we'll miss opening day."

Disney's imagineers and Tishman's construction people took a while to mesh. Many at Disney, utterly devoted to quality, defied the crunch of time. They wanted to tinker endlessly until they achieved perfection. "We knew what we wanted," says Howard Roland, Disney's construction contract administrator. "We had to keep reminding Milt this wasn't another office building. Disney is a creative company, and good ideas can't be cranked out like bricks."

More than most companies, Disney people pride themselves on their team spirit. They work through committees, where they seem to draw strength from each other's expertise. But on almost any construction job, particularly a giant maze like EPCOT, so many things happen fast that calling a huddle isn't always possible. Individuals must step up and make final decisions.

Besides Walker, Bongirno and Nunis, Disney's key people on EPCOT included Marty Sklar, WED's luminous vice president for creative development. Almost 30 years ago, when he was still a student editor for the University of California at Los Angeles *Daily Bruin,* Walker recruited him to become a Disneyland promotion writer. Sklar rose to direct WED's menagerie of script writers, graphic artists, set designers, sculptors, art directors, film-makers, lighting technicians, special effects experts, engineers and financial people. Throughout EPCOT's germination, they were strained to the limit, developing designs not only for that project but for Tokyo Disneyland, which was slated to open April 15, 1983.

Once design drawings were cleared, John Zovich, WED's husky chain-smoking vice president of engineering, was responsible for seeing that they got engineered—as he had done with Walt Disney World a decade before. He led his team of more than 260 engineers in churning out drawings until he suffered a heart attack in June 1981. He needed bypass surgery and was out of action for five months. Senior engineer Bud Stacy took over to see that the drawings got out.

Somebody had to orchestrate the flow of work between Tishman and Disney, and in January 1979 Carl Bongirno took the highly unusual step of choosing a non-Disney person—tall, amiable Jim Nagy, a Tishman man. Hailing from Detroit, Nagy was trained as an architect at Notre Dame, and he demonstrated an exceptional ability to resolve design-related problems fast on many other Tishman projects like Renaissance Center. During the construction of EPCOT, he had an office at WED.

There was the boisterous rah-rah you'd expect at a football game. A hundred-foot-long blue-and-pink "We Can Do It!" banner stretched across the WED offices. Everybody wore "We Can Do It!" buttons. Some things could happen only at Disney. For instance, Nagy's office filled with audio-animatronic chickens awaiting installation in various EPCOT and Tokyo Disneyland pavilions. Some people referred to Nagy as "the Pope," so on World Showcase Day, a funfest to buoy employee spirits, Nagy came dressed as the Pope—a gold mitre and costume used in *The Agony and the Ecstasy.*

Everything was in flux. In May 1979, Disney imagineers presented the Executive Committee with an overall design that would be twice as big as Walt Disney World's Magic Kingdom. Viewed from the air, the outlines of EPCOT would bear a distinct resemblance to Mickey Mouse's circular head with big ears. There would be Future World pavilions that demonstrated the wonders of industrial technology. Here would be the major shows and rides. EPCOT's trademark would be an 18-story-high aluminum geodesic dome called Spaceship Earth, which would dramatize the story of communications.

World Showcase would have pavilions representing various countries, including Israel, Morocco and United Arab Emirates, each fronting a 40-acre lagoon. Some pavilions would include scaled-down replicas of famous landmarks like the Eiffel Tower at the France pavilion, St. Mark's Square at Italy, the Temple of Heaven at China, Chateau Laurier at Canada and Independence Hall at American Adventure. Elsewhere would be representative cultural experiences like a pub at the United Kingdom and a Biergarten at Germany.

Estimated price tag: $793.3 million. The Executive Committee ordered that the budget be cut and scope of pavilions expanded.

Ideas were developed for pavilions to be called "Images and Imagination," "Costa Rica," "Africa" and "Scandinavia." Disney's designers insisted that quality shows required more money. Accordingly, at an August 1979 meeting, the Executive Committee was told that to do the job they wanted, the cost would be $870.1 million, and the job could be finished by October 1, 1982—provided the scope were set and overall designs approved promptly. Designers returned to their drawing boards and refined plans further.

When the Executive Committee met on December 10, 1979 they were presented with a scheme that would include six Future World pavilions—Spaceship Earth, World of Energy, Journey into Imagination, Land and a Future World Mall. There would be 10 World Showcase pavilions: American Adventure, Canada, United Kingdom, France, Germany, Italy, Costa Rica, Mexico and Japan. Disney executives weren't happy to hear that Living Seas, Denmark and Africa—other pavilions they wanted—probably couldn't be ready until a year after opening day. Nor would the science pavilion which, in its subsequent iterations, was referred to as Century III before becoming known as Horizons. The Executive Committee ordered that the estimated total cost, then $791.8 million, be cut.

What to do? At Canada, for instance, a couple of water features were taken out, and designers chose less fancy paving. The Mexico pavilion was made smaller, the show was redone, less expensive materials were used, and the total cost there was cut about $5 million to $40 million. Unlike the Future World, where pavilion costs were shared with corporate sponsors, Disney financed the entire cost of World Showcase pavilions.

Each meeting heralded more changes. By May 1980, when the opening day roster of pavilions was set, Morocco and Costa Rica were pulled, while China was added. The budget jumped to $800.2 million, then as plans were scaled back, the budget got cut back to $792.8 million.

Plans were modified continuously, since many sponsors signed on after designs were well along and requested changes of their own. Exxon, for instance, became a sponsor (World of Energy) on March 29, 1979. Kraft (Land) followed on June 1, 1979. American Adventure gained two sponsors, with Coca-Cola signing on December 21, 1979 and American Express on February 12, 1980. Kodak became a sponsor (Journey into Imagination) on February 15. Then AT&T (Spaceship Earth) and General Electric (Horizons), both on July 10, 1980. Sperry (Communicore) didn't come on board until September 15.

"The budget for the Energy pavilion was reworked seven times," Nagy recalls. "The Land pavilion expanded and contracted several times on paper. Spaceship Earth was downsized from a 195-foot diameter to 165 feet. We analyzed numerous versions of the American Adventure pavilion. On and on."

At groundbreaking, October 1, 1979, Gerstman and his people inspected the 600 acres of swampy land where EPCOT was to go. They saw a sobering tangle of pines, oaks and palmettos. Out in the wilderness were Florida panthers and rattlesnakes up to 6 feet long.

Gerstman insisted that the top priority was to prepare the entire site. "I wanted all the parking lots in the first package that went out to bid—to accommodate construction workers, we needed room for perhaps 3,000 cars, and the closer they could be parked to the job site, the better. We needed temporary roads so trucks could bring in 16,000 tons of steel, 500,000 board feet of lumber and everything else for the job; temporary electrical power and water for the contractors; permanent utilities for the various pavilions. We had to clear out swamp muck so we could create the lagoon."

Gerstman wanted to put out to bid a $75 million to $100 million site-preparation package that would include on-site utilities and monorail foundations. This would be big enough to attract the biggest heavy construction contractors in the country.

Disney executives urged a more conservative approach, because pavilion designs were still on the drawing boards. How could anybody know exactly where the utilities would go?

Gerstman's blood began to boil. "If we go out there, and we can't move workers and equipment, you will have mind-boggling claims from contractors who claim you delayed their work and cost them money. How are workers going to get out there? Where are they going to park? Where do you get power?

"Sure we might put down a lot of pipe, for instance, which wouldn't be used because the needs of a sponsor resulted in a pavilion being different than we anticipated. But the location of most utilities would probably be right, and we'd have a lot fewer headaches than if workers have to install utilities later, around everybody else on the jammed-up site."

One Disney executive asked if Gerstman realized how much all the trees were worth, noting that there was "a tremendous amount of timber on the 600 acres, and somebody would pay us perhaps $25,000 to cut it down and haul it away."

"What are you talking about?" Gerstman fumed, "This is an $800 million project. I don't want somebody out there selling trees, messing around for months so you can earn $25,000. I don't care whether our contractor turns those trees into matchsticks, as long as they get this crap off the site, and the work moves forward. If a job starts out behind, you'll be playing catch-up all the way."

Though Roland agreed with Gerstman about the trees, he didn't believe it was feasible to get designs far enough along to justify laying all the utilities on the first pass. The projected dimensions of pavilions changed as ideas evolved for the shows and rides that would go inside. Sometimes these changes required shifting the location of a pavilion. Consequently, no permanent utilities other than storm drainage in the initial contract. For $48 million, Tishman bought a major site preparation from a joint venture of Florida and Philadelphia contractors.

Roland: "I soon realized it was a mistake not to install permanent utilities initially. A piecemeal approach introduced tremendous complications. After this experience, we felt more confident relying on Milt's judgment. He turned out to be right more often than not."

The actual site preparation was a staggering task. Canals had to be dug around the perimeter, to provide drainage for future parking lots. More than a hundred pieces of massive equipment were brought in—bulldozers, push-loading scrapers, draglines, backhoes, front-end loaders, vibratory drum rollers and hydraulic dewatering pumps. Altogether, some 54 million tons of earth, muck and sand were moved.

Earth movers didn't try to bulldoze out the lagoon, since a comparable effort at Walt Disney World left equipment mired in muck. Instead, flatbed trucks brought in an ocean-going dredge that removed muck as much as 15 feet deep. That took three months. But the dredge couldn't budge two gigantic tangles of roots and stumps. Solution? These were covered with 27 feet of sand, which pushed the mess below the lagoon bottom. Pumping sand in took three more months.

Soil engineers performed 730 test borings around the lagoon site, but these could only provide clues about below-ground conditions. The tests didn't reveal the size of an ancient sinkhole which the dredge hit. Filled with soft organic material like peat, a sinkhole can't support much weight. So the site design was modified to make the sinkhole part of the lagoon, and General Motors' World of Motion was located farther away from it.

As the site was prepared, Disney's people worked frantically on their construction drawings. Changes in one aspect of a complex show and ride entailed changes elsewhere. If the show and ride changed enough, the building enclosing it had to be changed. When a design was estimated to exceed the budget—as happened with the Spaceship Earth, Mexico and Land pavilions—it was returned to the drawing board. Thousands of drawings went back and forth.

Clearing the site intensified pressure on Disney's designers, because it made them realize construction was actually moving forward. EPCOT was no longer the abstract vision they had contemplated for years.

With work underway for real, Gerstman became frustrated when he felt Disney's designers were holding up the job. He felt a strong personal responsibility to keep the job on schedule, even if it were the client's screwing around that introduced delay.

He wanted to hit the designers and engineers with angry letters, but Roland told him no. In many cases, design approval was delayed by a sponsor. The China pavilion, for instance, didn't get underway until November 1981—just 10½ months before it had to be completed. Producing the scenic film shown inside took longer than that.

Again and again, Gerstman insisted he had to make Disney people understand how critical the schedule was. Roland continued to forbid him to send any letters. Gerstman got on the phone and called designers directly until they complained to Roland. He glared at Gerstman for going back on his word. "You told me not to *write* letters, and I didn't," Gerstman replied.

"Milt never accepted any restraints right away," Roland shrugs. "He was ferocious the way he would keep pushing. I admired all his positive energy, difficult though he was sometimes."

Despite these clashes, Gerstman found kindred spirits at Disney. "The Disney people are so dedicated," Gerstman says, "that you become swept up. You eat and sleep Disney. You work seven days a week, and there are never enough hours. I was on the job site by 6:30 in the morning, and I didn't return home until 12 or 14 hours later. Sometimes after midnight."

Gerstman was a lion on a leash. "I was used to being the Emperor where whatever I say goes," he says. "If I needed to call the architect, consulting engineer, contractor or anybody else, I just picked up the phone and told them what must be done. Not this time. I found myself in a democracy where many people had authority. Art directors made the turnstiles spin at Disney, and they could order something demolished and done over for show business reasons—hang the schedule! How to prevail here was a new challenge!"

In June 1981, Disney's EPCOT project director left to devote all his efforts to Tokyo Disneyland. Nagy became the new EPCOT project director. Tishman paid him, but he wore a Disney hat and represented Disney at construction meetings. Increasingly, he found himself amidst a tornado of drawings.

Since EPCOT was such a huge project, it needed more than one general contractor. When enough pavilion design drawings were ready, Gerstman combined them in $25 million to $50 million packages and invited perhaps a dozen general contractors to bid on each package. There would end up being 15 to 20 "generals" who would be responsible for dealing with a multitude of subcontractors.

Gerstman's way of handling bid negotiations was a revelation to Disney. If the bids came in over budget, instead of talking only with the lowest responsible bidder, he continued for quite a while with at least three, so there would be competitive pressure to lower bids further. "Often there's more than one way to achieve the quality you're after, and a contractor might recommend lower-cost construction methods which our architects overlooked. So I'd ask the contractors: How might bids change if certain materials were substituted? What would the numbers look like if materials came from different suppliers? What if different techniques were used to install the materials? We'd give the contractors a week to submit revised bids."

On the usual construction job, as more pavilion design drawings were finished, they'd be sent only to the low bidder, but here they went to all three contenders. He kept the pot boiling rather than award a contract right away. Again, Gerstman asked for revised bids. "You'd be surprised at the results," he says. "Somebody who wasn't originally the lowest bidder may want a job badly and cut $100,000, $300,000, $700,000 or more out of their bid and wind up lowest. We called this process 'wringing out the bids.'

"We had to watch the contractors," Gerstman adds. "Some tried to sell us a bill of goods. They'd say nobody else could do a job but them.

"Take, for instance, Spaceship Earth. Several contractors who erect steel complained they couldn't get steel prices from a leading fabricator. Often this fabricator preferred to erect their steel as well as fabricate it, instead of supplying it to another erector.

"I called an executive I knew at the fabricator and said I wouldn't tolerate his company playing around with this bid. Give the erectors legitimate bids! Well, he denied that his people would ever do such a thing. We awarded that steel fabrication job to another company, and they did fine."

Roland: "I believe the way Milt handled the bidding helped us save tens of millions of dollars. This was crucial, because we knew we'd be giving away a lot of money when the inevitable change orders came."

One of the first buildings put out to bid was the cast and wardrobe facility, where Tishman people would locate their offices during construction. That way, they'd be right on the job site. Some Disney people thought the field offices should be a couple miles away. "We put our foot down on that," Gerstman says. "How can anybody respond to you a couple miles away? It was ridiculous—they thought they were building Walt Disney World over again. Not with this job!"

Disney's people were at odds with Tishman over the awarding of the contract for monorail foundations, which would cost around $30 million. John Zovich especially felt a strong loyalty to a Tacoma, Washington contractor who had done the job at Disney World's Magic Kingdom a decade before. Tishman noted that although it was a quality job, there had been expensive delays. Three Disney people had been assigned to keep track of those foundations as they were shipped on railway flatcars across the country, an added expense necessary only because the contractor was located so far away. A snowstorm anywhere en route could easily halt work for a week. Tishman didn't want EPCOT vulnerable like that.

In the 10 years since the Magic Kingdom had been built, Tishman insisted, many concrete contractors had come along who could satisfy the requirements at EPCOT. Zovich wasn't buying. Nagy, though, persuaded him at least to consider other concrete contractors. Disney's staff evaluated the qualifications of nine. Zovich, Roland, Gerstman and Nagy visited six. Over Zovich's objections, an Idaho contractor was selected. To avoid the risk of delay, they fabricated the monorail tracks on the EPCOT site.

"You buy me dinner if it doesn't work out," Zovich said to Nagy.

"I'll buy you dinner if you prove to be right." The job was done without a hitch, and the cost was about $4 million less than would have been the case with the Tacoma contractor. Zovich bought dinner for nine at Jimmy's, a plush Beverly Hills restaurant.

Gerstman put the pressure on contractors early. From the very beginning of the job, his project managers met with contractors every other Friday morning around 8:00. Each contractor presented written reports of what they had done. Every contractor was given copies of other contractors' reports, so they could see who was setting the pace and who was lagging. If a contractor was behind schedule, Gerstman didn't accept excuses. He wanted to know how they planned to catch up. He and his people monitored progress every day.

Every pavilion posed problems that were trickier to resolve because of the time constraint. Taking more time cost more money and increased the risk of missing the sacred opening day.

The Italy pavilion required elaborate plasterwork seldom done anymore, so it wasn't easy to find artisans. Steel girders didn't fit together at the Land pavilion because of mistakes in shop drawings, so new steel girders had to be made. The wood floor in the Japan pavilion became soaked with water, buckled and had to be done over. China's Temple of Heaven had an elaborate fiberglass roof which leaked, so beneath it was built a functional roof.

"You can't let people say they'll make up tomorrow what they should have done today," Gerstman snorts, "because today is gone forever."

The Tishman people weren't just insistent about deadlines. They were martinets about quality. "You get consistent quality," Gerstman insists, "only if a strong person is around to demand it. Workers who know they are being constantly looked at will automatically do a better job. You don't get quality by delegating everything to the subcontractors, letting them do whatever they want.

"I remember walking across the EPCOT site when I noticed some crooked concrete curbs. Maybe the workmen were in a hurry, or the wooden forms slipped before the concrete had set—it didn't mater. I got the subcontractor and ordered that the curbs be ripped out and repoured immediately. Probably this cost a couple thousand dollars, but it would cost more later. The longer a mistake stays in place, the more difficult and costly to correct."

As concrete was poured, some was funneled into 6-by-12-inch cylinders for tests. After seven days of curing, concrete should have a certain amount of strength. Accordingly, at EPCOT one concrete core was removed from its cylinder and put into a compression machine that increased stress until the core shattered, thereby determining actual strength. Similar tests were performed after 14 days and 28 days, when concrete was considered fully cured.

Structural work? Before foundations were poured, Disney surveyors checked the position of anchor bolts and the elevation of base plates that would help secure columns. High-strength bolts were tested with a torque wrench to determine that the right amount of tension had been applied. There were millions of welds, and they were subjected to ultrasonic, nondestructive testing, which assessed the soundness of the bond and revealed the presence of any foreign material or cracks in the weld. The elevations of steel beams were verified by surveyors.

Supervisors checked whether floors were level as concrete was being poured. They saw that concrete was troweled properly to assure the right smoothness. On the first floor, they painted lines to represent partitions, so that if there were any miscalculations, they'd be discovered as early as possible. This avoided having to jackhammer through many floors and damage the structure.

Electrical work: "We begin by seeing whether conduits are the proper size," Gerstman explains. "You have to put a certain amount of cable through a conduit, and sometimes as the result of a design error, the conduit is too small to accommodate the wires. Our people perform what are called Meggar tests, which check the integrity of insulation around the wiring, because this is what helps protect against short circuits and fires. We check the soundness of connections in hundreds of electrical panel boxes where cables are terminated."

More details: Pipes were hydrostatically tested to see whether they could withstand specified pressures. Windows were tested in an independent laboratory for resistance to wind and rain, and their installation was checked. Drywall was checked to make sure it was straight. The fit of ceilings, doors, everything was checked. Smoke bombs were used to see whether fire safety systems could purge smoke as fast as they were supposed to.

The biggest failing on the part of general contractors," Gerstman says, talking about both schedule and quality issues, "was that they didn't do their homework. They relied too much on subcontractors to get the job done. We had some contractors who underestimated the number of foremen and superintendents needed here, and they lost control.

"As a construction manager, you must lead. People expect you to lead. They want to be told where they're going to work, how they're going to deliver materials. This can't be done by memo. You must always be on the spot, talking with people."

There were cases where a strong subcontractor ran a weak general.

Such a subcontractor worked where he wanted to, even if it caused serious logistical problems and losses for other subcontractors. Strong subs like to work their own schedule rather than observe the schedule of the job.

"Everybody would like to say they'd start their work after other subs were finished," says Dave Meyers who succeeded Gerstman as construction boss at the World Trade Center, then joined him at EPCOT as construction manager. "But if everybody waited around, we'd still be building EPCOT. You must work wherever you can, as opportunities arise."

Beginning in June 1981, various contractors were responsible for pouring the 600,000 square feet of pink concrete walkways. Their natural preference was to finish paving one area, then move truckloads of concrete forms and equipment to the next area. But this wasn't possible, because work was going on at virtually all of the pavilions.

Gerstman wanted contractors to pave the areas nearest the lagoon, then, in effect, zigzag around as areas became available. "No question this was difficult," Meyers concedes, "but we had only so many days to pour the massive amount of concrete. If we didn't get that done, we knew we'd never get EPCOT completed on time."

In this case, even Gerstman's forceful presence wasn't enough. To increase pressure, he summoned contractors to a white trailer which had Disney field offices. It was called the War Room. There they met with Nunis, Bongirno, Roland, Nagy and other supervisory people involved.

Nunis and Bongirno were intimidating as they expressed concern of an owner worried about their huge investment. Though Nunis didn't yell much, he was feared because of his determination to hold people responsible for their actions. He talked like a football coach. "Come on guys," he'd say, "this is a job we have to get on track."

Bongirno would dig into practical details. Do you have enough men? Enough equipment? How do you plan to move those materials around? He was more sympathetic, and the contrast with Nunis seemed to give these sessions greater impact.

Roland was there for follow-through. If a contractor promised to put more workers on the job, if they agreed to bring more equipment onto the job, if Disney approved a night shift at time and a half pay—Roland spelled out these as well as myriad other agreements. "We wanted no misunderstanding about who was to do what," he says.

In this case, short-term goals were set to keep the concrete pour moving forward at about 50,000 square feet a week—a large amount by any measure. There were daily meetings with Gerstman, Meyers and their associates who wanted to know how the men and equipment were going to be deployed, why the job wasn't moving faster.

Then there was the great thrust block caper. On a Friday afternoon, just months before the opening, newly installed underground chilled water pipes were being tested. They burst, because surges of high pressure moved the pipes around enough to overstress the lines. First, these had to be removed. The apparent solution was to lay in thrust blocks—steel-reinforced concrete anchors about 18 feet long, 18 feet wide and 4 feet thick to secure the pipes. Disney's customary committee couldn't be assembled right then, so Nagy, representing Disney, approved the $1.5 million job. "What was at stake," he explains, "was the opening of the park. If we didn't start construction on those thrust blocks immediately, walkway concrete couldn't be placed, and there would be delays all along the line."

Disney staff pitched in where they could. The Walt Disney World weather station provided weather reports about every 10 minutes, so workers would be alerted in time to protect freshly poured concrete from the devastation of sudden local thunderstorms. Since there wasn't electric power in some places during several late-night workathons, Disney brought in a hook-and-ladder fire truck to project light over a wide area, enabling more than a hundred concrete finishers to continue their work. Disney chefs arrived to grill hundreds of hamburgers, which helped maintain morale.

The "year out" Executive Committee meeting, September 8, 1981, was an anxious time of reckoning. "If you give me four Future World pavilions and six World Showcase pavilions," Nunis declared, "I can operate a viable theme park. Spaceship Earth, of course, is a must."

Well, World of Motion, World of Energy, Land, United Kingdom, France, Canada and American Adventure were on schedule—structures rising. Germany's structure proceeded more slowly than expected. None of the other pavilions were beyond the foundation level. China wasn't even started yet.

"Until now," John Tishman said, "we've concentrated on controlling risks. Now, with the end in sight, we must accelerate the work with selected overtime. We'll have to fast-track China—start construction before all the drawings are finished."

Almost every day, something would threaten to delay the project. Subcontractors demanded money because a job took more time than they bargained on. "Extra money?" Gerstman would ask, incredulous. "What extra money? Forget it!" He would pay contractors only for extra production, not for the inconvenience of coordinating with other contractors—an inevitable part of a big job like this.

A carpentry subcontractor tried arm twisting at the China pavilion. He notified Tishman construction manager Dave Meyers that he wouldn't deliver about $775,000 worth of woodwork unless he got a bonus.

"Keep your woodwork, we don't need it," Meyers bluffed.

Although Disney has a shop where this kind of thing could be done, they were jammed with work. Fortunately, the subcontractor didn't know that.

The rattled subcontractor called Gerstman and pleaded with him to accept his woodwork rather than order anew from Disney—he didn't want to be stuck with it. Delivery followed promptly.

On Rosh Hashanah 1981, Gerstman and Roland were heading for temple when they were notified via walkie-talkie that drywall laborers had suddenly called a strike at the France and Japan pavilions. They arrived to learn how the drywall subcontractor had skipped to South America with their $50,000 payroll and work records, and they resolved to stay "on the clock." According to union rules, workers owed money may remain at the site and accumulate time until they're paid.

Gerstman guaranteed the situation would be resolved promptly and asked workers to leave the site since their shift was over. He promised that the next day he, Roland and the union business agent would meet with the contractor who bore the liability. Together they'd reconstruct missing work records. Everybody would get pay plus benefits they were entitled to.

Workers balked. Gerstman reminded them that since he was making a legitimate proposal, union regulations required them to call off their job action while the proposal was being pursued. Everybody returned home.

On another occasion, a union pension trustee called Gerstman. "The structural steel subcontractors owe us $60,000 for our pension fund," he menaced, "and unless you pay by the end of the day, we'll picket the entrances to EPCOT."

"Charlie," Gerstman said, "I don't know anything about your problem. I won't lift a finger to help you. You do whatever you feel you have to. Picket the place. But don't you ever come at me with threats again."

There were no pickets, and Gerstman and the union pension trustee met the next day. Employers were supposed to pay about 10 percent of payroll into the pension fund every payroll period, and this pension trustee let the subcontractor go too long without paying. The pension trustee was personally liable for the shortfall, because under the rules he hadn't done his job. It is up to the union to go after the subcontractor. But the trustee panicked and tried to pressure Disney through Gerstman. Approached more reasonably, Gerstman helped him collect the money.

A plumbing-and-heating subcontractor ordered his sheet metal subcontractor—many subcontractors parcel out work to more specialized trades—to slow work on the Mexico pavilion and East Restaurant complex. The plumbing-and-heating subcontractor ignored his general contractor's demands to accelerate work. The plumbing-and-heating subcontractor said he was losing money on the job and demanded that Gerstman pay a $1 million claim. Apparently he expected Gerstman would cave in, anxious about the opening-day deadline.

Instead, Gerstman tore up the claim report and called in the burly general contractor: "This is the second time I'm hearing this shit. Get him off the site! Replace him! If I see that plumber on the site tomorrow, I'll have him put off by security!"

Within hours, the contractor returned. "Milt, he wants another chance."

"That's up to you," Gerstman growled, "but the bastard better shape up. I don't want to hear another peep out of him."

The plumbing-and-heating subcontractor returned to work, put more people on the job and got it back on schedule at his expense. Then he sued his general contractor to recover his losses—case still pending.

"You have to know what your rights are under the contract, so you can be tough," Gerstman reflects. "You must be an engineer, contractor and lawyer rolled up into one. Tough means I could stop your payments. I'm in a position to give you more work. In this case, the plumber was bonded, and if I notified his bonding company that he was at fault, he'd be in trouble."

During final months, Gerstman put additional pressure on everybody. Saturdays at 7:00 in the morning, he, Nunis, Bongiorno, Roland, Nagy and other executives toured the site. All contractors and subcontractors were expected to be at their sites. Those who were on schedule got praise. Laggards were grilled: Why wasn't work completed? What would be done about it? How much would be accomplished by next Saturday?

One Saturday, the executives discovered that the nearly finished Kodak-sponsored Journey into Imagination pavilion was cluttered with scaffolding and gear that prevented Disney's people from doing their work. "I was vile with the general contractor," Gerstman acknowledges. "I yelled at him in front of his subcontractors. I reamed out the general contractor and his subcontractors for holding up the job. Nobody there escaped."

They protested they were behind schedule because Disney's people demanded so many changes—a familiar line, since construction troubles are routinely blamed on design changes. Gerstman described how the subcontractors could complete their job while they started to remove scaffolding, but they were negative, quick to give reasons why an idea couldn't work. He lashed at them again, ordered them to follow his procedure. He stormed out.

Nunis said: "Don't you think you were a little hard on them, Milt? Wouldn't it be good to give them a pat on the back?"

Gerstman snapped: "It's better for them to see I can walk out mad. Threaten the bastards. They won't want to hear that again. You can't always be Mr. Nice Guy. If they perform next week, that will be time enough for a pat on the back."

Both Disney and Tishman people were alarmed that by being so publicly critical of the general contractor, Gerstman had undercut the contractor's authority. This could mean problems, since the contractor still had to deal with his subcontractors. Roland was asked to speak with Gerstman, but he declined. "I can't tell Milt how to handle this job when it's almost done," he protested.

The following week, the Imagination pavilion was immaculate. The ceiling was finished, the scaffolding was gone. Nunis told Gerstman: "Sometimes you hit them, and sometimes you kiss them. I guess there's method to your madness."

"It was easy to be tough on contractors when they were at fault," Meyers concedes, "but we realized this was an exceptionally difficult job with changes and a deadline which remained fixed. Keeping the job on track was often due to the pure power of personality."

The contractors Gerstman sometimes wrestled with were multi-million-dollar companies who had attorneys aggressively pressing their claims for more money. Yet according to Howard Roland, claims were resolved for only about 25 cents on the dollar.

Gerstman knew how to harness pride, as was apparent in his handling of Communicore. This was one of the most critical pavilions, since it was the gateway to EPCOT and displayed wide-ranging technologies. If on opening day it were a mess of scaffolding, canvas and dirt, everybody would see it. Communicore was behind, because designs were seven months late.

Gerstman put on two shifts around the clock and, to help spur them on, he gave a special commendation at weekly progress meetings. He announced a Subcontractor of the Week who had performed the assigned tasks and done the most to help move the job along. There wasn't any actual award—no plaque or bottle of booze—but people appreciated the recognition nonetheless. Some subcontractors expressed disappointment when they weren't selected.

Gerstman created competitions to make the grinding work more of a game. In May 1982 he told people with Inland Construction Co., responsible for the Italy pavilion, that on August 15 there would be a special forty-eighth birthday celebration for Roland, to which Disney top brass would be invited. It would be held at the Italy pavilion restaurant—if it was ready. Otherwise, the dinner would be at the France pavilion.

Then he told people with Palmer-Smith Co., contractor for the France pavilion, that the celebration would be at the restaurant there if it was ready. In the event they couldn't handle the challenge, the Italy pavilion would host the affair.

On the appointed day, *both* restaurants were finished and approved by health inspectors. The executives had Fettucini Alfredo at the Italy pavilion, then moved to the France pavilion, where they finished the meal with fancy French dishes. Roland's birthday cake had a huge confectionery tennis ball, a tribute to one of his favorite pastimes.

"Since this proved to be a motivator," Roland laughs, "Milt, John Tishman and Jim Nagy announced more high-level gatherings. After a while, it seemed we were using almost any excuse for one. The idea ceased to work, so we discontinued it."

Gerstman: "There was one occasion where Disney's chefs-in-training gave us a trial run. We were warned to try just a little of everything, since there would be so many dishes representing all the countries at EPCOT. Well, I remembered my mother's dictum from our early years of poverty—eat everything in front of you. I did, and I could hardly walk out of there."

During the summer, at Nunis's suggestion, workers were invited to bring their families to the job site on Sundays, so they could see what the project was all about. There were models and films to show how the pavilions would look. Trams took people around, and there were refreshments.

The biggest push was for a Labor Day celebration. There was a feverish burst of overtime. Long past midnight, Gerstman, Nagy, Nunis and Roland went from pavilion to pavilion, checking progress and showing workers they were on the job, too.

Labor Day was a preview for workers and their families. They could see models and drawings that showed what the various pavilions would look like. Trams took people around the site as guides explained how progress was unfolding before their eyes. Refreshments were served in cheerful circus tents. Workers who labored all night to install lighting fixtures at Germany were so proud of their work that they spent virtually the entire day at their pavilion, drinking German beer.

Hard though everybody pushed, it was seldom enough for Orlando Ferrante, vice president of Disney's MAPO subsidiary, named after Mary Poppins, which manufactured key components for shows and rides at EPCOT as well as Tokyo Disneyland and the other theme parks. Ferrante was a former football lineman at the University of Southern California, where he had known Dick Nunis and Ron Miller. He went on to play professionally for the San Diego Chargers before joining Disney.

Ferrante was anxious about his production deadlines, because approved drawings came through late. There were to be some 450 computer-guided audio-animatronic figures—Mark Twain, Benjamin Franklin, Michelangelo, 20-foot-high dinosaurs and talking broccoli, among others. Computer software had to be written, ride systems produced and synchronized with extraordinarily complex shows. Disney's designers aim for shows that offer so much action that you can't grasp everything at once. It's their way of inviting you back.

When construction workers fell behind schedule, they further complicated Ferrante's job. What to schedule for production first, when and how to install it—changes poured in daily to the 1,300 people Ferrante had working at WED's Glendale, California facility and 1,000 at Walt Disney World. Some 90,000 hours were required just to manufacture the show and ride for the American Adventure pavilion. Ferrante was pressed tighter against the October 1 opening day.

Since much of the equipment involved precision electronics, Ferrante preferred that it be installed only after a pavilion was dust-free and air-conditioned. But with construction lagging, he charged into pavilions like a brawny lineman. "You have to force the issue," Ferrante told me. "You can't let the job slide."

The actual installation of all the audio-animatronic figures was handled by Neil Gallagher, a tall, graying man who started as a Disney studio machinist and became head of their in-house Buena Vista Construction Company. As taciturn as Gerstman is garrulous, Gallagher is a bulldog who commits himself to an important Disney job before he really knows where he'll get the resources, and somehow the job gets done. He helped finish Walt Disney World's Magic Kingdom after the general contractor was fired. More than once Gerstman took critical work away from a lagging subcontractor and gave it to Gallagher.

Perhaps the toughest squeeze came during July 1982 at Exxon's Universe of Energy pavilion, where audiences were to be rotated on an 80-foot-diameter air-float turntable. After the turntable was installed, it was discovered that the concrete pad beneath couldn't withstand the high air pressure. Because the concrete flaked, air pressure couldn't be maintained. So the whole thing had to be disassembled, and the concrete pad was jackhammered away. Workers poured a new mix of concrete with a harder, smoother finish. The turntable was installed again, but this didn't work either. Once more, it was disassembled, concrete was jackhammered away, and a turntable pad constructed from quarter-inch-thick steel. It worked, but more than a month was lost.

Shows and rides were being installed as carpenters, plasterers, painters and other people were still in pavilions. As a result, more repairs and touch-up had to be done after all those people left. It was a price for making the deadline.

Though Gerstman was boss, even he had to bow before Disney's show people. One of the most exacting was tall, balding, reserved John Hench. An animator who started with Walt Disney in 1939, he worked on some of the studio's most sensational achievements like *Cinderella, Peter Pan* and *Fantasia*. He won an Academy Award for his special effects in *Twenty Thousand Leagues Beneath the Sea*.

Every pavilion had something redone to capture the magical "Disney touch." The French marketplace, modeled after Les Halles in Paris, was repainted a darker green to be more authentic. Woodwork in the Canadian restaurant had to be stripped and refinished, so it would be lighter.

At the Mexico pavilion, there was a temple modeled after the great temple at Chichén Itzá, the Yucatan Peninsula. It had more than 30 gorgeous gargoyles, but it was decided that for greater authenticity they had to be torn out and moved up 24 inches at a cost of perhaps $15,000. "It broke my heart to see that beautiful work undone," says Gerstman, "but I respected Disney's devotion to quality."

At the United Kingdom pavilion, Disney people scorched half-timbering and beat it with chains to achieve a weathered look. Later a well-meaning workman filled in all the nicks with a caulking compound. Disney art directors were furious and established a new policy: Once they approved a look, nobody was permitted in the area without special permission.

Landscapers were asked for miracles. Directed by Horticultural Director Tony Virginia, a debonair Italian with a Southern California drawl, they had to plant some 10,000 shrubs, 12,500 trees and 5 million square feet of grass. EPCOT would be ablaze with annual flowers like gerbera daisies, phlox, mums, begonias and petunias. Virginia traveled around the United States searching for hard-to-find varieties like contorted hazelnut and weeping mulberry trees for the China pavilion. Canadian pines didn't survive at the Canada pavilion, because of Florida's climate, so Virginia flew halfway around the world to Taiwan, where he located a species that looked the same and did well.

Landscapers started planting before construction workers were finished with pavilions, and this multiplied the pressures. If a contractor had to reenter an area for a job which should have been completed earlier, they would replace landscaping at their expense. It was still Tony Virginia's headache to finish. By opening day, his people did over almost a third of the landscaping. A construction crew, for instance, sandblasted all the curbs in EPCOT, spewing sand over shrubs, trees, grass and flowers—much of which had to be replaced.

The day before EPCOT opened, a helicopter hovered near the entrance, immortalizing the scene on film. The powerful downdraft, however, decimated the Super Graphic garden below. Overnight, Tony Virginia's landscapers had to obtain and plant 10,000 flowers—blue salvia, yellow and orange marigolds. "Not too many horticulturists know what to do about helicopter damage," he chuckles.

Such was the stress at EPCOT that many key people gained weight. Bongirno and Zovich were big gainers. Ferrante tipped the scales over 250 pounds. It didn't help that the standard Disney construction-site lunch was fried chicken, potato chips, chocolate chip cookies, soft drinks and apples. "I don't know how healthy apples got in there," Nagy laughs—he along with Gerstman somehow managed to stay trim.

Not everything was finished by October 1, 1982. But enough was done that EPCOT could open with six Future World pavilions—Spaceship Earth, Communicore, Land, Journey of Imagination, Universe of Energy and World of Motion. A remarkable nine pavilions were ready in World Showcase: United Kingdom, France, Italy, Germany, China, Japan, Mexico, Canada and American Adventure. By any standard, this was a prodigious feat.

After opening day, there was plenty of work left to do, and for a while, Gerstman continued his dizzy pace. Then several weeks later, Gerstman said to Dave Meyers: "Do you realize this will be our last Saturday on the job?" They felt mixed emotions of relief and regret as they cut back the work schedule to five days a week. They had time to talk with each other.

On December 11, 1982, John Tishman and the Disney executives held a banquet at which they honored Gerstman for his contributions. They gave him an engraved Mickey Mouse watch, and he has worn it ever since. "If anybody tells me I'm in a Mickey Mouse operation," he beams, "I'd say that's a mighty fine compliment."

A year after EPCOT opened, total annual attendance at Disney's Florida empire almost doubled to 22.7 million, and it has remained above 20 million since then. EPCOT is probably the biggest drawing card in the United States, with about twice as many visits as recorded by the Smithsonian museum complex in Washington, D.C.

How do you follow up a once-in-a-lifetime challenge like EPCOT? John Tishman didn't have much time to worry about that, immersed as he was in dozens of projects around the United States for himself as well as other companies. While busy with EPCOT, Tishman was asked to handle many other projects. His people took over as development manager for PPG Place, the neogothic glass headquarters building in Pittsburgh designed by Philip Johnson and John Burgee, when that project fell six months behind schedule. The Tishman organization managed construction for South Street Seaport, the Rouse Company's festive marketplace in New York. Tishman handled the renovation of Carnegie Hall. They do more construction work in New York than anybody else, more than a billion dollars worth annually.

Jim Nagy succeeded Gerstman as head of Tishman's Florida operations in April 1983. He, Dave Meyers and other Tishman people built the 814-room Hilton Hotel at Disney World Village in 12 months—it opened in October 1983.

Within six months after EPCOT opened, Gerstman moved to Atlantic City, where he would be Tishman's construction executive for a luxurious Hilton casino hotel. While Gerstman plunged into his new assignment, his wife Edie rented a house in Margate, less than 10 miles south of Atlantic City. She was as adaptable as he, settling quickly into the community—she taught yoga to senior citizens and served on several committees at the local Jewish community center.

When, in the spring of 1985, Hilton was denied a gaming license, they sold the casino to Donald Trump for a lusty $320 million. Contract completion date was July 1, 1985, but Trump hoped to start the cash flowing quicker. Gerstman had Trump's Castle Casino & Hotel open by June 17.

The most opulent Atlantic City casino yet, it was true to Trump. Operating profits were reported in an astonishing two weeks—most other casinos didn't hit black ink for perhaps six months. When, shortly after opening, *60 Minutes* filmed a segment on the brash real estate entrepreneur, one of the gilded settings was Trump's Castle Casino & Hotel. Trump called Gerstman, who was in his cramped construction trailer office and asked him to be part of the segment. "Milt," he exclaimed, cameras rolling, "this place is fabulous!"

As gamblers dreamed of a jackpot beneath crystal chandeliers, Gerstman returned to his trailer. He put his white hard hat on a dusty file cabinet and talked about his two children and two grandchildren. He relished the next job. "Whatever it may be," he smiles, "I'll do the best I can, and nobody will do any better."

INDEX